The State and the Legacies of British Colonial Development in Malawi

The State and the Legacies of British Colonial Development in Malawi

Confronting Poverty, 1939–1983

Gift Wasambo Kayira

LEXINGTON BOOKS
Lanham • Boulder • New York • London

Published by Lexington Books
An imprint of The Rowman & Littlefield Publishing Group, Inc.
4501 Forbes Boulevard, Suite 200, Lanham, Maryland 20706
www.rowman.com

86-90 Paul Street, London EC2A 4NE

British Library Cataloguing in Publication Information Available

Library of Congress Cataloging-in-Publication Data

Names: Kayira, Gift Wasambo, author.
Title: The state and the legacies of British colonial development in Malawi : confronting poverty, 1939–1983 / Gift Wasambo Kayira.
Description: Lanham: Lexington Books, 2023. | Includes bibliographical references and index. | Summary: "This book examines the discourse of development in Malawi and how it unfolded through a milliard of experts and institutions that expressed interest in the plight of the poor and yet did little to achieve their goals between the 1930s and 1983"—Provided by publisher.
Identifiers: LCCN 2022046144 (print) | LCCN 2022046145 (ebook) | ISBN 9781666921656 (cloth) | ISBN 9781666921663 (epub)
Subjects: LCSH: Poverty—Malawi. | Rural development—Malawi. | Malawi—Economic conditions—20th century. | Great Britain—Colonies—Economic policy.
Classification: LCC HC935.Z9 P6185 2023 (print) | LCC HC935.Z9 (ebook) | DDC 339.46096897—dc23/eng/20220927
LC record available at https://lccn.loc.gov/2022046144
LC ebook record available at https://lccn.loc.gov/2022046145

To my loving Mother

Contents

List of Figures, Tables, and Maps

Preface

A popular and contemporary saying in Malawi is *Pa ground sipali bwino* (the terrain or ground is not good) or *Pa ground paterera* (the terrain is slippery). Both refer to cases where one does not have money in a hopeless economic environment. There is another saying, *Chuma chili mnthaka* (Wealth in the land, or literally, in the soil), which contrasts with the above sentiments. Dr. Hastings Kamuzu Banda, Malawi's first president (1964–1994), popularized the latter to encourage people to invest in farming. Malawians accept both sayings, declaring the importance of agriculture while acknowledging that the land and its claimed wealth are elusive to many. The struggle to reconcile the two sentiments also reflects the fight against poverty in the country. It is this struggle that is central to this book. Such a struggle involved interventions by British colonial administrators and, after independence, more interventions by state leaders and other international bodies such as the World Bank. It is also a struggle over ideas on how to arrest poverty, how they were contested and yet continued to influence each successive generation of those who intervened on behalf of the poor. I highlight conflicts between the colonial discourse on welfare and development and nationalist discourse on development, politics, and the economy, and international parastatals and the postcolonial state.

It is also a book that represents an internal struggle. It is a struggle of my memories surrounding the distinction between the rich and the poor. In primary school, we sang a national anthem that extolled Malawi as a country that was rich in resources, with soil so "rich and fair." But it was also at school that I saw distinctions between the rich and the poor. Such distinctions included dress. Some pupils had shoes, others did not. There are also memories of my mother expressing her frustration at the cost of living and hoping for something better. Such an internal struggle is not just about childhood; it is about the choice to learn history. It is about realizing that poverty is also about policies and how they impact people. It is also about having to interrogate those policies as a Malawian, researcher, and member of faculty. As I question them, I am forced to examine how my thinking about poverty and development has changed over the years. These experiences and my interest in the field of "development history" inspired the writing of this book. The book, therefore, is also a way of writing back to development theories for failing to provide a deeper historical context to many of the economic challenges the country and its people grapple with. I consider inclusion and emphasis on history as a way of understanding poverty's historical origins and the measures undertaken to address the problem.

The book is articulated through the lens of imperial and transnational frameworks. I have used the imperial framework to contextualize the politics of development the British carried out during the colonial era, as well as how the colonial government conceptualized notions of poverty. Through the transnational framework, the book focuses on the relationship between Malawi and other nations and international non-state actors. While there may be problems unique to Malawi, the transnational outlook enables a comparison with other countries while putting the country's story within the broader politics of poverty and development. It is a story I have constructed through a multi-sited research undertaking, taking me through archival centers in Britain, the USA, and Malawi.

I have deliberately focused on a timeframe spanning over five decades to examine forms of transition within the state; from the colonial time when the country was known as Nyasaland to a period twenty years after independence when the country was now known as Malawi. Such a timespan also allows one to appreciate the extent to which the vestiges of colonial legacy lingered in the newly independent country and the extent to which postcolonial Malawi could own its policies. For example, through the book, I explore how some development interventions could not reach the implementation stage because of the competing discourses discussed above.

This is not a book focusing on villains and heroes. It is a book about efforts that the state players believed would work and their different interpretations of those efforts. It is also about the intentions and motives behind those efforts and whether they succeeded or were frustrated. Even as the focus is on what I have referred to as the key actors—the state, the World Bank, and other international agencies—this is not with the assumption that ordinary Africans were simply on the receiving end of expert intervention. As the book demonstrates, Africans were landowners even during colonial times, and they were capable of questioning systems and policies, particularly those relating to the land tenure system. Even those Africans who did not own land could still articulate their concerns. The book demonstrates how the peasantry could overturn the official discourses, forcing development practices to proceed on their terms. Therefore, this book is also about power and the kaleidoscopic ways it played out.

As the book focuses on the decades referred to above, it also invites reflections on the way forward for Malawi and for its counterparts. Agriculture continues to be the main source of income. The people are digging and cultivating, even in the face of challenges and expensive farm inputs. The state is also digging for answers, for solutions. The book in itself is a form of digging, searching for truths, and engaging in a continual search on how to confront poverty. It does not promise absolute truths but reflects my form of digging throughout the years.

Acknowledgments

This book would not have taken its current shape without support from several individuals and institutions. Dr. Joseph Hodge of West Virginia University deserves a special mention for introducing me to the role of British colonial experts and how they have shaped development histories. Drs. Robert Maxon, Tamba M'bayo, and Michele Stephens of the same insitution match Hodge's generosity with taking time off their busy schedules to listen to my thoughts. So too, were Drs. Hendrina Kachapila Mazizwa, Anne Chiponda, Timwa Lipenga, and Emmanuel Ngwira of the University of Malawi. They read the manuscript and made suggestions that improved its quality. Such goodwill extended to the anonymous peer reviewers of the manuscript and Sydney Wedbush, an Associate Aquisitions Editor at Lexington Books. Together with the production team, Sydney provided unparalleled support and guidance.

Also deserving acknowledgment is the contribution of staff in the multiple archival and documentary centers I consulted and the local farmers in Lilongwe, Malawi. The latter spared their time to share with me their local experiences on development projects. Staff at the Malawi National Archives, the British National Archives at Kew in London, the Bodleian Library of Commonwealth and African Studies (Weston Library) in Oxford, and the World Bank Group Archives in Washington, DC, freely provided me with the materials I needed for this work. I received similar support from staff members of the downtown campus library of West Virginia University and the H. K. Banda Archive at the University of Indiana Library. I should also thank the University of Malawi management for providing me with financial support to workshop the manuscript. Dr. Park Muhonda of Oregon State University and Mr. Jonathan Gwaligwali, a cartographer at the University of Malawi, deserve special mention. Park helped to draw all the maps in this book except for Map 3.3, which Jonathan drew. Lastly, I should thank my family. My wife, Jean, and our children, Shalom and Joel never ceased praying for my success, even though I denied them my presence to concentrate on this project. This book bears testimony to their answered prayers.

List of Abbreviations

ADMARC	Agriculture Development and Marketing Corporation
ADS	Agricultural Development Service
Ag. DofA	Acting Director of Agriculture
BLCAS	Bodleian Library of Commonwealth and African Studies
CDA	Colonial Development Act
CDC	Colonial Development Corporation
CDF	Colonial Development Fund
CDWA	Colonial Development and Welfare Act
CDWF	Colonial Development and Welfare Fund
CmDC	Commonwealth Development Corporation
CO	Colonial Office
DOD	Department of Agriculture
DofA	Director of Agriculture
FAO	Food and Agricultural Organization
FCB	Fabian Colonial Bureau
FMB	Farmers Marketing Board
FRG	Federal Republic of Germany
GDP	Gross Domestic Product
GNP	Gross National Product
IBRD	International Bank for Reconstruction and Development
IDA	International Development Association
IMF	International Monetary Fund
KfW	Kreditanstalt für Wiederaufbau
LDCs	Less Developed Countries
LLDP	Lilongwe Land Development Project
MCP	Malawi Congress Party
MNA	Malawi National Archives
NAC	Nyasaland African Congress
NTGA	Nyasaland Tung Growers Association
OAU	Organization of African Unity
ODA	Overseas Development Administration
ODM	Ministry of Overseas Development
OFC	Overseas Food Corporation
OPC	Office of the President and Cabinet

ORDA	Overseas Resources Development Act
PPAS	Project Performance and Audit Study
PRC	Peoples Republic of China
PWDC	Post-war Development Committee
ROC	Republic of China
S/S/C	British Secretary of State for Colonies
SCA	Smallholder Coffee Authority
STA	Smallholder Tea Authority
SVADP	Shire Valley Agricultural Development Project
TNA	The British National Archives
UNDP	United Nations Development Program
UNO	United Nations Organization
US	United States
VIPCOR	Viphya Corporation
WB	World Bank
WBGA	World Bank Group Archive

Introduction

While growing up in rural areas of northern Malawi in the 1990s, I lived in two distinct economies that defined the experiences of rural farming communities. The first related to smallholder coffee producers, who lived a relatively better life. The first cup of locally processed coffee that I ever had was in my grandfather's house. I remember seeing him cultivating a plot of coffee trees. While he sold a good portion of the harvested coffee beans through a cooperative outlet, he retained a portion of it for family consumption. Coffee, a beverage that is hard to find these days, constituted part of our daily breakfast. Smallholder coffee farmers such as my grandfather benefitted from state support and seemed to have enjoyed a relative degree of autonomy over the land they cultivated and its products.

I also remember visiting tenants on tobacco farms where my mother used to work. A frequent narrative on such farms was of tenants who made losses every growing season. As part of their contracts, tobacco estate owners provided the tenants with food rations and all the relevant agriculture input to produce the crop. Sometimes the owners would have a tractor work a farmer's field, particularly for virgin land that a hoe would do little to open for cultivation. All the expenses were recouped at the point of sale at the end of the growing season. A poor harvest spelt disaster for the tenants. For some, the proceeds were barely enough to cover for the expenses incurred. Others had a negative balance that was forwarded to the next growing season. If the coffee economy aimed at empowering rural farmers, the tobacco one had the goal of supporting large-scale commercial producers.

I could not reconcile these two experiences and wondered why the Malawian state did little to replicate the coffee farmers' experience and, instead, allowed the tenancy system in tobacco farms to dominate despite its seemingly exploitative nature. Over the years, my reading of literature on the plight of the poor and Malawi's developmental challenges did not address this concern. There is a tendency to ignore the first scenario and emphasize the exploitative nature of the state, often depicting it as a leviathan institution least interested in the struggles of the poor.[1] An autonomous postcolonial state, so goes the argument, took after the nature of its colonial predecessor and pursued policies that constrained the rural poor, while enriching large-scale farmers and other players. It is an argument that begged more questions than answers. Dependent as it were on external resources, I wondered whether the state in Malawi was truly autonomous. Again, I could not comprehend how a state would legitimize its rule over the local people with policies designed to exploit the many ordinary farmers placed under its care. More significantly, I had questions on whether there are alternative ways of telling the legacies of British colonialism in Malawi beyond the dominant exploitation narrative.

This book is, in part, a response to the many initial concerns I had regarding the behavior of the colonial and postcolonial state in Malawi and its responsibility as a guardian of the development process. It contributes to histories of development by weaving analysis around the following questions: What were the origins of the British ideas on rural poverty, and how did they play out in colonial Malawi? How did development practice of the colonial era impact the postcolonial state and its quest to confront poverty? In what ways did postcolonial development ideas and practices mediate with those of international organizations and intergovernmental agencies, and what were the results of that mediation? Although the notion of poverty features prominently, this book is not about the history of the poor. The questions it raises, moreover, depart from those seen in typical studies on that subject.[2] Instead of asking questions such as whether the poor existed in pre- or colonial Africa, or questions about their identities and the causes of their poverty, or how they survived, it asks questions about the interventions that existed to confront poverty, the ideas that drove such programs, and the character of the state that development practice reveals over time.

In addressing the highlighted questions, this study brings together multiple actors, and how the ideas they held on poverty played out in Malawi, a less-studied former British protectorate located in south-east Africa. It begins by analyzing how Britain sought to address the challenges of the poor at home in the latenineteenth century and how similar ideas were later debated in the context of British Africa and Malawi before and after independence in 1964. The book's substantive chapters reveal concerns state authorities had over the welfare of poor Africans, which were never fully reconciled with the pressing demand of stabilizing the country's economy. Reconciling the two objectives was a subject of debate that pitted various actors against each other, including politicians and bureaucrats, the settler community and educated Africans, international non-state actors, and state aid agencies. The contestations and debates which emerged left behind results that fundamentally contradicted the effort to mitigate poverty.

The book takes off from the premise that despite committing itself to raising the living standards of rural Africans, the state in Malawi, both colonial and postcolonial, failed to fulfill this mandate between the late-1930s and

1983. It is, therefore, a study of the struggles the state endured in fulfilling the mandate of arresting rural poverty. Its chapters show that none of the development interventions of the postcolonial period were without deeper historical colonial antecedents. Postcolonial state's attempts to introduce private property rights to communal land with the intention to increase its productivity and improve the welfare of Malawians, or to support industrial projects that would accommodate local interests, or greater still, promote rural development interventions explicitly targeting the poor communities, were not without a precedence. These ideas and practices were first debated and implemented during the British colonial era but without much success, which caused them to be abandoned. In examining these commonalities, the book points to a story that displays first, the cyclical nature of development history in the country and second, how state power was contested in ways that frustrated the state's mandate to arrest poverty.

In contrast to the existing scholarly tradition where actions of state actors are, for the most part, interpreted within the confines of domestic politics, the study employs an imperial and transnational analysis that goes beyond the confines of a nation-state. A transnational approach emphasizes doing history in ways that bring together themes, personalities, institutions, or historical phenomena that cut across nation-states.[3] In the context of this study, a transnational approach allows me to emphasize how multiple actors and institutions beyond the geographical boundaries of Malawi helped to frame the country's development history. For the colonial era of this study, an imperial analysis substitutes a transnational approach to locate Malawi within a broader context of the British Empire. In adopting this approach, the book responds to recent scholarly appeals to write histories of development in more global and transnational terms.[4] By reflecting on how multiple actors interacted, the book also decontextualizes the developmental state in Malawi and helps us to see beyond it. Instead of seeing like a state or analyzing development through the lens of state officials and bureaucrats only, it also brings in the analysis the many non-official and non-governmental agencies who participated not only in debates about development and rural poverty but also in the formulation and execution of development projects. Other than the concerns they registered for the poor, many of these agencies and organizations had other ambitions to fulfill, and they did so by appealing to the language of development.

In this way, the book contributes to scholarly work that emphasizes the role of Western experts as guardians of the development process.[5] Many of these individuals first served in the British Empire before working with the specialized agencies of the United Nations Organization.[6] After independence, Malawi retained several of the ex-colonial officers in its civil service, whose role scholars are yet to systematically analyze. This book shows how these experts interacted among themselves and with government bureaucrats and politicians. Although this group worked through a network, it was not monolithic. There were cracks within it and failure to produce positive results often magnified experts' differences in ways that reveal the anxieties they had as harbingers of development.

This study also contributes to the debate on weak and/or strong states and how such a characterization of the state relates to the failure of development in Africa. If measured against well-bureaucratized and decentralized Western states, the postcolonial Malawian state was weak. According to neo-Weberians, strong states are those that are well institutionalized and decentralized with state bureaucrats objectively performing their tasks unrestrained.[7] The opposite is true for weak states which are usually authoritarian with politicians capturing state institutions, rendering them weak and inefficient. The Malawian state was, for the most part, authoritarian with Dr. Hastings Kamuzu Banda, the country's president between 1964 and 1993, making most of its economic and political decisions. This book points to another cause of state weakness. Despite having a relatively well bureaucratized civil service reinforced by the white expatriate staff, the Malawian state remained weak in the sense that there existed contending, competing, and often contradictory interests of the various groups which registered concern in the country's development process. More significantly, external influence on the country was pushing the state towards a more authoritarian attitude as it sought to protect its sovereignty. In consequence, the state failed to achieve meaningful progress in certain areas and often opted for policy options it did not envisage.

Finally, this study joins those empirically based studies that question post-structuralist development scholars for their tendency to reduce development into a discourse of power relations or an instrument of control and domination.[8] None of the developmental actors under study, whether state bureaucrats, local politicians, or international actors from aid organizations, had complete control over the development process in Malawi to wield unlimited power. The same applied to local Africans, the very beneficiaries of the war on poverty. They too displayed agency and often forced experts to execute projects in line with their interests as opposed to blueprints of development experts. Throughout the discussion, therefore, the book emphasizes one overarching theme—the limits of state power in the unfolding of development history in Malawi—and shows how this theme played out in various debates on and practices of development and welfare from the 1930s to 1983.

The book makes use of sources obtained from the Malawi National Archives and the British National Archives at Kew in London, the archival holdings of the World Bank, Oxford Bodleian Library of Commonwealth and African Studies (Weston Library), and Dr. H. K. Banda Archive in

Indianapolis, USA. It also taps on interviews conducted among local farmers in Malawi and several other published works. Together, these varied sources from multiple centers afford the book an imperial and transnational touch otherwise missing in most works on Malawi's history. Postcolonial records from the Malawi National Archives the book uses are particularly unique for their originality. Although accessible to the public, most of them are yet to be processed into public archives. Using them requires time and patience, for one must assume the role of an archivist before obtaining some usable data. Other than merely supplementing official documents, which often emphasize the modernizer's perspective of development, the oral sources are equally invaluable for they present the lived experiences of the very targets of the war on poverty and hence offer an alternative explanation to that of experts regarding how this war failed in Malawi.

Malawi presents an ideal case for a study of this nature. Today, it ranks among the poorest countries of the world with a Gross National Income (GNI) per capita of $360 USD. The United Nations Human Development Index ranks the country on position 172 out of 185 countries.[9] Since 1980, the country's income per capita has remained stagnant to register significant improvements in people's welfare. Over 50 percent of its population is poor and survives on less than one US dollar per day. 25 percent of the poor lives in extreme poverty.[10] Most rural people can hardly afford decent accommodation, a well-balanced diet with adequate calories, and safe drinking water. Women-headed households, which constitute about 25 percent of the poor over the past three decades, have been hit the most. Unlike men, women have limited opportunities to engage in off-farm activities, which can supplement the surplus from subsistence farming. With the collapse of estate agriculture in the early 1990s, opportunities for wage labor have diminished, forcing rural-urban migrations to soar at an increased pace. The collapse of state-run industries in the wake of the Structural Adjustment Reforms has left the poor in urban areas with limited alternatives. Lacking adequate education qualifications and skills to afford better jobs in the civil service and the private sector, the urban poor have resorted to street vending, brick making, and sand mining, supplementing their income with bicycle and ox-cart taxiing. Others have clandestinely left to work in South African households and retail outlets. Across the country, the central region fares better in terms of poverty levels than the South and the North. Higher population densities in the Southern region shrink land for cultivation in rural areas and the number of non-skilled jobs in urban spaces.[11]

The current situation in Malawi is not different from that of the distant past. Even when the country was under British colonial rule (1891–1964), the protectorate, first known as British Central Africa and later Nyasaland, was the poorest territory in East and Central Africa. Lacking any minerals worth the name, it relied on tea, tobacco, and cotton production, supplementing her agriculture-based economy with labor exports. This position did not change when the protectorate became part of the Central African Federation between 1953 and 1963.[12] It was the imposed nature of the Federation and the minimal economic benefits it presented to Malawi that helped to drum up support towards politics of mass nationalism in the country under the leadership of the Nyasaland African Congress (NAC), which was renamed Malawi Congress Party (MCP) in 1959. Led by Dr. Hastings Kamuzu Banda, the country achieved self-governing status in 1961, with Banda as the Prime Minister. Full political independence from Britain came in 1964. When the country became a republic in 1966, Banda's position changed to that of the President. Henceforth, the country became a *de facto* one-party state until 1994 when Banda and his MCP lost in the 1994 multi-party general elections. Political independence did not mark an economic break with the past. Agriculture remained the mainstay of the country's economy where over 90 percent of its rural population engaged in subsistence production.[13] Because of its weak economic position, the country became a space accommodating different ideas and practices of rural and industrial development, with the latter loosely defined here as a deliberate intervention to raise the country's economic capacity, address poverty, and improve the living standards of the rural and urban population.[14] This book pays attention to how the state struggled to arrest poverty among the rural poor from the 1930s to 1983. Understanding state effort in Malawi requires, in the first place, unpacking the politics of development and exploitation.

POLITICS OF DEVELOPMENT AND EXPLOITATION

Although Malawi presents us with a good case for studies on development and poverty, particularly because the country remains among the poorest in the Global South, there is not enough discussion that addresses the subject of poverty through the lens of development history.[15] A few notable titles by historians and others have their own problems. There is a tendency to conflate development with politics or reduce development stories to narratives of exploitation. Paul Chiudza Banda's book is one such example of those that locate the development project within the context of Malawi's political history.[16] Central to Banda's book is the theme of counterinsurgency, which emphasizes how the authorities viewed those who opposed its actions between 1891 and 1994. It depicted them as insurgents, rebels, guerrillas, or enemies of the state. In doing so, the state deployed what Banda describes as the "stick and the carrot." Public executions and hangings, detentions, deportations, and use of paramilitary groups were significant aspects of the stick. The carrot was manifested through the implementation of development projects and related welfare programs to appease the insurgents. What emerged, Banda notes, was a developmental state that seemed to have been primarily interested in solving political problems. In displaying the nexus between development and politics, Banda's work joins similar volumes such as that by historian Frederick Cooper, which projected the same argument.[17] For Cooper, like Banda's work shows, the post-1940 British colonial and welfare development, which the Colonial Development and Welfare Act of 1940 inaugurated, aimed at solving certain political problems irate Africans caused in British Africa. Although the argument is persuasive, it is not without weaknesses. If not robbing the development project of its history, it risks blinding us from seeing the intentions of specific individuals who had long campaigned for improved welfare of Africans before and after the outbreak of certain violent episodes only in political terms. This book goes beyond the politics-development nexus to examine how some state bureaucrats and non-state actors saw development projects as avenues for fulfilling certain personal ambitions. Such interests would better materialize by uplifting the living standards of rural societies such that they became disappointed when projects did not produce intended outcomes, even if they served political aims.

Guy Mhone's edited volume is a good representation of the literature that advances an exploitation narrative.[18] Mhone's book discusses the country's developmental or structural adjustment crisis of the late-1970s and attributes it to a political model the state adopted at independence. Like several other articles taking a similar line of thought, the book emphasizes how the postcolonial state in Malawi perfected colonial tactics of exploitation and domination by deliberately pursuing policies whose aim was to extract economic surplus from the peasantry, a rent-seeking behavior that was ruinous to the rural farming communities but enriching for the largescale estate farmers. Focusing exclusively on postcolonial period, with the colonial era as a mere reference point, the book misses out on the historical context which gave rise to much of development planning of the 1960s and later. But in failing to interrogate this context, the book presents a predictable analysis of events and simplistically links the colonial past with the postcolonial present. In so doing, it commits a historical sin of reading history backwards based on consequences rather than intentions. This study challenges Mhone's book for reading historical events based on the late-1970s outcomes as opposed to state intentions, and how they unfolded in practice. Although state policy in the 1970s was increasingly predatory for many ordinary farmers, that behavior was less an adoption of colonial economies of exploitation than the immediate postcolonial developments which included the conflictual interaction taking place between Malawi, the World Bank (WB), and Britain's Ministry of Overseas Development (ODM), whose outcome forced the state to pursue some exploitative policies it never envisaged.

By emphasizing an exploitation narrative, moreover, these scholars reversed the earlier perspective advanced by scholars such as David Humphrey and S.N. Acharya. The latter two praised the state for promoting an export-oriented economy, which brought dividends in the early years of independence.[19] Carolyn McMaster and T. D. Williams also belong to this category of scholars. Although McMaster documented the country's foreign policy as it evolved in the 1960s and 1970s, her coverage of the theme of development was sketchy and at best highlighted, in 14 pages, what the country achieved in the areas of agriculture, trade, and aid management, much of it from Britain.[20] William's work is less remarkable for the theme of development than it is notable for its excessive praise of President Banda. Like McMaster, he singles out Banda's foreign policy as having contributed to economic growth in the country although much of it, he acknowledges, never trickled down to the majority poor.[21] The two scholars typically argued that Banda was a maverick leader who shrewdly interacted with Western powers and those within the African region in ways that benefited the country's economy.

Although the conclusions of the scholarship of the 1970s differed from what scholars of the 1980s and 1990s projected, their unit of analysis was the same—an autonomous state whose actions either grew or ruined the economy. They also agree that the rural poor were not the major beneficiaries of the economy, whatever growth it registered in the 1970s. Again, in both cases, external influence did not play a significant role. Although this political economy literature explains well Malawi's history of miracle and mirage, it exaggerates the power and autonomy of the postcolonial developmental state and its intentions. This book shows that the Malawian state did not operate as an autonomous entity. The character of the state in Malawi becomes clear when we decenter the state, factoring into the analysis the multiple forces that acted on it, particularly those external state and non-state agencies that registered interest in the country's development process. A seemingly autonomous state pursuing its own vision of development is reduced to one among several competing development actors. What emerges, instead, is a fractious and less hegemonic state caught up in political dynamics in which the power to decide on and implement development ideas and practices rested with multiple actors whose negotiations often produced a *modus vivendi* that left in its trail the accumulation of some and exploitation of others, or a total modification or rejection of the original development goals.

To avoid the trap of deterministic analyses inherent in the highlighted literature—where actions of state actors, whether colonial or postcolonial, are bent on exploiting rural farmers—this book sets aside the "exploitation narrative" as a frame of reference. In this way, it is better placed to ask new questions about the intentions of individuals or groups within and without the country—what they sought to achieve for rural farming communities, and sometimes themselves, and how their strategies manifested in specific historical contexts. Answers to these questions provide a vantage point from which to understand the behavior of the very state that presided over the development process in Malawi. This book, therefore, reverses the order of analysis. Instead of taking the state as a starting point, it begins by reframing analysis through the lens of "development history" and how it unfolded through the agency of multiple groups, individuals, and institutions to bring about certain outcomes. In doing so, it avoids dismissing the development project or rejecting the state's attempts to improve rural societies as a mere illusion and an attempt to control the society for ulterior motives as the post-structuralist inspired development literature once insisted.

Arturo Escobar, Wolfgang Sachs, Gilbert Rist, and somewhat problematically, James Ferguson and James Scott, belong to the category of those scholars that question the state-led and expert-driven "development project."[22] These scholars were disappointed with the failure of state-led development projects to address poverty in the Global South by the turn of the 1980s. Inspired by the post-structuralist movement of that decade, they condemned development as an idea and practice of ending poverty and improving the standards of living among rural and urban communities. They argued that "development" was a mere discourse of power relations, a weapon of control whose history they mostly traced to 1949. That was the year when the US president, Harry S. Truman, launched an offensive against global poverty. From multiple angles, these scholars also condemned states for aligning matters of development with security concerns at the height of the Cold War confrontation.[23]

In a more local setting, Scott took issue with self-acclaimed planners and experts who, touting themselves as agents of the "high state modernist ideology," remained insensitive to the agency and specific challenges of the local people and their environments. Typical examples of such projects include the depression-era Tennessee Valley Authority (TVA) scheme in the US, which inspired that country's post-war modernization drive; Britain's large-scale colonial development projects of the post-war era; and several other state-led rural development projects of the 1960s and 1970s in Africa. These projects emphasized top-down "modernization" strategies and a belief that Western technology and expertise was all that was required to transform "backward" societies into "modernized" ones. It is not surprising that most of these social engineering projects failed because of this self-proclaimed but dominating high state modernism.[24] Anticipating Scott, Ferguson earlier argued that despite their failure, such projects served as "anti-politics machines"—that is the idea of using development projects to depoliticize the question of poverty and gloss over the sufferings of the local people. Well-qualified state experts, whether knowingly or not, help to construct this machinery using their technical expertise. Through them, notes Ferguson, the state reframes political questions of land, resources, and low wages, into technical ones with a technical solution in the name of development projects.[25] But these seemingly apolitical projects give rise to a vast expansion of state power and extension of influence into rural areas. In other words, Ferguson suggests that there are unintended effects that run contrary to the stated intentions. In the case of Lesotho, where Ferguson locates his study, politics and development reinforced each other, with the latter helping to provide a language which those in authority used to define their proper roles and those of a centralized government bureaucracy.[26] Because of its predatory effects on the many local people, Escobar suggested a complete deconstruction of the Western-led development project, in favor of what he called a post-development regime rooted in indigenous systems of resource production with local people in control of the development process.[27]

These arguments have attracted criticisms from students of development history, not so much for conflating development and politics, as for robbing development of its history and reducing it to a mere discourse of power relations.[28] The historicists, which include names such as Frederick Cooper, Michael Cowen, Robert Shenton, Joseph Hodge, and David Ekbladh, have sought to rescue development from the obscurity of discourse to which it was thrown. They reject the idea that development is a post–World War II invention. Instead, they highlight the deeper roots of the development and/or modernization project. Whether as an intentional course of action aimed at raising production and productivity, or a course of action aimed at raising the living standards of the poorer segments of societies, development, they insist, predated the post-war era.[29] This book interjects into this debate and criticizes them both for privileging expert at the expense of local voices. It thus joins scholars who have shown how the colonized local people negotiated their involvement in colonial projects.[30] Unlike these works, I demonstrate that this level of negotiation went beyond the colonial era such that the local people were able to influence official blueprints of development projects even within the context of postcolonial authoritarian regimes like that of Dr. Banda in Malawi. They presented some alternative perspectives that came to influence official blueprints. In this way, rather than depicting development projects as weapons of control, the book shows the kaleidoscopic ways in which that power played out, with experts often accommodating local demands. Development is primarily a project of the state. As such, a book of this nature, emphasizing the intersection between local and international actors, requires an interrogation of the state.

CONTEXTUALIZING THE AFRICAN DEVELOPMENTAL STATE

Although emphasizing development ideas and practices and how they unfolded over time, existing studies tend to leave out the state uninterrogated.[31] This book, therefore, pays attention to the history of development and the behavior of the state that presided over the development process. This task is methodologically enriching because it reveals two approaches crucial to studying a developmental state in Africa—the retrospective and prospective approaches. The approaches help us to understand the internal logic of the state without missing out on the broader dynamics that define it which are captured through an imperial/transnational analysis. A retrospective approach begins from the known present and seeks to provide answers to historical phenomena by searching the past, either in poor leadership or state policies, the very assumptions of rational choice theories.[32] Much of the political economy literature advancing an exploitation narrative in Malawi borrows from this approach, where everything is predetermined. A prospective approach departs from the view that historical processes are highly predictable. It deliberately ignores the known present as the starting point and, instead, seeks to understand how different actors and forces combined to bring about specific outcomes.

Nowhere is this opposition more apparent than in the works by Crawford Young and Bruce Berman. In analyzing the colonial and postcolonial African states, Crawford Young settles for a retrospective approach. For Young, a retrospective examination of the African state has the potential to unravel fundamental continuities between the colonial and postcolonial periods. It possesses the potential to expose the very pitfalls of the colonial state, which came to define its successor state.[33] Such an approach has one fundamental problem—it reads history backward, embarking from the known present and seeking to explain it through the past, often using a particular model. Bruce Berman challenges Young for adopting an approach that presents deterministic modes of explanation. "By beginning from a presumably known present [such as the 1980s economic crisis] and searching backwards to uncover the cause of a [given] outcome," notes Berman, "we are inclined to ignore or eliminate as extraneous all those factors or events that do not appear to be directly linked to the current situation."[34] As a consequence, the state is reduced to a black box with clearly determined outputs.[35] Instead, Berman suggests a prospective approach that is flexible enough to accommodate the unpredictability of the historical process.

A retrospective approach places well on a single continuum the colonial and postcolonial state, making it easier to understand historical continuities and discontinuities. As Berman observes, however, the approach is less useful in dissecting the specific ways in which the constituent parts of the state interacted with each other and with other development players. Uncritically using such an approach is most likely to leave us with abstracted analyses of the country's development direction and, its challenges explained through terms such as "predatory state," "poor leadership," "neopatrimonialism/politics of the belly," "weak institutions," and "bifurcated state."[36] Each of these terms represents specific scholarly arguments explaining the African state and its failure to bring about development in Africa. In his *Politics of the Belly*, Jean-François Bayart argues that development failures in Africa result from corrupt leadership bent at perpetuating patrimonial politics in which politicians (as patrons/big men with huge bellies) always seek to please the local people and others (clients) often through corrupt practices. These individuals use parastatal organizations to extract state resources, which are further distributed among their clients to strengthen patrimonial ties. He calls this "politics of the belly" because state resources are channeled towards fulfilling personal interests of corrupt politicians. In their *Africa Works*, Chabal and Daloz share this argument. They argue that African states are weak, lack legitimacy, and therefore do not conform to the ideal "neo-Weberian state" introduced earlier and discussed at length in the subsequent paragraphs. African states are, therefore, ill-suited for a development assignment. Nevertheless, they still work despite this failure. They call this the "political instrumentalization of disorder" because politicians benefit from this very disorderliness by projecting themselves as architects of development.

Mahmood Mamdani's "bifurcated state" thesis locates the problem of development in Africa in the differential laws, rooted in the colonial moment, but which the African postcolonial state perpetuates. While the countryside (with subjects) operates under customary law in which non-elected chiefs are in control (even distributing communal land), the urban areas (with citizens) fall under the civil law (with the state bureaucracy in control). What emerges is the informalization of the state that fails to measure up to well institutionalized Western states. Such states are incapable of achieving development. For Mamdani, this is not surprising. His case of Uganda showed how the country failed to shed off the ghost of British indirect rule in which both civil and customary laws co-exist. Sara Berry and others, such as Goran Hyden, argue that Africa's problems today stem from the absence of development-conscious institutions. African institutions conflict with capitalist relations of production. Berry argues that Africans often access resources through informal patrimonial and other networks and further invest resources not in the productive sector, but in these very networks. Hyden used the case of Tanzania to project the "uncaptured peasantry" thesis, which located the failure of development in Africa in peasant behavior. He argued that African peasants are averse to change and resist capitalist penetration (they remain uncaptured) which can help to economically transform Africa. Seeking to defend their autonomy, African cultivators have either withdrawn from the market or resisted state plans aimed at reshaping their economic behavior. Hyden's thesis puts undue emphasis on the power of capitalism and suggests a total eradication of peasant economies as the first step to achieving development.[37]

With minor variations, Berry, Hyden, and Bayart speak a similar language of patron-client relationships or cultural and economic institutions. Such is also the case with a more recent edited volume by Dan Banik and Blessings Chinsinga on Malawi. Rather than addressing the theme of development as a deliberate intervention to address poverty and grow the country's economy for the benefit of the masses, the book explores constraints to development, focusing especially on how weak political institutions could be strengthened and reoriented towards achieving development.[38] These works share the same weakness of reductionism, not least because they collapse a rather complex problem of Africa's development into one of "institutional weakness" or the problem of "weak states" introduced above. This weakness, in their view, is precipitated by forces internal to Africa, either the behavior of political and other state bureaucrats or archaic African institutions. There is little attempt to move beyond the confines of a nation and interrogate how African states interact with other external forces. This is somewhat understandable. Dissatisfied with the now challenged 1970s underdevelopment or dependency perspective which emphasized problematic economic ties between Africa or the Global South and the Western world, these scholars presented an internalist analysis to the continent's challenges. One criticism of the dependency school, which drew the attention of the works in question, centered on the way this perspective pushed the blame for Africa's impoverishment towards Western players and their economic allies on the ground while shielding the ills of politicians in Africa or the continent's institutional weaknesses. The internalist alternative they presented, however, brings in other costs to analysis. The internalist argument is a substitute that is overly deterministic in ways fitting Young's retrospective approach. Though useful, such a retrospective analysis forces analysts to relate the postcolonial to the colonial state with little regard to other intervening forces, in the process creating leapfrogging legacies.[39] This book shares their argument on the weakness of the African states. With Malawi, however, the state's weakness was less a result of failure to measure up to a Western state or an outcome of archaic and resistant African institutions, than the contending voices this study presents. As it will become apparent, external and internal pressures acting on the state undermined its developmental assignment.

In any case, these arguments reflect the notion of a neo-Weberian state, which has gone a long way in influencing scholars such as Crawford Young and other political scientists. The neo-Weberian concept of the state borrows from Max Weber's thinking about what states seek to achieve and how they ascertain both legitimacy and autonomy. Neo-Weberians typically group states under two or three dominant categories, which include states that are strong, weak, or those that have failed (failed states).[40] Without falling into the trap of oversimplification, states that conform to Western democratic principles are considered strong and capable of delivering development. They have efficient and well-decentralized bureaucracies. States that depart from Western democracy often assume an authoritarian character and are considered weak and incapable of delivering public services. Under such states, political regimes usually capture the state machinery, rendering it weak and incapable of effectively performing its duties. Failed states mostly refer to those where neither politicians nor state bureaucrats have control of the government machinery. Instead, competing, usually armed groups, constantly fight over the control of a given country.

Under the first two categories, states achieve legitimacy by dominating or exercising hegemony over the rest of the society.[41] This state behavior reinforces its autonomy from other segments of the society such as civil society groups or outside influence. This conception of the state almost sunk into the dustbin of history in political science literature for a good part of the 1950s. It resurfaced later in the 1980s as a significant unit for analyzing national politics.[42] Associated with names such as Theda Skocpol, Peter Evans, Dietrich Rueschemeyer, Eric Nordlinger, Stephen Krasner, and others, state-centered analysis re-emerged to challenge literature which had robbed the state of its autonomy and reduced it into one operating at the mercy of societal forces.[43] The first three authors are behind the celebrated 1985 edited volume, *Bringing the State Back In*, which served as a manifesto of their mission. There is not space in this book to delve deeper into these debates. One extract from Skocpol's earlier work, however, deserves citing at length because it represented this thinking most clearly. "The state properly conceived," she argued, "is no mere arena in which socio-economic struggles are fought out. It is, rather, a set of administrative, policing, and military organizations headed, and more or less well-coordinated by, an executive authority. Any state first and fundamentally extracts resources from society and deploys these resources to create and support coercive and administrative organizations."[44] Despite variations in their arguments, these scholars viewed the state as an autonomous entity, with individuals or state institutions making independent decisions irrespective of any societal pressure. "The statist approach," summarizes Mitchell, "always begins from the assumption that the state is a distinct entity, opposed to and set apart from a larger entity called society."[45] This scholarship emphasized a state-society dichotomy in which the two were independent of and/or opposed to each other. Under this conceptualization, the power to decide on the socio-political or economic direction of a country rested not with the society but with the state and its machinery.

Building on this view, Crawford Young argued that the postcolonial African state, just like many others, has always been autonomous and operates according to a particular state logic, what he calls the "reason of the state." The reason of the state comprises six imperatives—hegemony, autonomy, security, legitimacy, revenue, and accumulation.[46] What is anomalous in the African context, however, is that the reason of the state (which should guide state bureaucrats) is not distinguishable from interests of a given political regime, often guided by the ambitions of the political elites. For Young, most bureaucrats have worked in conformity to the will of the authoritarian political leaders. Young sees this dominance of political interests as the source of Africa's economic challenges. He, therefore, suggests the need to decolonize the African state to make it more inclusive. For Young, autonomous as they are, authoritarian states—which he expresses through a Congolese phrase of Bula Matari or stone crusher—are inherently weak and ill-suited for a development assignment. But this state autonomy that Young, and indeed, most neo-Weberians emphasize should not be exaggerated. Whether the state achieves its legitimacy through well-decentralized institutions capable of delivering services to the people and where the people in question respect the state's authority; or through dictatorial tendencies where the state achieves legitimacy through political regimes that instill fear in the people, state power is always contested, either through a ballot, protests, or open violence. To maintain legitimacy, the state may settle for compromises rather than forcing its will on society; in other cases, building political regimes on patron-client relationships that are deeply rooted in society helps to cultivate legitimacy. However, such behavior also makes the state less autonomous than imagined. Similarly, for economically weak states, the need to secure funding from outside sources weakens their power to act autonomously from outside aid agencies.[47]

It is an argument in futility to insist on state autonomy under these circumstances just as it is problematic to argue that political leaders always subject state bureaucrats to their will as Young would want us to believe. As Naomi Chazan has illustrated, even under the most authoritarian regimes, "politics, power, and control are not of necessity coterminous with the state *nor is the state bureaucracy a mere agent of the ruling elite*" [italics added].[48] In Tanzania, Leander Schneider recently showed how local government officials retained their autonomy to act independently despite operating within the overall authoritarian framework of Julius Nyerere's villagization program.[49] The reason of the state, therefore, should not reduce it, as Migdal shows, into an undifferentiated entity pulling towards a single direction.

Doing so is reifying and anthropomorphizing the state hence obscuring the dynamics and patterns of the struggles in which it is caught. Migdal suggests a "state in society" approach that should see the state from below while acknowledging how various components, "often impelled by conflicting interests and pulling in different directions relate to one another."[50] What Migdal overlooks, however, is the role of other actors and forces outside national politics. Nevertheless, his work points to the need for analysts to examine statecraft as a process, one that is defined by a web of relationships in which multiple actors play their roles which are sometimes conflicting and at odds with each other.

The development history this study documents displays these interlocking but web-like relationships that defined the state in Malawi. In doing so, it joins Berman's work on Kenya and, to a lesser extent, Hodge and Phillips, whose works also speak to the prospective approach.[51] At the center of all these works is the kind of paralysis that characterized the working of the colonial state. Phillips argued that colonialism in British West Africa was a makeshift settlement, "an attempt to hold together in harmony a number of conflicting processes, a complex of objectives . . . frequently challenged by administrators, and ultimately incompatible."[52] Phillips framed her thesis as a critique of the popular British West African policy, which relied more on African than capitalist systems of production during the inter-war period. She attributed the resilience of African production systems, including communal land tenure, to the weaknesses of the state, which failed to play its role as an agent of European capitalist groups.[53] "Constrained on one side by the existing capitals [sic] which demanded cheap labor, cheap transport, and cheap land . . . and threatened on the other side by fears of political disorder," she argued, "the colonial states could not formulate a satisfactory strategy for capitalist development."[54] Although Phillips' overall conclusion reduces the West African states into agents of the capitalist class—they could have served this class better had they been strong enough—her analysis is novel and dovetails well with what we see in Hodge and Berman's prospective approach.

Hodge showed how multiple but often conflicting voices characterized decision-making during the late British colonialism in Africa. Local administrators often ridiculed the expatriate staff for their patronizing ideas. Unlike Phillips, who locates this kind of paralysis in the structural limitations and administrative frictions, Hodge goes beyond this to examine how "contradictory and ambivalent aims of the colonial mission itself" gave rise to this quandary. While some officers were keen at saving the empire from collapsing, others concerned themselves with fulfilling Britain's mission of modernizing and improving the colonial societies.[55] The reconciliation of these objectives proved difficult, if not impossible, to achieve.

It is Berman's work that discusses at length how such a prospective approach played out in colonial Kenya. His work shows the semi-autonomous nature of the colonial state in Kenya.[56] While retaining its autonomy from European settlers and the African society, the state did not lose its metropolitan ties. Again, although connections with the metropole made it strong, reliance on African allies for personnel weakened its autonomy. More significantly, the colonial state in Kenya was locked in contradictory objectives. Although it sought to support capitalist groups for the economic independence of Kenya, there were limits regarding the extent it could pass labor and land policies subjecting the peasantry to capitalist interests. In fact, following the Great Depression and the subsequent collapse of settler agriculture in the early 1930s, the state switched towards supporting African agriculture. Besides, the state bureaucracy in colonial Kenya was neither monolithic nor uniform. The interests of the prefectural leadership were often at variance with those of technical administrators, just like the metropolitan interests sometimes deviated from those of the officers on the ground. In brief, the Kenyan state operated within the confines of a dialectic process, the outcome of which was the articulation of several goals, interests, and objectives.[57]

Despite its strength, the prospective approach advocated by Berman and, much earlier Lonsdale and Berman, is necessarily Marxist and privileges class struggles which the state moderated. Theirs is a thesis that examines "political conflicts" and "administrative misunderstandings" as aspects of a capitalist economy such that the contradictions the state coped with are those relating to its role as a "protector of capitalist social relations."[58] Such an explanation describes well the behavior of the colonial state. However, it is inadequate as a frame with which to explain state relations with external post-war state bureaucrats and postcolonial non-state institutions whose operations were not always driven by capitalist interests. These weaknesses notwithstanding, the prospective approach we see in Berman, Phillips, and Hodge presents many advantages for the current study. It departs from an unknown future and seeks to reconstruct the history of development through a myriad of players whose actions were unfixed and undetermined. It disassembles the "black box" and seeks to understand how multiple actors helped to open or close certain development options and analyzes the effects of their actions on the country's economic progress. This book pays attention to historical-specific forces that acted on development players both within and without the country.

Its relevance notwithstanding, the prospective-retrospective opposition is less rewarding. Neither of the two offers the explanatory power to adequately capture the country's history of development, particularly as it relates to raising the living standards of the poor. The prospective approach privileges doing history as a process, emphasizing how certain decisions were made and with what results. This order of the daily routines is significant, especially in a study that emphasizes development as history. The approach, however, is incomplete without a framework that presents us with relative linear view of historical events and how they unfolded over time. Moreover, even if we disassembled the black box as Berman insists, the layered behavior of an aircraft such as taxiing, taking off, air detours, and landing throws back a certain degree of linearity inherent in Young's retrospective approach. Insisting on this dichotomy robs scholars of the benefits of a fruitful dialogue between the two approaches. Needless to state, doing history is, in many ways, thinking retrospectively. The prospective approach was a useful lens with which to discuss the nature of the colonial state. It remains an excellent corrective to the weaknesses of retrospective studies on historical change and continuity with their tendency to place causes and outcomes on a single continuum without due regard to the unpredictability of the daily and specific routines that produced them. The chessboard analysis in a prospective approach, however, is less useful in tracing how ideas and practices of development have unfolded over time. This book is, in part, a contribution to a scholarly dialogue between these two approaches and how they play out in practice. While emphasizing the "behind the scenes" daily struggles of development experts and administrators, it also pays attention to the enduring legacies of their actions.

CHAPTER OVERVIEW

This book is organized around six chapters. Chapter one discusses the discourse of British colonial development and welfare as it unfolded from the late nineteenth century to the 1960s. It brings together various politicians, bureaucrats, and individuals of informed opinion, notably those that subscribed to the liberal ideals of the Fabian Society and how they sought to defend the interests of the poor in Britain and, later, in Africa. It shows how these ideas later informed or resonated with debates on international development when the World Bank and other Western state agencies sought to arrest poverty in Less Developed Countries from the 1950s onwards. The chapter provides a conceptual framework for understanding the case studies that proceed it. It shows how these debates on poverty and development influenced how the war on poverty proceeded in Malawi.

The second chapter examines how the administrators in colonial Malawi interacted amongst themselves, with the colonized, and the Colonial Office (CO) in their struggles to stabilize the protectorate economically and improve the living standards of Africans from the 1930s to 1964. The chapter discusses the heated debate on land tenure reforms that pitted these groups against each other, making progress difficult to achieve. It highlights the multiple meanings different players attached to land, each emphasizing those that yielded the best political rather than economic benefits. Land reform proposals of this era, however, shaped the postcolonial customary land legislation, making the latter less a break with the past than the fulfilment of an old technocratic debate on land. Like the second, chapter three discusses the competing interests over the emerging tung oil industry and how they pitted the Department of Agriculture (DOA) officials against non-African planters/settlers, and the Colonial Development Corporation (CDC) administrators against local authorities in Nyasaland from the late 1930s to the early 1950s. It shows how officials within the DOA sought, without success, to defend African interests. However apologetic their actions were, they were not without other ulterior motives. Worried that planters were usurping their role of guiding the economic agenda of the protectorate, they used the African card to block the planters' growing influence. Such fears also dictated their interaction with the CDC, which was involved in the tung oil industry from the late-1940s.

The interaction between the postcolonial state, Britain, and the World Bank (WB) is highlighted in chapter four. The chapter focuses on how Malawian politicians and development experts responded to the patronizing behavior of the ODM and WB officials and the subsequent results of such responses. At issue here is how the ODM and the WB periodically policed Malawi's policy decisions in various areas such as the country's failure to craft a well-articulated plan to guide the development process and its obsession with capital intensive development projects with less direct effects on the poor. To defend its autonomy, Malawi struck back, but in ways that promoted an economic culture hostile to the welfare of the rural poor. If the postcolonial state is considered to have taken over the exploitative tendencies of its colonial predecessor as much of the Malawian political economy literature contends, I argue that the analysis reads Malawi's history backwards. I suggest paying attention to the intervening forces of the 1960s and 1970s to understand the unique character of the Malawian postcolonial state.

Reforms towards private rights to customary land resurfaced during the postcolonial era and were first attempted in the World Bank-supported Lilongwe Land Development project (LLDP). Chapter five discusses this project, which was designed to intensify maize and groundnut production among rural communities working in registered individual plots of land. None of the objectives were achieved. Instead, the LLDP became a space where competing ideas about rural development were projected. The WB interpreted the dismal performance of the scheme in terms of poor commodity prices the state marketing board presented to farmers. Beyond doubting their expertise, they viewed the LLDP as a test case, using its failure as justification for turning towards neoliberal reforms that would break such state monopoly over rural agriculture. Farmers too negotiated land titling reforms as proposed and, instead, forced WB experts to register land under village titles. As a result, rather than breaking with custom, I argue, the project ended up reinforcing the same custom. More revealing is how the project shows cracks between WB experts. Having failed to make sense of the low production figures, experts from the WB headquarters resorted to accusing their colleagues in Malawi of doing a poor job without understanding the overall socio-political environment in which the project operated.

Finally, chapter six carries on the theme of industry and development introduced in chapter three. It shows how the postcolonial state struggled to raise investment capital towards a proposed pulp and paper-making industry in the 1960s and 1970s. When Malawi signed a contract with a consortium of European investors from Finland, Sweden, Britain, and the then Federal Republic of Germany in 1978, the WB blocked the contract because, in its opinion, it rendered Malawi's economic interests incidental to those of the foreign investors. Unlike in the past, when the country's leader, Dr. Banda, often disagreed with the WB and Britain's decisions on the country's development direction, this time around, Banda bowed down. A rigid Western-oriented foreign policy evolving in the context of Cold War politics, the chapter argues, condemned the country to its traditional Western donors and closed prospects for soliciting funding from the East.

The six substantive chapters of the book flow chronologically. Thematically, however, they read in pairs, pulling together chapters two and six and chapters three and five, with chapters one and four acting as a connecting thread. Such a layout is deliberate. Other than breaking the colonial/postcolonial divide, the paired chapters allow me to emphasize common themes and how they played out during the colonial era before they were carried over to the postcolonial period. In this way, the book highlights better the legacies of British ideas and practices of development, spotting both continuities and discontinuities, and the multiple ways in which they were appropriated, contested, or changed during and after the colonial period.

NOTES

1. A good representation of this literature includes Guy Mhone, (ed.), *Malawi at the Crossroads: The Post-Colonial Political Economy* (Harare: SAPES Books, 1993). See also proceedings of the 1984 Edinburgh conference on Malawi's economic pattern published under the title *Malawi: An Alternative Pattern of Development: Proceedings of a Seminar held in the Centre of African Studies,* University of Edinburgh, 24 and 25 May, 1984.

2. For this history see a seminal work by John Iliffe, *The African Poor: A History* (Cambridge: Cambridge University Press, 1987).

3. See Andrew Zimmerman, "Africa in Imperial and Transnational History: Multi-Sited Historiography and the Necessity of Theory," *Journal of African History* 54, no. 3 (2013): 331–40; Akira Iriye and Pierre-Yves Saunier, *The Palgrave Dictionary of Transnational History* (New York: Palgrave Macmillan, 2009); Simone Turchetti, Néstor Herran, and Soroya Boudia, "Introduction: Have We Ever Been 'Transnational'? Towards a History of Science across and beyond Borders," *British Journal for the History of Science* 45, no. 3 (2012): 319–36; Pierre-Yves Saunier, *Transnational History* (New York: Palgrave Macmillan, 2013).

4. I am indebted to the following works for pointing scholarship towards that direction: Joseph Morgan Hodge, "Writing the History of Development (Part 2: Longer, Deeper, Wider)," *Humanity: An International Journal of Human Rights, Humanitarianism, and Development* 7, no. 1 (2016): 125–74; David C. Engerman and Corinna R. Unger, "Introduction: Towards a Global History of Modernization," *Diplomatic History* 33, no. 3 (2009): 375–85.

5. Donna C. Mehos and Suzanne M. Moon, "The Use of Portability: Circulating Experts in the Technopolitics of Cold War and Decolonization," in Hecht Gabrielle, ed. *Entangled Geographies: Empire and Technopolitics in the Global Cold War* (Cambridge: MIT Press, 2011): 43–72; Joseph M. Hodge, "British Colonial Expertise, Post-Colonial Careering and the Early History of International Development," *Journal of Modern European History* 8 no. 1, (2010): 24–46.

6. See Joseph Hodge, *Triumph of the Expert: Agrarian Doctrines of Development and the Legacies of British Colonialism* (Athens, OH: Ohio University Press, 2007)

7. Neo-Weberian literature seeks to expand the ideas about the state earlier raised by a German scholar, Max Weber (1864–1920). Weber had tremendous influence on the disciplines of sociology and political science. See Philipp Lottholz and Nicolas Lemay-Hébert, "Re-reading Weber, Re-conceptualizing State-building: From Neo-Weberian to Post-Weberian Approaches to State, Legitimacy and State-building," *Cambridge Review of International Affairs* 29, no. 4 (2016): 1467–1485.

8. Typical examples of this empirically based scholarship include Monica M. van Beusekom, *Negotiating Development: African Farmers and Colonial Experts at the Office Du Niger, 1920–1960* (Portsmouth, NH: James Currey, 2002); Rohland Schuknecht, *British Colonial Development Policy after the Second World War: The Case of Sukumaland, Tanganyika* (London: Global Book Marketing, 2010); Tania Murry Li, *The Will to Improve, Governmentality, Development, and the Practice of Politics* (Durham: Duke University Press, 2007).

9. See live data from https://data.worldbank.org/indicator/NY.GNP.PCAP.CD?locations=MW&year_high_desc=true, Accessed on January 28, 2019. Without oversimplifying the concept, GNI per capita measures the average net worth of a productive individual citizen in a given country per year. It is usually measured in US Dollars and assumes that the country's wealth is shared equally among the citizenry. For illustrative purposes, the USA's GNI per capita for the year 2018 was US$62,850. See https://www.macrotrends.net/countries/USA/united-states/gni-per-capita, Accessed on January 28, 2020; UNDP, *Human Development Report* (New York: UNDP, 2019), 302.

10. The country has a population of 17,563,000 people where more than 90 percent of it lives in rural areas. See Government of Malawi, *Malawi in Figures* (Zomba: National Statistical Office, 2019): 5, http://www.nsomalawi.mw/images/stories/data_on_line/general/malawi_in_figures/2019 percent20Malawi percent20in percent20Figures.pdf, Accessed on January 28, 2019.

11. See World Bank, Republic of Malawi Poverty Assessment (Washington, DC, World Bank Group, 2016), 2–10, https://openknowledge.worldbank.org/bitstream/handle/10986/26488/MalawiPovAssess.pdf?sequence=1&isAllowed=y, Accessed July 26, 2022; National Statistical Office, Integrated Household Panel Survey, 2010–2013: Household Socioeconomic Characteristics Report (Zomba, Malawi: National Statistical Office, 2014), 67–73.

12. The Central African Federation (CAF) was a loose political structure linking the governments of Nyasaland, Southern Rhodesia (Zimbabwe), and Northern Rhodesia (Zambia). Each of the countries had independent territorial Legislative Councils but sent representatives to the Federal Assembly in Southern Rhodesia where the Federation was headquartered.

13. At independence in 1964 Malawi had a total population of 4,032,326 people with 90 percent living in rural areas. The country occupies 45,747 square miles, including 9,422 square miles of Lake Malawi. See Government of Malawi, *1977 Statistical Survey* (Zomba: National Statistical Office, 1977), H.K. Banda Archive, Indiana University Library, Box 3, Folder 17.

14. I address the nuances of the discourse of development in chapter one.

15. Exceptions include John McCracken's *A History of Malawi*, 1859–1966 (Oxford: James Currey, 2012), which dedicated a chapter on general development projects of the 1950s; Literature of the 1970s such as that by Louis-James Nthenda, "H.M. Treasury and the Problems of Nyasaland Public Finance, 1919–1940," PhD Dissertation, Oxford University, 1972; Leroy Vail, "The Making of an Imperial Slum: Nyasaland and its Railways, 1895–1935," *Journal of African History* 16, no. 1 (1975): 89–112; Leroy Vail, "Railway Development and Colonial Underdevelopment: The Nyasaland Case," in Robin Palmer and N. Parsons, eds. *The Roots of Rural Poverty in Central and Southern Africa* (Los Angeles: University of California, 1977), 365–95. Typical studies of the 1980s and 1990s with a similar colonial era focus include John McCracken, "Experts and Expertise in Colonial Malawi," *African Affairs* 8, no. 332 (1982): 101–16; William Beinart, "Agricultural Planning and the Late Colonial Technical Imagination: The Lower Shire Valley, 1940–1960," in *Malawi: An Alternative Pattern of Development*, 93–148; Owen J. M. Kalinga, "The Master Farmers' Scheme in Nyasaland, 1950–1962: A Study of a Failed Attempt to Create a 'Yeoman' Class," *African Affairs* 92, no. 368 (1993): 367–87; Colin Baker, *Development Governor: A Biography of Sir Geoffrey Colby* (London: I. B. Tauris, 1994). I comment on some of these works in subsequent chapters of the book.

16. See Paul Chiudza Banda's *The State, Counterinsurgency and Political Policing in Colonial and Post-colonial Malawi, 1891–1994* (Lanham, MD: Lexington Books, 2020).

17. Frederick Cooper, *Decolonization and African Society: The Labor Question in French and British Africa* (Cambridge: Cambridge University Press, 1996).

18. Mhone (ed.), *Malawi at the Crossroad.*

19. David H. Humphrey, "Malawi's Economic Progress and Prospects," *The Eastern Africa Economic Review* 5, no. 2, (1973): 71–104; S. N. Acharya, "Development Perspectives and Priorities in Sub-Saharan Africa," *Finance and Development* 18, no. 1, (1981b): 16–24.

20. Carolyn McMaster, *Malawi: Foreign Aid and Development* (London: Julian Friedman Publishers, 1974), 73–87.

21. T.D. Williams, *Malawi: The Politics of Despair* (Ithaca: Cornell University Press, 1978), 261–300. See page 266–67 for statistical figures on that economic growth between 1964 and 1972.

22. Arturo Escobar, *Encountering Development: The Making and Unmaking of the Third World* (Princeton, NJ: Princeton University Press, 1995); James Ferguson, *The Anti-Politics Machine: "Development," Depoliticization, and Bureaucratic Power in Lesotho* (Minneapolis: University of Minnesota Press, 1994); Wolfgang Sachs (ed.), *The Development Dictionary: A Guide to Knowledge as Power* (London: Zed Books: 1992); Gilbert Rist, *The History of Development: From Western Origins to Global Faith* (London: Zed Books, 1997); James C. Scott, *Seeing Like a State: How Certain Schemes to Improve the Human Condition Have Failed* (New Haven: Yale University Press, 2008). For a critical review of works by Escobar, Ferguson, and Sachs see Arun Agrawal, "Poststructuralist Approaches to Development: Some Critical Reflections," *Peace and Change* 21, no. 4 (1996): 464–77.

23. I return to these issues in chapter two.

24. Scott, *Seeing Like a State,* 3–52; 88–89. For a critique see Daniel Immerwahr, *Thinking Small: The United States and the Lure of Community Development* (Cambridge, MA: Harvard University Press, 2015), 41–42; Robert Chambers, *Rural Development: Putting the Last First* (London: Routledge, 2014). On a lighter note, Immerwahr acknowledges that despite expert dominance, the TVA also encouraged "grassroots participation." For a book which seeks to trace the historical foundations of "community development" to the distant American past other than the more contemporary period as most scholars do, such an observation is not surprising.

25. Ferguson, *The Anti-Politics Machine,* 256.

26. Ibid., xv.

27. Escobar, *Encountering Development,* 15.

28. See a special issue of the *Journal of Modern European History* 8, no. 1 (2010). Frederick Cooper's introductory chapter, "Writing the History of Development," 5–23, is enlightening in its critique of the post-development school.

29. See Michael Cowen and Robert W. Shenton, *Doctrines of Development* (London: Routledge, 1996), 7; Michael Cowen and Robert Shenton, "The Origin and Course of Fabian Colonialism in Africa," *Journal of Historical Sociology* 4, no. 2 (1991): 143–74; Joseph Hodge and Gerald Hödl, "Introduction," in Joseph M. Hodge, Gerald Hödl, and Martina Kopf, eds. *Developing Africa: Concepts, Practices and Twentieth-century Colonialism* (Manchester: Manchester University Press, 2014), 2–4; David Ekbladh, *The Great American Mission: Modernization and the Construction of American World Order* (Princeton, NJ: Princeton University Press, 2011).

30. Beusekom, *Negotiating Development;* Schuknecht, *British Colonial Development Policy after the Second World War*.

31. Frederick Cooper is an exception to this observation. His studies on the colonial and post-colonial histories of development seriously engage the developmental state. He breaks the boundaries of histories of development to critique and borrow from Africa's political economy literature. See his *Africa Since 1940: The Past of the Present* (Cambridge: Cambridge University Press, 2019); *Colonialism in Question: Theory, Knowledge and History* (Berkeley, CA: University of California Press, 2005): 3–30; 153–203. While the former examines the behavior of colonial and post-colonial states, discussing, among others, the political aims of development projects and the ways in which politicians raised resources for such projects, the latter reflects on empire states, their behavior, and fluidities. A significant contribution in both is how we should interpret the legacies of colonialism. His analysis breaks the colonial-postcolonial divide.

32. Rational choice theorists such as Robert Bates view African leadership as having workable policy options at their disposal and yet they deliberately choose unworkable ones which usually harm the very poor in the societies but present some political dividends to leaders. See Robert H. Bates, *Markets and States in Tropical Africa: The Political Basis of Agricultural Policies* (Berkeley: University of California Press, 1981).

33. Crawford Young, *The African Colonial State in Comparative Perspective* (New Haven: Yale University Press, 1997): 9; Crawford Young, *The Postcolonial State in Africa: Fifty Years of Independence, 1960–2010* (Madison: University of Wisconsin Press, 2012): 3–31.

34. Bruce J. Berman, *Control and Crisis in Colonial Kenya: The Dialectic of Domination* (London: James Currey, 1990), 25. Berman is joined by Cooper who faults literature on the decolonization of the British and French Empires in Africa for presenting a deterministic analysis of the process because of reading history with the 1960s as the starting point. See Cooper, *Decolonization and African Society,* 4–7.

35. Berman, *Control and Crisis in Colonial Kenya*, 32.

36. The following works are associated with these terms: Mahmood Mamdani, *Citizen and Subject: Contemporary Africa and the Legacy of Late Colonialism* (Kampala; Cape Town; London: Fountain Publishers; David Philip; James Currey, 1996); Patrick Chabal and Jean-Pascal Daloz, *Africa Works: Disorder as Political Instrument* (Oxford: James Currey, 1993); Jean-François Bayart, *The State in Africa: The Politics of the Belly* (Cambridge: Polity Press, 1993); Sara Berry, *No Condition Is Permanent: The Social Dynamics of Agrarian Change in Sub-Saharan Africa* (Madison, WI: University of Wisconsin Press, 1993); I could also add Göran Hydén, *Beyond Ujamaa in Tanzania: Underdevelopment and an Uncaptured Peasantry* (Berkeley: University of California Press, 1980).

37. Hyden's thesis should be located in the general Marxist debates of the 1980s which blamed colonial capitalism for having failed to exploit Africa enough in the sense that it left active pre-capitalist economies or failed to integrate Africans fully into a capitalist market economy (i.e., did not transform colonies by creating land and labor markets). Instead of blaming Western capitalism or colonial economies

generally, Hyden shifts our attention to the resilience of the African peasantry or mode of production which rendered Western capitalism weak to achieve its transformative purpose. See also Anne Phillips, *The Enigma of Colonialism: British Policy in West Africa* (London: James Currey, 1989).

38. See Dan Banik and Blessings Chinsinga, *Political Transition and Inclusive Development in Malawi* (London: Routledge, 2016).

39. According to Frederick Cooper, leapfrogging legacies denote analyses that assume that historical event A influenced event C, ignoring the influence of event B. See his *Colonialism in Question*, 17.

40. See Lottholz and Lemay-Hébert, "Re-reading Weber, Re-conceptualizing State-building," 1467–1485.

41. Max Weber et al., *From Max Weber: Essays in Sociology* (New York: Routledge, 1967): 78.

42. One of the reasons why scholars discarded the state as a conceptual framework had to do with the rise of new political institutions in the mid-twentieth century including political parties, pressure groups, mass media, and others. Under such circumstances, the use of a "political system" was desirable because it accommodated all such groups. See Gabriel A. Almond, "The Return to the State," *American Political Science Review* 82 (1988): 82. For a general introduction of the debate to the usefulness of the state as a unit of analysis see Timothy Mitchell, "The Limits of the State: Beyond Statist Approaches and Their Critics," *The American Political Science Review* 85, no. 1 (1991): 77–96.

43. See Eric A. Nordlinger, *On the Autonomy of the Democratic State* (Milton Keynes, UK: Lightning Source, 1981); Theda Skocpol, *States and Social Revolutions: A Comparative Analysis of France, Russia, and China* (Cambridge: Cambridge University Press, 1979); Theda Skocpol, Peter B. Evans, and Dietrich Rueschemeyer, *Bringing the State Back In* (Cambridge: Cambridge University Press, 1986); Stephen D. Krasner, *Defending the National Interest: Raw Materials Investments and U.S. Foreign Policy* (Princeton, NJ: Princeton University Press, 1978).

44. Skocpol, *States and Social Revolutions*, 29.

45. Mitchell, "The Limits of the State," 89.

46. Young, *The African Colonial State in Comparative Perspective*, 35–42.

47. In other words, a gate-keeper state, to use the language of Frederik Cooper, cannot wholly ascertain its independence from its financial source. See his *Africa Since 1940*, 298–304.

48. Naomi Chazan, "Patterns of State Society Incorporation and Disengagement in Africa," in Donald S. Rothchild and Naomi Chazan, eds. *The Precarious Balance: State and Society in Africa* (Boulder: Westview Press, 1988), 123.

49. See Leander Schneider, *Government of Development: Peasants and Politicians in Postcolonial Tanzania* (Bloomington: Indiana University Press, 2014).

50. Joel S. Migdal, *State in Society: Studying How States and Societies Transform and Constitute One Another* (Cambridge: Cambridge University Press, 2010), 115–16.

51. See Berman, *Control and Crisis in Colonial Kenya*; Hodge, *Triumph of the Expert*; Phillips, *Enigma of Colonialism*.

52. Phillips, *The Enigma of Colonialism,* 14.

53. In this way, Phillips challenges Crawford Young's conception of a *Bura Matari* state.

54. Ibid., 156.

55. Hodge, *Triumph of the Expert,* 61.

56. In that the colonial state was not divorced from the Colonial Office.

57. See Berman, *Control and Crisis in Colonial Kenya*, 1990.

58. John Lonsdale and Bruce Berman, "Coping with Contradictions: The Development of the Colonial State in Kenya, 1895–1914," *Journal of African History* 20, no. 4 (1979): 490.

Chapter One

The Poor and British Development Discourse in Africa, 1909–1970s

This chapter provides a framework for understanding British ideas of colonial development and welfare and how they evolved. The discussion is relevant because much of what the state tried to achieve for the poor in Malawi mirrored the debates on poverty and development as they unfolded within the British Empire. British politicians, bureaucrats, advisors, lobbyists, and several other individuals engaged each other continuously on the theme of African progress throughout the first half of the twentieth century. At the center of the debate was the question of framing a colonial policy that addressed metropolitan development needs without sacrificing specific economic and political interests of colonial peoples placed under the care of Britain; or the goal of raising production and colonial productivity while improving African living standards.[1] Equally contested were strategies for achieving these goals. While some supported capitalist-oriented and market-based economies, others were in favor of merely improving what they considered to be indigenous "traditional" economies. British politicians, Colonial Office officials, and administrators in the colonies, never agreed on these alternatives such that the colonial policy that evolved in British Africa oscillated between these opposing poles, depending on individual interests or the specific historical forces acting on the empire at the time. The chapter argues that the ideas these debates generated presaged how the war on poverty unfolded in colonial and, later, postcolonial Malawi. Because the debate on colonial development and welfare remained unsettled, equally unpredictable and less deterministic is the history of development practice in the country.

Four distinct moments defining Britain's engagement with the colonial societies on development and welfare provide shape to this chapter. The first began as an extension of the late nineteenth century metropolitan debate on how to safeguard the interests of the poor and unemployed segments of British society. Concerns for the British poor became dominant with the onset of the agricultural depression in the late nineteenth century and forced politicians to explore solutions to the problem. African colonial societies were involved in the debate because part of the solution to the problem lay in exploiting or developing colonial resources. The second moment began in the late 1930s and had its climax in 1940 when the British Parliament passed the Colonial Development and Welfare Act (CDWA). It is generally agreed that the Act symbolized Britain's commitment to colonial development and welfare. While in the past colonies mostly relied on self-generated resources for development, from 1940 on Britain committed to supporting dependencies through development grants.[2]

The third phase witnessed the passing of the 1948 Overseas Resources Development Act (ORDA), which created two public corporations—the Overseas Food Corporation (OFC) and the Colonial Development Corporation (CDC). The two public corporations aimed to produce resources in the colonies for metropolitan industries. In creating them, Britain was responding to the post-war Sterling Crisis that the Second World War created. If the CDWA favored the interests of African colonial subjects, the ORDA rendered concerns for African development incidental to metropolitan economic needs. The final phase began from the 1960s and was marked by Britain's engagement with its former colonies. This was an era when the UN aid organizations and the Western bilateral donor agencies took an active role in addressing the problem of poverty in the former colonies, now turned into Less Developed Countries (LDCs).

In discussing these phases, the chapter pays attention to ideas of development associated with some key figures, notably those affiliated with different political parties and organizations in Britain. It was those individuals identified with the Liberal, the Liberal Unionist, and, later, the Labour Party, that had a tremendous influence on Britain's position on colonial poverty and other ills. The Labour Party features prominently in the discussion because, over time, it lobbied not just for the interests of the working class in Britain, but also the many colonial societies whom it regarded as victims of capitalist exploitation. Individuals from such organizations as the Fabian Society and the Fabian Colonial Bureau (FCB), founded in 1884 and 1940 respectively, had a tremendous influence on Labour's colonial policy in diverse areas. By discussing the ideas that some selected members of the Fabian Society and the Labour Party held, the chapter displays better how development practice unfolded in Malawi. The subsequent sections discuss the phases in question.

FROM THE POOR IN BRITAIN TO THE EXPLOITED IN AFRICA, 1890S–1940

In 1905, Britain's Liberal Prime Minister, Henry Campbell-Bannerman, had this to say: "we desire to develop our undeveloped estates in this country; to colonize our own country; to give the farmer greater freedom and greater security in business . . . to make the land less of a pleasure ground for the rich and more of a treasure house for the nation."[3] Campbell-Bannerman's remarks came in the wake of domestic challenges of poverty and urban unemployment Britain grappled with in the closing decade of the nineteenth century. Much of this resulted from the late nineteenth-century agriculture depression that created a surplus rural population. Urban overpopulation was imminent and forced politicians and intellectuals to identify solutions to avert the impending social and political chaos. Joseph Chamberlain, a Liberal Unionist who was appointed the Secretary of State for Colonies (S/S/C) in 1895, saw the solution to domestic challenges in developing what he described as the "imperial estate," by which he referred to the colonial territories which had come under British occupation from the late nineteenth century.[4] Chamberlain called upon Britain to use public resources and set-up necessary infrastructure that was significant enough to attract private enterprises—settlers, plantation owners, and mining magnates. Such projects included road, railway, and dock construction. Another significant aspect of his plan was to promote investment in research, especially in the areas of agriculture, medicine, forestry, and others. He saw this aspect as helping Britain to overcome problems of production.[5] With this in place, Britain would develop its old and new markets in the colonies, attract investors, and employ the surplus population while addressing her economic problems.

Campbell-Bannerman's 1905 speech illustrates well the rejection of Chamberlain's ideas while projecting an alternative approach. By 1909, the Liberals had passed a Development Act which sanctioned the Treasury to finance development projects within Britain. Among other aspects, the Act addressed the problem of unemployment prevalent among the poor by introducing state-financed agricultural schemes, rural industries, and land reclamation projects.[6] Such projects would help to arrest rural-urban migration and hence contain social pressure such groups potentially presented in urban areas.[7] The Liberals, including such names as Sydney and Beatrice Webb, who became staunch members of the Fabian Society, and Henry Rider Haggard, celebrated David Lloyd George's 1909 Development Act.[8] The Act advocated for agrarian and rural development practices that targeted rural and urban British communities as opposed to supporting industry and high-level infrastructural projects in the colonies as Chamberlain advocated. They tolerated state-financed infrastructural projects in so far as these targeted the destitute rural and urban classes.

The two opposing solutions discussed here are relevant in the way they clarify two meanings that the concept of development carries—either as a deliberate intervention to raise production and productivity and hence achieve economic progress, or a deliberate course of action aimed at raising the living standards of people placed to the care of the state.[9] Both of these aspects arise out of the premise that development can be a subject of what Cowen and Shenton call an "immanent and objective process." The first aspect assumes that a natural process towards progress has failed to raise production and productivity. It is, therefore, necessary that deliberate effort be made to produce progress. This conceptualization resonates well with Chamberlain's thinking of "developing" the imperial estate to address Britain's economic challenges. The second aspect assumes that the unregulated natural process of progress has created "progress" for some, but impoverished others. It departs from the premise that societies can achieve "bad progress," which, while empowering some, disempowers others, rendering them unemployed and poor. Such an outcome necessitates a deliberate intervention to ameliorate the effects of bad progress and improve the living standards of those caught up on the wrong side of development.[10] Chamberlain's solution lay in developing colonies and creating jobs for the surplus population while addressing the general economic problems Britain faced. The Liberal project aimed at ameliorating the problem of progress that the unregulated late nineteenth-century industrialization created. It sought to directly target the poor in Britain by providing them with employment and improving their living standards.

But certain development practices or interventions, such as the ones Chamberlain advocated, could also be destructive and create more chaos. Some segments of British society feared that Chamberlain's proposal would have the effects of exploiting African societies. Radical Liberals and others warned British society about intruding in African economies along the lines of Chamberlain's proposal. Chief among them were members of the "Liverpool School" whose task dovetailed with that of the Fabian Society and the Labour Party. Considering themselves as advocates of African rights and interests, which was an extension of similar roles they played in Britain, they helped to formulate significant ideas on colonial development and welfare whose legacy went beyond the colonial period.

Named after the strong links its advocates had with the Liverpool merchants in Britain, the Liverpool School became dominant from the 1890s. Its members included Mary Kingsley, an English ethnographer and writer who had visited West Africa several times, John Holt, a merchant who plied his trade on West African coast, and E. D. Morel, a politically connected journalist.[11] They distinguished themselves as defenders of African political and economic rights, which late nineteenth-century imperialism threatened. Rather than providing answers to the debate on the surplus population in Britain, the group took issue with Britain's capitalist activities, especially concessionary and plantation companies, for their disastrous effects on the indigenous communities. Instead, they advocated for British imperialism that would safeguard both the political and economic freedom of Africans. To achieve this, the group advised Britain to rely on existing structures of production in Africa while encouraging African peasants to grow cash crops the Liverpool merchants could trade. Freedom of trade for Africans, they argued, was a common practice that characterized old trading deals. For them, imperialism threatened this freedom. The group condemned what Bernard Porter describes as the manifestations of capitalist exploitation in both West and Central Africa. Among others, they criticized the dominance of "monopoly companies, the exploitation of natural resources for profit, gold-mining, and forced labor" which exploited Africans.[12]

None of the members of the Liverpool School was more influential than Morel. The youngest of the three, Morel criticized British imperialism for disrupting African economies and traditions in West Africa. He argued for freedom of exchange, with Africans left to manage their economies and directly dealing with traders of their choice. He advocated for direct intervention only insofar as it would build African institutions and help to empower them both economically and politically. For Morel, commerce and the communication infrastructure associated with it, should have served as vehicles for building up Africans, rather than imposing on them "laws and institutions unfamiliar to him [sic]."[13] Morel's ideas on native land rights became nuanced through the Congo Reform Movement (1904–1913), an organization that advocated for the rights of Africans in King Leopold II's Congo, which Morel served as its secretary. Displeased with massive land dispossession there, he became critical of deliberate policies that deprived Africans of their rights to land, not just in Congo but within the British Empire and other parts of the world. Morel associated imperialism with human rights abuses in the South African and Southern Rhodesian mines and rubber plantations of Putumayo in Latin America.[14] In consequence, "Morelism" (as a doctrine constituting Morel's ideas) offered a solution—which was to abolish the exploitative system of plantations, introduce indirect as opposed to direct rule, promote free instead of monopoly trade, and peasant rather than company proprietorship.

By the time Morel's ideas matured, colonial rule was well established in British Africa such that there was little gain in advocating for old imperialism based on trade. In Southern and Eastern Africa, for instance, white settlers already owned vast tracks of land. Thus, Morelism merely checked the nature of colonial exploitation while advocating for a better way of harnessing resources in Africa. Members of the Liverpool School, therefore, were imperialists just like Chamberlain. The distinction between the two groups centered on the nature of the imperial trusteeship they projected. The concept of "trusteeship" has a long history that deserves a summary here. It should be traced back to the ideas of Claude Henri de Saint-Simon (1760–1825), a French scholar who had tremendous influence on such disciplines as Philosophy, Political Science, Sociology, and Economics. In the area of social progress, Saint Simonians (referring to all those who believed in his ideas), became disappointed with progress as a natural and spontaneous process and its failure to produce order. Consider unregulated production capitalism as an example and how it empowers the capitalist class while disempowering the proletariat at the same time. Saint Simonians sought to provide order to this kind of imperfect progress by suggesting that certain people be appointed to regulate it—the trustees. They had in mind bankers as possible trustees or experts that would guide societies towards perfect progress in an orderly fashion. Later, Auguste Comte (1798–1857), who was raised in the Saint Simonian tradition, perfected Saint Simonian model by elevating priests and sociologists, the people whom he regarded as having a better understanding of the society, as guardians of progress. He theorized his ideas through what has been passed down as a theory of "positivism," which was the last of the three stages through which he traced the development of human society.

The Comtean model did not completely drop bankers as trustees, however. From the late nineteenth century, the Fabians believed in the principle of trusteeship as the best way of guiding progress. As will become clear, they rejected Chamberlain's ideas as representing Saint-Simonian version of trusteeship which, having relied on bankers, who by nature are interested in making profits, would only create further chaos in the development process. Instead, they replaced bankers with state officials. State bureaucrats, so they argued, were better placed to act as trustees and guide societies towards "positive" progress. The concept of trusteeship assumed a political meaning in the late nineteenth century and helped to justify European imperialism—the whole idea that Europe was only acting as a trustee to help the conquered societies achieve progress. The concept gained more ground with the formation of the Mandates Commission of the League of Nations in 1919, which allowed allied powers to take over colonies that once belonged to Germany and her allies in the hope that they could be assisted to achieve economic progress and political maturity before they were ushered towards political sovereignty.[15]

For Chamberlain, true trusteeship required developing the imperial estate for the benefit of Britain and its colonies. But the strategy of achieving this required the agency of European enterprises with the state merely helping to set up the necessary economic infrastructure and technical assistance. The strategy also required reorganizing African economies. Chamberlain's ideas, therefore, represented what Kenneth Robinson points to as a transformative doctrine of imperial trusteeship, according to which Britain held the responsibility to transform African societies through Western science, expertise, and technology.[16] In contrast, Morel and his colleagues, and as will become apparent, the Fabians, pushed for a "preservationist doctrine of imperial trusteeship"—the whole idea of developing African resources along "native" lines, with state officials providing some guidance. Morelism, therefore, longed "for patience, honesty, and a just recognition of human rights amongst the people we govern, no matter their color, intelligence, or degree of natural mental evolution."[17] This approach would help to contain the disorder associated with capitalist activities.

It is this idea of whether to achieve development along native lines or through European enterprise that was at the center of the debate on colonial development strategies throughout the first half of the twentieth century. Another point of contention centered on the question of whose interests the British Empire needed to protect. For Morel and his colleagues, Britain was merely interested in addressing its domestic problems with little interest in African welfare. The solution Morelism presented, however, would not immediately address both the metropolitan and colonial economic interests, even if they so desired. Advocates of British imperialism doubted the capacity of the African economy to meet the growing European demand for African products without reorganizing it. More significantly, however, is what Marshall Berman has described as the "darker side of development."[18] As described earlier, unregulated progress or development interventions could potentially create chaos, enriching some while pauperizing others. It is here that Morel's ideas would not align with those of Fabians such as Sydney Olivier, although Morel too became a confessing Fabian.[19]

Olivier, who served as the Governor of Jamaica between 1907 and 1913, distinguished himself as a defender of the rights that the conquered societies held over land. Unlike Morel, however, he objected to allowing peasants total freedom—where, as individual proprietors, Africans could participate in free exchange willy-nilly within the overall context of *laissez-faire* exchange, as Morel advised. Rather than promoting individualism among the peasantry, Olivier and the rest of the Fabians emphasized collectivism, with British officials slowly guiding Africans towards progress as communities or individuals within communities. Thus, with its calls not to intrude into African economies, "Morelism" did not convince members of the Fabian Society that it was a workable strategy for improving the lives of the people placed under their care in Africa and meeting Britain's demands for African products. In other words, Morelism was a less useful guide to "develop" Africa for itself, and the broader global population, as Lord Lugard's Dual Mandate would emphasize a few years later. Similarly, the Fabians were reluctant to accept the Chamberlainite position, which the members of *The Round Table* would carry forward after the First World War. The *Round Table* was a journal which started in 1910 and pulled together contributions from those British politicians who believed in Chamberlain's ideas of developing the imperial estate by laying down basic infrastructure that would attract private investors.[20] For the Fabians, Chamberlain's thesis was not a workable solution either because, by failing to contain the excesses of capitalism such as land alienation, proletarianization, and individualism, it could produce chaos and, therefore, was not in conformity with Britain's sense of trusteeship over the colonies.

Drawing his data from Kenya, Norman Leys, another prominent Fabian figure of the time who was dismissed from his medical post there (after which he came to Nyasaland) owing to the critical position he held on land alienation, argued that both the settler and peasant economies were essential and called upon the state to defend them both as a necessary means of sustaining the Kenyan economy. Like Olivier, he dismissed the Liverpool School's call to preserve precapitalistic African economies. Leys saw attempts to halt the forces of capitalism as an unrealistic undertaking. Instead, he called for a fair system of land redistribution that reflected Britain's sense of trusteeship over the colonies. Such interventions would help to protect Africans from the excesses of production and market capitalism.[21] While serving as the chairperson to the Labour Party Advisory Committee on Imperial Questions (LPACIQ), Leonard Woolf, another significant member of the Society, saw land in Africa as the property of the local community. The government had the responsibility to develop village agricultural communes and cooperatives for the benefit of Africans, without sacrificing other broader interests.[22]

The Fabian emphasis on African community life did not lack a deeper historical context. It was expressed in opposition to liberal ideas of achieving progress or improvement in India by promoting English institutions and private property rights laws. As both Metcalf and Hodge observe in their separate studies, between the 1770s and 1830s, British politicians and intellectuals debated the central role land would play in improving Indian lives.[23] Such figures as Lord Cornwallis, who served as the Governor-General of India between 1786–1793, argued that economic progress in India could be achieved through a policy that targeted the Indian hereditary landlords, the Zamindars. Cornwallis reasoned that if the state granted the Zamindars private rights to land, and their proprietary rights were recognized amidst competing claims to land, they would be motivated to invest in it and achieve high agricultural productivity. High productivity, in consequence, would help to expand commerce for the benefit of both Indians and British East Indian Company's trade dealings.

Cornwallis implemented these ideas in 1793 through a Permanent Settlement Act of that year, which helped to establish a Zamindar-dominated Settlement Scheme in Bengal. The Act recognized the Zamindars as owners of specified portions of land for a fixed revenue payable to the state. It also granted them powers to sell or transfer land. Under the Bengal Settlement Scheme, the Zamindars would work their land through peasants contracted to them. Critics of Cornwallis' ideas viewed the settlement project as potentially disrupting of Indian community life. Instead, they suggested that the "project of improvement"—improving the Indians and hence justifying British rule in India—could proceed through the agency of peasants (the ryots) and along the lines of community production.[24] Such an approach would preserve a sense of community crucial to achieving progress in India. These commentators were joined by later critics who argued that because of their rent-seeking behavior, the Zamindars were inherently "parasitic." Using them as agents of improvement/progress would only lead to the exploitation of more peasants. Many of these critics were admirers of Jeremy Bentham and James Mill, the renowned English Utilitarians of the late eighteenth and early nineteenth centuries. Though they advocated for progress through the agency of peasants, they were no fans of traditional Indian civilization and culture. Utilitarians supported peasant-centered improvement only in so far as it would eventually give rise to propertied individuals or "yeoman" farmers. They regarded the latter group as critical agents of economic change in India.[25]

During the first half of the nineteenth century, it was Utilitarian ideas that dictated much of India's agrarian reforms, with peasants clandestinely accessing individual landholdings, often taking on board the responsibility to settle previous debts on the titles. Excessive land revenues demanded by the state forced peasants to resell their land and relegated some to tenancy arrangements on the same land they previously owned. In part, the chaos that emerged fed into the 1857 Indian Rebellion in which Indian soldiers revolted against their superiors in the British East India Company's military, in the process killing several whites. The reform project had failed. Britain dropped attempts, albeit not entirely, to improve the Indians through the introduction of Western institutions of land ownership and other aspects. While the Indians might have been improvable, such reforms were considered politically dangerous to British rule on the subcontinent. Consequently, Britain ruled India through the traditional institutions of the region. Metcalf has described this change as representing the "rule of difference" in contrast to that of "similarity." Under the latter approach, Britain sought to transform Indian socio-economic life into the very replica of British society, an exercise that failed.[26]

Elsewhere, Michele Stephens has shown how the liberal ideology played out in Mexico during the second half of the nineteenth century. The liberals linked land, modernization, and civilization as constitutive parts of an "ideology of progress" and regarded communal landholdings prevalent among the Huichol (native Indians) of Mexico's Sierra Madre and other regions as a threat to that progress. For example, Porfirio Diaz's regime (1876–1880, 1884–1911), tried with minimal success to force individual landholdings among the native Indians. Such attempts were part of the wider reform movement of the late nineteenth century which aimed at improving the "ignorant" and uncivilized native Indians.[27] Similar to the case of British India, the reform program failed to improve the Indians in Mexico, leading some intellectuals to seek to defend their way of life, arguing that the people in question were naturally averse to reforms and not improvable.

Similar arguments played out in Jamaica between the 1830s and 1860s. As Catherine Hall has documented, the Baptist Missionary Society took upon itself the task of civilizing the predominantly black society in British Jamaica. Blacks, so they argued, were caught up in "savagery, heathenism, and superstition."[28] By Christianizing and campaigning for the emancipation of slaves, the Baptist missionaries hoped to improve these communities. The planters, who sought to defend their economic interests, condemned missionaries for pursuing what they perceived as unrealistic goals of improving blacks and other related communities. Their arguments became pronounced in 1831 and 1865 when blacks rebelled against the colonial state on the island. The 1831 Rebellion was staged following rumors that the king in Britain had emancipated slaves and that the planters in Jamaica denied them their freedom. The riots lasted for a week and left much property destroyed. Total emancipation followed in 1838. The 1865 event, which was the most extensive rebellion, took place at Morant Bay in Jamaica. Droughts, the failure of the crops, unemployment, oppressive taxes, oppressive justice system and police brutality, combined to bring about the rebellion that led to the loss of European lives and destruction of property. More significantly, the protesters used the same language of freedom that the missionaries taught them to demand equality on the island.[29] In response, Governor Edward John Eyre declared martial law that led to the execution of more than 400 protesters. For the planters and other segments of the metropolitan society, freed slaves could not be improved. Baptist missionaries condemned the rebellion but did so in ways that cast the blame on poor administration of the island.

One could add to these stories the late nineteenth- and twentieth-century case of the Sulawesi people of Indonesia. As Tania Li shows, seeking to improve the "backward" and "uncivilized Sulawesi," the Dutch removed these "uncultured" people from their isolated hamlets in the mountains, and forcibly resettled them in the concentrated villages in the valleys. Here, they were forced to produce rice in colonial settlement schemes through modern ways of agricultural production. Contact with more "enlightened," sedentary communities of the valley was regarded as a necessary step in civilizing the Sulawesi peoples. Having failed to adapt to their new locations, many of them died of malaria or returned to the mountains where they continued with their swidden agricultural practices.[30] The project of improvement had failed but with terrible consequences on the government's capacity to guide the process of "improvement."

All these cases served as a warning to the British activities in Africa. Other than condemning capitalist exploitation in East and Central Africa, the Fabians argued against policies of haphazardly intruding into community life without weighing the political and social costs involved. Instead, they sought a new form of colonial trusteeship that safeguarded Africa's indigenous institutions, while protecting them from the ravages of markets. This object included supporting either the community or individual African farmers within the confines of communal life. Not surprisingly, much of the Labour Party literature they influenced displayed these aspects. In 1926, for example, the Labour Party argued against principles of individualism, stating in its policy conclusions that "land in Africa, [as a general policy], should be treated by the administration as the property of the native community or communities." The governments had the responsibility to develop the "economic resources of the land for the benefit of communities."[31] Among the seven principles it outlined on matters of land, none of them emphasized individual land tenure. Instead, Labour policy insisted that "native land tenure should be maintained and, where necessary, strengthened by legislative enactment."[32]

Though acknowledging the role the Fabians played in shaping the discourse of colonial development, especially in matters of land and African welfare, British officials in Africa also debated these ideas during the early phase of colonial rule. Lord Lugard, for one, was averse to reforms that encouraged individual land ownership. Unlike the Fabians, he tolerated communal tenure systems because he saw private rights to land as a product of an evolutionary process. For Lugard, who hatched these ideas while serving as the Governor-General of Nigeria between 1914 and 1919, private property was more advanced but he did not think Africans were ready for it. He believed that with the passage of time, Africans would adopt private property.[33]

But most members of the Fabian Society feared that capitalist activities had already set private land ownership in motion, leaving in its trail a kind of disorder synonymous to that of India in which individualism created chaos in form of peasant indebtedness, landlessness, and political unrest. Such activities, warned Olivier in 1929, were creating "a demoralized and uncontrolled African proletariat" and considered the resultant resentment as "the encroaching danger [of revolt] in Africa."[34] The 1933 Labour publication—*The Colonial Empire*—which influential Fabian figures (C.R.

Buxton, W. McGregor Ross, and Leonard Woolf) helped to draft, presented a similar concern:

> The serious responsibility for the welfare of these many millions of [African] peoples which rests on the British electorate and the Governments they appoint has never been adequately recognized by the British people. In territories where there has been a self-conscious and vigorous white minority, expropriation of native lands and exploitation of native labour have been permitted and defended by successive British governments. The methods of our capitalist system have been transplanted overseas, and tribal and family life has been broken up by taxation designed to compel the male population to work for the white employer. [We must halt this level of chaos or we will soon face the consequences].[35]

Concerned with addressing such problems, Labour's policy advocated for agricultural cooperatives, designed to assist Africans in their economic undertakings by producing and marketing products as communities. The policy also lobbied for increased funding towards improving African welfare, while rebuking East and Central African governments for pursuing land, taxation, and marketing policies that disadvantaged Africans.

The 1938 publication by Lord Hailey, *An African Survey*, further articulated the problems Africa was facing especially as they related to the question of land and progress.[36] Hailey's report was one outcome of a decade-long (1929–1939) project which aimed to understand the potential scientific knowledge held for resolving Africa's social and economic problems. As a first step, however, the exercise required the acquisition of up-to-date knowledge about the specific problems of Britain's tropical African colonies.[37] With post-Depression industrial strikes in British Africa looming in the background, authorities awaited the findings of Hailey's survey with great anticipation. Published in 1938, it dedicated several sections to the question of land tenure systems in tropical Africa. A significant question raised by the study was whether it was necessary to introduce reforms from above to facilitate the individualization of land in African societies. In general, the report affirmed the superiority of private rights to land over communal land ownership. But it also dispelled philosophical fallacies that had guided debate on communal land tenure systems:

> "Communal" or "collective" [sic] tenures do not necessarily involve insecurity for the cultivator. . . . Insecurity on the part of the cultivating occupier is, indeed, an incident much more common to the relations of landlord and tenant than to the "collective" system prevailing in Africa.[38]

With such an observation, the report inadvertently reinforced the Fabian view of supporting Africans within the circles of communal life. Moreover, Hailey shied away from suggesting reforms towards land individualization despite observing that in some African colonies, "a more definite advance in the direction of individualization [was justified] by economic and social conditions."[39] Having served in India where attempts to create individual proprietorship in land created indebtedness and uncontrolled differentiation with adverse social effects on the Indian peasants, Hailey feared that top-down reforms towards land individualization would have similar effects on the African continent. Instead, he favored a "system of occupancy" where Africans would enjoy usufruct rights to land as opposed to one in which individuals would have proprietary rights over registered land. Unlike the latter case in which holders had the freedom to dispose of their land, he saw the former constituting "less of a break with traditional social structure and the prevailing system of cultivation."[40] Even with this, Hailey advised that governments might adopt either of these routes, depending on the rural economy they wanted to create. The debate on land, as the next chapter will show, pitted the CO officials against local colonial administrators in the 1940s in Malawi. The two groups tussled over proposals towards "native" land individualization as one way of achieving higher productivity in African land. Significantly, the debate coincided with the passing of the 1940 CDWA, another defining moment in Britain's engagement with Africa.

FROM THE CDWA TO ORDA, 1939–1950S

It was Malcolm MacDonald, not a subscriber to Fabian ideals, who helped to frame the Colonial Development and Welfare Bill of 1939 while serving as the S/S/C under the National Government. The Bill passed into an Act of Parliament in 1940—the Colonial Development and Welfare Act (CDWA)—and dedicated £5 million per year in grants from the British imperial treasury for ten years towards development and welfare in the colonies. The Act also set aside £500,000 per year for ten years towards research.[41] Britain renewed this Act on several occasions—1945, 1949, 1950 (under a Labour government) and 1955, 1959, 1963 (under the Conservatives). It committed more resources for colonial development with each subsequent renewal. The CDWA launched what has gone down as Britain's developmentalist colonialism. The commitment placed on addressing the development challenges and welfare of the colonial peoples was unprecedented. It did not lack a historical context, however. Gupta has argued that a shift towards Britain's active involvement in colonial development was a direct response to the recommendations of the Royal Commission's report on the West Indies.[42] The British Parliament set up the Royal Commission to investigate the post-Depression political unrest there. However, as Cooper has argued, the 1940 CDWA, which took effect in earnest after 1945, was equally responding to similar political unrests in Africa.[43] Africans rejected the limited roles that the colonial project had assigned to them. Combined with the economic challenges the Great Depression presented, Africans responded through strikes and unrests. Peasants in rural areas, as McCracken has illustrated with colonial Malawi, resorted to burning their produce rather than presenting them to what they described as unscrupulous marketing boards.[44]

These immediate political problems arising "from below" should not negate the pressure that the critics of the state had long raised concerning African welfare. In significant ways, these unrests and protests vindicated earlier Fabian criticism of the imperial project in Africa, and the Labour Party's demands for significant economic and political reforms. This time around, the Fabian Society's affiliates and others were joined by the international community in demanding colonial reforms, without absorbing themselves in the latter's anti-colonial sentiments.[45] In pushing for the CDW Bill in 1939, MacDonald was also responding to these deep-seated historical demands for better African welfare. That Britain regularly replenished the Colonial Development and Welfare Fund shows that the Labour Government, and later, the Conservative Government, continued to embrace the CDWA. Much of Labour's postwar policy for the colonies, however, was presented under the guidance of the Fabian Colonial Bureau (FBC), a Fabian Society research body. The FCB, enjoying the input from the new generation of Fabian leadership, including Arthur Creech Jones, who became the FCB's chair in 1943, and Rita Hinden, its executive secretary, celebrated Britain's concern for the welfare of colonial societies. It was under its guidance that Labour's policy on African dependencies became nuanced, incorporating even the contentious political objectives of self-government within the Commonwealth.[46]

In her work on Fabian Socialism, Patricia Pugh has argued that the development reforms of the 1940s aimed at preparing colonies for independence, a view that later gained Robert Pearce's attention. Stephen Constantine, Paul Kelemen, and Frederick Cooper have challenged that thesis. The development drive of that period, they argue, aimed at revitalizing and extending the life of the colonial state when multiple fronts criticized it.[47] Labour literature, notably the edited volume by Arthur Creech Jones, the *New Fabian Colonial Essays* to which Rita Hinden contributed a chapter, affirmed the latter view. Although committed to improving the living standards of the colonial societies, Labour saw such an object attainable within the context of continued British trusteeship, and one in line with its protective vision. Reflecting on how Labour responded to critics of empire, Hinden noted in 1959:

> Anti-Imperialism? Yes. But non-interventionism? No. We must intervene, but somehow it must be for the other man's good. We must be trustees, not

imperialists. The only difficulty was to know precisely where one role ended, and the other began, or to convince the colonial peoples that there was any real difference.[48]

As noted, Labour kept on replenishing the Colonial Development and Welfare Fund, dedicating much of the resources towards the areas of African agriculture, health, education, and agricultural research.

Between 1947 and 1951, Labour deviated from the objectives of welfare and development, passed the Overseas Resources Development Act (ORDA) which pursued development projects that made African interests incidental to those of the metropole. Arthur Creech Jones, who at the time was serving as the S/S/C and a staunch member of the Fabian Society, supported this turn of events.[49] A series of postwar economic and social challenges, including the war debt of about £40 billion from which Britain never fully recovered; the food shortages of 1946; Sterling Crisis of 1947, and pressure from the patronizing US, necessitated that shift. During this time, Britain had a dollar deficit of about £600 to £700 million per year. The Labour Government turned to colonies for a solution to these problems. Intensified colonial development would serve several objectives. First, it would create new markets for British products and hence replace those lost during the Second World War. Second, colonial development would supply British industries with cheap raw materials during such a difficult economic environment. Third, and perhaps the most important, accelerated colonial development would address the problem of foreign exchange and balance of payment deficits. As Nicholas White put it, Britain desperately needed "foreign exchange (and especially dollar) earning for colonial exports to purchase food and goods vital for metropolitan reconstruction but which were extremely scarce in Western Europe."[50] As a consequence, the Labour Government passed the ORDA of 1948, which established two public development corporations. These were the Colonial Development Corporation and the Overseas Food Corporation. Both the CDC and OFC had the responsibility to develop colonial agricultural resources for the benefit of the metropole.[51]

The CDC and OFC had a borrowing potential of £110 million and £55 million, respectively. Although these were public corporations, the CDC, whose activities were more robust than those of the OFC, was mandated to partner with private enterprises or colonial governments in its operations. The aspect of private enterprise makes the CDC's *modus operandi* similar to what Chamberlain had earlier advocated when he argued for the idea of developing the "imperial estate." Established under an Act of Parliament, the CDC was, in principle, independent of the CO, and often directly managed projects in the colonies through its own staff or partners.[52] In practice, however, the S/S/C was the minister responsible for the CDC to the British Parliament and had the powers to appoint the CDC's Board of Directors. Moreover, the S/S/C approved loans advanced to the CDC for its colonial projects. The presence of the S/S/C in both the CO and CDC does not illustrate unity in the two offices. As chapter three will show, there was friction between the CO and the CDC.

The operations of the CDC in the early years could be placed within two periods, the expansionist and contractionist phases. The former extended from 1948 to 1950. During this time the CDC was under the chairmanship of Lord Trefgarne, a former Director of Barclays Overseas Development Corporation.[53] Within this period, the CDC funded and implemented 50 projects across 22 colonial territories. These projects attracted a total approved expenditure of £31 million. In eight of the 50 projects that were operational in 1950, the CDC partnered with private investors. Disappointments with the performance of the projects under the first phase led the CDC to abandon 21 projects, which was a major distinctive feature of the second phase, which extended from 1951 to 1954 under the chairmanship of Lord Reith, a former founding Managing and later Director General of the BBC.[54] One abandoned project was the infamous Gambia Poultry Farm, which concerned itself with the mass production of eggs for export to Britain. Another abandoned project is the Viphya Tung Scheme discussed in chapter three of this book. By 1951, the CDC was about to write off £825,000 already advanced towards the poultry scheme in the Gambia. Thirty-thousand birds had died, and the CDC lacked adequate knowledge to produce enough feed.[55] Such experience was common across many of the CDC's projects. With time, the number of CDC-supported projects declined. During the phase of contraction, it only financed sixteen projects over which it had sole responsibility. It attracted private investors for a few of its projects, while others were written off. In 1954, the Corporation jointly launched seven new projects with private enterprises.[56]

The OFC is remembered for the failed East Africa Groundnut Scheme which occurred between the late 1940s and early 1950s. It aimed at producing groundnuts on a large scale to supply oil manufacturing industries in Britain. Capitalized at £40 million, the Groundnut Scheme was designed to yield an average of 700,000 tons of groundnuts annually on an area of over 3 million acres, which would be produced using mechanized agriculture. Failure to systematically examine soil and climatic conditions combined with the difficulties of supplying and using imported technology reduced the Scheme to a white elephant.[57] By privileging industrial production, the ORDA replicated the very tenets of the 1929 Colonial Development Act which served similar purposes albeit with some minor differences. But it also went much further by getting directly involved in production in the colonies through the creation of state corporations. While colonial governments took a more direct and active role in devising development projects under the 1929 CDA, the two public corporations created under the ORDA assumed this role directly with the senior staff from CDC or OFC planning and executing projects. Although it was expected that staff from these public corporations would liaise with their colleagues in colonial governments for the successful implementation of their projects, the latter's council was rarely positively considered. Differences of opinion often made colonial governments' staff to withhold its advice and patiently wait for results of the corporations' projects which were mostly disappointing.

If the ORDA represented a shift away from the goals of colonial development and welfare which the CDWA embodied, this shift was not without opposition within Labour circles and beyond. Failure to reconcile the two opposing policy objectives, one supported by the CDWA and the other by the ORDA, pitted metropolitan bureaucrats against each other. Conflicts often emerged between the Corporation and CO; the Treasury and the CO; and the CDC officials in London and the local personnel in the colonies. Among others, conflicts revolved around whether the CDC should concern itself with capitalist interests or also fulfill colonial welfare development objectives. The most vigorous opposition towards the goals of the ORDA, arguably, came from the Association for World Peace whose 1952 report to the British audience condemned Labour for reneging on its call to address poverty in colonial societies and others. Harold Wilson, a member of the FCB and a future Prime Minister, provided chairmanship to a committee that authored the report. The other FCB members serving on the committee were Rita Hinden and W. Arthur Lewis, who served in the Colonial Economic Advisory Committee in the 1940s. The report registered dissatisfaction with the immediate postwar colonial projects such as the East African Groundnut Scheme, arguing that

> We must not think of colonial development mainly in terms of providing markets for our products and employment in our factories; nor must we embark on costly projects like the groundnuts scheme primarily for the purpose of more margarine on British tables and only incidentally with the idea of helping [poverty-stricken] Africans.[58]

The report condemned capitalist exploitation that had characterized Britain's pre- and postwar era. It questioned colonial governments in the two territories, arguing that what passed as economic developments [in these regions]—railways, roads, port and harbor installations—were for the most part limited to the works necessary to support the major private enterprises of the area.

The *War on Want* further questioned the International Bank for Reconstruction and Development (IBRD, later World Bank) for its traditional approach to development which left out most of the poor in the global South. Instead, it suggested that the United Nations establish an International

Development Authority to promote the socio-economic advancement of the world's under-developed areas. The objectives of such an authority would include, among others, deciding and administering the distribution of grants-in-aid; co-operating with the under-developed countries in preparation and coordination of plans for economic development; providing technical assistance and resources for preparing plans for economic development; and helping in implementing development plans.[59]

The subsequent publications of the Labour Party, notably, *Towards World Plenty*; *Economic Aid*; and *New Fabian Colonial Essays*, acknowledged such self-criticisms and recommitted the Party to addressing the concerns of poverty in British dependencies and other "developing countries."[60] Although the Party never stopped theorizing about the future of the Commonwealth, being out of power throughout the decolonization of African colonies in the 1950s and early 1960s, it was unable to implement many of its ideas. The 1964 national election victory presented a renewed opportunity for the Labour Government to project those ideas to its liberated former colonies and elsewhere. Despite the 1947–1951 interlude, the Labour Party remained a major advocate for the poor. It was through the newly created Ministry of Overseas Development (ODM) in 1964 that Labour mediated much of the Government's relations with former colonies and others. At this point, however, several other actors, both state and non-state, joined in the campaign to arrest poverty in the Third World countries. The following section discusses how ideas on development and poverty evolved from the 1960s when many African nations attained their independence.

AID AND THE POOR: A POST-1960 TRANSNATIONAL DEVELOPMENT DISCOURSE

When the *War on Want* challenged Britain and the IBRD to address the plight of the colonial poor, it spoke to a discourse that came to link aid, development, and poverty. British theorists and administrators contributed to this discourse, having debated these ideas on poverty throughout the first half of the twentieth century. The climax of that debate came in 1964 when the Labour Government, having been out of power since 1952, formed a new ministry, the ODM. Headed by Barbara Castle, the ODM combined the functions of the Department of Technical Co-operation (established in 1961) with those aspects on aid hitherto scattered across several different government departments, including the CO.[61] Though not replacing the CO, the ODM worked closely with it and the Foreign and Commonwealth Relations Office and took charge over matters on development aid and technical assistance in dependencies, High Commission territories, and former colonies/protectorates.

ODM's mission mirrored previous Labour policy for the African colonies. Its manifesto on aid captured this very well in a 1965 White Paper:

> The objective of the British aid programme is to help developing countries in their efforts to raise living standards. Our purpose is therefore to promote social and economic development. But development means more than reducing poverty and unemployment. It means fulfilling aspirations towards steady and continued social and economic progress. Our aim is to do what lies within our power to help the developing countries to provide their people with the material opportunities of using their talents, of living a full and happy life and of steadily improving their lot.[62]

In ways that reflected the concept of trusteeship, the White Paper emphasized Britain's moral obligation towards the LDCs as the main motivation dictating her aid policy. Labour was again at its best in committing aid and loans with little anticipation of quick economic returns:

> Even though aid may be in the form of loans which have to be repaid and on which we receive interest, it involves the transfer of economic resources without the expectation of a full economic return. Its primary aim is to supply the country receiving aid with goods and people needed for development. A clear distinction should therefore be kept between aid and commercial credit.[63]

The Labour Government, it appears, had learned some lessons from the criticism it endured following the passing of the ORDA in 1948. That Act had dented Labour's image and it was necessary to remedy it. As noted, Harold Wilson, who became the Prime Minister of Britain in 1964, was the chair of the committee which produced the *War on Want*. Throughout the 1950s, Labour's literature insisted on developing a colonial policy that was supportive of the interests of colonial peoples. Having been in opposition for a long time, the 1964 victory was an opportunity to finally take a new approach. In other words, the formation of the ODM marked both a continuity and a break with the past. While the ODM translated into practice Labour's previous insistence on advancing the interests of the colonial societies, most of which had gained independence by 1964, its objectives also marked a break with the shadow of the ORDA.

This shift contrasted with the Conservative Government's earlier concern to redirect aid towards those areas that would strengthen the Commonwealth's economic capacity. In the 1957 White Paper, the Conservative Government clarified that "the special responsibility which HMG [Her Majesty's Government] has for colonial dependencies ceases when they achieve independence." Britain, therefore, did not envisage "Government to Government loans as a normal means of assisting such countries," but rather that the interests of the ex-colonies could "better be served if they build up their own credit and thus make use of the facilities for raising money on the London market or elsewhere."[64] By 1958, this trend relaxed, but the general tenor remained the same. It was Labour that brought in fundamental shifts in British aid policy.

Jim Tomlinson has argued against exaggerating the philanthropic motives Labour attached to aid, noting how concerns for economically strengthening the Commonwealth were as important for Labour as they were for the Conservative Government. Such figures as Harold Wilson saw a strong Commonwealth as an alternative to joining the European Economic Commission. Therefore, like the Conservatives, Labour tied British aid to investments with a possible significant economic return on the Sterling Area. Despite periodic oscillation, however, there was a significant shift in the amount of aid Britain allocated to former colonies when the Labour Government came to power in 1964. And, as Tomlinson rightly acknowledges, the declining trend in aid between 1966 and 1971 resulted from Britain's balance of payment problems which forced the Treasury to set, in 1966, a £205 million cash ceiling on the ODM's disbursement of aid.[65] The Wilson government was on a path towards rehabilitating Labour's image, which had been badly tarnished by the late 1940s' projects. Postcolonial societies became sites where Britain undertook such an exercise. The strategy mostly involved, but was not limited to, a focus on small-scale projects that targeted the poor. But this discourse that linked aid, development, and the poor was not unique to Britain's ODM. The WB as well as the bilateral agencies of other countries, particularly the US and the Federal Republic of Germany (FRG), shared this strategy.

Two defining moments mark the WB's engagement with the poor. The first began from the 1940s to early 1960s. During this time, the aims of development targeted the poverty of countries but not specific individuals in them. The strategy for achieving economic growth or raising a country's Gross National Product (GNP) focused on developing infrastructural facilities such as ports, railway lines, dams, and energy plants. During this period, the WB was a conservative institution, keen at playing the role of a commercial entity as opposed to a public development agency.[66] Between 1961 and 1965, the WB lent out almost half of its resources towards electricity plants and transportation in developing countries. It dedicated only 18 percent of its development funds to agriculture, with only 3 percent reserved for social services. This trend held even after it had created the International Development Association (IDA) in 1960, a WB affiliate aimed at providing "soft" loans to Third World countries.[67]

The 1968 ascendancy to the WB presidency of Robert McNamara marked a shift in the aims and strategies of the WB, albeit one that was already underway. The shift was already noticeable during the era of George Woods, that is 1963 to 1968. McNamara should be given credit for his massive campaigns to mobilize resources towards development projects that targeted the urban and rural poor. An American who previously served as the Secretary of Defense under Kennedy's and Johnson's administrations, McNamara became increasingly frustrated with the failure of the big "showcase projects," like the kind the CDC promoted in the late 1940s and early 1950s, to address poverty and raise the living standards of over two-thirds of the global population. Many of these people lived in the Third World. If the previous approach helped to raise GNP for some countries, this growth in national income did not trickle down to the poor who were living in both absolute and abject poverty. Given the low investment in agriculture, moreover, a crisis in production and productivity was looming and exposing millions of the poor to the risk of famine. McNamara expressed these fears in his September 24, 1973, speech to the WB Board of Governors in Kenya, which was only restating a shift that was already discernable since the early 1960s. His call to developed countries emphasized the need to devote more resources towards poverty alleviation, by targeting the individuals (both rural and urban poor) in LDCs.[68] Thus, the WB did not abandon the object of achieving economic growth in the Third World countries but paid particular attention to the plight of the poor by reshaping both the aims and strategies of achieving development.

Poverty within states became a significant focus of the Bank's efforts with much of its funding directed to rural or urban development projects. As Robert Ayres noted, "over 50 percent of the Bank's lending for agriculture and rural development from 1974 to 1978 was accounted for by 210 rural development projects defined by the Bank as those projects in which more than half of the direct benefits are expected to accrue to the poor."[69] Malawi was already benefiting from the shift toward rural development since the late 1960s. Between 1967 and 1971, 64 percent of the loans IDA disbursed to the country went to projects benefiting the rural and urban poor, representing $29,850,000 of the $46,500,000 in total granted.[70] The Bank established several technical departments whose missions to the LDCs helped to provide expertise in areas of project proposal preparation and, after funding was approved, implementation and evaluation.

What is also significant about this era is how the WB is said to have internationalized the problem of poverty, making it a global concern. For example, Martha Finnermore acknowledged that concerns about poverty and redistribution of resources had long circulated in government departments and the academy, and argued that these "views did not become globally influential until they found a powerful organizational home [at the Bank during McNamara's era]."[71] There is little debate about the role the Bank played to popularize the anti-poverty drive. The "globality" of these ideas, however, should rest more in the ways diverse societies and technocrats believed in them than their being attached to the WB. The British technocrats, as noted, had earlier embraced these ideas for relatively similar reasons.

President Harry Truman, for one, had already declared war against global poverty in his fourth point of the inaugural address he made on January 20, 1949. As Truman observed at the time, "more than half of the people of the world," he stated, "are living in conditions approaching misery. Their food is inadequate. They are victims of disease. Their economic life is primitive and stagnant. Their poverty is a handicap and a threat to them and to more prosperous areas."[72] Truman made his speech within the context of the war against Communism (which he saw as a threat to global peace) such that the objectives of development and "security" soon became intertwined. Poverty-stricken societies were havens of social dislocation, and at risk of falling into the arms of the Soviets. By raising the living standards of the poor in the global South, America would stabilize those societies. Truman saw the US as having the necessary capital and expertise to achieve this goal. America's capacity to transform poor societies through financial capital, technical expertise, and advanced technology was part of what Michael Latham calls an American ideology of modernization. That ideology had deep historical roots which are beyond the scope of the current study.[73] Suffice to state that the US-led 1961 Alliance for Progress and several other development interventions of the 1950s and 1960s in the Middle East, India, Southeast Asia, and Africa, constituted a part of the modernization drive.[74]

The Alliance for Progress was a comprehensive economic and political plan that targeted Latin American countries. It had the overall aim of increasing the rate of economic growth there, with a bias towards redistributing national income in ways that included the poor. It had a budget of over US$80 billion to spend towards reforms and improvements in such areas as agriculture, health, and education, which was almost four times the amount America provided towards economic aid in Asia between 1950 and 1971.[75] Several projects dotted Latin America in the 1960s, and many of them proved disappointing. At the level of politics, the Alliance for Progress aimed at spreading liberal democracy in the region. Within the US, the 1964 Economic Opportunity Act provided for relatively similar programs and serve as a reminder to the 1909 Development Act the Liberals pushed through in Britain. The Opportunity Act targeted the predominantly rural and urban societies of the Appalachian region where a third of the population lived in poverty. The region's per capita income was 23 percent lower than the average in the US.[76]

The Appalachian Regional Commission was set up by Congress to coordinate the effort and helped to mobilize human and financial resources to contain poverty in the region. Much of its work, carried out through the Area

Development Districts of the Community Action Program, was modelled after Roosevelt's Tennessee Valley Authority (TVA) projects and US work in India and other parts of Asia in the 1950s.[77] Daniel Immerwahr has noted that the strategies the US employed in India, the Philippines, and other parts of the world, which placed community participation at the center of development activities, "were imported into the United States as part of the war on poverty" described here.[78] Immerwahr contends that America's small-scale modernization strategies in India and the Philippines represented the country's belief in small-scale and/or community development projects that were democratic enough to tap on local traditions and agency, an argument which runs counter to the typical transformative modernization drives often associated with the US's activities in the global South. In other words, while the US development policy is typically associated with large-scale multipurpose projects pioneered by the TVA, equally important to note for Immerwahr are other small-scale community-based projects the US supported, which seem to have co-existed with the former.

This debate notwithstanding, serving as the Secretary of Defense in Kennedy's and Lyndon B. Johnson's administration (1961–1968), and a close advisor to both, McNamara easily fit into the WB which had already taken a direction towards addressing global poverty in ways that were different from their previous approach. McNamara's previous experience in the US's counterinsurgency campaign at the height of the Cold War, including his involvement in the Strategic Hamlet Program in Vietnam of the early 1960s, no doubt proved useful in influencing his dealings with rural societies of the LDCs. The strategy for project implementation which saw the WB commanding both capital and technical expertise, was characteristic of the modernization drive of the US and, as more recent literature shows, several other European powers whose contribution has thus far been obscured by the US's modernization offensive.[79]

Scholars of the former Federal Republic of Germany (West Germany), for example, have gone a long way to compare that country's modernization discourse to that of the US and the United Nations' agencies. The major turning points discussed above also characterized West Germany's policy on aid, albeit with minor differences. Even though the country's investment aid in the 1950s went towards industrial plants, railway lines, and other infrastructural projects of the LDCs, that policy did not sacrifice concerns for the poor. It emphasized narrowing the gap that existed between the rich and poor countries.[80] Following the founding of the Ministry for Economic Co-operation in 1961, the FRG became more pro-active in the fight against poverty. The Ministry for Economic Co-operation, as Unger argued, recognized the limits of industrial development as a strategy of addressing people's poverty: "Instead of building high-tech steel mills in the 'middle of nowhere' and naïvely expecting them to modernize the surrounding areas and populations, [it paid] greater attention . . . to local conditions and interests."[81] A 1961 Cabinet paper signed by the FRG's three ministries coordinating aid provision emphasized the problem of poverty in the LDCs and how to address it. Titled "Of German development policy and the principles of financing foreign aid," it stated that, "in co-operation with the other countries of the Free World, it is the intention of the Federal Republic to support the developing countries in their effort to build a sound political, economic and social order to increase the standards of living and to integrate these countries into the world economy."[82]

That shift was followed by increased resource mobilization, with the FRG engaging its official development bank—the *Kreditanstalt für Wiederaufbau* (KfW)—for that purpose. To ensure that aid achieved its aims, the FRG disbursed funding as part of a package that included technical know-how; a case in point being that of India. In the early 1960s, the FRG went about establishing model villages with experts guiding the local communities there.[83] Unlike the US experts who often moved from place to place, in India, notes Unger, German experts lived in rural areas for extended periods, teaching farmers modern practices of mixed farming which included livestock production. The FRG envisaged that such a strategy would "increase agricultural productivity, raise the general level of income, level social discrepancies, and solve the perceived problem of 'overpopulation'" [sic].[84] If the FRG's aid policy visibly sought to address poverty among communities of the LDCs, it was not devoid of other higher objectives, chief among which was to re-establish [West Germany's] reputation following the horror of the Second World War. The other centered on stabilizing the population of the LDCs to avoid losing them to Eastern communist countries. Other than these political and ideological concerns, equally significant was the desire to create industrial markets in the LDCs for FRG's industries and manufacturers.[85] It was in this area that the KfW featured the most.

CONCLUSION

It is worth emphasizing that although the discourse of aid and poverty became more nuanced under the leadership of the WB and, as others have shown, the many UN aid agencies in the 1960s and 1970s, it did not lack historical antecedents as we have seen in this chapter. Concerns on how to address the challenges of the poor and achieve development date back to the late nineteenth-century and captured the interest of diverse intellectuals, bureaucrats, and politicians. Throughout the first half of the twentieth century and beyond the debate on the aims and strategies of achieving development revolved around the fear of what development could achieve—either creating order or unleashing disorder. Whether in debates on land as a gateway to achieving agricultural productivity and hence improve the living standards of Africans, or in those of industrial and rural development, actors who intervened in the development process were conscious of these opposing poles, and never agreed on the best workable option. The Fabians and the Labour Party which they influenced, particularly guarded against African exploitation. These past contributions notwithstanding, Corinna Unger warns against ignoring the changes and discontinuities in the aims of development across the colonial/postcolonial eras. She points to the multiple interests the "postcolonial" Western governments and non-state actors attached to the discourse of aid, poverty, and development, ranging from strategic, diplomatic, business, and philanthropic interests.[86]

Worth emphasizing also are the strategies employed to address poverty. Almost all the players involved in the war on poverty—Britain, the US, FRG, and the WB—deployed and supported technical experts in the LDCs. Between the 1960s and 1970s, therefore, former colonies became spaces in which poverty-oriented development practice played out. What remains unclear, however, is how recipient governments responded to such ideas and practices and the effects of that encounter. This study is, in part, a response to this omission. Subsequent chapters will discuss the extent to which these ideas on arresting poverty played out in practice in Malawi and with what outcomes. The result is a study that shows how development practice in Malawi mirrored but also deviated from the broader contours of the debate on colonial development and welfare in twentieth century. Because the debate in question was never resolved, the history of development in Malawi, and indeed the struggle to arrest poverty in the country, was far less deterministic than is otherwise portrayed by the existing literature.

NOTES

1. See Hodge and Hödl, "Introduction," 3.
2. The only exception was in 1929 when Britain reoriented its policy towards supporting colonial development through the Colonial Development Act of that year.
3. Speech by Britain's Liberal Prime Minister, Henry Campbell-Bannerman, 1905, cited in Cowen and Shenton, "The Origin and Course of Fabian Colonialism in Africa,"147.
4. During this time, Chamberlain served under the coalition government of the Conservative Party and Liberal Unionists.
5. Stephen Constantine, *The Making of British Colonial Development Policy, 1914–1940* (London: Frank Cass, 1984), 10.

6. See Michael Cowen and Robert Shenton, *Doctrines of Development* (London: Routledge, 1996), 282–86.

7. Michel Cowen and Robert Shenton, "The Origin and Course of Fabian Colonialism in Africa,"148.

8. At the time, David Lloyd George was the Chancellor of the Exchequer. He became the last Prime Minister of the Liberal Party (1916–1922). After 1922, it was the Conservative and the Labour parties that were the most dominant.

9. See Hodge and Hödl, "Introduction," 2

10. See Cowen and Shenton, *Doctrines of Development,* 7.

11. For a comprehensive discussion of the Liverpool School see Kenneth Dike Nworah, "The Liverpool 'Sect' and British West African Policy, 1895–1915," *African Affairs* 7, no. 281 (1971): 349–64; Bernard Porter, *Critics of Empire: British Radicals and the Imperial Challenge* (London: I.B. Tauris, 2008), 239–90.

12. Porter, *Critics of Empire*, 239. Ironically, Morel once tolerated monopoly companies to ply their trade in Sierra Leone, the case in point being that of William Hesketh Lever (of Lever Brothers), a merchant who was offered a 21-year monopoly to erect a power mill for purposes of extracting oil in West Africa. See K. Dike Nworah, "The Politics of Lever's West African Concessions, 1907–1913," *International Journal of African Historical Studies*, 5 no. 2 (1972): 251.

13. Porter, *Critics of Empire*, 258.

14. Ibid., 267–69. See also E.D. Morel, *Affairs of West Africa* (London: Frank Cass & Co., 1968), 285–34. The first edition of Morel's book came out in 1902. Kenneth Nworah wrote a preface to the 1968 edition.

15. For a further discussion of the relationship between the concept of trusteeship and progress or development generally, see Cowen and Shenton, "The Origin and Course of Fabian Colonialism in Africa," 156–57; Hodge and Hödl, "Introduction," 4; Kenneth Robinson, *The Dilemmas of Trusteeship* (London: Oxford University Press, 1965), 1–28.

16. Kenneth Robinson, *The Dilemmas of Trusteeship*, 25.

17. John Holt, cited in Nworah, "The Liverpool 'Sect' and British West African Policy," 354; Robinson, *The Dilemmas of Trusteeship,* 25.

18. See Hodge and Hödl, "Introduction," 4.

19. Cowen and Shenton, "The Origin and Course of Fabian Colonialism in Africa," 154.

20. Most members of the Round Table once served in the Alfred Milner's government in South Africa and included figures such as Milner himself, who later served as the S/S/C between 1919 and 1921; Leo Amery, who served in similar capacity from 1924–1929, and Philip Kerr (the prime minister's private secretary during the First World War). They championed British development activities in Mandate Palestine along the lines as Chamberlain theorized. See Jacob Norris, *Land of Progress: Palestine in the Age of Development* (Oxford: Oxford University Press, 2013): 7–9.

21. Paul Kelemen, "Individualism is, Indeed, Running Riot: Components of the Social Democratic Model of Development," in Mark Duffield and Vernon Hewitt, eds. *Empire, Development and Colonialism* (Woodbridge, UK, Byodell and Brown, 2009), 189.

22. Luke Reader, "'Not Yet Able to Stand by Themselves': Leonard Woolf, Socialist Imperialism, and Discourse of Race, 1925–1941," *Trans-Script* 1 (2001): 102–30.

23. Thomas R. Metcalf, *Ideologies of the Raj* (Cambridge: Cambridge University Press, 1994), 17, 28–45; Hodge, *Triumph of the Expert,* 30–33.

24. Early critics of Cornwallis' ideas included Thomas Munro, Mountsuart Elphinstone, and Charles Metcalfe, all of which administrators in East India Company and contemporaries to Cornwallis. See Hodge, *Triumph of the Expert*, 30–31.

25. Hodge, *Triumph of the Expert*, 31.

26. Metcalf, *Ideologies of the Raj*, 28–45.

27. Michele McArdle Stephens, *In the Lands of Fire and Sun: Resistance and Accommodation in the Huichol Sierra, 1823–1930* (Nebraska: University of Nebraska Press, 2018), 50, 54, 61–62, 64.

28. Catherine Hall, *Civilizing Subjects: Metropole and the Colony in the English Imagination, 1830–1867* (Chicago: University of Chicago Press, 2002), 88.

29. Ibid., 105–6; 245.

30. Li, *The Will to Improve*, 62–82.

31. See Labour Party, *The Empire in Africa: Labour's Policy* (London: The Labour Party, 1926): 7.

32. Ibid.

33. Lugard, *The Dual Mandate in British Tropical Africa,* 280–81.

34. Lord Olivier, *Imperial Trusteeship* (London: The Fabian Society, 1929), 14.

35. The Labour Party, *The Empire in Africa,* 3. For a discussion of the influential role that Leonard Woolf played see Reader, "Not Yet Able to Stand by Themselves," 102–30.

36. Lord Hailey, *An African Survey: A Study of Problems Arising in Africa South of the Sahara* (London: Oxford University Press, 1938).

37. See Tilley, *Africa as a Living Laboratory: Empire, Development, and the Problem of Scientific Knowledge, 1870–1950* (Chicago: University of Chicago, 2011) 2–3; 27. Lord Hailey, the chairperson of this specific study, was an experienced colonial administrator who had retired from his post as a governor of the United Provinces in India. See Hailey, *An African Survey,* v.

38. Hailey, *An African Survey*, 869. For a discussion of such fallacies see Martin Chanock, "Paradigms, Policies, and Property: A Review of the Customary Law of Land Tenure," in Kristin Mann and Richard Roberts eds. *Law in Colonial Africa* (London: James Currey, 1991): 61–84.

39. Hailey, *An African Survey*, 869.

40. Ibid., 869.

41. Through the CDWA Britain sponsored more research and experts to work in the colonies after 1940. The large number of British technical experts has made D. A. Low and J. M. Lonsdale to dub the post-war era as the age of second colonial occupation. See D.A. Low and J. M. Lonsdale, "Introduction: Towards the New Order 1945–1963," in D. A. Low and Alison Smith, eds. *History of East Africa*, vol. 3 (Oxford: Clarendon Press, 1976), 12–16.

42. Partha Sarathi Gupta, *Imperialism and the British Labour Movement, 1914–1964* (London: MacMillan, 1975), 244; Michael Havinden and David Meredith,

Colonialism and Development: Britain and its Tropical Colonies, 1850–1960 (London: Routledge, 1993), 218, 226.

43. The political problems were reported by Hailey, *An African Survey* and whose findings Malcolm McDonald anticipated.

44. John McCracken, "Planters, Peasants and the Colonial State: The Impact of the Native Tobacco Board in the Central Province of Malawi," *Journal of Southern African Studies* 9, no. 2 (1983): 172–92.

45. Both the USA and the League of Nations became increasingly critical of the colonial powers' utter neglect of African welfare.

46. See Paul Kelemen, "Planning for Africa: The British Labour Party's Colonial Development Policy, 1920–1964," *Journal of Agrarian Change* 7, no. 1 (2007): 76–89.

47. Patricia Pugh, *Educate, Agitate, Organize: 100 Years of Fabian Socialism* (London: Methuen & Co., 1984); Robert Desmond Pearce, "The Colonial Office and Planned Decolonization in Africa," *African Affairs* 83 no. 330 (1984): 77–93; Constantine, *The Making of British Colonial Development Policy;* Kelemen, "Planning for Africa," 76–89; Cooper, *Decolonization and African Society.*

48. Rita Hinden, "Socialism and the Colonial World," and in Arthur Creech Jones, ed. *New Fabian Colonial Essays* (New York: Praeger, 1959), 11.

49. Joseph M. Snyder, "The Fabianization of the British Empire: Postwar Colonial Summer Conferences and Community Development in Kenya and Uganda, 1948–1956," PhD Dissertation, West Virginia University, 2017 uses this turn of events as an example of how Fabian ideas often fractured when its key members serving in the government pursued policies that fundamentally deviated from what they professed.

50. Nicholas J. White, "Reconstructing Europe through Rejuvenating Empire: the British, French, and Dutch Experiences Compared," *Past and Present,* Supplement 6 (2011): 214.

51. Great Britain, *Overseas Resources Development Act, 1948* (London: HMSO, 1948). Sourced from MNA S19/1/1/1.

52. Because the S/S/C was a responsible minister for the CDC to the British Parliament, he appointed its Board of Directors.

53. Christopher Brain and Michael Cable, *Pioneering Development: CDC Diamond Jubilee, 1948–2008* (London: CDC Group plc, 2008), 12.

54. Ibid., 34; See also E. R. Wicker, "The Colonial Development Corporation, 1948–1954," *Review of the Economic Studies* 23, no. 3 (1955–1956): 216.

55. Great Britain, *Parliamentary Debates* (Commons), 5th Series 482 (December 13, 1951), https://www.theyworkforyou.com/debates/?id=1951-03-13a.1317.7, accessed January 18, 2020.

56. Wicker, "The Colonial Development Corporation," 216.

57. Hodge and Hödl, "Introduction," 16.

58. Association for World Peace, *War on Want: A Plan for World Development* (London: Association for World Peace, 1952), 9.

59. *War on Want*, 73–74.

60. Labour Party, *Towards World Plenty* (London: Labour Party Publications, 1952); Labour Party, *Labour's Colonial Policy: Economic Aid* (London: Labour Party, 1957).

61. Great Britain, *Overseas Development: The Work of the New Ministry*, Cmnd. 2736 (London: HMSO, 1965), 27. See also Charlotte Riley, "The Winds of Change are Blowing Economically: The Labour Party and British Overseas Development, 1940s–1960s, in W. M. Smith and Chris Jeppesen, eds. *Britain, France and the Decolonization of Africa* (London: UCL Press, 2017), 43–46.

62. Great Britain, *Overseas Development*, 6.

63. Ibid., 7.

64. Great Britain, *Role of United Kingdom in Commonwealth Development*, Cmnd. 237 (London: HMG, 1957): 6, Cited in Jim Tomlinson, "The Commonwealth, the Balance of Payments and the Politics of International Poverty: British Aid Policy, 1958–1971," *Journal of Contemporary European History* 12, no. 4 (2004): 417.

65. Tomlinson, "The Commonwealth, the Balance of Payments and the Politics of International Poverty," 424–25; See statistics on page 424; the ceiling was lifted in 1969.

66. Martha Finnermore, "Redefining Development at the World Bank," in Frederick Cooper and Randall Packard, eds. *International Development and the Social Sciences: Essays on the History and Politics of Knowledge* (Los Angeles: University of California Press, 1997), 203–27.

67. Robert L. Ayres, *Banking on the Poor: The World Bank and World Poverty* (Cambridge: The MIT Press, 1984), 4. "Soft" loans is used here to emphasize the IDA credit which had a zero or low interest rate. Loans would be payable within a period of about 50 years with a ten-year grace period.

68. McNamara's address to the World Bank Board of Governors, Nairobi, Kenya. September 24, 1973, http://documents.worldbank.org/curated/en/930801468315304694/pdf/Address-to-the-Board-of-Governors-by-Robert-S-McNamara.pdf; See also Ayres, *Banking on the Poor*, 5.

69. Ayres, *Banking on the Poor*, 5.

70. See World Bank IDA Aid to Malawi, 1971, MNA, 1-8-9R/17841.

71. Finnermore, "Redefining Development at the World Bank," 204.

72. The fourth point of President Truman's inaugural address, January 20, 1949. Reprinted in Association for World Peace, *War on Want,* 89.

73. Michael E. Latham, *Modernization as Ideology: American Social Science and "Nation Building" in the Kennedy Era* (Chapel Hill and London: The University of North Carolina Press, 2000), 5. On the deeper roots of America's modernization ideology see also Ekbladh, *The Great American Mission;* Nils Gilman, *Mandarins of the Future* (London: John Hopkins, 2007).

74. For a discussion of America's fight against poverty as an aspect of counterinsurgency in Iran, Ghana, and Guatemala; India and Southeast Asia generally see Michael E. Latham, *The Right Kind of Revolution: Modernization, Development and U.S. Foreign Policy from the Cold War to the Present* (Ithaca: Cornell University Press, 2011); Nick Cullather, *The Hungry World: America's Cold War Battle Against Poverty in Asia* (Cambridge: C.U.P., 2013).

75. Cullather, *The Hungry World, 6*

76. See Appalachian Regional Commission, *Moving Appalachia Forward: Appalachian Regional Strategic Plan, 2005–2010* (Washington DC: The Appalachian Regional Commission, 2004), 3.

77. For a detailed discussion of America's modernization projects in the 1950s India, See Cullather, *The Hungry World*, 134–158; Immerwahr, *Thinking Small.*

78. Immerwahr, *Thinking Small*, 9, 11–12; 135, 137.

79. A good discussion of how different European countries engaged with non-Western societies in matters of poverty was presented in a special issue of the *Journal of Modern European History* 8, no. 1 (2010). Corina Unger, "Histories of Development and Modernization: Findings, Reflections, Future Research," In H-Soz-Kult 09.12.2010. 1–22, See 10–13, https://www.hsozkult.de/literaturereview/id/forschungsberichte-1130. Accessed on March 17, 2019.

80. Heide-Irene Schmidt, "Pushed to the Front: The Foreign Assistance Policy of the Federal Republic of Germany, 1958–1971," *Contemporary European History* 12, no. 4 (2003): 482.

81. Unger, "Histories of Development and Modernization, 54.

82. Cited in Schmidt, "Pushed to the Front," 484. The three ministries were Economics Ministry—*Bundesministerium fur Wirtshaft*; Foreign Ministry (AA)—*Auswartiges Amt*; and Ministry for Economic Co-operation—*Bundesministerium Für Zusammenarbeit.*

83. Ibid., 484; Corinna R. Unger, "Modernization à la mode,": West Germany and American Development Plans for the Third World," *GHI Bulletin*, no. 40 (Spring 2007): 151

84. Unger, "Modernization à la mode," 153–54.

85. Ibid., 154; Corinna R. Unger, *International Development: A Post-War History* (Bloomsbury, PA: Bloomsbury Academic Press, 2018).

86. Unger, "Histories of Development and Modernization," 17.

Chapter Two

The Land-poverty Nexus in Colonial Malawi, 1930s–1965

In 1939, the British Secretary of State for the Colonies (S/S/C), Malcolm McDonald, wrote the East African governors, stating:

> I have the honour to inform you that the problems of land tenure in Africa have for some time past been under my consideration. . . . It seems to me . . . that some attempt should be made to inquire systematically into the principles which govern native land tenure, and which should regulate the record or registration of titles in native held lands. . . . The purpose of this dispatch, therefore, is to suggest to you . . . the lines upon which the matter might be approached and a definite procedure of investigation. . . . I am anxious that there should be no delay in proceeding with the work and should be grateful for a reply at an early date.[1]

MacDonald's dispatch came immediately after Lord Hailey's 1938 publication, *An African Survey,* which had outlined the multiple problems confronting British Africa, one of which was the chaotic and unregulated process of land individualization in the colonies. Denied of private rights to land, some selected Africans were already breaking loose from the communal land tenure system and made claims of ownership to land without appropriate certification. Coming in the wake of the 1939 Colonial Development and Welfare Bill, which MacDonald's office was preparing, the proposed tenurial reforms were also a necessary step to improving the welfare of Africans by raising land productivity through the provision of private rights to land.

But if MacDonald hoped his proposals represented a forward move to achieve progress in the colonies, the colonial government in Malawi rejected the reforms because of their destabilizing effects on African communal life.[2] The colonial state in Malawi was unmoved until 1956 when it accepted the proposals. During this time, however, the educated African elites, who had for long clamored for leasehold land titles, opposed the reforms. They threw back the same language the colonial authorities used in their previous opposition—the whole idea that such reforms were against African tradition.[3] Beyond appeals to "African tradition," how else should we explain these objections to proposals on private rights to land? What fears did the groups in question have, and how did they affect their reception of the proposed changes? How do we interpret the 1950s change of mind on the part of the authorities in Nyasaland? In what ways did the land reform proposals of the 1950s influence similar reforms of the postcolonial era?

This chapter addresses these questions to understand the enduring debate on land tenure and development in Malawi and how it relates to the failure of the war on poverty. For a predominantly agrarian society, land is a significant resource such that a search for answers to the development challenges of the country should begin by analyzing the debates surrounding the use and ownership of land, and particularly the relationship between land and increased agricultural productivity. As one British report once highlighted, "to attempt to consider . . . the economic development of British Africa without a careful examination of the land question is impossible."[4] The chapter uses the exchange as introduced here to illustrate how different interest groups understood the nexus between land tenure and development in colonial Malawi, and the implications the debate had for the country's postcolonial state.

In their contribution to this debate, both Martin Chanock and Joey Power argued that the colonial government in Malawi attached a political significance to the customary land tenure system and used it to entrench its rule.[5] The "fear of social dislocation, often cast in the protective framework of concern over the indebted peasantry and a landless class," argued Chanock, "prevented the colonial authorities from granting legal rights to land to many African farmers."[6] He considered this a problem that spilled over to postcolonial African regimes with their tendency to deny rural Africans rights to land or render them subordinate to other interests. Earlier, Bridglal Pachai supported this thesis. He posited that the colonial state in Malawi bequeathed the communal land tenure system to the postcolonial government, a formidable task which the latter attempted to rectify by passing the 1967 Customary Land Development Act. The legislation sought to provide individual titles to smallholder farmers and was first applied to the World Bank-supported Lilongwe Land Development Project in central Malawi. This legislation, therefore, is said to have represented a break with the past.[7]

There is little doubt that land in colonial Malawi, as was the case with other colonial societies elsewhere, was a target of colonial power or, at least, imbricated in politics. In northern Nigeria, for example, Steven Pierce has demonstrated the impossibility of separating paradigms of land tenure from paradigms of governance, not least because control over land translated into control over people.[8] Sara Berry, Parker Shipton, and Mitzi Goheen, among others, have all illustrated a similar thesis, further noting how economic and political meanings of land intersect.[9] Even those scholars that criticize the "property rights school" for its failures draw a similar conclusion in which economic matters (changes towards individual land tenure) often give rise to serious social and political effects.[10] The nexus between the political and economic meanings of land is unquestionable.

What is in doubt, however, is the effect of colonial land tenure regimes, or political practices generally, over the postcolonial states. In her contribution to such continuities, Berry has demonstrated how many of the conflicts over access to land and related resources which characterized the colonial era, continued to the twentieth and twenty-first centuries.[11] However, she also acknowledged that these were not specific to the colonial era and, indeed, characterized much of the politics of land before the advent of colonial rule. In this way, Berry effectively challenged Chanock's thesis for reinforcing the invention of tradition school which posited that the colonial regimes immobilized African societies for political ends.[12] Berry's critique helps one to understand how the debate on land tenure has unfolded in Africa. However, her argument concerns itself mostly with chiefs and other local players. This chapter goes beyond the local politics of land and shows how different interest groups, from the CO in London, to local administrators, the white settlers, and Africans in colonial Malawi, contested and debated the land question and the legacy of that debate for postcolonial Malawi.

I agree with Chanock and others that the colonial authorities in Malawi defended communal land tenure for political purposes. In doing so, they drew on the long history of Fabian paternalism and its tendency to regard Africans as communitarian. However, historical developments of the late colonial period (1950s–1964) do not display attempts to subordinate African land rights to the colonial administrative machinery as Chanock and Pachai emphasize. Such assertions are only attainable when we consider the pre-1950s debate on land and leapfrog to the postcolonial era without due consideration to political developments lying in between.[13] The chapter argues that beginning in the mid-1950s, the colonial state struggled, without success, to provide Africans with rights to land although these sought to promote different but related political objectives. Nationalist opposition to the colonial state threatened settler interests in land, forcing the administration to secure freehold titles by broadening the sector with private rights to land. This would make it difficult to achieve a targeted land expropriation or nationalization in the event that Africans took over power in Malawi. In other words, the acceptance of the CO proposals on land tenure reforms in the mid-1950s in Malawi had more to do with political than economic interests. The suggestion to grant legal land rights to Africans and opposition to it, therefore, were both products of the politics of decolonization emerging in the late colonial period. The colonial administration re-imagined land tenure as a weapon with which to protect settler interests. African elites, instead, opposed the reforms by appealing to the same Fabian notions of trusteeship that previously sustained communal land tenure system.

In this way, the chapter demonstrates how the groups at the center of the land tenure debate—the CO officials in London, colonial administrators in Malawi, and Africans—appealed to similar ideas of Fabian preservative trusteeship to achieve certain ends. In other words, they all spoke the same language of trusteeship, albeit at different times and for different reasons. Such contending interests frustrated efforts to experiment with other development ideas, particularly as they related to African land. Nevertheless, it was the same land reform proposals of the late-colonial period that later influenced the customary land legislation of the postcolonial state. The 1967 Customary Land Act, therefore, marked less the triumph of the postcolonial state over colonial mistakes than the fulfilment of the land reform vision of the late-colonial period. It was, at best, a continuation of debates that began in the colonial period.

THE CO AND LAND TENURE REFORMS, 1930S–1955

When the British declared a protectorate over Central Africa, later Nyasaland in 1891, land fell under three categories—freehold, crown land (public land), and after 1936, native trust land (reserved for Africans). Europeans acquired much of the freehold land between the 1870s and 1890s. Between 1889 and 1891, for instance, African chiefs signed 63 treaties which effectively transferred land to European planters, missionaries, and companies.[14] When Sir Harry Johnstone took charge of the protectorate as the first Commissioner and Consul General of Nyasaland in 1889, he re-evaluated previous land transfers and granted "Certificates of Claims" to qualifying planters and others. Those certificates granted freehold title to the landholders as understood in the Western sense. By 1894, 15% of the protectorate's land was held in title, representing 3,705,255 acres (1,500,000 hectares) of land under 72 European title holders, and one African.[15]

Between 1891 and 1936, the colonial debate on land centered on how best to secure land for Africans amidst intense land alienation in the protectorate. For example, to protect Africans who were settled on the alienated land, the Certificates of Claims carried a "non-disturbance" clause which prohibited planters from disturbing the economic life of these Africans. The non-disturbance clause was ambiguous, however, because it did not accommodate the growing African population. Consequently, some Africans eventually settled in estate areas not covered under the non-disturbance clause.

For instance, in the 1920s, over 15000 Africans lived within a 320,000-acre Livingstone-Bruce estate of the Shire Highlands region in the Southern Province.[16] This group paid rent to the estate owners in form of labor. The practice marked the beginning of the much-hated colonial *thangata* system of labor where Africans worked on the plantations in selected months in lieu of rent. Thangata was a pre-colonial tradition in which communities pooled their labor together to work fields of those who participated in these labor parties. The work was reciprocal and accompanied by beer drinking and feasting. During the colonial era, the system took a different shape as described here. Thangata was common in the Shire Highlands region where complaints over land and its related labor abuses contributed to the 1915 Chilembwe Uprising. Led by an American-trained Baptist minister, John Chilembwe, Africans protested, among other things, poor working conditions and Thangata. They killed the European manager of the Livingstone-Bruce estate and wounded several others.[17] Before then, however, the government was aware of the challenges Africans faced related to land. One problem centered on the failure of planters to develop their freehold land when some Africans lacked it. To contain the growing frustration among Africans, the government raised land taxes, which forced settlers to sell idle land. In addition, it passed the 1912 Land Ordinance, which discontinued the issuance of freehold titles in favor of leases of 21 or 99 years, depending on the purpose to which land was put.[18]

Other than the 1915 Chilembwe uprising, which raised awareness regarding African frustration with matters of land, the 1924 East African Commission, covering Nyasaland, Kenya, Uganda, Northern Rhodesia, and Tanzania also had similar results. It was J. H. Thomas who helped to institute this parliamentary commission while serving as the S/S/C in the Labour Government. Led by William Ormsby-Gore, at the time a Conservative member of the British Parliament and the future S/S/C, it aimed to investigate, among others, the economic conditions under which Africans lived and to suggest solutions for improving their welfare.[19] It was also tasked to provide suggestions on how best to accelerate economic development in British Africa. The Commission decried a lack of security of tenure for Africans on both crown and estate-owned land. It singled out Nyasaland and Kenya as territories with the worst record. The report argued that in these territories, no subject agitated the African mind "more continuously than the question of their rights to land."[20] To help safeguard African interests in land, the report recommended creating Trust Boards, which would have administrative oversight on "native" land. The Trust Boards would include the following individuals: The Governor, who would also act as the chairperson of the Boards; the Chief Native Commissioner; three Senior Commissioners; two representatives of Africans, and two representatives of non-Africans unofficial population.[21]

The climax of this campaign for protecting African land rights to Nyasaland came in 1936 when the government passed the Nyasaland Protectorate (Native Trust Land) Order-in-Council. The legislation provided a legal mechanism for safeguarding indigenous peoples' rights over the land they occupied, effectively protecting it from alienation towards settler agriculture.[22] Among others, African land was vested in the office of the S/S/C such that any further alienation had to pass through this office. Although protecting African land from alienation, the legislation did not spell out changes in communal land tenure system. An opportunity presented itself later in 1939 and the 1940s, when officials at the CO theorized the possible shape of Britain's post-war development policy. That shift coincided with the Colonial Development and Welfare Bill which was passed into an Act of Parliament in 1940. Because of the growing interest in the welfare of Africans, the shift initiated a closer examination of African land tenure systems and coincided with increasing faith in proprietary rights over land as a gateway to economic progress.[23]

As noted, MacDonald, and the CO generally, felt that many colonies in British Africa were rife for a move towards land individualization and certification. Land "reform" from below was already occurring and the CO wanted to have control over the process. Joey Power has illustrated how some Africans in Malawi, whom she refers to as the "Petit-Bourgeoisie" (loosely defined as the lower middle class), were pressing for individual land ownership and were clandestinely claiming portions of land, often without official land titles.[24] In other words, for colonial Malawi and indeed for British East and Central Africa generally, "traditional power was giving way, as a result of the development of capitalist relations, to a more individualized economy," a process that needed to be tamed to avoid chaos.[25] While proposals on land reforms came from above, it is equally significant to acknowledge this local pressure and demand for individual titles from below.

Lord Hailey's *An African Survey* influenced MacDonald, especially because, as previously noted, it pointed to such a chaotic process. Not surprisingly, in his 1939 dispatch cited earlier, MacDonald warned the colonial governments against what he described as colonial inaction on matters of land tenure which, if not encouraging a "fatalistic attitude of *laissez-faire*," helped to breed "a chaotic evolution towards land individualization."[26] To systematically deal with the problem, MacDonald suggested setting up a committee of land experts in London to liaise with colonial governments on these changes. These arguments did not win the support of administrators in colonial Malawi who argued that the 1936 Native Trust Land Order-in-Council had already settled the question of land tenure in the protectorate.[27] Moreover, colonial authorities in Malawi considered a study on indigenous tenure systems as potentially raising local suspicion because it increased the number of other inquiries the protectorate welcomed in the immediate past. These administrators, noted the acting governor, K.L. Hall, preferred the "development of cooperative movement" to land individualization as a strategy of "achieving proper utilization of land and of progress in the sphere of economic development."[28] The former did not conflict with communal land tenure system. Besides, Hall warned the CO to ensure that a system of land registration, whatever shape it took, did not undermine the powers chiefs had over land allocation.

It was Governor Donald-Mackenzie Kennedy who later captured the mood better upon his return from holiday: "We are bound to flounder and blunder if we take into our own hands the allocation to individuals of lands normally held on communal tenure." Instead, he advised not to undermine the confidence and assistance of native authorities, further emphasizing that "without the confident assistance of native authorities . . . we may put up a good-looking scheme here and there: as years pass, our successors will find us out."[29] The colonial state in Malawi was not the only one that resisted these proposals. In East Africa, Uganda also objected to the CO dispatch.[30] Even with this opposition, the CO retained its confidence and looked forward to a future moment when "it [would be possible] to revert to the study of this problem."[31] That opportunity came when Arthur Creech Jones was appointed the S/S/C in October 1946. Before then, however, the CO set up a committee on post-war reconstruction in the colonies under the chairmanship of Lord Hailey to keep alive the debate on land tenure reforms in British Africa. Much of its exchange, occurring between 1941 and 1943, later helped to produce Charles Kingsley Meek's *Land Law and Custom in the Colonies* whose publication in 1946 almost coincided with Creech Jones' appointment as the S/S/C and helped to shape the latter's ideas on land changes.[32]

A British Government Anthropologist who previously spent much of his time researching on Nigerian societies, Meek produced a study which Malcolm MacDonald had in mind. His work went beyond MacDonald's expectations and, perhaps, even those of Lord Hailey, who contributed an introductory chapter. Not only did Meek examine the indigenous systems of land tenure in the British dependencies in Africa, but also covered extensively other parts of the empire, including Malaya, Ceylon, Cyprus, and British West Indies. Despite their variations, these colonies had similar bifurcated land tenure systems. They allowed the settler communities freehold or leasehold titles in land while the majority native peoples owned land through customary laws. Despite its extensive coverage, Meek's work, like Hailey's *An African Survey*, was shy in taking a position on how East African governments could approach the problem of land tenure. It thus remained more of a theoretical than a practical guide for official policy. More significantly, while Meek's work had a sympathetic reception at the CO, it was not spared of criticisms in the colonies.

The 1947 publication of Sir Philip Mitchell's analysis of the problems of rural Africa deserves highlighting, because it represents better the views of those who doubted the practicality of land tenure reforms in Africa.[33] Mitchell sought to compile some notes on Kenya's agrarian problems with a view of providing a workable solution. Anticipating renewed commitment to land tenure reforms following Meek's publication, he warned his colleagues by reiterating his earlier position:

> It should be noted that the tenure and use of land and the ownership of stock are a part of the fabric of all African society and at present inextricably interwoven with clan and family obligations, with birth, marriage and death, and with the beliefs and observances of each tribal community. These things are far more than merely property rights, as in our conception and no approach to the problem which neglects that consideration can hope to succeed. We have got to get the people and their simple but remarkably effective indigenous authorities and institutions as well as their newly developed political leaders with us, or we shall all of us pay the price to nature.[34]

In his conclusion, he unapologetically addressed adherents of land reforms as "ignorant people [who were] continually clamouring for quick results [while] charging the government with weakness and incompetence because it does not do so." Instead, he retreated to Lugard's concept of evolutionary changes in African land tenure, noting that no degree of "walloping can bring about profound social changes and extensive agricultural . . . reforms, [because] these are slow processes."[35]

Such upfront criticisms, however, did not derail Arthur Creech Jones' proposals for post-war development where land tenure reforms ranked high on the agenda. Creech Jones sought to provide a practical solution to the problems that communal land tenure presented. His dispatch to the colonial governors set out in clear terms what needed to be addressed in Africa: "There can be no doubt that existing agricultural practices are almost everywhere incapable of yielding a production which will support the standards of life at which we are aiming for the African."[36] Creech Jones did not believe changes in the methods of land utilization were the only strategy of achieving greater agricultural productivity for the improved welfare of Africans. Moreover, he saw the standards the CO set for African welfare as impossible to attain on a purely agricultural basis. It appears this was a general feeling at the Colonial Office that such figures as Sydney Caine, the head of the CO's Economic Bureau shared in the 1940s.[37] Earlier, Lord Hailey had noted that "if an African has to depend only on the results of his agriculture, poverty and malnutrition are . . . likely to continue to hinder him in making any material advance in the standards of life."[38] In his dispatch, Creech Jones suggested a revolutionary strategy which combined land tenure reforms, local government reforms, secondary industry, and cooperatives as the structure for lifting British Africa out of poverty.

Like Hailey and Meek, Creech Jones believed there was a nexus between land utilization strategies and land tenure-systems. He saw private rights to land solving other problems such as those on inappropriate land utilization and soil erosion. Emphasizing one without the other was a mere palliative and less in conformity to Britain's commitment to raising the welfare of Africans. Creech Jones' proposal is surprising and deserves a comment. He was one among staunch Fabians who did not believe in breaking Africans out of their communal life, exactly what land individualization would achieve. Economic and political developments of the post-war era necessitated shelving his faith in certain Fabian ideals, particularly those on African land tenure and governance. As Kelemen has illustrated, from the 1940s there was an urgency to reform colonialism by introducing certain Western institutions such as those of local government, trade unions, and, in this case, property rights to land. All these, as stated, were related to the aims of improving African welfare when the international community criticized Britain for ignoring her role of trusteeship.[39]

The inclusion of local government reforms in his proposal was deliberate. Creech Jones understood the concerns African governments registered—not to alter the supposedly traditional institutions that sustained chiefly powers, the very linchpin of colonial governance. Instead, the S/S/C suggested that Native Authorities should give way to local district assemblies, which would draw membership from educated Africans and a cross-section of society in each colony. The switch from chiefs as key collaborators to educated Africans presented some advantages. Educated Africans would better understand the contribution of land individualization and registration to agricultural productivity. Their inclusion in the ambits of power would also help to diffuse opposition educated Africans leveled against the colonial state. Though Creech Jones prescribed what he believed was a solution to the challenges of economic progress in Africa, the reality in the colonies was different. Nyasaland responded in ways that reminded Creech Jones of the extent to which he had strayed from traditional Fabian ideals of preservative trusteeship which Labour literature had clearly articulated.

DEBATING CREECH JONES' PROPOSALS IN POST-WAR NYASALAND

The responsibility to act on Creech Jones' dispatch fell on the Chief Secretary in colonial Malawi whose call to act on this dispatch generated conflicting opinion in the protectorate. In summarizing the dispatch, he challenged his colleagues: "We are being asked to examine the problem of agricultural productivity [and consider] modifications that are necessary in the present system of land tenure and local government."[40] The Acting Director of Agriculture (Ag. DofA) dismissed the Chief Secretary' request for elaborate meetings to discuss the S/S/C's dispatch. He argued that his department already had in place comprehensive plans addressing the S/S/C's concerns: "I do not see that we can do more to further the Colonial Secretary's wishes than to press on with the development plans already projected."[41] The Senior Agricultural Officer (South) argued that rural progress had little to do with changes in land tenure. It centered on the attitude of African cultivators, many of whom he did not perceive were true agriculturalists.[42] Like the Ag. DofA, he too had confidence in the post-war development plan, a document that spelled out what Nyasaland was to achieve over a period of ten years before resources were released from the Colonial Welfare and Development Fund.[43] In his analysis, however, the Chief Secretary did not consider the highly cited plan as suggesting modifications in the system of local government and land tenure.

The Provincial Commissioner (North) condemned the idea of individual land rights because it concentrated land in the hands of Europeans, Indians, and capitalist Africans. He warned his colleagues that land mortgaging would lead to massive detribalization with disastrous social effects. The Central Provincial Commissioner did not think there was a workable strategy for the reform that would not conflict with the existing tenurial arrangements. He supported cooperatives, instead of the reforms, as the latter held a potential to undermine the traditional role of chiefs.[44] Authorities assumed, like many of the Fabian intellectuals, that cooperatives would not have destabilizing effects since Africans would produce or market their products either as communities or individuals within the confines of community life. African chiefs also rejected the changes, not so much because they disrupted their cultural practices but because they replicated what they saw as an existing practice. Unlike government officials who insisted that Africans owned their land communally, chiefs argued that land was already under individual cultivation within the communities. Individuals' access to land was guaranteed through chiefly trusteeship.[45]

Two individuals stood out in their support of the S/S/C's proposals—Richard W. Kettlewell, Senior Agricultural Officer (Center, later Director of

Agriculture), and C.C. Webster, the Senior Agricultural Officer heading the Tung Experimental Station (South).[46] Kettlewell supported the policy recommendation because he considered it as a step towards creating a "yeoman farmer" out of progressive native Africans. His ideas later crystalized into the Master Farmers Scheme in the early 1950s noted in Owen Kalinga's work. Kettlewell saw such changes taking shape through a policy of pushing out rather than concentrating Africans in rural land. "I suggest that the 'objective of government policy' [sic] in land tenure which the Secretary of State requires to be favored should have partial rural depopulation as one of its principal aims," Kettlewell advised his colleagues.[47] For Kettlewell, changes in land tenure were necessary. But the reforms would have rewarding effects if they targeted a group beyond ordinary farmers. Kettlewell's ideas aimed at moving peasants out of rural land to provide room for a few enterprising Africans and other players. The rest of the peasants were expected to provide wage labor to the few who would competently work the land along capitalist lines. Without such interventions peasants would be condemned to "small individual holdings which preclude any rise in the standard of living."[48] His ideas were reminiscent of an "enclosure movement" designed to remove the surplus population from rural land.

Kettlewell agreed with the S/S/C that secondary industry held potential to create jobs for ordinary Africans. Success in this area would also release more land for progressive farmers. He also affirmed the necessity of cooperatives. He warned, however, that by tying farmers to land, cooperative arrangements had the potential to forestall rural depopulation. Nevertheless, they were a better alternative to African collective farming at the heart of some colonial officials. The practice would allow Africans to consolidate their land and produce their crops collectively while sharing products or proceeds. "I think I am right" complained the Northern Provincial Commissioner, "the Senior Agricultural Officer, Lilongwe (Kettlewell), is opposed to the idea [of collectivism] and considers it impractical."[49] Kettlewell criticized the proposal on two counts. First, he argued that the protectorate did not have enough land to accommodate such agricultural experiments. Second, because most Africans owned land as individuals within communities, he saw the scheme only succeeding under Soviet style of compulsion. Such an approach would stifle individual liberties contrary to the beliefs of the British Empire—the Empire of Liberty. As a proponent of capitalist farming with "progressive farmers" serving as agents of development, Kettlewell's ideas contrasted with those of the Fabian intellectuals and his colleagues, who were concerned with forestalling rural depopulation by supporting Africans within the confines of their communal landholdings.

Though emphasizing cooperatives for the land-abundant North, Webster was hesitant to recommend them for the congested South. He saw the Southern province ripe for Lugard's last stage of evolution towards an individual land tenure system. Historically, much of the land alienation in the country took place in the Shire Highlands of the Southern Province, where it created landlessness among Africans. The influx of the Lomwe people from Portuguese East Africa (Mozambique) between the 1890s and 1940s, further contributed to high population density in that province. In 1946, Nyasaland set up a commission to investigate the problem of land shortage among Africans in the protectorate. Led by Sidney Abrahams, a member of the Privy Council and a lawyer who once served as an Attorney General in Uganda, it recommended that the government should purchase land from the white planters to resettle landless Africans.[50] The idea of resettling them came because Africans on private estates were spread unevenly. It was not possible for these Africans to keep the land they originally occupied. The best option was to buy portions of land where Africans would be resettled and taught better ways of cultivation. Most of the landless groups survived under the mercy of planters. These were Africans who paid rent in form of labor—the very Thangata labor system noted earlier. Webster criticized the recommendations for contradicting a natural path to progress which, for him, should have proceeded through individual land rights, all the while consolidating land in the hands of wealthy farmers. "The aim," he stated, "should rather be to remove the natives from the land. . . . They should be settled in model towns or villages and not given more than a quarter of land as a vegetable garden. Their means of livelihood would be as paid labourers on estates and secondary industries."[51] Like Kettlewell, Webster too wanted to create an African wage-earning class, drawn from the surplus rural population.

It is easy to explain these contradictory policy proposals. As Baker has argued elsewhere, many colonial administrators did not welcome landlessness because it bred "seeds of trouble" in the colony, a problem which some technical officers undermined. Authorities cited memories of 1915 Chilembwe uprising as a precursor to consequences of land dispossession among Africans. It is the same fear that forced administrators to view proposals towards individual tenure as a potential threat to the protectorate's stability. Moreover, Nyasaland lacked alternatives to absorbing those farmers who lost their land.[52] It is, therefore, less surprising that contradictory policy proposals played out, one of encouraging individualism and rural depopulation, the other of concentrating farmers in rural land. What emerged eventually was an ambiguous policy which neither forbade individual land ownership among Africans, nor encouraged deliberate reforms towards this direction. Government policy, however, was firm on cooperatives. It passed a resolution to experiment with community schemes in the hope that these would help to build farmers' cooperatives. In the 1950s, village land improvement and settlement schemes were attempted mostly in the Southern and Central provinces of the protectorate. Most, if not all, of them yielded disappointing results.[53]

In general, these schemes targeted multiple objectives, including teaching Africans effective soil conservation measures and modern crop production practices. The strategy operated at two levels. The first aimed at consolidating and rearranging the fragmented African land into appropriate landholding patterns arranged according to a land utilization plan. Such a pattern included marking land for specific purposes such as cultivation, grazing, and settlement. Thereafter, sound soil conservation measures were applied, including construction of diversion ditches, drainage passages, terraces, as well as contour bands.[54] The second strategy involved resettling African villages located in environmentally fragile areas into schemes which the government developed using modern technology (tractors). The Southern Province schemes illustrate well how the latter strategy operated, and the opposition Africans levelled against them. The Port Herald (Nsanje) scheme, for example, had the objectives of reducing pressure from the congested areas of the district. The strategy involved creating new settlements in Tomali/Mbewe, Mpheza/Pwaze, and Namphota areas. The state created a 15,000-acre space that sought to resettle 1000 families, each given eight acres of land. Ten boreholes were sunk to provide water to the settlers.[55]

If these schemes were instituted partly because they would maintain community life and hence a better alternative to detestable land tenure reforms, they were not spared of African opposition. Evidence shows that Africans resisted the state's attempts to resettle them in ways that surprised some officials: "The people of Port Herald District are not yet in a serious plight [to warrant resettlement. Instead,] they needed an area that would support their existing livelihoods" such as fishing, *dimba* production, and others.[56] It appears plans to resettle Africans in this area dated back to the 1920s and they met a similar resistance when the Mang'anja chiefs opposed the idea of resettling them to the Kololo-dominated lands in Chikwawa.[57] The Port Herald District Book of March 23, 1929, assured the headmen that the state had dropped all plans to reallocate them to Chikwawa.[58] Having resettled only 17 farmers, some authorities admitted that the scheme had failed.[59] The Namphota scheme suffered a similar fate. It only resettled eight families from three villages.[60]

In areas where the people accepted resettlement, the results proved disappointing. Farmers accumulated enormous debt, with others virtually starving. "Unless something can be done to assist them financially," complained the District Commissioner, "there will be a massive exodus to Northern Rhodesia."[61]

One reason for the failure of these schemes centers on top-down strategies that did little to command the confidence of villagers. Usually, government authorities relied on chiefs to convince their people about the benefits of proposed agricultural changes. However, as Peter McLoughlin notes, chiefs did not always have a firm hold over their people such that there was a disconnection between the "official mind" and local aspirations. Considering the soil and land conservation campaign as a less rewarding exercise personally, notes Erik Green, some chiefs took no pride in persuading Africans to move into these schemes. In the case of Thyolo and Mzimba districts, much of what the colonial authorities achieved in African agriculture was less a result of the intervention of chiefs than local interest or the use of force from above. Villagers often resisted conservation and land use measures which they perceived as less rewarding.[62] Thinking that exceptional land planning executed through meticulous technical detail and propaganda campaigns would work out a miracle, government officials ignored the sociological aspects of the reforms. There were minimal consultations with the local people such that matters to do with household economics—household food needs, new labor demands the consolidated plots presented—were often ignored.[63] These failure stories were a reminder to colonial authorities about the multiple meanings Africans attached to land. Beyond its economic purpose, land also provided a sense of identity and kinship such that failure to respect such ideas could only spell disaster for the reform program. Besides, coming in the 1950s when Africans were constantly opposing the Federation of Rhodesia and Nyasaland, the disturbances these schemes caused in resettling Africans were interpreted in political terms.

Around the same period, Kettlewell's proposals translated into the Master Farmers' Scheme. While encouraging community schemes, effectively fostering community life, the state also promoted individual cultivation, encouraging the most gifted and self-motivated farmers as trusted agents of economic progress. The state provided such individuals with rewards in form of agricultural inputs, plow technology, and monetary rewards. The intent, as Kelemen has observed elsewhere, was to build cohesive communities "but accompanied with the idea of unlocking its internal economic dynamism through self-help and [individual] entrepreneurship."[64] Even with that, however, targeted individual farmers did not evolve into a "yeoman class" as Kettlewell envisaged, and many of them pressed, without success, for freehold land titles. Moreover, when in 1955 Kettlewell presented a proposal for the provision of land titles to progressive African farmers, the Executive Council rejected the plan. It argued that the 1936 Nyasaland Native Trust Land Order-in-Council (amended several times) had settled the land question.[65] As noted earlier, that Order did not encourage individualism. It represented the earlier notion of Fabian-inspired colonialism whose aim was to protect Africans from the corruption of capitalist activities. And yet, a year later, after the Executive Council rejected Kettlewell's plan, the colonial state approved a robust African land reform (individualization) proposal which Nyasaland forwarded to the CO for support. How do we explain this sudden change of mind? The subsequent section addresses this question. Before achieving that, however, a few aspects require clarification.

Erik Green has argued that, unlike other colonies, Nyasaland did not experience a shift towards planning for economic improvement in the 1940s, despite the general shift brought about by the CDWA. For Green, there was no change in the aims and objectives of the colonial state. Instead, it was concerns over natural resources conservation that moved the state.[66] Green did not provide an explanation to this lack of a shift. Moreover, literature discussing colonial development planning in Malawi is silent about the changes of the 1940s.[67] Instead, it leapfrogs to the 1950s to examine the Master Farmers Scheme and land consolidation projects of that era. Other studies that discuss the development question emphasize Governor Geoffrey Colby's industrial projects of the 1950s. Although this literature discusses the land question, its focus is on how Governor Colby attempted to address land shortages among Africans. The tenurial aspects of land are left untouched.[68]

Green was right to argue that there was not a significant shift at the level of "rural" development practice in the 1940s which also helps to explain the scholarly silence. Elias Mandala shared a similar view. He took issue with such scholars as Beinart who viewed the village land improvement schemes of the 1950s as an aspect of the empire-wide development ideas and hence representing a break with the usual soil conservation paradigm. Instead, Mandala argued that the colonial state in Malawi was simply responding to the environmental challenges of the time.[69] Often overlooked in these arguments is that the 1940s and 1950s did not lack well-articulated development goals for improving African lives. Such goals, I argue, were intricately linked to the conservation paradigm and the protectorate's political dynamics. It is the tendency to emphasize the conservation discourse that obscures the developmental aspects. Land use measures constituted one aspect of the complete development package, the application of which conflicted with other political objectives. For the colonial state, economic progress would roll on the wheels of communal land improvement, settlement, and cooperative schemes, anchored on strict soil conservation measures. This was a better way to contain the political chaos some officials associated with land tenure proposals. Viewed from that angle, the land conservation campaigns of the late 1940s and early 1950s went beyond the soil conservation paradigm. They were an extension of the post-war development debate. Whether knowingly or not, bureaucrats in Nyasaland helped to promote preservative trusteeship we usually associate with the metropolitan-based Fabian membership, but in ways that met their specific political interests.

In the 1950s, however, these schemes triggered African resistance and became part of the rallying campaign against colonial rule in Malawi. Planned and executed during an era of strong opposition against the Central African Federation, educated African nationalists often drummed up support for mass nationalism by referencing harsh soil conservation rules and schemes.[70] The decade of the1950s, therefore, was an era of political uncertainties for both colonial administrators and settlers. The two groups feared that once the campaign against the Federation and for independence materialized, the African government might expropriate their land. In consequence, the state turned to the debate on land tenure reforms and reimagined land in ways that would ameliorate the effects of the political chaos that would emerge. The rest of the discussion in this chapter reflects on the thinking of the state in the 1950s, how it sought to use land tenure reforms to safeguard settler interests and the intense opposition it faced from Africans. This discussion is relevant because, apart from showing the limits of the state as a guardian of progress, it helps us connect postcolonial land tenure reforms to those of the late colonial period.

LAND AND POLITICAL SETTLEMENT IN THE 1950S MALAWI

While holding talks on land with officials at the CO in 1958, Sir Robert Armitage, the Governor of Nyasaland, expressed fears about a possible land expropriation in Malawi. The governor

> explained about the feeling of insecurity on the part of non-African landowners (who [at the time] held no more than 4% of the total land of Nyasaland). It was clear that even if safeguards for private ownership were written into the Constitution or into any other legal framework, it would be useless without having enforcing sanctions, and these could not operate from outside Nyasaland once Nyasaland attained self-government. Therefore, his feeling was that the best hope of security for landowners generally was to make freehold the rule rather than the exception in Nyasaland and to give more Africans a stake as freeholders in the maintenance of freehold tenure.[71]

Between 1956 and 1961, the colonial state in Malawi struggled to secure freehold land, most of which was supported under Johnstone's Certificates of Claims. Working under intense pressure from the settler community, which feared land expropriation under an African-dominated government, the state looked to the previous proposals on land reform as a solution to the impending problem. Once Africans were granted rights to land with both African and European land registered under the same land registry, the

Certificates of Claims would be regularized. Besides, targeted land expropriation would be difficult, although not impossible to achieve. But when on July 19, 1956, Armitage sent a proposal introducing freehold land tenure "as a rule rather than an exception" in Nyasaland, little did the CO know about its hidden agenda.[72] The events of the 1950s provided an opportune time for such reforms. The Conservative Government in Britain, with its insatiable quest for individualism, had taken over power in 1951. Again, it was around the same time that the East Africa Royal Commission released its report in 1955. The British Government set up this commission in 1953 to undertake an economic and social stocktaking of its East African colonies and recommend strategies of improving standards of living among Africans. Among the six objectives it had, three centered on land and agriculture. For instance, the Commission was charged to investigate and frame recommendations in first, the economic development of the land already in occupation by the introduction of better farming methods; second, the adaptations or modifications in traditional tribal systems of tenure necessary for the full development of land; and third, the opening for cultivation and settlement of land which was not fully used. Regarding the second aspect, the Commission considered reforms towards individual land tenure ownership as a policy objective "to pursue without exceptions."[73]

The 1956 Arusha conference report on African land tenure in East and Central Africa also provided context to Nyasaland's proposal on land reforms. Following the findings of the East Africa Royal Commission report, the S/S/C, Alan Lennox-Boyd, suggested to the east and central African governors the possibility for a conference to discuss further land tenure matters. The conference took place in Arusha (Tanganyika/Tanzania) between February 8 and 22, 1956. Like what Macdonald had highlighted in 1939, the report noted that in some parts of east and central Africa, land individualization was already underway but in more chaotic ways. Yet in others such as the Southern Province of colonial Malawi, the report decried the communal land tenure system which did little to promote economic progress. The report found colonial Malawi's case surprising. Despite high population densities in the Southern Province, which should have acted as an impetus towards individual land ownership, it had registered little in that direction. Instead, "customary communal tenure [had] become immobilized" through uxorilocal marriage and matrilineal inheritance: "The man lives at his wife's village and helps her to cultivate a garden on her family land; his heirs are his sister's children. This system gives the man no secure interests in the land he uses . . . and it discourages him from investing his labour or his capital in it."[74] While not advocating for haphazard reforms, the report advised African governments to consider providing secure and negotiable land title to Africans as a means of achieving greater agricultural productivity.[75] Such an intervention would help to guide the unregulated land individualization in some areas. But it would also help to break cultural institutions of land ownership and inheritance hostile to economic productivity in places such as the protectorate's Southern Province.

These recommendations provided a good context to the land reform proposals of the 1950s in colonial Malawi. Armitage's dispatch accompanying the land reform proposal affirmed the necessity of negotiable titles in African land: "Human beings will tend to put effort into a piece of land which he calls 'mine' than into any land which he calls 'ours' [sic]."[76] Providing a secure, negotiable, and registered title in land while allowing its devolution, was the major tenet of the land reform proposal. At the CO, S.R. Simpson (the Land Advisor to the CO who also attended the Arusha conference) described it as representing "a 'new look' and quite a different idea from vesting 'trust land' [sic] in the Secretary of State with the declared intention of preserving African law and custom."[77] It provided Africans with the legal mandate to lease or sell the land to a fellow African or transfer the title to successors. The proposal carried with it the African Wills Ordinance as part of the package, and it allowed willing Africans exemption from local inheritance custom.[78] By the time Armitage dispatched the proposal to the S/S/C, confidential discussions were underway with the African members of the Nyasaland Legislative Council and African chiefs. Both groups summarily dismissed the reforms as a threat to the African tradition of land ownership.

It was clear to many colonial authorities that Africans in the Legislative Council and others, all of whom were members of the Nyasaland African Congress (NAC), would not support the proposal. These included W.M. Chirwa (Federal Member of Parliament, MP); C.R. Kumbikano (MP); M.W.K. Chiume (Member of the Legislative Council, MLC); and H.B. Chipembere (MLC). Other members included N.D. Kwenje (MLC); D.W. Chijozi (MLC), and J.R.N. Chinyama (MLC). In his note to the CO, the Chief Secretary described this group of African representatives as bent on creating unnecessary delays and raising suspicion to an otherwise sound proposal.[79] To contain this opposition, Nyasaland requested for the S/S/C to visit, and between January 16 and 18 1957, he held discussions with African Provincial Councils in all three provinces of the protectorate. Other than challenging the reforms for their disruptive effects, chiefs and the other members of the Native Councils feared that the proposed reforms would lead to yet another spate of land alienation in the protectorate. The S/S/C assured Africans about the benevolence of the proposals, arguing they had nothing to do with land alienation as most of them had feared. That effort notwithstanding, the S/S/C left with a negative impression about the reforms. He considered the late-1950s as an inappropriate time to discuss land matters because of the mounting pressure for political independence.[80] Other than resistance from members of the African Provincial Councils, the S/S/C's position was no doubt influenced by a welcoming memo that NAC wrote him which deserves citing at length:

> We have time and again stated in no uncertain terms that Nyasaland is a black man's country and as such a black man by virtue of his birthright must rule it at all costs. . . . The question of land tenure is here with us suggested and put to the government by the very imperialist characters [settlers], who barely claim to have a stake in this country. At this juncture, we wish to declare here and now that Congress [NAC] is opposed to any ideas to reform land policy of this country in order to meet [the interests of settlers] and throw the poor African masses into a villainy of untold suffering. . . . In the circumstances we do reject the whole scheme regardless of whosoever is responsible for it. We feel strongly that we are capable of planning for any land development at our own initiative as soon as we are given the opportunity to do so and any European sponsored scheme affecting the land could not be accepted at present. Gone are the days of land schoolmasters. . . . The government should let us free to run such schemes by ourselves if there are any good intentions behind the suggestions. As a matter of fact, no scheme concerning land shall be acceptable until such time Nyasaland is extracted from the Federation.[81]

The February 1957 debate on land in the Legislative Council showed that Africans did not relent in their opposition to the land reforms. They suspected the proposal as a ploy to consolidate settler influence in Malawi through greater control over land. They also seem to have clearly understood the source of the pressure acting on the colonial administrators. "Mr. President," charged Kwenje in ways that serve as a reminder to the earlier debate on land among the Fabian intellectuals: "as far as we know, land in this protectorate is, in the final analysis, African land. That was the treaty that stands for protectorate. Land, or ownership of land, has just come in because the government has pressure to bear from the settlers of this country, who feel they should turn it into a colony."[82] Kwenje further emphasized his position by appealing to what he saw as an African tradition—that Africans recognized land as the sun which "should not be sold; the races will have to use the sunshine, and it should not be sold to others."[83] Another prominent member who drew on the language of land that the Labour Party documents emphasized twenty years earlier was Chipembere. "African land belongs to the whole tribe or the whole community together, and no single individual owns it," Chipembere charged, further challenging the right of chiefs to sell it to the white settlers in the 1890s: "It can, I think, be questioned quite successfully in a court of law and it can be proved, I believe, that the Certificates of Claim granted by Sir Harry Johnstone in 1893, were invalid."[84] Later, Chipembere called upon Africans to resist attempts to reorganize land and "make it a marketable article, a thing which our ancestors from whom we have received the land never knew."[85]

The position this group of African politicians took speaks to the very contradictions and contending interests with which the colonial state grappled. As Joey Power has shown, many in the group were part of the Petit-Bourgeoisie who frustrated attempts the colonial state made to promote the cooperative movement in off-farm activities. The Petit-Bourgeoisie included the employed missionary-educated Africans who ran their small-scale businesses through wage labor, and the uneducated self-employed artisans and other related traders. Because of its insatiable desire for individual enterprise, the group posed a threat to Indirect Rule. Besides, the colonial state viewed the group with suspicion. The state feared the group had political ambitions that needed to be tamed. In the 1940s and early 1950s, the colonial state moved to contain the Petit-Bourgeoisie by redirecting their energy towards cooperative retail businesses. If the colonial state considered cooperatives as a strategy of containing individualism in the protectorate, this group of African entrepreneurs rejected cooperatives. In the words of Power, the group "recognize[d] that cooperatives undercut the economic autonomy of individuals, depriving them of a crucial edge in an economy dominated by foreign capital and characterized by cut-throat competition."[86] The Petit-Bourgeois considered cooperatives as a weak business strategy with which to compete within the hostile colonial economy.

Undoubtedly, this group should have celebrated the land tenure reforms of the 1950s because they were in line with the ambitions of those who preferred individual accumulation. Africans serving in the Provincial and Legislative Councils, however, undercut such interests. Although believing in individual economic enterprise just like many of the Petit-Bourgeoisie, these Africans, as noted, blocked proposals towards individual land tenure reforms by appealing to custom. But they did so for political reasons. African elites used custom to frustrate the land reform proposal because, in their opinion, it would further the interests of the settler community. Their suspicions were not unfounded because beginning in the early 1950s, the white settlers became increasingly concerned about the security of their land. Colin Baker has illustrated how the "politics of castigation" that emerged in the wake of government's attempts to buy settlers' land to resettle Africans (often against the will of the settler community), pitted the two groups against each other.[87]

For example, earlier in 1954, the Convention of Associations in Nyasaland (a significantly powerful body that united diverse associations of the settler community in the protectorate), petitioned the then S/S/C, Oliver Lyttelton, about the conduct of Governor Geoffrey Colby. They condemned him for seeking to appease Africans at their expense.[88] What remains unclear is how the late colonial state sought to address settlers' concerns. The 1958 meeting at the CO whose record is cited above shows that the state was as anxious about the future of settlers' land as were the planters. There is little evidence to suggest that the CO treated the land reform proposal as a matter of urgency when Armitage disclosed its primary motive. Meanwhile Armitage continued to receive pressure from European settlers. The Nyasaland Tea Association Limited, under the chairmanship of Mr. A.R. Wilson, criticized what it saw as the government's inaction. It was joined by the Settlers and Residents Association of Nyasaland whose chair was Mr. T. R. Ness. Their concerns became more pronounced when Dr. Hastings Kamuzu Banda took over the leadership of NAC, following his return from Britain (through Ghana) in 1958.[89] His avowed declaration against what he called the stupid Federation of Rhodesia and Nyasaland (established in 1953 under opposition from Africans), and his quest for majority rule in the country, shook the settler community.

On January 18, 1960, the frustrated Tea Association challenged the government "to take immediate steps to remove all questions relating to the status of freehold alienated land from the legislative competence of the Nyasaland Legislative Council."[90] Instead, it suggested that matters of freehold land be placed directly under the S/S/C just like the native trust land, or under a federal regulatory body. What the settlers overlooked, however, was that such a request was politically unattainable. As noted earlier, Africans saw the Federation as a step towards annexing their land for white settlement. In fact, it was the same Federation that helped build up nationalist resistance thereby threatening settlers' interests in land. As early as 1954 when the proposal towards land titling reforms was discussed among government officials, the Federation was singled out as among the major threats to the proposal. Forewarning the District Commissioners (South) about a possible but difficult task lying ahead of them, the Provincial Commissioner remarked:

> It is almost certain that attempts to get Africans interested in this problem will be interpreted by some of them as a sign that the government is now putting into practice what all Africans feared would follow Federation, the alienation of African land to Europeans. You will have to combat such stories and point out clearly that Africans who can make the best use of the land . . . get some better security of tenure than they have under African law and customs.[91]

The suggestion to place all matters of white settlers' land under the jurisdiction of the Federal Assembly was most unlikely to win colonial administrators' support. Such, however, was the inaction the settlers referenced.

Pressure piled on Armitage who was still awaiting feedback from the CO on the 1956 land proposal. Concerned with the unnecessary delay, he sent a follow-up telegram on April 24, 1958, articulating the other hidden motive of the land reform proposal, which was to safeguard freehold titles of the settler community. The 1960 settlers' memo triggered a response from the CO with the S/S/C, now Iain Macleod, responding somewhat disappointingly:

> Generally speaking, the only "land policy" likely to survive under "popular government" [sic] must be one which commends popular support or, at least, does not excite opposition. Thus, a land policy which is sound in itself is as likely to survive as is any other sound institution, but it is doubtful whether administrative or legal steps taken in advance of the conferment of self-government to entrench a defective system will preserve it in the long run.[92]

The CO saw the Nyasaland position as complicated because the said freehold titles derived from rather dubious Certificates of Claim. Without promising success, CO advisors, chief among them being S.R. Simpson (the Land Advisor), suggested converting a Deeds Registry into a Registry of Title while compiling a register. With that in place, the "mere fact of registration would be proof of title" irrespective of the source of the title—Certificates of Claim. "Africans and Europeans would have their titles registered under the same law" thereby creating possible safeguards for the non-African freeholders.[93] Even with that, Macleod saw the greatest safeguards resting not so much in such legal frameworks or land reforms as in securing the goodwill of the majority government.

Heated negotiations regarding a land settlement took place between 1960 and June 1964 when Dr. Banda became the Prime Minister in 1962 under an African majority government. When it became clear that British colonial rule in Malawi was on its deathbed, administrators planned to secure settlers' land in multiple ways. First, they raised yet another land reform proposal, albeit one that retained chiefly powers over the allocation of titles in their areas of jurisdiction. The latter aimed to contain opposition from chiefs, hoping to negotiate with Banda's team on one front. Nevertheless, it emphasized the provision of rights to land, whether to families or individuals.[94] One other aspect missing in the previous proposal but included in the 1960 one was the provision of a Statutory Land Board. The latter would have regulatory powers over land and hence avoid placing it under the jurisdiction of the Prime Minister or any other political office in Nyasaland. As it turned out, Banda, like other nationalists before, dismissed the proposal by appealing to custom. Second, during constitutional negotiations that took place at the Lancaster House in London between July and August 1960 under the chairmanship of the S/S/C, Iain McCleod, the CO, and the local white administrators from Malawi proposed including the Bill of Rights to the constitution of the emerging government with the intension, among others, to protect settlers' economic interests. While Banda agreed to the proposal, the settler community saw it as a less effective way of preventing land confiscation because Banda, in their opinion, would not respect the Bill of Rights.[95]

The fears of the settler community became pronounced following the many public pronouncements Banda made concerning Certificates of Claim. During the preliminary discussion to the November 1962 Marlborough House (London) constitutional talks which the British Home Secretary, R.A. Butler, convened, Banda trashed the certificates and further argued that there "is no such a thing as private land under African customary law." For Banda, Europeans had mistakenly interpreted the fact that chiefs had allowed early settlers to use the land as a transaction of purpose.[96] Despite providing assurances that the majority government would not confiscate freehold land, settlers did not have confidence in such pronouncements. Unsurprisingly, the Settlers and Residents Association of Nyasaland petitioned the S/S/C, drawing his attention to Banda's contempt of the Bill of Rights.[97] Later, they challenged Butler's argument that the success of the Bill of Rights would depend, to a significant extent, on Banda's personal goodwill. Instead, they sent Butler excerpts from the *Malawi News* in which Banda urged his people "to carefully watch" every white man, calling them frustrated and bitter people. "These flaunt a pathological hatred towards Europeans," charged Ness, "mock Dr. Banda's views [on respecting the Bill of Rights]." Already, by 1963, Africans were encroaching into some selected estates in Cholo (now Thyolo) District in the South, something that strengthened the fears that Ness had. Ness was also worried with what he saw as government's inaction. "We must confess our doubts," he concluded, "as to the sincerity of your claim that our anxieties are appreciated."[98] These petitions forced Butler to convene a meeting in the company of Banda, Glyn Jones (Governor-General of Nyasaland), and others on September 24, 1963. Among issues discussed was the proposal to include in the Bill of Rights a provision that the Privy Council hear all appeals under it, establish a Statutory Land Board to advise on matters of land, and include in the constitution Banda's statement against land confiscation.[99] Banda agreed with the first aspect but rejected the last two. When Malawi gained independence in 1964, land in the country fell under the Office of the Prime Minister. It was executed under the Office of the Minister of Natural Resources. Banda held both offices.

One year after independence, the ODM in Britain deployed an Economic Mission, chaired by C de N. Hill, to investigate the economic problems of independent Malawi. Among others, the Hill report recommended reforms towards providing private rights to land, a proposal that had failed during the late colonial period. Because the report was critical of Banda's infrastructural projects, he trashed it, and with it the land proposal. In commenting on the report later in 1966, Banda stated: "We have every intention to consolidate landholdings wherever this is possible but there is no intention at this stage of introducing title deeds, freehold or leasehold, and certainly not as a reward for good husbandry."[100] That remark also coincided with a proposal to re-organize the 500,000-acre project in Central Malawi under the United Nations Special Fund Project. Banda reluctantly accepted to have S.R. Simpson, the former CO Land Advisor who was serving under the same post with the ODM, to advise on the possibility of the suggested reforms. Within three weeks, Simpson had proposed a robust customary land legislation that touched on four aspects. These included converting customary tenure to some form of recorded individual title; providing land and procedure suitable for the new landowners; protecting new landowners in their dealings; and converting existing documentary title to registered title.[101] With the aid of the State's Senior Counsel, A. C. MacDonald, he later drafted three Bills which were laid before Banda.[102] In passing them into law in Parliament later in 1967, Banda argued that "under existing laws in the country, the available land is being used uneconomically and wastefully," further repeating the language Armitage used before, that land that belonged to anyone belonged to none and "anyone's baby is nobody's baby at all."[103] Although the colonial state failed to secure white settlers' interests, the colonial debate on land reforms laid down an excellent foundation to land titling reforms that emerged after independence.

The 1967 Act, therefore, represented a continuity rather than a sharp break with the past. But what also continued was the dilemma the colonial state had to reconcile two goals of development. On the one hand was the need to achieve the protectorate's economic growth; on the other, the quest to improve the welfare or living standards of Africans, most of whom were poor. Although not ignoring peasant agriculture, the colonial state considered the settler economy as crucial to raising the protectorate's economic capacity. African nationalists condemned colonial officials for showing little interest in the welfare of Africans. It is through this lens that they read the 1950s land reform proposal. In their view, only an African majority government could balance the economic interests of various groups in the country. But as Chapter four of the book will show, although educated Africans criticized the colonial state for favoring large-scale farmers, they too did not fare any better after independence.

CONCLUSION

Students of British colonial development argue that the late-1940s witnessed a shift away from goals of rural welfare and development towards neo-mercantile objectives. What is often overlooked is how some members of the CO were equally concerned about colonial welfare and development during that era. Although seeking to address metropolitan economic concerns, they also theorized the possible ways of improving the living standards of the colonial societies, the case in point being that of faith in private rights to land. In Nyasaland, proposals towards land reform were caught up in the witches' brew of contending political and economic interests. During the immediate post-war period, communal land tenure systems among Africans were desirable because they sustained social and political order in the protectorate. Local administrators and bureaucrats defended it in ways that reminded the Labour Government how far it had strayed away from Fabian principles of trusteeship. However, that resistance to reform robbed the colonial state of an opportunity to experiment with some new ideas of development during the era of reform, particularly those on land tenure. The best it did was to attach an economic meaning to the communal land tenure system. That came with land consolidation schemes in the hope that these would compensate for the weaknesses of communal land tenure.

It was only after the mid-1950s that the colonial state in Malawi earnestly pushed for land individualization. This push, however, came after the politics of decolonization unleashed forces that challenged white planters' proprietary rights over land. Faith in the security that presumably came with freehold or leasehold tenure became tenuous, not least because what the planters saw as secure titles was a subject of the overall political climate of the time than the title itself. The threat of land dispossession, emerging in the wake of nationalist politics, forced the colonial state (under pressure from the settler community) to broaden the sector with private rights to land and hence cover up for the past mistakes. In that regard, the colonial state reimagined land tenure as an economic solution to the political challenges that nationalist politics presented. Africans rejected such proposals by re-appropriating and throwing back at the colonial authorities a similar language of trusteeship that guided the debate on land tenure during the interwar and post-war eras. That such a rejection came from the educated African elites, many of whom had previously sought for individual accumulation, reminded the colonial state about the difficulties of "coping with contradictions" which John Lonsdale and Bruce Berman emphasized in the case of colonial Kenya.[104] But it also points to one other significant aspect: Land tenure proposals of the 1950s in colonial Malawi were aimed at addressing the political problems emerging in the wake of the politics of decolonization. They were a response to the pressure the settler community exerted on the state. If development programs targeting rural communities are sometimes a response to certain political pressures as James Ferguson observed in the case of Botswana, acknowledging the multiple sources of these pressures beyond those Africans present is an assignment worth undertaking.[105]

In any case, by reflecting on the failure of the 1950s/1960s land reforms, the chapter puts on display the very nature of the colonial state in Malawi. It was one caught up in contending interests in which different groups appealed to Fabian language to achieve contrasting aims, and in the process frustrating the objectives of the state, albeit at different times. Save for changes in the aims, those proposals, however, crystallized in the 1967 customary land law of the postcolonial state in ways that display the colonial legacies quite remarkably. This chapter does not suggest drawing a linear relationship between the distant colonial past and the immediate postcolonial present. Instead, it proposes looking at the outcome as the climax of the enduring technocratic debate on land, itself an auxiliary to the broader concerns of addressing poverty and raising the living standards of African communities and other societies elsewhere. That debate was caught up in political, economic, and cultural interests, making progress impossible to achieve until new players, freed from political excesses of the late colonialism, came onto the scene after independence. Taking on the mantle of trusteeship, the postcolonial Malawian state, the ODM, and World Bank expressed faith in the power of private property. The limits of their actions are discussed in chapters four and five. Meanwhile, the failure of land reform paralleled the fate of a booming tung oil industry to which the Department of Agriculture looked to pursue the goals of African welfare and development in the protectorate.

NOTES

1. Malcom McDonald to Nyasaland Governor (also sent to other African Governors), November 29, 1939, MNA S43/1/11/1.
2. The debate leading to the objection in question is contained in Native Land Tenure, 1939–1940, MNA S43/1/11/1.
3. The African position is detailed in the Nyasaland Protectorate, *Proceedings of the Legislative Council*, 1st meeting of 71st Session, (February 7, 1957): 19–31.
4. William Ormsby-Gore, A. G. Church, and F. C. Linfield, *Report of the East Africa Commission*, Cmd. 2387 (London: HMSO, 1925), 23.
5. Martin Chanock, *Law, Custom and Social Order: The Colonial Experiences in Malawi and Zambia* (Cambridge: Cambridge University Press, 1985); Martin Chanock, "A Peculiar Sharpness: An Essay on Property in the History of Customary Law in Colonial Africa," *Journal of African History* 32, 1 (1991): 65–88; Joey Power, "'Individualism is the Antithesis of Indirect Rule': Cooperative Development and Indirect Rule in Colonial Malawi," *Journal of Southern African Studies* 18, no. 2 (1992): 317–47.
6. Chanock, "Paradigms, Policies, and Property," 71, 80.
7. Bridglal Pachai, "Land Policies in Malawi: An Examination of the Colonial Legacies," *Journal of African History* XIV, no. 3 (1973): 681–98. For a discussion of

the legal aspects of the Lilongwe Land Development Project see Clement Ng'ong'ola, "The Design and Implementation of Customary Land Reforms in Central Malawi," *Journal of African Law* 26, no. 2 (1982): 115–32.

8. Steven Pierce, *Farmers and the State in Colonial Kano: Land Tenure and the Legal Imagination* (Bloomington, IN: Indiana University Press, 2005): 14. A Similar view was earlier expressed by Phillips, *The Enigma of Colonialism,* 59–84.

9. Sara S. Berry, *Chiefs Know Their Boundaries: Essays on Property, Power, and the Past in Asante, 1896–1996* (Portsmouth, NH; Oxford, 2001), 36; Parker Shipton and Mitzi Goheen, "Understanding African Land-holdings: Power, Wealth and Meaning," *Journal of the International African Institute* 62, no. 3 (1992): 307–25.

10. The property rights school brings together those scholars who believe that increased productivity in agriculture could best be achieved through individual land tenure arrangements where landholders enjoy unlimited tenure security. The school criticizes communal land tenure systems. See Christian Lund, *Law, Power and Politics in Niger: Land Struggles and the Rural Code* (Hamburg: LIT Verlag, 1998); Christian Lund, "A Question of Honour: Property Disputes and Brokerage in Burkina Faso," *Africa* 69, no. 4. (1999): 575–94; Frank Place and S. E. Migot-Adholla, "The Economic Effects of Land Registration on Smallholder Farms in Kenya: Evidence from Nyeri and Kakamega Districts," *Land Economics*, 74, no. 3 (1998): 360–73.

11. Sara S. Berry, "Debating the Land Question in Africa," *Comparative Studies in Society and History* 44, no. 4 (2002): 638–68; Berry, *Chiefs Know Their Boundaries*; Sara S. Berry, *No Condition Is Permanent: The Social Dynamics of Agrarian Change in Sub-Saharan Africa* (Madison: University of Wisconsin Press, 1993).

12. The invention of tradition school argued that the colonial state had successfully codified the otherwise fluid and contested African traditions, including claims over land, making them reproducible within the confines of customary law. It therefore assumes that once the invention was complete, contestations over land and related aspects were muted. See Chanock, "Paradigms, Policies, and Property," 61–84; Terence Ranger, "The Invention of Tradition in Africa," in E. Hobsbawm and T. Ranger, eds. *The Invention of Tradition* (Cambridge: C.U.P, 1983), 211–62; Berry, *Chiefs Know their Boundaries*, 15–20.

13. As noted earlier in the introductory chapter, Frederick Cooper warns us to guard against leapfrogging legacies. See Cooper, *Colonialism in Question,* 17.

14. Bridglal Pachai, *Land and Politics in Malawi, 1875–1975* (Kingston, Ontario: Limestone Press, 1978), 33, 46. Crown land could be purchased by private interests and made freehold, before 1912 and leasehold after this year. After 1936, native trust land was also subjected to alienation but mostly to accommodate projects in which the state had some economic interests.

15. Nyasaland had 23,347,804 acres of land. See Ibid., 37, 41; Griffiths, "Land Tenure in Malawi and the 1967 Reforms," 9–10; *Native Trust Land Order-in-Council, 1936.*

16. See Ormsby-Gore et al., *Report of the East Africa Commission*, 110.

17. On Thangata see J. A. Kamchitete Kandawire, *Thangata: Forced Labor or Reciprocal Assistance? A Case Study of the Conversion of a Traditional African Institution into a Colonial Institution of Production with Special Reference to Southern Malawi* (Zomba, Malawi: Research and Publication Committee of the University of

Malawi, 1979). On Chilembwe Uprising see the seminal work by George Shepperson and Thomas Price, *Independent African: John Chilembwe and the Origins, Setting and Significance of the Nyasaland Native Rising of 1915* (Edinburgh: University of Edinburgh, 1963).

18. Griffiths, "Land Tenure in Malawi and the 1967 Reforms," 15.

19. Ormsby-Gore at al., *Report of the East African Commission: 1924* (London: HMSO, 1925), 3.

20. Ibid., 28.

21. Ibid., 30, 109.

22. For a discussion of the legal aspects of the Native Trust Land Order-in-Council see Ng'ong'ola, "The State, Settlers, and Indigenes in the Evolution of Land Law and Policy in Colonial Malawi," *International Journal of African Historical Studies 23, no. 1 (1990):* 51.

23. Pierce, *Farmers and the State in Colonial Kano,* 104.

24. Power, "'Individualism is the Antithesis of Indirect Rule,'" 317–47. I discuss this group in later sections of the chapter.

25. Kelemen, "Individualism," 197.

26. Malcom McDonald to Nyasaland Governor, November 29, 1939, MNA S43/1/11/1.

27. Kenneth Lambert Hall (Chief Secretary and Acting Governor, Nyasaland) to MacDonald, January 12, 1940, MNA/S43/1/11/1. The 1936 Native Trust Land Order-in-Council had only secured the rights and privileges of Africans by placing native trust land under the S/S/C and preventing its alienation. It had not, however, created markets in land. See Nyasaland Protectorate, *Nyasaland Native Trust Land Order-in-Council,* See also Pachai, *Land and Politics in Malawi,* 174–85.

28. K. L. Hall to MacDonald, January 12, 1940, MNA/S43/1/11/1.

29. Minute by the Governor Kennedy (Nyasaland) to the Chief Secretary, October 28, 1941, MNA/S43/1/11/1.

30. In Uganda, Governor Phillip Mitchell presented a major rebuttal to these proposals. See Phillip E. Mitchell to the S/S/C, March 5, 1940. MNA/S43/1/11/1.

31. Ibid.

32. See Charles Kingsley Meek, *Land Law and Custom in the Colonies* (Oxford: Oxford University Press, 1946), vi.

33. See Philip Mitchell, *The Agrarian Problem in Kenya* (Nairobi: Government Printer, 1948). The Official copy came out in 1947 even though printing was done in 1948).

34. Ibid., 14.

35. Ibid. The first chapter introduced Lugard's ideas on land.

36. Creech Jones to Nyasaland Governor, February 22, 1947, MNA S12/1/2/2.

37. See Cooper, "Development, Modernization, and the Social Sciences in the Era of Decolonization," 26–27.

38. Hailey, *An African Survey*, 980. Also cited in Rita Hinden, *Plan for Africa: A Report Prepared for the Colonial Bureau of the Fabian Society* (London: George Allen and Unwin, 1941), 65.

39. See Kelemen, "Individualism," 194.

40. Chief Secretary to Ag. DofA (also copied to several officers in the protectorate), March 22, 1947, MNA S12/1/2/2.

41. Ag. DofA to Chief Secretary, April 4, 1947, MNA S12/1/2/2.

42. Senior Agricultural Officer (South) to Chief Secretary, April 30, 1947, MNA S12/1/2/2.

43. Nyasaland formulated its ten-year development plan in 1945 with a total budget of £7.5 million which was originally promised (spread over ten years). This plan did not propose any changes in African communal land tenure along the lines the S/S/C suggested. On a different note, Nyasaland received £2 million only towards its ten-year plan. By 1947, the budget was revised downwards by £3 million. See Postwar Development Plan, 1945–1955 (Revised 1947), TNA CO 525/208/4.

44. See Provincial Commissioner (North) to Chief Secretary, May 30, 1947, MNA S12/1/2/2; Provincial Commissioner (Center) to Chief Secretary, June 14, 1947, MNA S12/1/2/2. Detribalization is exactly what many Fabian intellectuals had feared because it broke apart the sinews of "tribal"/community life.

45. Record of discussion, August 8, 1947, MNA S12/1/2/2.

46. Other than Kettlewell and Webster, it would have been interesting to see how Christian missionaries contributed to this debate on African agriculture and welfare. This omission is a subject of the records under consideration. Missionaries do not feature in these conferences. While missionaries would have embraced the CO proposals as a step towards liberating Africans from the burden of tradition, it is doubtful they would have accepted a drastic path of reform. Like the colonial authorities, they, too, were paternalistic and protective of the "natives."

47. Kettlewell to Chief Secretary, May 28, 1947, MNA S12/1/2/2; Kalinga, "The Master Farmers' Scheme in Nyasaland," 367–87.

48. Record of the Central Province Conference, September 12, 1947, MNA S12/1/2/2.

49. Record of Northern Province Conference, October 4, 1947, MNA S12/1/2/2.

50. Sidney Abrahams, *Nyasaland Land Commission*, Vol. 1 (Zomba: Government Printer, 1946).

51. Webster to Chief Secretary, June 16, 1947, MNA S12/1/2/2.

52. Colin Baker, Seeds of Trouble: Government Policy and Land Rights to Nyasaland, 1946–1964 (London: British Academic Press), 1993, A Transcript of Land Colloquium on Malawi, November 22, 1980, BLCAS, MSS/Afr./s/1742.22.28.

53. For a comprehensive discussion of the 1950s village improvement schemes and others see Beinart, "Agricultural Planning and the Late Colonial Technical Imagination"; Peter F. M. McLoughlin, "Land Re-organization in Malawi, 1950s–1960: Its Pertinence to Current Development." in Sayre P. Schatz, ed. *South of the Sahara: Development in African Economies*. (Philadelphia: Temple University Press), 1972,128–39.

54. McLoughlin, "Land Re-organization in Malawi, 1950s–1960," 131.

55. Record of the meeting held in Provincial Commissioner's office, Blantyre, February 11, 1956, MNA PCS1/16/1.

56. District Commissioner (Port Herald) to Provincial Commissioner (South), February 27, 1957, MNA PCS1/16/1. Dimba is a common term among different ethnic

groups in the country synonymous to Dambo. Dambo denotes a wetland and/or flood land, but one that is not water-logged. It should be distinguished from a swamp. It supports the production of such crops as rice, maize, beans, sugar, and other vegetables. Elias Mandala presents a better description of the Dambo while discussing its ecological significance for colonial societies in the Lower Tchiri Valley of the country. See his *Work and Control in a Peasant Economy*, 5–7.

57. Unlike the Mang'ganja who are native to both Nsanje and Chikwawa Districts, the Kololo came to the region (Chikwawa) from Barotseland (at the time under the Lozi state) as porters to Dr. David Livingstone in the 1860s. The colonial state saw the Kololo as more enlightened than the Mang'anja even though tradition has it that the former were less inclined to farming than the latter. See Elias C. Mandala, "The Kololo Interlude in Southern Malawi, 1861–1895," M.A. thesis, University of Malawi, 1977.

58. District Commissioner (Port Herald) to Provincial Commissioner (South), February 27, 1957, MNA PCS 1/16/1.

59. Memo by P. M. Lewis, Chairman of Chikwawa Land Use Committee, October 17, 1957, MNA PSC 1/16/1.

60. Land Usage Schemes—Namphota, 1956, MNA PCS 1/16/8.

61. District Commissioner (Chikwawa) to Provincial Commissioner (South), May 1, 1956, MNA PCS 1/16/8.

62. McLoughlin, "Land Re-organization in Malawi, 1950s–1960," 133; Erik Green, "Indirect Rule and Colonial Intervention: Chiefs and Agrarian Change in Nyasaland, ca. 1933 to the Early 1950s," *International Journal of African Historical Studies* 44, no. 2 (2011): 274.

63. McLoughlin, "Land Re-organization in Malawi, 1950s–1960," 137.

64. Kelemen, "Individualism," 198.

65. That plan is articulated in Richard W. Kettlewell, *An Outline of Agrarian Problems and Policy in Nyasaland* (Zomba: Government Printer, 1955); See also Richard W. Kettlewell, *Agricultural Change in Nyasaland, 1945–1960* (Stanford, CA: Stanford University Press, 1965): 249–51. On rejection of Kettlewell's plan see Nyasaland Protectorate, *Proceedings of the Legislative Council*, 69th Session, (May 3, 1955), 2–3.

66. Erik Green, "A Lasting Story," 247–68.

67. Kalinga, "The Master Farmers' Scheme in Nyasaland, 1950–1962"; Beinart, "Agricultural Planning and the Late Colonial Technical Imagination," 93–148; McLoughlin, "Land Re-organization in Malawi, 1950s–1960," 128–39.

68. See McCracken, *A History of Malawi*; Baker, *Development Governor*; Pachai, *Land and Politics in Malawi;* Pachai, "Land Policies in Malawi," 81–698.

69. See Mandala, *Work and Control in a Peasant Economy*, 217.

70. See Beinart, "Agricultural Planning and the Late Colonial Technical Imagination," 93–148; McLoughlin, "Land Re-organization in Malawi, 1950s–1960," 128–39.

71. Note of discussion with the Governor of Nyasaland, London, April 17, 1958, TNA CO 1015/1407. In attendance at the meeting were R. S. Simpson (the CO Land Advisor), E. H. Hall, and S. D. Holdershaw.

72. Armitage to Lennox-Boyd, July 19, 1956, TNA CO 1015/901.

73. Great Britain, *The East Africa Royal Commission Report, 1953–1955,* Cmd. 9475 (London: HMSO, 1956), ix, 56. The Africa Bureau presented a strong critique to the report, trashing it for raising unrealistic land tenure proposals. See Africa Bureau, *Reflections on the Report of the Royal Commission on East Africa* (London: Africa Bureau, 1956), 27.

74. Great Britain, *Report of the Conference on African Land Tenure in East Africa and Central Africa: February 1956* (London: HMSO, 1956): 3.

75. Ibid., 5.

76. Armitage to Lennox-Boyd, July 19, 1956, TNA CO 1015/901.

77. Minute by Simpson, CO, October 22, 1956, TNA CO 1015/901.

78. Note on African Land Tenure in Nyasaland, December 28, 1956, TNA CO 1015/901. A primary target here, as the Arusha Conference report had noted, was matrilineage, a system of inheritance predominant in the Southern Province. Unlike the patrilineal North, married men lacked tenure security because of settling in the wife's place. Upon the death of the wife, the tradition released men to resettle in their original homes.

79. Chief Secretary to J. C. Morgan (CO), December 28, 1956, TNA CO 1015/901. See also Notes of a meeting held in the Council Chamber at the Secretariat (Zomba), July 28, 1956, and again August 1, 1956, TNA CO 1015/901.

80. Extract from the record of the meetings—Southern Province (January 16, 1957); Central and Northern provinces (January 18, 1957), TNA CO 1015/1407.

81. National African Congress memorandum to the S/S/C, January 1957, TNA CO/1015/1748.

82. Nyasaland Protectorate, *Proceedings of the Legislative Council*, 1st meeting of 71st Session, (February 7), 1957, 31

83. Ibid., 31.

84. Ibid., 22.

85. Henry Chipemebere, A letter to the African people of the Southern Province of Nyasaland Protectorate, February 1957, TNA CO 1015/1748.

86. Power, "'Individualism is the Antithesis of Indirect Rule,'" 318–19; Joey Power notes that most of the Petit-Bourgeoisie did not have political interests

87. See Colin Baker, *Development Governor,* 125–36; Baker, *Seeds of Trouble.*

88. See also magazine cutting, "Matters of Moment," *East Africa and Rhodesia,* May 27, 1954, TNA CO 1015/850.

89. Banda's return to lead the Nyasaland African Congress galvanized politics of mass nationalism. Three years later in 1961 Malawi became a self-governing territory with Banda as the Prime Minister. In 1963 the Federation of Rhodesia and Nyasaland was dissolved, and the country gained independence in 1964.

90. A. R. Wilson to the Chief Secretary, January 18, 1960, TNA CO 1015/2188. Even with the Federation in place, matters of land and, agriculture, generally, remained under the jurisdiction of territorial governments. The demands of the Tea Association should be read against this background.

91. Provincial Commissioner (South) to District Commissioners (South), March (specific date not legible), 1954, MNA PCS 1/16/9.

92. S/S/C to Governor, Nyasaland, March 11, 1960, TNA CO 1015/2188.

93. Ibid.

94. African Land Tenure and Land Policy in Nyasaland, 1960–1965, TNA DO 183/110; A Transcript of Land Colloquium on Malawi, November 22, 1980, BLCAS, MSS/Afr./s/1742.22.28.

95. See the discussion under the file Titles to Land, Nyasaland, 1960–1962, TNA CO 1015/2188.

96. Notes/Recollections on Dr. Banda's visit, September 9, 1963, TNA DO 183–210.

97. T. R. Ness (Chairperson) to Butler, March 27, 1963, TNA DO 183/110.

98. Ness to Butler, May 7, 1963, TNA DO 183/110. See also *Malawi News*, February 22, 1963, and March 15, 1963, Newspaper Cutting, TNA DO 183/110.

99. Note of a meeting held in London, September 24, 1963, TNA DO 183/110.

100. Banda's Comment on the Hill Report, February 1966, TNA OD 31/039.

101. See Report by S. R. Simpson, November 16, 1966, TNA OD 31/039. Simpson benefitted from both the land reform proposals of Nyasaland and those of colonial Kenya, particularly the Swynnerton plan. The Swynnerton project, among other objectives, aimed at providing secure land rights mostly to the Kikuyu following the political disturbances of the 1950s. It was named after Roger K.M. Swynnerton, the Assistant Director of Agriculture. See Colony and Protectorate of Kenya, *A Plan to Intensify the Development of African Agriculture in Kenya* (Nairobi: The Government Printer, 1954).

102. These were The Customary Land (Adjudication and Development) Bill; The Registered Land Bill; and The Local Land Boards Bill. See TNA OD 31/039. Report by S.R Simpson, November 16, 1966, TNA OD 31/039.

103. Malawi Government, *National Assembly Parliamentary Debates*, 4th session, 1966–1967, 403. Also cited in Clement Ng'ong'ola, "The Design and Implementation of Customary Land Reforms in Central Malawi," 115.

104. Lonsdale and Berman, "Coping with the Contradictions," 487–505.

105. See Ferguson, *The Anti-Politics Machine.*

Chapter Three

Whose Interests? The State, Industry, and Rural Development, 1930s–1953

On August 17, 1932, the Nyasaland governor received a letter from the Imperial Institute in London whose contents set apace what emerged as a promising tung industry in the protectorate.[1] The letter presented a report on the economic value of the sample of tung fruits which the Director of Agriculture (DofA) had forwarded there for laboratory tests. It was Kew Research Station that supplied the first seeds of tung trees (*Aleurites Fordii*) to Nyasaland in 1928. The government planted the seeds in the Kanjedza Forest Reserve near the commercial town of Limbe (Southern Province). At the Imperial Institute, Dr. L. A. Jordan, the Director of the Research Association of British Paint, Colour and Varnishes Manufacturers, and a member of the Imperial Subcommittee on Tung Oil, worked on the sample which weighed just one and a quarter pounds. "The oil expressed from the seed," he wrote in his report, "is of outstanding quality as regards colour and acid value, while its chemical characteristics are in accord with those usually recorded for the species. On test, the oil is found to dry in [a] normal manner yielding a satisfactory film and would appear to be suitable for incorporation into varnish, etc." Although the sample was too small to accommodate "extended tests of a practical character," the report was assuring for a protectorate whose economy mostly relied on migrant labor, and the cultivation of tea, tobacco, and cotton.[2] Coming in the wake of the 1929 Great Depression, the Board of Agriculture in Nyasaland received the report with enthusiasm. Besides *Aleurites Fordii*, the DOA planted another species of tung trees (*Aleurites Montana*) at the Zomba Experimental Station. The sample yielded similar results at the Imperial Institute. Meanwhile, the acreage in tung trees increased from 65 acres in 1933 to 341 acres in 1935, winning the interest of the white planters, many of whom were traditional tea growers.[3]

This chapter examines the difficulties the colonial authorities in Malawi endured in their quest to safeguard the interests of Africans in the booming tung oil industry from the 1930s to 1953. For many colonial administrators, such as those serving under the DOA, the tung oil industry presented an opportunity to absorb the surplus population from the rural areas. It would create employment for Africans and help to improve their living standards. The industry would also encourage the growth of a class of enterprising farmers noted earlier in the first chapter, by affording them direct participation in the cultivation of tung oil trees. At the same time the debate on land tenure unfolded in the 1940s, the tung oil industry was also evolving and reached its maturity in the late-1940s when London passed the Overseas Resources Development Act in 1948. With that Act in place, the Colonial Development Corporation (CDC) was set up and became an active player in tung tree production in Malawi. The following questions guide the flow of this chapter: How did the tung industry evolve and who were the major actors involved? Does its evolution reflect a state whose aim was to serve the interests of market capitalism? To what extent did the local colonial bureaucrats defend African interests when faith in postwar resource extraction policies the Overseas Resources Development Act (ORDA) inaugurated challenged the objectives of development and welfare in the Empire? Beyond the concerns for the poor Africans, what specific interests did these colonial bureaucrats have? These questions are significant because the existing literature, concerned with reinforcing the exploitation paradigm, fails to provide adequate answers.

As noted in the introductory chapter of this book, scholars project an "exploitation narrative" where the colonial state in Malawi is said to have deliberately entrenched a policy regime in which land, taxation, and pricing policies favored the settlers or large-scale producers.[4] This narrative, however, is a weak framework and barely useful in providing answers to the questions raised here. And, as Erik Green has pointed out, the narrative has some methodological flaws, especially because of its tendency to concentrate on the Southern Province of the protectorate where much of the land alienation took place. For Green, the existing evidence justifying the "violence" of the colonial state is elusive. Even during the interwar period, state policy was fluid, sometimes supporting the settler agriculture, at other times the peasantry.[5]

To understand the challenges of African production in the country, Green pointed out how labor barriers (unrelated to state policy), among other factors, negatively affected African production. Using the examples of the estate and labor migration economies of Thyolo (South) and Mzimba (North), respectively, he showed how a "structure of partial integration" forestalled progress in African agriculture.[6] In Thyolo, peasants were partially integrated into the wage economy that estate agriculture presented, just like they were partially linked to South African mines through labor migration in Mzimba. Shortage of labor, in consequence, combined with a lack of agricultural technology to undermine the success of African agriculture. Another work questioning the "violence of the state thesis" is Colin Baker's *Seeds of Trouble*. As noted in the previous chapter, his work discusses the state attempts to purchase land for "landless" Africans beginning from the late 1940s.[7] It therefore depicts the state as a benevolent actor concerned with African welfare. What also needs emphasizing, as Baker likely acknowledges, is that plans to buy land for resettling Africans did not have the welfare of Africans as a primary aim. Threatened with the possible negative consequences of landlessness among Africans, the state sought to pre-empt a possible African revolt on the lines of the 1915 Chilembwe uprising. Nevertheless, Baker's work, like that by Green, departs from the "exploitation narrative."

This chapter joins critics of the exploitation school by examining how the late-colonial state attempted to reconcile the neo-mercantile demands of the postwar era with concerns for the colonial poor. It weaves the discussion around two themes. First, the chapter examines the significant role European planters and the DOA played in developing the tung oil industry in the protectorate. Taking advantage of the growing demand for tung oil on the global market after the collapse of Asian markets, planters moved towards tung production and helped to establish what the colonial authorities saw as a significant industry. To fulfill their ambitions, the planters formed the Nyasaland Tung Growers Association (NTGA) and transformed it into a powerful lobby group. Among other achievements, the group helped to establish the Tung Experimental Station and the Viphya Tung Scheme, the latter of which was taken over by the CDC in 1948. Despite registering successes, local administrators and advisors resisted some of their proposals because they conflicted with concerns over the welfare of Africans. In significant ways, in fact, officials under the DOA saw planters as a threat, not least because the latter's proposals often pre-empted the work that they thought the Department should have primarily undertaken. In this way, the chapter also points to the power struggles that emerged when both state bureaucrats and planters sought to control the development process in Malawi. While planters turned to the influential positions they occupied in government circles to advance their ambitions, officials under the DOA used the African card—the idea of defending African welfare—to contain the latter's growing influence. Such an observation should not downplay concerns state authorities had in promoting African welfare. It should act as guard against interpreting the intentions of state bureaucrats in overly apologetic terms.

The second theme revolves around the Viphya Tung Scheme and its subsidiary, the Limphasa Rice Scheme. The latter aimed at producing rice and maize to feed the workers under the CDC-Viphya Scheme. Of significance here is how the local agricultural officers and other administrators viewed these CDC-run projects. Local players condemned these schemes for their exclusive focus on metropolitan interests that had little to do with the welfare of Africans. Putting hopes in the Limphasa Scheme, a project which potentially targeted the interests of Africans, administrators ended up disappointed when they realized that the CDC's design actually excluded Africans. The chapter concludes by reflecting on what the two themes reveal about the nature of the late colonial state in Malawi.

By emphasizing the zeal select colonial authorities displayed in defending what they perceived to be the interests of Africans, the chapter questions some of the findings of the exploitation school. In referencing this tradition, the chapter does not intend to challenge, nor do the conclusions drawn justify the benevolence of colonialism. Rather, the intention is to show how the narrative often misunderstands the nature of the late colonial state and its legacies. Also, less clear when viewed through the lens of this tradition, is the nature of the post-war reformist state, including what it sought to achieve for Africans and the limits of its actions. By critically examining the intentions of the late colonial state, and the outcomes of its development interventions, we can better understand its intentions and actions from a more critical plane. Such an analysis provides an opportunity to better understand the behavior of the bureaucrats who served the late colonial regime in Malawi and helps us to avoid deterministic analyses of its legacies for the postcolonial state.

This chapter, therefore, complicates previous historical literature by demonstrating how certain individuals, particularly officials within the DOA, sought to defend African interests. It also reveals how complex the late colonial state was, with multiple groups—local administrators, the planters, or CDC officials—projecting diverse and often contrasting agendas, and in the process undermining the goals of mitigating poverty. Such a conclusion is perhaps less novel because it simply confirms what other historians have found in the context of East and West Africa.[8] However, these scholars privilege an economic explanation rooted in Marxist political economy. The various contending economic interests reduced the state to a referee, though not an entirely disinterested one, moderating such interests. This chapter, and indeed the book more generally, goes beyond economic "reductionism," to examine how other forces beyond the Marxist political economy influenced state actions with relatively similar results. Like Lonsdale and Berman, however, it shows the fluidity of the state and how different groups competed for its attention. These multiple voices frustrated the war on poverty, despite achieving certain strides.

THE FORMATIVE YEARS OF THE TUNG OIL INDUSTRY, 1930–1944

Following the favorable tests on Nyasaland tung tree samples at the Imperial Institute, the government sped up plans to establish a Land and Agricultural Bank in the protectorate to support the emerging industry. It was Hubert Winthrop Young, the Nyasaland Governor, who appointed a committee to explore the possibility of establishing a Land and Agricultural Bank in 1934. Once established, the bank would provide funding to planters and others who wanted to invest in the protectorate.[9] The government, however, did not wait for the outcome of the discussions on the Land Bank which, ironically, was never established. It determined to support selected promising farmers. On October 16, 1936, a preliminary meeting of the Governor (Harold B. Kittermaster), the DofA (Dr. W. Small), and the Treasurer, favorably considered the request for funding from J. Aitchison of Mlanje (now Mulanje) District. Aitchison, a member of the Board of Agriculture in Nyasaland who had been less successful with tobacco production, had raised 130 acres of tung trees and was seeking to extend his plantation with an additional 50 acres. To that effect, he required a loan of £252. The three-man meeting found such an application legitimate and one that could not wait for the Land and Agricultural Bank. Because of the economic potential the tung oil industry presented to the protectorate, the three accepted the request.[10] The application received a similar response at the CO when, in his quest to support such planters as Aitchison, the Governor sought the approval of the S/S/C to use resources from the Colonial Development Fund.[11]

Between 1936 and 1939, many traditional tea planters in Cholo (now Thyolo), Mulanje, and parts of Zomba Districts registered interest to diversify towards tung tree production (see Map 3.1 below). The districts in question have climatic conditions that naturally favored tung tree production. As a result, acreage under tung tree plantation increased from 341 acres in 1935 to 4,356 in 1939. To coordinate their activities, the planters formed the Nyasaland Tung Growers' Association (NTGA) in 1938, drawing its membership from those who mostly straddled tung tree and tea production. By March 1940, the NTGA had 29 members, all of whom were top managers of the tea and tung plantations with an esquire title suffixed to their names. Notable among these included Mr. Malcolm P. Barrow, Manager of the Nyasa Tea Estate, who for many years served as the Chair of the NTGA and a member of the Executive Council in Nyasaland; Hon. W. Tait-Bowie of the Blantyre and East Africa Ltd., who was the Vice Chair; Mr. E. C. Peterkins of Makungwa Estate in Limbe; and Mr. J. Aitchison of Nalipiri Estate in Mulanje.[12] Two issues captured the NTGA's attention between its formation in 1938 and the mid-1940s. The first centered on the need to create a tung experimental or investigational station with the explicit purpose of promoting tung production in the protectorate. The second was erecting a tung oil factory, including the supply of an oil expression plant. Both were of utmost concern to the tung tree growers. Although acreage under tung tree plantations increased, there was little effort to conduct detailed research on the best agricultural practices in tung tree production. Again, given that by 1939 tung trees were nearing maturity, planters needed a factory to process the fruit before exporting the oil to Britain. During their meeting on March 31, 1939, the NTGA resolved to set up both the experimental station and the factory in Thyolo District. The Association also agreed to request the government for a grant from the CDF towards financing the two projects. It subsequently sent a deputation to the Governor to discuss the two issues.[13] In attendance at the meeting on the government side were the Governor, the Acting Chief Secretary and the DofA. Messrs. Barrow, Aitchison, and Peterkins represented the NTGA. The planters argued that the government needed to take responsibility to support such a promising industry whose risks the planters had exclusively borne.

Both issues received a sympathetic hearing, with the Governor suggesting raising an application to the S/S/C to the effect that "this government [should] make an advance of £6000 to the Association . . . as a loan from the CDF."[14] It was the research station component, however, that significantly captured the government representatives' attention. Also discussed at the meeting was the proposal to accommodate African interests in the emerging tung oil industry. Members of the NTGA rejected that suggestion, arguing that it was premature to include Africans during the experimental stage of the industry. The DofA, for one, registered interest in both the research station and African participation in tung tree production. In his memo to the Chief Secretary requesting him to table these matters at the Executive Council, he emphasized the last two aspects while omitting the proposal for the tung oil factory. In preparing his notes, the DofA had consulted widely, including such people as Sir Frank Arthur Stockdale, who was serving as the CO's first Agricultural Advisor to the S/S/C from 1929–1940. Stockdale encouraged the DofA to emulate the attention which the Dutch agricultural authorities in Java gave to tung trees, such as the "multiplication by bud grafting of desirable mother trees."[15] To promote the tung oil industry in Nyasaland, Stockdale planned to transfer Mr. C.C. Webster from Nigeria to Nyasaland. Webster, a holder of a Bachelor of Science in Agriculture, had sound knowledge in tung tree production and would be of help in developing the industry in the protectorate. The DofA found Webster to be the ideal person to head the proposed research station.

Concerning African participation in the industry, the DofA had already issued tung seeds to Africans around Domasi in Zomba, albeit on an experimental scale. When the Executive Council met in December 1938, it provisionally approved the request for a loan towards the experimental station, further advising the DofA to prepare a detailed scheme for submission to the Colonial Development Advisory Committee in London. The Council rejected the request for African participation in the industry. It advised that "until [tung oil industry] possibilities in Nyasaland had been more definitely determined, natives should not be encouraged to grow tung trees and no further issues of seed should be made to them."[16] Evidence, however, suggests that the DofA did not immediately raise a proposal on the experimental station.

The two issues not effectively resolved—the question of a tung oil factory and African participation—would, in 1940, determine much of the relations between the NTGA on the one hand, and government officials on the other. The government was of the view that the NTGA's request for a tung nut crushing mill was less a priority, especially so because one planter, Souter, already had a similar factory at Chiromo in the South (see Map 3.1). Souter had expressed willingness to let planters use his mill. When the DofA inspected Souter's plant, he found it ideal for the task at hand. Not satisfied with the government's position, the NTGA commissioned yet another team to inspect Souter's mill. Led by Mr. E. C. Peterkins, the second inspection team produced a report which disqualified Souter's factory. "My conclusion on the test and machinery," Peterkins reported, "are as follows":

> [The] building is good and is situated near the [railway] line at Chiromo and capable of further expansion; [the] present machinery is not suitable for tung; power is not sufficient for an expeller plant if one were installed; [and] situation [location is] too remote when considering the return of residue.[17]

These technical shortfalls as detailed in their report made the NTGA reject Souter's plant. However, we should not rule out the fear of enriching one planter, who was relatively new in the protectorate. The demand for a cooperative mill financed through a government-guaranteed loan came after protracted negotiation among planters. Some planters, including Barrow, preferred to run private mills. During a meeting with members of the Executive Council in November 1938, Barrow was reported not to have opposed the cooperative mill, but he "wished to retain the right to put up a factory for those [planters] who wanted to." The decision to use a private mill elsewhere, it appears, did not sit well with such interests.[18]

Two days after receiving Peterkins' report, the NTGA adopted it. In forwarding the report to the Ag. DofA, the memo requested that "government be asked to apply for a loan of £6,000 from the Colonial Development Fund to import an up-to-date tung oil extracting plant." Besides, it reminded the government about the previous resolution on the tung experimental station,

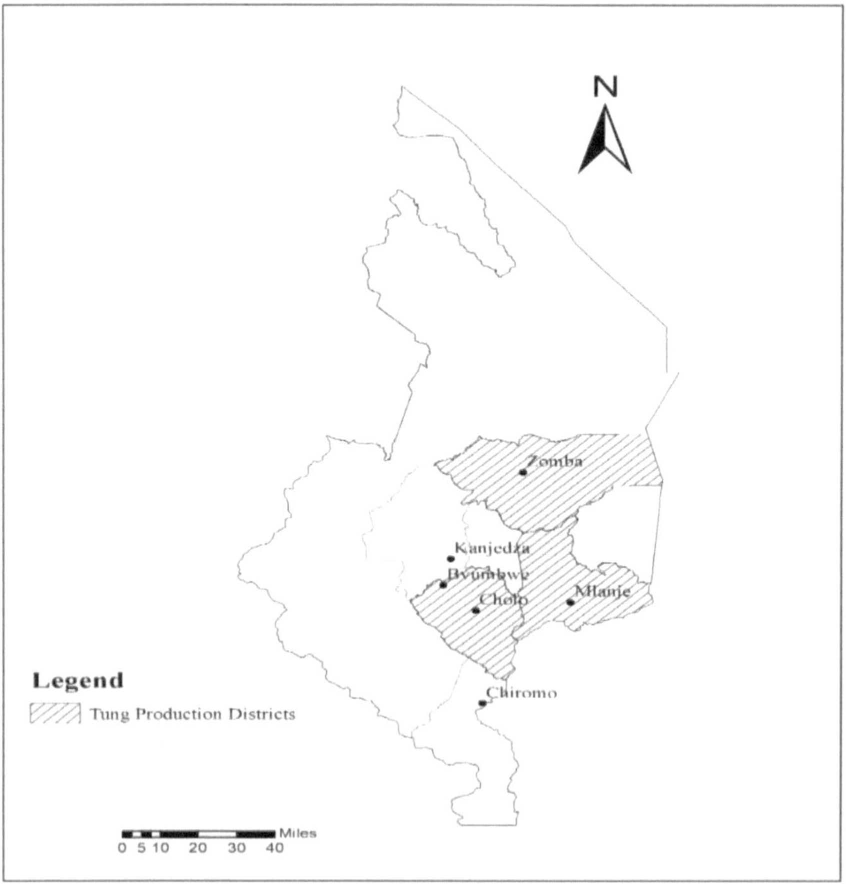

Map 3.1. Tung production districts and centers in the Southern Province, 1930s–1950s
Source: Drawn by Dr. Park Muhonda, Oregon State University.

further advising the Ag. DofA to act on the request.[19] Other than responding to concerns of maturing tung fruit, the Second World War also explains the urgency with which the NTGA pushed their demands. The war had blocked tung oil markets from Southeast Asia and China, creating demand elsewhere. The fall of the Far East, notably Singapore, sustained that demand beyond the 1940s.

When the Executive Council discussed the demands of the NTGA on April 4, 1940, the response was disappointing:

> Council advised that the Association should be informed that while government regarded the new tung industry with sympathy and considered an application to the Colonial Advisory Committee was justified in respect of a tung experimental

> station, a similar view could not be taken with regard to the commercial side of the industry.[20]

The Governor, in consequence, forwarded the £14,498 proposal on the tung experimental station to the CO where it received overwhelming support from the Colonial Development Advisory Committee. In approving the grant, the CO insisted that the officer heading the station should periodically liaise with similar research stations in the USA, Netherlands East Indies, and Indochina where experimentation in tung tree production had gone well ahead of that of Malawi.[21] Meanwhile, the government acquired 500 acres of land in Thyolo (valued at £1000) from the British Central Africa Company where it erected the station.[22] By the late 1940s, C.C. Webster had taken charge of the only tung experimental station in the British Empire. In the 1940s, the station boasted the presence of a chemist, whose task was to regulate the quality of tung oil to make it conform to global standards.

One reason the idea of establishing a tung research station had a positive reception at the CO has to do with the nexus between science and development or faith in scientific research as a prerequisite to colonial development, which had already taken shape in the British Empire from the late nineteenth century. It was Joseph Chamberlain, S/S/C from 1895 to 1903, who saw scientific research as complementing his vision of developing the imperial estate through private enterprise. He is the one who helped to promote both the London and Liverpool schools of tropical medicine and the Botanical Gardens at Kew. From the 1940s when the CDWA was passed, the CO created so many research departments whose experts swarmed to British Africa in an unprecedented way. In the case of East Africa, the 1924 East African Commission lead by Ormsby-Gore and discussed in chapter two, deplored a lack of research centers to investigate the potential colonies held for the production of economic crops and industrial development. The Commission encouraged governments to provide funding to existing research stations and create others. The tung research station under consideration responded to this call.[23]

Though the decision on the tung experimental station pleased the planters, the NTGA did not welcome the response to the mill proposal. It insisted that the association send a deputation to the Governor to discuss the proposal on the mill. The Ag. DofA, however, considered such a request unnecessary. In fact, it was the DOA which, to a more significant extent, influenced the Executive Council's decision on the tung oil plant. Following receipt of the NTGA report on Satour's mill, the Ag. DofA launched extensive research to understand the motives behind the NTGA's resolutions. His analysis, which he accompanied with detailed figures of the profits many of the planters made in other crops over time, considered the planters' request an abuse of the Colonial Development Fund.[24] "Ever since the Association made its first approach to the government," he stated, "it has not been clear why . . . individuals who, as far as we know, have plenty of money, should find it necessary to apply to government for financial assistance."[25] For the planters, however, it was necessary that the government should share in the risks of developing the industry, an argument that never convinced such officers as the Ag. DofA who stated: "It looks very much as though the Association wished government to take a risk which they themselves regard so well." The Ag. DofA was equally worried about the broader implications a favorable response would have, further noting that "the £6,000 if provided as a grant would ultimately be found by the British taxpayer, the weight of whose burden needs no emphasis. [Moreover], it would not be a grant to assist persons who are unable to help themselves and who have no other means of subsistence."[26]

The Ag. DofA was not alone in his observation. He was joined by the DofA, who saw it necessary that the government should take a firm position on the request. "I have felt all along," he briefed his colleagues, "that we are being bounced back into providing the tung tree growers with [a] cheap plant," further stating that the planters were in the habit of "deriving benefits without risk." Like Strangways, he cited the case of Mr. Tait Bowie, whose company, the Blantyre and East Africa, boasted, respectively, tea profits of £25,054, £37,488, and £35,181 in the years 1936, 1937, and 1938.[27] Convinced by such sentiments, the Executive Council rejected the proposal. Opposition from the DOA notwithstanding, planters continued to invest in the tung oil industry and resorted to using privately acquired plants to process tung fruits. As the following table shows, between 1941 and 1944, tung oil exports increased albeit at an experimental scale from 10,456 Lbs. to 100,000 Lbs.[28] Mr. Webster's work at the tung station contributed to the progress of the industry in the Southern Province. Through his original research in budded tung tree stumps at the Tung Experimental Station, he produced several clones for distribution to the planters, affording the latter a break from over-reliance on tung seedlings.[29]

The above discussion illustrates the significant role the planters played in developing the tung oil industry in the protectorate. Through the NTGA, they turned themselves into a powerful lobby group that helped to establish the tung experimental station, a project which won the attention of the DOA and other imperial authorities. The group sold its ideas to the government in ways that shaped the future of the protectorate in agricultural research and other areas. The tung experimental station it helped to set up outlived the colonial era and continued to serve independent Malawi in various areas of agricultural research under the name of the Bvumbwe research station. Although distinguishing themselves as ardent planners, cunning and calculative, much of the successes of planters, at least up to 1944, depended on the specific interests of other groups, chief among them being the personnel at the DOA.

If the discussion points to the positive role planters played in the development of the tung oil industry in the protectorate, it also reveals the struggle for control over the protectorate's development agenda. The DOA's opposition to the NTGA's request on the mill should be read beyond the idea of good stewardship over government money. As noted in the first chapter, the CDF, whose resources the planters requested, aimed at supporting development projects in the colonies under the 1929 Colonial Development Act. Despite its private nature, the tung oil industry fits very well into such projects. Both planters and government officials seem to have clearly understood the purpose of the CDF. In fact, when planter Aitchison requested for a loan to expand his tung fields in 1936, officials had in mind the CDF as a possible source of funding. The same was true when planters first raised the proposal for establishing a tung nut crushing mill. It was the S/S/C who suggested advancing a sum of £6,000 from the CDF towards the mill. The planters requested no more than this amount. As will become clear in the subsequent sections, one reason for the DOA's objection to the NTGA's request centered on the latter's growing influence in guiding the development process of the protectorate. This influence needed to be tamed before the group replaced the DOA, the main body responsible for setting the protectorate's development agenda, particularly in the area of natural resources' utilization. Control over resources was one strategy of containing the NTGA's influence. An appeal to African welfare and participation in the booming tung oil industry was another. The subsequent section is concerned with the latter point. Taking the discussion beyond the 1940s, it argues that although legitimately concerned with advancing the welfare of Africans, officials from DOA also used the "African card" as means through which to suppress the growing influence of the tung growers in the protectorate.

AFRICAN INTERESTS AND THE VIPHYA TUNG SCHEME, 1945–1948

On October 11, 1944, Mr. M.P. Barrow submitted a proposal to the Nyasaland Post-war Development Committee (PWDC) seeking to expand tung tree production in the protectorate. Barrow noted that tung tree production in the country had passed the experimental stage. Targeting mainly the Viphya Plateau in the North which shared similar climatic conditions to those of Thyolo and Mulanje, his proposal requested the PWDC to support planters in their quest to develop the region through extensive and rapid estate tung tree production. Barrow considered such a scheme a necessary step towards raising Nyasaland to one of the top producers of tung oil in the world. Besides, by locating the scheme in the North, Barrow saw it transforming that province which had carried the image of a "Dead North" because of its lack of meaningful economic activities. Besides the Viphya, the proposal suggested extending tung plantations in existing production zones of Thyolo and Mulanje. In significant ways, Barrow recommended extending tung tree production to such districts as Mwanza, Zomba, and the Upper Lower Shire (South); Mchinji, Ntcheu, and Ntchisi (Center); and the Upper Henga Valley (North). Other than Mulanje, Thyolo, Zomba, and Viphya where tung tree planting would be under the white planters, Barrow's proposal opened the rest of the areas to African cultivation, albeit under strict supervision (see Map 3.2 below). The following figure provides projected acreage under each of these areas:

Table 3.1. Tung tree production and land allocation under Barrow's Scheme.

European Production	*Acreage*
Mulanje	10,000–20,000
Thyolo	25,000–30,000
Zomba	10,000–16,000
Eastern Viphya	50,000–100,000
Total	95,000–166,000
African Production	
Upper Henga Valley	15,000–15,000
Kirk Range Area (Ntcheu)	5,000–10,000
Ntchisi	3,000–5,000
Mchinji	3,000–5000
Total	26,000–35,000

Source: M. P. Barrow, The possibilities of intensive development of the tung industry in Nyasaland Protectorate on a large-scale by means of assistance from Government and the Colonial Development Fund, submitted to the Nyasaland Post-War Development Committee, October 11, 1944, MNA S12/1/18/3.

In presenting the proposal, Barrow argued that his scheme had received Webster's support. Moreover, like in the earlier requests, he saw the success of the scheme as dependent on the government's financial assistance. He suggested, therefore, the Colonial Development and Welfare Fund (CDWF) as a potential source of funding.[30]

Before discussing it at the PWDC, the proposal passed through the scrutiny of the DOA. Reaching the Ag. DofA's desk, he rejected it with a simple note: "the [tung oil] industry will develop with or without state aid, and it is merely the question of the 'tempo' [sic] of the development." For him, the planters did not need government support to promote the industry. They lacked interest and considered tung tree production as a merely "side issue." With rather

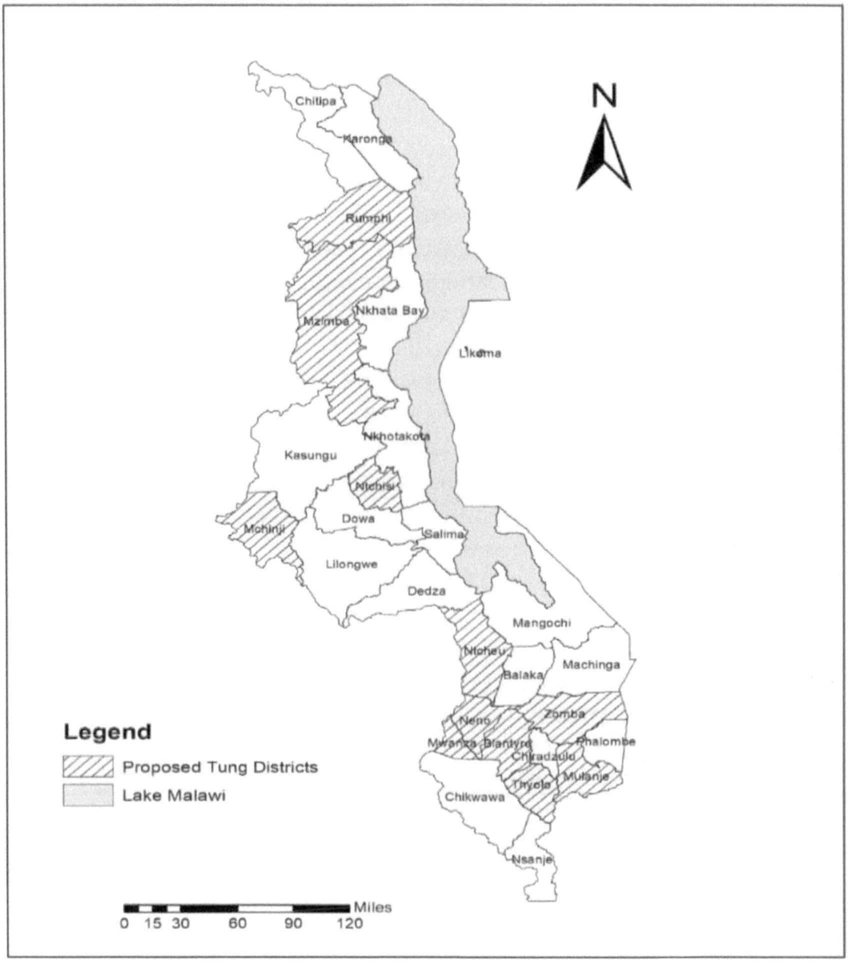

Map 3.2. Barrow's proposed tung tree production areas in Nyasaland, 1940s
Source: Drawn by Dr. Park Muhonda, Oregon State University.

sarcastic remarks, he argued that financial aid would not "produce a Garden of Eden unless the landlords [were] prepared to make a wholehearted effort on their part."[31]

Two objections to Barrow's scheme dictated the discussion among government officials. The first had to do with its failure to accommodate Africans in the Viphya and the traditional tung tree production areas in the South. As highlighted in Table 3.1, Barrow's scheme allocated much of the land for tung tree production to European growers. For the DOA, the bias against African growers represented Barrow's ploy to sustain European dominance in the industry. It was clear to the DOA that although citing the approval of Webster,

Barrow had twisted Webster's land allocation figures which he provided upon the former's request. Webster allocated more land to Africans than what we see under Barrow's scheme as Table 3.2 shows below.

A comparison of Tables 3.1 and 3.2 shows a reversal of Barrow's proposed acreage for both European and African land. For the DOA, Webster's figures were realistic for a scheme of that nature, especially because it favored Africans as principal tung tree growers. In justifying his scheme, however, Barrow argued that the Eastern Viphya, like much of the Thyolo and Mulanje areas, had a steep topography that did not lend itself to African cultivation. He claimed Africans were not good husbandmen and would soon expose the land to soil erosion.[32] Again, fearing that Africans would steal tung fruits from European plantations should the two groups grow the crop in proximity to each other, Barrow did not allocate acreage for African production in the popular districts of Thyolo and Mulanje. Many agricultural officers shared those fears. In the words of Webster, however, Barrow took "a rather pessimistic view of the African capabilities regarding tung growing." He further noted that Africans in other colonies, notably in West Africa, grew "perennial crops such as cocoa, oil palms, citrus and coffee. . . . Tung did not present greater difficulties than these other crops."[33] Webster's remarks probably referenced the land-abundant North. As noted in the previous chapter, he later harbored a pessimistic view about encouraging African production in the congested Southern Province.

Table 3.2. Tung tree production and land allocation under Webster's Scheme.

European			*African*		
Southern province	*Min*	*Max*	*Southern province*	*Min*	*Max*
Mulanje	10,000	20,000	Blantyre and Central Shire	5,000	10,000
Thyolo	25,000	30,000	Mwanza and Neno	5,000	5,000
Zomba	10,000	15,000	Zomba	5,000	5,000
Total for European	45,000	65,000			
			Northern province		
			Upper Henga Valley	15,000	15,000
			Eastern Viphya	50,000	100,000
			Central Province		
			Kirk Range Area	5,000	10,000
			Mchinji Hill Area	3,000	5,000
			Nchisi Area	5,000	10,000
			Total for African	93,000	160,000

Source: Produced from the minute by the DofA, November 9, 1944, MNA S12/1/8/3.

Second, the DOA rejected Barrow's proposal because the Eastern Viphya area which was allocated to Europeans was Native Trust Land protected under the 1936 African Trust Land Order-in-Council. Barrow's scheme effectively promoted further alienation of African land, which the Order sought to prevent. Though the proposal was a sound one, its primary focus, at least in the eyes of the DOA, should have been to encourage Africans as tung tree growers and not to alienate more of their land. Already keen to integrate Africans in tung tree production, the DofA claimed he "had in mind the possibility of getting the natives to work that land [Eastern Viphya] under European supervision." He, therefore, shared Webster's sentiments who "regard[ed] this a possibility."[34]

Equally supportive of these ideas was the Ag. DofA. Underpinning his support was what could pass as the Fabian concern for the colonial poor. "[In] primitive countries such as Nyasaland," he stated,

> colonial development is aimed at social and economic advancement of the [African] inhabitants . . . in order that they may improve their standards of life. . . . One of the principal means of achieving this object is . . . for him to manage his own enterprises. . . . [By allowing Africans to grow tung], we [will] improve [their] standards of life and provide for British exports.[35]

Barrow's scheme ran the risk of perpetuating African exploitation. It, therefore, represented the very antithesis of such an object. Such fears did not escape the attention of the DofA whose minute on the labor demands of the scheme deserves emphasis here:

> [On the terms as Mr. Barrow presents], the European should be able to make a net profit of £7.14 per acre . . . while the African labourer is to get 30/- [shillings] per acre. The European can superintend some hundreds of acres and so obtain some hundreds of £7.14s [sic]. While the native can, presumably, work about 6 acres and earn at the most £9 or £10 a year. I do not think this is a fair division of profits when one bears in mind that the capital and the land are to be provided by the state. . . . I subscribe to the general view that we should do what we can to develop the tung industry, but we should give the African a greater share in the scheme than is contemplated in Mr. Barrow's report.[36]

That task of developing the industry in favor of Africans fell on the Ag. DofA who, together with Webster, presented an alternative proposal of the tung scheme later in 1945. Like Barrow, who appealed to Webster's expertise, the Ag. DofA secured the support of both Webster and Mr. Gervas F. Clay. Clay, a member of the CO staff, was appointed the Joint Development Advisor to Northern Rhodesia (Zambia) and Nyasaland in 1945. He was scheduled to visit Nyasaland early that year. The Ag. DofA saw his coming as an opportunity to drum up support towards his proposal, especially because Clay had distinguished himself as one sympathetic to the African cause. Already, in debating Barrow's proposal, the Ag. DofA had suggested that the PWDC hold off its decision until Clay gave his comments. In introducing his proposal to the Chief Secretary, the Ag. DofA reiterated his previous position, further adding that it was apparent from various comments that Barrow's scheme was unacceptable because it did not sufficiently accommodate African interests. "It seemed necessary, therefore," he stated, "to have [an] alternative proposal ready for discussion on Mr. Clay's arrival and to this end, I conferred again with Mr. Webster."[37]

Focusing on the Eastern Viphya, the new proposal made four propositions. The first suggested allocating blocks of undeveloped land to selected but willing Africans capable of growing the tree under strict European supervision. The second option recommended that the government use its resources to develop the land before assigning portions to Africans. In both cases, the government would shoulder all related expenses, such as those to do with road development, office construction, and input loans, recouping them once the scheme reached its productive stage. Under the two options, the goal was to assist African growers set up a producer and marketing cooperative on the lines of the Bugishu Coffee Scheme in Uganda which had won the praise of administrators for its efficiency.[38] The plan sought to encourage a Viphya cooperative and one with potential to set up a tung oil company. The third alternative differed from the first two only in terms of the management style. Rather than devolving the scheme's management to the farmers, the government would run it, eventually establishing either a cooperative society or a limited liability company with exclusive rights over the scheme. Africans would participate as shareholders in such firms.[39]

With the first three options in place, the Ag. DofA boasted that they had designed the scheme "to secure greater prosperity to the African," further emphasizing how the scheme would bring about "substantial improvements in [Africans'] basic standards of living." Such optimism, however, should not be exaggerated, nor did it display consensus among officials who contributed to the proposal. Some uncertainties become clear under the fourth alternative. That option, where Clay, Webster, and the Ag. DofA never reached a consensus, sought to use European enterprises to develop and manage the scheme. Under this option, Europeans would lease one bloc of the Viphya and run their respective farms as private entities. Africans would occupy the other bloc, growing the tree on arrangements akin to a supervised tenancy system.[40] The Ag. DofA never believed in the last alternative. He was of the view that the government develop the scheme without the aid of Europeans. He only accepted it as a bitter compromise and one that accommodated Barrow's proposal.

Here, the ambiguous nature of the new scheme was clear. By failing to settle for a workable option, it was subject to multiple interpretations by the higher committees. The failure of the three-member committee to agree on certain aspects of the proposal, moreover, illustrates the challenge colonial authorities grappled with in reconciling the economic interests of both Africans and Europeans. Earlier, the DofA considered developing the Viphya for the benefit of Africans as a necessary step. But "how to give that share [was] a matter for discussion," further noting that "unless we make the scheme attractive to the European [planter], he will not be interested."[41] Despite assembling a team of experts to work on the new proposal, the Ag. DofA understood the politics involved. Some planters were members of the PWDC and served in the Legislative Council.[42] Barrow, the author of the original proposal, was a member of the PWDC together with William Tait-Bowie, the General Manager of Blantyre East Africa Company who retired in 1946. It is this dilemma of evolving a scheme without European involvement and yet one that would win their political support that explains Ag. DofA's openness: "The question [of] whether European enterprise should or should not be associated in the development of the Viphya is as much one of policy as of economies, and we reached no final agreement. Doubtless, there will be an opportunity for discussion with [the] government on the subject."[43] That opportunity never came. If the DOA influenced the Executive Council on the tung mill decision, appeals to African welfare did not work this time around. The Department soon watched, helplessly, as the proposal on Viphya tilted more to the European than African side, with some selected members of the NTGA as key actors in the emerging Viphya Scheme.

When the PWDC met on August 2, 1945, it was Barrow's scheme that was under consideration, with the record of discussion silent on the Ag. DofA's proposal. The Committee recommended rapid, large-scale tung tree development at Viphya, further advising the government to provide land for that purpose. It further suggested that the government help to set up a tung oil company where the public would have 75% of shares with the rest reserved for itself.[44] Such a recommendation might have appealed to planters, many of whom had the potential to buy shares. What did not receive serious consideration was the question of African participation in the scheme. The PWDC, nevertheless, recommended allowing Africans to grow tung trees within the vicinity of the Viphya under strict European supervision. Such a proposal, however, was cast to a distant future.

A September 1945 Executive Council meeting ratified, with minor variations, these recommendations, including a three-member subcommittee which the PWDC had established to assist the government in setting up the tung oil company.[45] Ironically, Barrow was appointed a member of that subcommittee in the company of Sir William Tait Bowie and others. It tasked the two (Barrow and Tait Bowie) to draft the company prospectus, a decision the Executive Council approved. When the subcommittee visited Viphya for an initial assessment, it produced a report that shaped the subsequent developments of the scheme. Barrow and Tait Bowie, both of whom were members of the NTGA, reported the difficulties they faced in producing the prospectus. Because the Viphya had had no history of tung tree production, they argued, it was impossible to raise one without baseline data. They requested the government to either form a small syndicate or itself undertake, with the help of the NTGA, to develop the area. The preliminary progress at such a pilot scheme would dictate the nature of the company to emerge.[46]

It is difficult to explain how a syndicate, as proposed, could undertake such an assignment for a project whose risks were myriad. At the time, the Viphya, which was covered predominantly in bush and uncleared, lay far beyond the major commercial centers of the protectorate, notably those in the Southern Province. Moreover, because its economic returns remained unclear, throughout the late 1930s and early 1940s planters in the Southern Province constantly lobbied the government to actively support the tung oil industry. It is not surprising then that the Executive Council settled for the second option, taking on board even its hidden costs.

It was Barrow and his colleague who advised the government to use the Colonial Development and Welfare Fund to develop at least 500 acres of the area and grow the tree for the first three years.[47] They projected the tentative cost of £27,000 per year. Emphasizing their point, they insisted that the "government should undertake the initial development by establishing plantation roads, tung nurseries and the nucleus of administrative buildings. . . . When the company is formed, it should refund these preliminary expenses to the government. [However, when the project proves less attractive, the government shall accept the loss]." More significant is how the fresh proposal ignored African participation. "Because of the steep and broken nature of the ground necessitating proper soil conservation measures," Barrow and Tait Bowie emphasized plantations rather than "native village cultivation methods."[48] It appears the fear of pilferage dictated such sentiments, forcing Barrow and Tait Bowie to push African growers out of the area.

Anticipating such a turn of events, the Ag. DofA earlier warned the Chief Secretary about approving a scheme exclusively for the white planters. Pre-empting Barrow and Tait Bowie's sentiments, he argued against excluding Africans on the claims "that the proximity of European and native plantations will result in much stealing of the tung fruit."[49] Noting the difficulties emerging in developing an African-dominated scheme, the Ag. DofA settled for the tenancy system as a workable compromise. Under such a scheme, Africans would be allocated tung tree plots where they would grow the tree under European planter's supervision. That suggestion, however, was already among the options in the alternative proposal he raised with support from Webster and Clay.

What the DOA feared came to pass. The Executive Council approved Barrow's and Tait Bowie's request, committing the government to the scheme. Equally assuring for the planters was the S/S/C's response that came following the Governor's submission of the request for funding from the CO. Though noting the anomaly of the lack of African participation, the S/S/C expressed optimism that the Governor would address it. He approved the expenditure of £27,000 as requested.[50] The dream of securing African participation in the scheme had fractured. According to these plans, African participation in the tung industry was only guaranteed as wage laborers, initially on the pilot scheme and later, on European-owned plantations.

Following the S/S/C's approval, the government appointed Mr. Charles E. Boardman to lead the operations at Viphya while Barrow and Tait Bowie completed arrangements for a prospective company. Boardman's posting as a Tung Development Officer had less to do with his skills in the tung industry than his knowledge of the Northern Province. A former agent of the South African-based Witwatersrand Native Labor Association (WNLA), Boardman was familiar with the region and its peoples through his labor recruitment tours. He was considered the right person to head a scheme that depended highly on local African labor. Boardman selected Mzuzu as the administrative headquarters of the scheme and, with the help of the DOA, established tung tree nurseries at Mazamba and Chikwina, both located within the same radius (See Map 3.3 below).

Between 1947 and 1948, Boardman was joined at Mzuzu by John da Silva, Derek Dunne, and Joe Slomcgzsky, who served, respectively, as Accountant, Agricultural Assistant, and Land Surveyor.[51] As Boardman's experimental scheme took off, two problems emerged. The first centered on the question of land, and the second on low wages for African workers. Regarding the first aspect, the Viphya Scheme had encroached the Native Trust Land of Chief M'mbelwa without appropriate consultations. It had also cleared off part of the Lunyangwa Forest Reserve without the knowledge of the District Commissioner or the Conservator of Forests. A rather anxious M'mbelwa queried the Provincial Commissioner of the Northern Province, forcing the latter to provide an explanation on land encroachment. While M'mbelwa did not have the intention or real "powers" to withhold land, he was worried that neither his office nor his sub-chiefs were aware of the plans to extend the Viphya to Native Trust Land.[52] For a scheme whose success depended on local cooperation, M'mbelwa's query was a cause for concern. But it was not unprecedented. Earlier in 1945, Chief Kabunduli of the Nkhata-Bay side of the Viphya raised similar concerns when the scheme extended to Native Trust Land.[53] For the Provincial Commissioner, it was necessary to seek the

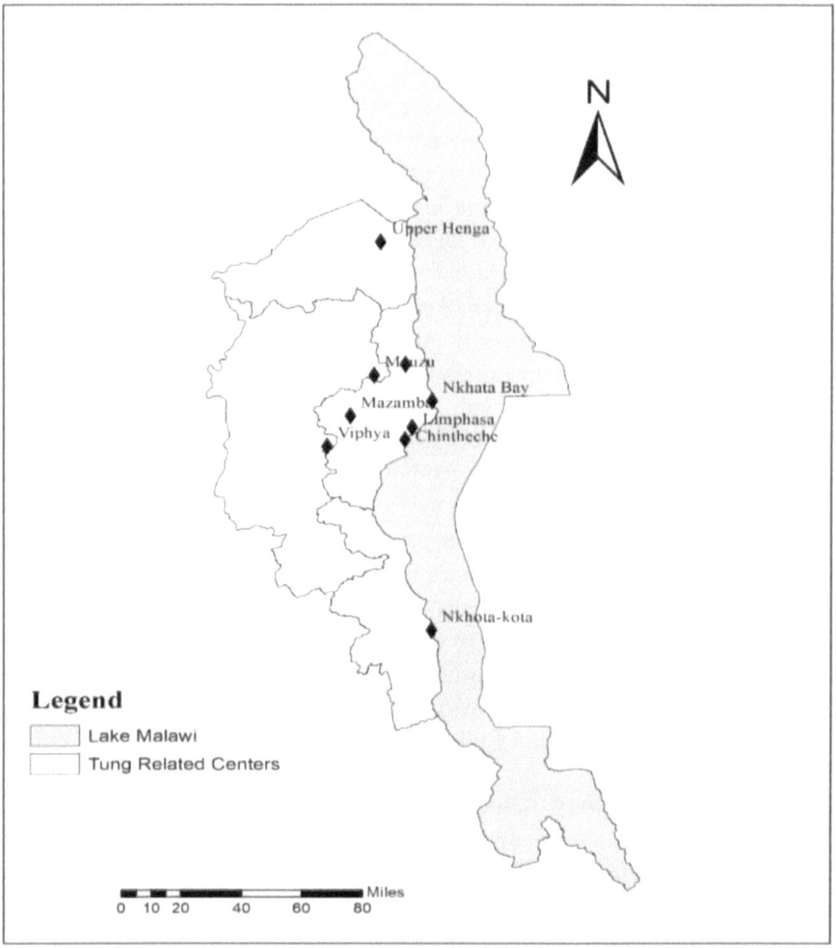

Map 3.3. The Viphya and related tung tree growing centers, Northern Province, 1940s
Source: Drawn by Dr. Park Muhonda, Oregon State University.

consent of chiefs and their people before encroaching their land. He did not hide his frustration to the Chief Secretary such that his memo deserves citing at length here:

> You are no doubt aware that as a Provincial Commissioner, I have fostered this scheme from its inception, and done what I could to smooth out difficulties as they arose, but I must protest that the casual attitude of indifference displayed by those people responsible for the development of the scheme to the interests of any, but those of themselves, may well result [in] arousing antagonism which might easily jeopardize the ultimate success of the scheme, particularly so when it becomes divorced from Government as a departmental project.[54]

The Provincial Commissioner was not the only one who accused the Viphya personnel. Earlier in 1945, the Conservator of Forests registered similar concerns when he noted that the Viphya team had cleared off part of the Kaning'ina Forest Reserves without prior consultation. Both the Conservator of Forests and the Northern Province Commissioner feared that since Africans were legally prohibited from encroaching these forests, they were most likely to view the Viphya as representing a state ploy to alienate land. Furious of the approach Boardman took, the Conservator of Forests objected most strongly to how "he had been deliberately ignored by the persons responsible, and . . . the entire lack of cooperation shown by [Boardman and colleagues]."[55] This kind of departmental exchange is significant to note, mainly because it points to how local pressure from African chiefs reveals the attitude officials outside the DOA held towards the Viphya. While the DOA previously wrestled with planters, both the Provincial Commissioner and Conservator of Forests feared that Boardman and his team were intruding in somewhat contentious affairs of land which only the administrators in question would competently handle.

Low wages for Africans who worked in the Viphya in such tasks as tree felling, field clearing, and tree planting, was another problem that captured the authorities' attention. Wages were paid weekly at a daily rate. Adult male taxpayers received a pay of 6d (pence) per day. Women received a wage of 4d per day. Older and younger children received a daily wage of 3d and 2d respectively. An adult male who worked for 90 days was eligible for a bonus of 7/6d (7 shillings, 6 pence). An adult male who worked for three months would receive a total wage earning of £2.12.62, which translated into about £11 in a year, including bonuses. This was a relatively low yearly wage compared to what others received elsewhere.[56] In fact, the £11 was equivalent to the yearly wage, which the DOA had earlier projected when he challenged Barrow's scheme, arguing it would lead to an unfair distribution of income in the protectorate.

Even though these were low wages, Africans accepted the rates because the Viphya Scheme authorities promised to provide free food rations covering breakfast, lunch, and dinner, a position which the Northern Province Commissioner communicated through the *barazas* he held with chiefs and the prospective laborers. As it turned out, Boardman and his team defaulted on the pledge of three daily meals and forced workers to pay for the evening meal. Later, they stopped providing the last meal altogether, a scenario that forced some workers to withdraw their labor. Others protested erratic meal rations and the poor quality of food, forcing the Provincial Commissioner to report in 1946 that "a third pound of maize meal, and 4 ounces of beans per man for the mid-day meal was not regarded as 'liberal' [enough]."[57] It was such poor labor conditions that made Chief M'mbelwa of Mzimba to remark in 1946 that "it looks as though our first effort at development in the 'Dead

North' [sic] is going to be destroyed in its infancy unless labour conditions are made acceptable to the local people."[58] Evidence on whether wages in the Viphya improved has been hard to find. Interesting to note, however, is how the scheme manager accused the Provincial Commissioner of giving Africans wrong information on wages and meals. Whatever departmental politics were involved, authorities were aware that Africans held the last word for the success of such a labor-intensive project. "Unless remedied, [these problems of low wages and poor food rations] are likely to harm the future development of the [Viphya] Scheme, which is absolutely dependent on an adequate and contended labour force," noted the Provincial Commissioner of the Northern Province.[59] As a consequence, the free evening meal was re-introduced, and no other charges were assessed on food rations.[60]

These problems notwithstanding, the government formalized activities relating to the tung industry in the protectorate by enacting appropriate legislation to regulate it—the 1946 Nyasaland Tung Ordinance.[61] Section six of the Ordinance provided for the establishment of a Tung Board with oversight powers over the tung oil industry in the protectorate.[62] The Board mostly drew its membership from the NTGA. Its first members included M.P. Barrow, who also served as its chairperson, the Financial Secretary, Director of Agriculture, William Tait Bowie, P. E. Hansen, E. C. Peterkins, J. Kaye Nicol, L. J. Rumsey, and C. C. Webster.[63] This team held its first meeting on April 26, 1946.

Earlier in August 1945, Barrow and Tait Bowie had released a sketch of the company, which was no different from the suggestions the PWDC had outlined. Capitalized at £500,000, it had the task of developing five 25,000 acre-blocks of tung plantations, each producing 6,000 tons of tung oil per year. Its total land area was pegged at 75,000 acres (30,351 hectares), leased for 99 years. As envisioned, the government would have 25% of the shares.[64] The dream to form a company, however, died at the proposal stage. In 1948, the Colonial Development Corporation (CDC) took over the Viphya Scheme. As discussed in the first chapter, the CDC was a public corporation set up under the Overseas Resources Development Act of 1948 as part of the postwar development offensive.[65] Economic pressure emerging in the wake of the Second World War forced Britain, and the Labour Government, in particular, to turn to colonial resources in ways that replicated the prewar effort. Whether acting alone as a public corporation or in partnership with colonial governments, or private enterprises, the CDC financed and managed about fifty development projects within the British Empire between 1948 and 1954. One of them was the infamous Gambia Poultry Farm introduced earlier in this book. Another was the Viphya Tung Scheme under consideration here.[66] With the CDC takeover of the Viphya, neither planters' interests, nor those of Africans, materialized. Mostly managed by metropolitan experts and administrators, the Viphya Tung Scheme that emerged prioritized the economic concerns of the weakening British Empire. Even with that, the DOA carried on with its fight for African interests. Much of its "advocacy" work, took place within the confines of the Limphasa Scheme. The latter was an auxiliary project to the CDC-run Viphya Scheme whose aim was to produce food for the CDC's Tung Scheme's wage laborers.

DOOMED FOR FAILURE? THE CDC AND THE LIMPHASA SCHEME, 1948–1953

The CDC takeover of the Viphya Scheme coincided with Geoffrey Colby's appointment to the governorship of the protectorate in 1948. Colby, whom Colin Baker described as a "development governor," was a believer in capital-intensive projects with potential to transform the protectorate's economy.[67] Within the period he was in Nyasaland, 1948–1956, the CDC planned and executed several agriculture-related projects, most of which proved disastrous and incurred massive losses. Other than the Viphya Scheme, the other projects the CDC financed included the Nyika Pulp Wood and the Kasunga Flue-Cured Tobacco projects. John McCracken has summarized these developments such that there is no need for repeating the same here.[68] Suffice it to state that between 1948 and 1954, the CDC had invested over £1million in Nyasaland for development projects. The Viphya Scheme was the most ambitious among those that attracted the CDC capital.[69]

The CDC's involvement in the Viphya followed the invitation of the colonial government in Malawi. Evidence suggests that local administrators in the protectorate misunderstood the operations of the CDC despite receiving a briefing by the S/S/C.[70] For instance, when the latter advised colonial governments to prepare projects for CDC financing in 1947, the colonial state in Malawi raised a proposal requesting the CDC to provide £125,000 towards the Viphya Scheme. In local administrators' opinion, the Corporation would only provide funding such that all operations were to be undertaken by the proposed Nyasaland tung oil company on the arrangements outlined earlier. However, the CDC was not a public bank. As noted, it was a public corporation with the mandate to finance and manage projects whether as a sole proprietor or in partnership with other public or private enterprises. In the case of Malawi's Viphya Scheme, the CDC operated as a sole proprietor. It also deployed its own staff and managers, many of whom settled at its headquarters in Mzuzu.[71]

In general, the CDC divided the Viphya into blocks of plantations. Both Africans and European planters did not have shares in it. Despite deviating from original plans, the government welcomed it mostly because of other advantages it presented to the protectorate. Already, the DOA had in mind the Limphasa Dambo as a potential area through which to secure African participation in the scheme. Politically, the Viphya scheme was likely to socio-economically transform the Northern Province which, until that time, did not register an economic activity worth the name. Besides, the Viphya would employ laborers from that province, which was notoriously famous for its outward labor migration.[72]

Seeking to extend the area under tung tree cultivation from 500 to 20,000 acres, the CDC set aside £1,410,000 for the Viphya Scheme. This funding represented the highest level of CDC's financial commitment to its Malawi projects.[73] The sum also included funding for the construction of a 59-mile road connecting Mzuzu with Nkhata-Bay harbor, the lake outlet for tung oil (refer to Map 3.3 above).[74] In 1949, the CDC deployed its staff to Nyasaland, most of which were former military officers with little experience in agricultural production. The CDC had also successfully imported several hundred tons of assorted heavy-duty machinery. These included plows, harrows, winches, seed planters, and others. Much of this equipment was ferried by road from Lindi, a small port on the Indian ocean coast in present day Tanzania to Mbamba Bay, another small port on the Tanzanian side of Lake Malawi. Through flying boats which the CDC had hired from British Overseas Airways Corporation, the machinery was ferried to the Malawi side of the lake where it was transported by road to Mzuzu.[75] The determination to ensure that the Viphya scheme became a reality was strong. By 1953, however, it was clear that the scheme would not meet its targets, having cultivated only 3,200 acres of tung trees. Again, it constructed just eight miles of the 59-mile Nkhata-Bay-Mzuzu Road. Besides, oil prices on the global market went down when China and other Eastern countries resumed oil exports to the Western countries after the war. In consequence, the CDC scaled down the project in 1953 and later abandoned it, having accumulated a loss of over £700,000.[76] Following independence in 1964, the Malawi government cleared off part of the Viphya plateau for a softwood plantation.

The Limphasa Scheme was no exception to this failure story. It drew its name from the Limphasa *Dambo* located east of the Viphya Plateau (See Map 3.3).[77] Plans to produce rice in the area had a long history and one that preceded the Viphya Scheme. As early as 1941, the DOA proposed to produce rice in the Dambo as part of the Nkhata-Bay District agricultural projects. The idea at the time was to provide the local Tonga people an opportunity to earn money from within the protectorate and thus contain the spate of migrations to the South African and Southern Rhodesian mines.[78] For many colonial administrators, outward labor migration, despite its economic benefits to Nyasaland, was indicative of a lack of promising economic alternatives in the protectorate, particularly in the Northern Province. Labor migration was also a source of social dislocation because it separated families. By encouraging economic activities in the North, officials would be solving such social problems.

Convinced of the economic importance of the Limphasa Dambo, the District Commissioner of Chintheche/Nkhata-Bay held *barazas* in the area briefing the Tonga Chiefs about government plans. He urged them to set aside land for rice production, citing the benefits the crop had brought to the population of Nkhota-Kota District (refer to Map 3.3). The latter had excelled well at rice production and marketing through cooperatives.[79] Already, within the Limphasa Dambo, about 100 families grew rice for consumption. The DOA planned, as the first step to promote rice production in the area, to provide such farmers and others, with improved rice seeds and markets. Despite this level of commitment, officers within the DOA warned against expecting quick results. The lack of roads to the area and the remoteness of the Dambo relative to the main district centers (Chintheche and Nkhata-Bay) proved to be significant obstacles in promoting rice production there.[80] Instead, the DOA nominally concerned itself with distributing free rice seeds and setting up markets in the major district centers. An opportunity for a grand rice scheme presented itself with the Viphya Tung Scheme in place.

When in 1946 the Viphya Scheme officers raised the question of food to feed their workers (estimated at 5,000), the DofA was quick to sell the Limphasa project. He wrote to the Chief Secretary:

> The Limphasa Swamp offers distinct possibilities for rice and maize production on a large scale provided proper drainage, dams and an irrigation scheme were undertaken. Such a scheme would necessitate rigid control of water duties and cropping. I suggest that the area should be examined by the water expert. . . . I do not anticipate the examination of the area would take very long.[81]

The DOA considered this an opportunity to develop the Limphasa Dambo into a scheme with Africans producing rice and maize under the direction of DOA officials. It envisaged a smaller scheme of about 1000 acres in which Africans, working their plots with family labor, would be producing rice and maize for workers at the Tung Scheme. In that way, Africans would be indirectly participating in the tung oil industry.[82]

When the CDC took over the Viphya, it embraced the idea and set aside the sum of £149,000 (later raised to £220,000) for rice and maize production in the Dambo.[83] Contrary to the DOA expectations, however, the CDC headquarters designed it as a large-scale scheme occupying 6,000 acres of land. Alarmed by the colossal nature of the project, the DOA objected to the proposal, suggesting it be scaled down to 1,000 acres. The CDC settled for 3,000 acres, arguing that the DOA's proposed 1,000-acre scheme was economically unproductive. In response, the DOA insisted on 1,200, later raised to 1,300 acres. To limit the Corporation's ambitions, it argued that any acreage beyond 1,000 needed the support of a land survey and a formal application to alienate land.[84]

Equally unsettled was the question of how the Limphasa Scheme would operate. The DOA wanted the CDC to develop the scheme and leave the cultivation of crops to Africans who would work under the supervision of government officers. This plan was in line with earlier proposals on the Limphasa Dambo. Such hopes faded when the CDC brought in machinery from Britain to work the scheme as its auxiliary project, effectively pushing Africans out, and at best reducing them to wage laborers for such tasks as rice planting. Again, the CDC deployed its personnel who managed the scheme and worked it by means of machinery, including the use of combined harvesters.

After three growing seasons, the project failed and incurred a loss of £146,000 when the CDC discontinued it in 1953.[85] Among other reasons, experts' failure to understand the hydrological cycle of the region combined with the challenges of imported technology to foil the project. In his confidential report to the CO, the Chief Secretary expressed his disappointment with the scheme's failings, reminding the CO about the reports it received on the Corporation's Gambia Egg and Poultry Scheme: "Heavy rains in the dry season made ploughing and subsequent cultivation impossible for protracted periods with the equipment available and only a comparatively small area of rice was eventually planted." Besides, "much of the equipment proved quite unsuitable since the wheeled-tractors became bogged as soon as the land was at all wet, and certain of the ploughs were never used."[86]

The CDC management, in consequence, reduced production to 500 acres, hoping to accommodate Africans who would cultivate an equivalent acreage along the lines as the DOA had earlier proposed. That proposal never took off because after the 1949 famine, the food situation in the protectorate had tremendously improved.[87] As a result, the CDC bought maize and rice from African peasant producers at a much cheaper cost than what it would cost to produce these products under the Limphasa Scheme. When the scheme closed in 1953, it had only cultivated about 500 acres.[88] Ironically, in 1969, the postcolonial government set up a vibrant rice settlement scheme in the same locality following the pattern the DOA had earlier proposed. The government developed the scheme and allocated small plots to farmers who worked under the supervision of government-deployed staff. The new scheme has served local farmers beyond the twentieth century.[89] While its mode of operation differed from that of the CDC, it borrowed from the proposal the DOA had raised before the former took over rice production in the Dambo.

Technical challenges militated against the success of the Limphasa Scheme. But many of the officers within the DOA and the CO did not interpret it that way. Richard Kettlewell, who at the time was serving as the DofA in Nyasaland (and future Minister of Natural Resources with Dr. Hastings Banda as the Prime Minister), did not believe the Limphasa Dambo was unsuitable for rice production. In memorializing the project later in 1979, he faulted the CDC personnel for their incompetence and unguided belief in large-scale development projects.[90]

Earlier, Kettlewell had this to say when G. W. Nye, the CO's Agricultural Advisor, asked for his comments on the negative reports the scheme had consistently produced:

> If only the Corporation [CDC] would realize that there is so much we do not know and cannot predict about Africa, instead of adopting the attitude that money, machines, and enthusiasm are [all] that is required to show a backward little country like Nyasaland how to progress, their operations would be far more successful.[91]

Nye had formed his opinion well from Kettlewell's remarks. "I am satisfied," he briefed his colleagues at the CO, "that had the Limphasa Dambo been developed by the DOA, it would now be a satisfactory rice production area [with the potential to raise the living standards of African producers]."[92] For Nye, because the CDC refused the advice of the local administrators, it was just a matter of time before it failed. It is less surprising that Nye concluded his briefing with a simple note: "It is quite time that the CDC learned that you cannot hurry in Africa."[93] For most of the staff at the CO, the CDC's proclivity towards large projects that could hardly match its expertise was a cause for concern. Many of them formed the opinion to the effect that the "CDC [was] altogether unsuitable for experimental work on colonial agriculture . . . and agricultural development unless it [was] in close association with local government."[94]

Though Kettlewell's concerns were legitimate and reflected similar criticisms of the CDC's approach elsewhere within British Africa, the nature of his criticisms reveals the degree of frustration that local administrators registered when foreign experts took over what they perceived as their legitimate roles—to champion colonial progress. Like officials at the CO, Kettlewell and his colleagues within the DOA, condemned the CDC for adopting what they considered to be a wrong-headed approach to development—the whole idea of reducing agricultural projects into extractive industries with the potential to generate quick economic results through the agency of metropolitan experts. CDC's activities were rarely based on careful research and trials at the local level. The top-down as opposed to the bottom-up approach militated against the success of most of their schemes.

The administrators in Nyasaland further faulted the CDC for ignoring rural development goals they attached to CDC-run agricultural projects. In this way, their concerns illustrate how the post-war dilemma of evolving development enterprises without sacrificing the goals of welfare development played out at the local setting.[95] Even though their voice is rarely recognized, officials within the DOA joined the metropolitan audience in condemning the post-1947 development euphoria which ignored welfare objectives in the colonies. Whether knowingly or not, they helped to preserve the Fabian concerns for the colonial poor. For example, after the CDC-run Limphasa Scheme had failed, Kettlewell lobbied, without success, to have the DOA take over the project.[96] Despite the failure to revamp the project, the initial vision to develop a scheme whose focus was to improve the living standards of the Tonga people finally took shape under the postcolonial government. Set up under the banner of rural development, the state developed 1000 acres of the Dambo, allocating smaller plots to farmers who cultivated them under the direction of agricultural experts. The Limphasa Settlement Scheme of the postcolonial state, therefore, represented the fulfillment of the rural development ideas hatched during late colonialism. Recognizing the legacies of late colonialism in this way affords us an opportunity to understand the multifaceted nature of the colonial state and its legacies, which earlier historical studies somewhat overlook.

On a lighter note, despite its failure, the CDC had some unintended effects on colonial and postcolonial Malawi. First, it created Mzuzu, its headquarters, as the new provincial headquarters of colonial Malawi. Hitherto, Mzimba Boma was the main administrative center of northern Malawi. When the Viphya Scheme failed, the government took over its infrastructure in Mzuzu, which included some office blocks, staff houses, and an airstrip. The Provincial Commissioner's office shifted from Mzimba to Mzuzu in 1955. Mzuzu, which was already boasting a township because of the CDC's presence, grew into a vibrant town. Today, it is one of the four towns with city status in Malawi, the other three being Blantyre, Lilongwe, and Zomba.[97]

CONCLUSION

In concluding this discussion, it is worth restating that literature on colonial history in Malawi emphasizes the exploitative nature of the colonial state, a legacy which the latter is said to have bequeathed to postcolonial Malawi. The state is said to have deliberately framed policies aimed at exploiting the peasantry for the benefit of the planters. The study agrees, as much as the Labour literature at the time did, that colonial states in East Africa no doubt assumed that character. However, such a thesis should not obscure the reformist nature of the postwar developmentalist state which, for the most part, remained fluid and contested with some administrators seeking to serve what they perceived to be the interests of Africans. In fact, save for some selected works noted in the introductory chapter of this study, much of the "exploitation literature" assumes a direct continuity between the interwar and postcolonial periods without considering the developments of the postwar era. As a result, what emerges are leapfrogging legacies in which Malawi's postcolonial economic/development history is read selectively. Focusing exclusively on the exploitative nature of colonialism leads to deterministic analyses in which the interests and actions of state bureaucrats are predictable and bent on assisting the planters and the "capitalist class" to exploit the peasantry. Though significant, such a retrospective analysis of the colonial state is incomplete. Beyond condemning us to a predictable legacy of the colonial state, it also ignores the otherwise discrete and contending interests of different groups that constituted that state. This chapter has used the example of the tung oil industry to understand how the colonial state in Malawi balanced the postwar objectives of promoting secondary industry and rural development and with what results. The analysis points to the effort that certain individuals made to defend African interests, particularly those serving under the DOA. Their actions, however, were constrained by other contending interests, chief among them being those of European planters.

Seeking to advance their interests in the emerging tung oil industry, planters often took an edge over the DOA and shrewdly lobbied the Government to support their proposals. Although some proposals appealed to the interests of the DOA (such as the creation of a tung experimental station), others fundamentally conflicted with the DOA's concern for African welfare. As a result, officers within the DOA often found themselves persistently on the opposing side. The reactionary attitude of the Department reveals a certain degree of anxiety among officers who saw their role as setting the pace to the agricultural direction of the country effectively replaced by the planters and, later, the CDC. It is tempting to suggest that while legitimately concerned with the welfare of the poor Africans, members of the DOA equally used the "African card" to contain the growing European planter influence. They did so by projecting themselves as trustees for the Africans, a language that Fabian membership understood so well. In making judgments about the actions of officers under the DOA, we should not ignore the power struggle that emerged as different parties sought to control the protectorate's development agenda, with each registering both successes and failures.

In any case, the actions of the DOA, at least in the years under consideration, afford us a break from analyses that reduce the Department to an agent of European capitalists. Though agreeing with European planters in certain areas, they objected to others, depending on the specific interests at stake.

Like the planters, their success also depended on the interests of other groups within the protectorate and beyond. Thinking of the actions of the state actors in this way and how certain decisions were made and/or failed requires that we dissect the notion of a monolithic state to understand the ways in which its very constitutive parts helped to limit or promote progress in Nyasaland. In doing so, there is a need to think "beyond the state" and include other non-state actors such as the Nyasaland Native Tung Growers Association.[98] Its achievements, especially that of the tung experimental station that survived beyond the colonial era, also help us to rethink the way we remember planters. They were not just authors of exploitation as existing literature has made us believe.

Thus, similar to the previous chapter, the contradictions to which the state responded in this chapter are clear. Unlike Lonsdale and Berman's thesis or that of Philips, which tend to privilege an economic explanation rooted in Marxist political economy, this chapter goes beyond the economic reductionism inherent in their works.[99] Personal interests and concerns over who should take the lead in guiding the economic direction of the protectorate were equally important forces to note. The quest to secure African participation in the tung industry was not an afterthought, coming in the wake of a "crisis" in the settler-dominated economy as was sometimes the case in Kenya or as Wiseman Chirwa has argued in the case of Malawi's tobacco industry.[100] Inclusion of Africans in the tung industry was part of the plan and a strategy of promoting African welfare, albeit not without other ulterior motives. Like Lonsdale and Berman, however, this chapter shows the fluidity of the state and how different groups competed for its attention. Despite achieving certain strides, these multiple voices frustrated the war on poverty particularly as it concerned ordinary Africans. The next chapter discusses how concerns for African welfare influenced the postcolonial state and with what results. It discusses a similar conflictual relationship that emerged between the Malawian state on the one hand, and Britain's Ministry of Overseas Development and the World Bank on the other. The last two institutions became actively involved in the war on poverty in postcolonial Malawi.

NOTES

1. Harold Brown (for the Director General of the Imperial Institute, London) to Nyasaland Governor, August 17, 1932, MNA S12/1/18/1.

2. Imperial Institute Report, Tung Fruit (*Aleurites Fordii*) from Nyasaland, August 1932, MNA S12/1/18/1.

3. Cited in the Extract of the Report of the Land Bank Committee, 1936, MNA S12/1/18/1.

4. Leroy Vail, "The State and the Creation of Colonial Malawi's Agricultural Economy," in Robert I Rotberg, ed. *Imperialism, Colonialism and Hunger: East and Central Africa* (Lexington: Lexington Books, 1983), 39–88; McCracken, "Planters, Peasants and the Colonial State"; Elias Mandala, "We Toiled for the White Man in Our Own Gardens; The Conflict between Cotton and Food in Colonial Malawi," in Allen Isaacman and Richard Roberts, eds. Cotton, Colonialism and Social History in Sub-Saharan Africa (London: James Currey, 1995), 285–306; Elias Mandala, "The Triumph of the Peasant Option and the Parasitic Cotton Sector in Malawi, 1891–1995," in Karin Hofmeester and Pim de Zwart, eds. *Colonialism, Institutional Change and Shifts in Global Labour Relations* (Amsterdam: Amsterdam University Press, 2018), 173–203.

5. Erick Green, "Peasant Production and Limits to Labour," PhD Dissertation, University of Lund, Sweden, 2005.

6. Green's argument dovetails with typical Marxist literature of the 1980s which argued that colonial capitalism did not have transformative effects in Africa because it did not exploit Africa enough. One reason for this failure in Malawi, Green argued, bordered on the inability of colonial economies to provide workable alternatives that would help to break ties Africans had with their traditional economies.

7. Baker, *Seeds of Trouble.*

8. For East Africa see Berman, *Control and Crisis in Colonial Kenya*, Lonsdale and Berman, "Coping with Contradictions." For details on West Africa see Phillips, *The Enigma of Colonialism.*

9. See The Land Bank, 1939, TNA CO 525/178/10.

10. Memo from DofA to Chief Secretary, October 19, 1936, MNA S12/1/18/1.

11. The Colonial Development Fund (CDF) was established under the 1929 Colonial Development Act. The tung oil industry in Malawi initially benefitted from the CDF before the CDC financed large-scale tung tree production. In general, between 1929 and 1938, Nyasaland used a total of £726,534 from the CDA. Ironically, only 4% of this figure went to agriculture. The rest was spent on such aspects as water supply projects, public works, telegraph and telephone system, education, and others. See Colin Baker, "The Development of Agricultural Administration in Malawi," *The Quarterly Journal of Administration* 8, no. 3 (1973/4): 269; Banda, *The State, Counterinsurgency and Political Policing in Colonial and Postcolonial Malawi*, 121.

12. List of the NTGA's membership, March 7, 1940, MNAS12/1/18/4.

13. Record of the NTGA meeting, March 31, 1939, MNA S12/1/18/4; Record of the discussion between representatives of NTGA and government, Zomba, November 15, 1938, MNA S12/1/18/1.

14. Ibid.

15. Cited in memo by DofA to the Chief Secretary, December 6, 1938, MNA S12/1/18/1.

16. Memo from Chief Secretary to the DofA, December 15, 1938, MNA S12/1/18/1. The Executive Council included the Governor, Chief Secretary, Attorney General, the Financial Secretary (previously known as the Treasurer), and after 1949, two non-official members, usually from the white settler community. During this time, many of the white planters were already serving in the Post-War Development

Committee—a powerful body that determined the development process of Nyasaland from the 1940s onwards. It was chaired by the DofA.

17. E. C. Peterkins to the Chair, NTGA, March 2, 1940, MNA S12/1/18/1.

18. See Record of discussion between representatives of the NTGA and Government, November 11, 1938, Zomba, MNA S12/1/18/1. The report by the DofA, May 8, 1939, MNA/S12/1/18/4 shows that Barrow objected to the idea of a cooperative mill. However, it does not provide reasons for this decision. Tony Woods has illustrated the major divisions among planters (unofficial group) playing out between 1895 and 1924. It appears such divisions transcended the period Wood studied. See Tony Woods, "The Myth of the Capitalist Class: Unofficial Sources and Political Economy in Colonial Malawi, 1895–1924," *History in Africa* 16 (1989): 363–73.

19. Secretary, NTGA, to Ag. DofA, March 5, 1940, MNA S12/1/18/1. The post of an Acting Director of Agriculture was synonymous to that of a Deputy Director and does not symbolize the absence of the Director of Agriculture. At the time, the DofA was Mr. A. S. Richardson, and the Ag. Director was Mr. Fox Strangways.

20. Executive Council Minute, April 4, 1940, MNA S12/1/18/1.

21. Secretary of State (Malcom MacDonald) to the Nyasaland Governor (D. M. Kennedy), April 13, 1940, MNA S12/1/18/4.

22. Minutes of Nyasaland Lands and Survey Department, October 31, 1940, MNA S12/1/18/4.

23. See Joseph M. Hodge, "Science, Development, and Empire: The Colonial Advisory Council on Agriculture and Animal Health, 1929–1943," *Journal of Imperial and Commonwealth History* 30, no. 1 (2002): 1–26; Ormsby-Gore et al., *Report of the East African Commission;* The report is also summarized in "Science and Administration in East Africa," *Nature* 115 (January 10, 1925): 37–38, https://doi.org/10.1038/115037a0, accessed January 19, 2020.

24. For such details see memo from Comptroller of Customs to the Chief Secretary, March 13, 1940, MNA/1/1/18/1.

25. Minute by the Ag. DofA March 18, 1940, MNA/1/1/18/1.

26. Ibid.

27. Minute by DofA (Mr. Richardson), March 19, 1940, MNA/1/1/18/1.

28. Minutes, Correspondence in Tung Development, 1945, MNA S12/1/18/3.

29. S. G. B. Williams, "The Beginnings of Mzuzu with Some Biographical Notes on Some of the Viphya Tung Project Managers," *The Society of Malawi Journal* 22, no. 1 (1969): 46.

30. Ibid.

31. Minute by the Ag. DofA, October 17, 1944, MNA S12/1/18/3.

32. M. P. Barrow, "The Possibilities of Intensive Development of the Tung Industry in Nyasaland Protectorate," 1944, MNA S12/1/18/3.

33. Minute by Webster, January 1, 1944, MNA S12/1/18/3.

34. Minute by the DofA, November 9, 1944, MNA S12/1/8/3.

35. Minute by the Ag. DofA, February 6, 1945, MNA S12/1/8/3.

36. Minute by DofA (Mr. Garnett), November 20, 1944, MNA S12/1/8/3.

37. Minute by the Ag. DofA to the Chief Secretary, January 16, 1945, MNA S12/1/18/3.

38. See United Nation Economic Commission for Africa, *The Cooperative Movement in Africa* (Addis Ababa: UNECA, 1962), 102–106.

39. Proposal for African involvement in the Viphya, 1945, MNA S12/1/18/3. It remains unclear how the government would recoup the expenses made on the scheme under the options as proposed. It appears the Ag. DofA and colleagues were mostly concerned with securing African participation in the tung oil industry without a careful calculation of the cost to the government.

40. Proposal for African involvement in the Viphya, MNA S12/1/18/3.

41. Minute by the DofA to the Chief Secretary, November 20, 1944, MNA S12/1/18/3.

42. Established in 1943 to provide oversight to the development of Nyasaland in several areas such as agriculture, health, education, and communication, the PWDC committee had the following membership: The Chief Secretary, who also served as the Chairperson, the Financial Secretary, and six unofficial members mostly drawn from the settler community. See Chiudza Banda, *The State, Counter-insurgency and Political Policing in Colonial and Post-colonial Malawi*, 199.

43. Minute (on the proposal) by Ag. DofA, January 12, 1945, MNA S12/1/18/3.

44. Minutes of the Post-War Development Committee, August 2, 1945, MNA/FS/1/6/1. The public in question mainly referenced the planters, a group with economic means.

45. Minutes of the Executive Council, September 5, 1945, MNA S12/1/18/3.

46. Minutes of the Executive Council, September 21, 1945, MNA S12/1/18/1.

47. As noted in the previous chapters, the Colonial Development and Welfare Fund was established under the 1940 Colonial Development and Welfare Act. The fund should be contrasted with the Colonial Development Fund established under the 1929 Colonial Development Act. The two served relatively similar purposes with the former having a bias towards projects which targeted the welfare of Africans.

48. Cited in Minutes of the Executive Council, September 21, 1945, MNA S12/1/18/1.

49. Minute of the Ag. DofA to Chief Secretary, May 1, 1945, MNA S12/1/18/1.

50. S/S/C to the Governor (Nyasaland), November 11, 1945, MNA S12/1/18/3.

51. Williams, "The Beginnings of Mzuzu with Some Biographical Notes on Some of the Vipya Tung Project Managers," 46–47.

52. M'mbelwa's views are cited in memo from the Provincial Commissioner (Northern Province) to the Chief Secretary, July 24, 1946, MNA S12/1/18/3.

53. Also cited in memo from the Provincial Commissioner (Northern Province) to the Chief Secretary, July 24, 1946, MNA S12/1/18/3.

54. Provincial Commissioner (Northern Province) to the Chief Secretary, July 24, 1946, MNA S12/1/18/3.

55. J.B. Clements (Conservator of Forests) to Chief Secretary, July 31, 1946, MNA S12/1/18/3.

56. Viphya Tung Development Scheme Wages, 1946, MNA S12/1/18/3. Robin Palmer notes that in the tea growing districts of Thyolo and Mulanje, tea pluckers were paid a wage of 6 shillings per day in 1941. Compare this with the daily wage of 6 pence workers in the Viphya were paid. See Robin Palmer, "Working

Conditions and Worker Responses on Nyasaland Tea Estates, 1930–1953," *Journal of African History* 27, no. 1 (1986): 110. Using a backward conversion from https://www.in2013dollars.com/uk/inflation/1940?amount=11, the £11 the Viphya workers earned per year in 1946 is equivalent to approximately £619.84 (US$807.45) in 2020. However, the minimum wage for non-skilled jobs for the year 2020 in Malawi was MK420,000 (Malawi Kwacha), about £438 ($US571). The war on poverty is more real in twenty-first century Malawi than it was in the mid-twentieth century.

57. Provincial Commissioner (Northern Province) to Chief Secretary, May 20, 1946, MNA S12/1/18/3.

58. Cited in Memo from Provincial Commissioner (Northern Province) to Chief Secretary, May 20, 1946, MNA S12/1/18/3. The remarks were recorded during a meeting the Provincial Commissioner held with the Native Authorities in Mzimba.

59. The Provincial Commissioner (North) complained about this in his memo to the Chief Secretary, May 20, 1946, MNA S12/1/18/3.

60. Chief Secretary to Provincial Commissioner (North), June 12, 1946, MNA S12/1/18/3.

61. See Nyasaland Protectorate, *The Tung Ordinance no. 11 of 1946* (Zomba: Government Printer, 1946). The Tung Ordinance was first gazetted on November 24, 1945.

62. Drawing its powers from the Tung Ordinance, the Tung Board, among others, granted and regulated licenses to those seeking to grow tung trees and open tung nut processing factories; fixed fees on all licenses issued in relation to tung industry; fixed the maximum fees tung factory owners would charge in processing planters' tung nuts. The Board also regulated the marketing of tung oil outside the country and fixed, from time to time, the amount of tax payable to the government.

63. See Second Annual Report of the Nyasaland Tung Board, May 23, 1947, MNA S12/1/18/3.

64. Record of the discussion, PWDC Sub-Committee on Viphya Tung Scheme, August 25, 1945, MNA S12/1/18/3.

65. The CDC was established in 1947 but the legislation formalizing it, the ORDA, was passed in 1948.

66. The Overseas Food Corporation (OFC), a sister corporation to the CDC also established under the ORDA of 1948, was popular for the failed East Africa Groundnut Scheme noted earlier in chapter one.

67. To emphasize this position, Colin Baker titled his biography *Development Governor.*

68. The Nyika project, set up under the Nyika Forestry Syndicate in the North, aimed at producing 380,000 tons of paper a year out of 250,000 acres of cedars it planned to plant beginning from 1952. By 1957, the syndicate had pulled out citing political opposition and other concerns over land. It only spent about £24,000 and planted just a few acres of pine trees. Located in Kasungu District, the tobacco project made losses when it failed to raise the protectorate to a status of one of the major global producers of flue-cured tobacco. See McCracken, *A History of Malawi.*

69. For a brief discussion of the Viphya Scheme under the CDC see Canaan R. K. Phiri, "The Viphya Tung Scheme, 1945–1968: A Futile Strategy to Awaken the Dead

North," History Seminar Paper, 1987/88, No.6. Chancellor College, University of Malawi.

70. The briefing came through the S/S/C's dispatch to Nyasaland of June 22, 1947, MNA S19/1/1/1. The CDC was formed in 1947 but formalized through the ORDA in 1948.

71. See Williams, "The Beginnings of Mzuzu with some Biographical notes on some of the Viphya Tung Project Managers," 1–6.

72. See Green, "Peasant Production and Limits to Labour."

73. McCracken, *A History of Malawi*, 244.

74. Memo from Chief Secretary to Colonial Office, February 14, 1953, TNA CO 1015/622.

75. See Brain and Cable, *Pioneering Development,* 18.

76. Transcript of the Nyasaland Colloquium on Finance, 1982, 22, BLCAS MSS. Afri.s.1742 m-40. See also McCracken, *A History of Malawi*, 244. In the subsequent paragraphs, I attempt to provide an explanation to this failure which was not unique to Malawi.

77. Dambo, like Dimba denotes a wetland and/or flood land, but one that is not necessarily water-logged. It is ideal for the cultivation of different crops mostly during the dry season.

78. Rice Production in the Limphasa Valley, 1942, MNA S12 1/12/2. South African and Norther Rhodesian mines were preferred because wages there were higher than estate wage labor in the Southern Province of the Protectorate.

79. District Commissioner (Chintheche/Nkhata-Bay) to DofA, January 15, 1941, MNA S12 1/12/2. The efficiency of the Kota Kota (now Nkhota-kota) Produce and Trading Society, Ltd., was later emphasized in the 1946 Nyasaland Annual Report. See Nyasaland Protectorate, *Nyasaland Annual Report, 1946* (Zomba: Government Printer, 1948): 4.

80. Memo from Provincial Agricultural Officer (W. W. T. Webb), Center, to DofA, Zomba, June 22, 1942, MNA S12/1/12/2. The Provincial Agricultural Officer (Center) was asked for advice because the most prominent Rice Cooperative of Nkhota-Kota fell in his province.

81. DofA to Chief Secretary, January 3, 1946, MNA S12/1/18/3.

82. That idea of ensuring African participation in the Viphya through sales of foodstuffs was earlier emphasized in the protectorate's 1946 Annual Report. See *Nyasaland Annual Report, 1946,* 16. See also Ag. DofA to Chief Secretary, October 15, 1947, MNA S19/1/1/1.

83. Limphasa Scheme CDC Quarterly Report, September 1951, TNA CO 1015/622; See also McCracken, *A History of Malawi*, 244.

84. Memo from the Chief Secretary to CO, February 14, 1953, TNA CO 1015/622.

85. CDC Abandoned projects, 1953, TNA CO 1015/622.

86. Memo from Chief Secretary (Zomba) to CO, February 14, 1953, TNA CO 1015/622. Compare this to the description of the technical challenges Wicker presents for the Gambia Egg Poultry Project in Wicker, "The Colonial Development Corporation," 222–23.

87. Nyasaland had the worst of its famines after the war in 1949. Two years of dry spell had affected the food situation in the protectorate such that most of the relief food had to be imported from outside the protectorate. The famine affected food acquisition for the Viphya Scheme workers. For a discussion of the 1949 famine and its effects on peasant production see Megan Vaughan, *The Story of an African Famine: Gender and Famine in Twentieth-century Malawi* (Cambridge: Cambridge University Press, 1987). Elias Mandala also highlights the magnitude of the famine in his *The End of Chidyerano: A History of Food and Everyday Life in Malawi, 1860–2004* (Portsmouth, NH: Heinemann, 2005).

88. Quarterly report of the Limphasa Scheme, June 1952, TNA CO 1015/674.

89. Paul Kishindo discusses at length the post-colonial Limphasa Rice Scheme. See his "Farmer Turnover at Settlement Schemes: The Experience of Limphasa Irrigation Rice Scheme, Northern Malawi," *Nordic Journal of African Studies*, 5, no. 1 (1996): 1–10.

90. Dr. William Beaver interview with Richard Kettlewell, October 11, 1979, BLCAS MSS.Afr.s.22–28. The relative success of the post-colonial scheme (which occupied a similar acreage of 1000) confirmed Kettlewell's sentiments.

91. Kettlewell to G. W. Nye (Deputy Agriculture Advisor, Colonial Office), August 19, 1952, TNA CO 1015/622.

92. Colonial Office Minute, August 26, 1952, TNA CO 1015/622.

93. Ibid.

94. Ibid.

95. Such a conclusion reflects the conflicting development mandate of the Colonial Office during this period. One represented by the CDWA and aiming at promoting rural development; the other by the Overseas Resources Development Act that aimed at producing resources for the benefit of Britain. The CDC fell under the latter. Michael Cowen has discussed at length how that dilemma played out at the metropole. See his "Early Years of the Colonial Development Corporation," 63–75. Wicker also discussed the concept of the "Conflicting Mandate." See Wicker, "The Colonial Development Corporation," 221–26.

96. Kettlewell to Nye, August 19, 1952, TNA CO 1015/622.

97. See Williams, "The Beginnings of Mzuzu with Some Biographical Notes on Some of the Viphya Tung Project Managers," 46–50; Phiri, "The Viphya Tung Scheme, 1945–1968."

98. There is a tendency among development students to privilege the role of government technical experts and scientists in analyses of the inter- and post-war development science, often neglecting the significant role that other groups played. A typical example is Hodge, *Triumph of the Expert.*

99. Berman, *Control and Crisis in Colonial Kenya*, 1990; Lonsdale and Berman, "Coping with Contradictions"; Phillips, *The Enigma of Colonialism.*

100. Wiseman Chirwa, "'The Garden of Eden': Sharecropping on the Shire Highlands Estates, 1920–1945," in Alan H. Jeeves and Jonathan Crush, eds. *White Farmers Black Labour: The State and Agrarian Change in Southern Africa, 1910–1950* (Portsmouth, NH: Heinemann, 1997), 271, argued that between 1925 and 1929, colonial policy on tobacco production in the protectorate shifted. While the state ignored

African tobacco producers in the past, the crises of the Great Depression forced the DOA to shift attention away from supporting tobacco-growing European settlers towards encouraging peasants who, because of their local knowledge of the crop, remained resilient and mostly withstood the challenges the economic recession presented. The Director of Agriculture is quoted to have stated that the economic future of Nyasaland did not lie in the settler community, but rather, in African producers. Such is also a story we find in Berman's *Control and Crisis in Colonial Kenya*, where the colonial state moved to support African producers of economic crops following the challenges of the Great Depression. In contrast to such "crisis-led decisions," in seeking to secure African participation in the emerging tung industry in Nyasaland, the DOA, as noted, was moved by entirely different motives, either interest to promote African welfare, or the use of an "African card" as a strategy with which to contain the growing influence of planters.

Chapter Four

Confronting Poverty

The State, ODM, and World Bank Triad, 1960s–1970s

While addressing Malawi Parliament on January 18, 1966, Dr. Hastings Kamuzu Banda had this to say:

> I'm sick of experts, I am. They come here with their minds already made up, and they write a report not based on facts . . . but just what they think should be. . . . I feel sick that people sitting in the offices, either in London, or Washington or elsewhere, civil servants who just sit down and lecture at Oxford who say this is uneconomic, it makes me really sick! I was furious when I read that British Economic Mission supplement. When I see that man again [Hill], I mean the man who was chairman [of ODM's Economic Mission to Malawi]. . . . He had better not come here again. Nonsense! In fact, [he] did not even write a report based on facts.[1]

This excerpt from Dr. Banda's speech points to the emerging conflictual interaction that characterized the relationship between the Malawian state and Western experts from 1964 to the early 1970s.[2] Throughout the period in question, experts from Britain's Ministry of Overseas Development, the World Bank, and the United Nations Development Program, disagreed with Malawi on several policy directions. The major disagreements related to Malawi's decision to transfer the national capital from Zomba in the Southern Region to Lilongwe in the Central Region, and to construct a Nacala rail link connecting land-locked Malawi to the Indian Ocean through Mozambique (see Map 4.2 below). Added to these projects was Banda's insistence on constructing a lakeshore road running from Fort Johnston (now Mangochi) in the South to Karonga in the North. Western experts argued that the projects in question would strain the economy and divert resources away from the most immediate needs of the country, especially investments in rural agriculture and other social amenities. Besides, experts questioned Malawi's decision to drop the five-year development planning in 1967, a tradition that was inaugurated in the post–World War II era. Because the country lacked any development plan worth the name after that year, they argued, Malawi was less equipped to confront its developmental challenges in a more coordinated manner. Malawi argued that long-term development planning was irrelevant for a country that relied on outside sources of funding to finance its recurrent and development budget. Long-term plans were regarded as rigid and made it difficult for the state to introduce urgent changes in the development process.[3] Instead, Malawi replaced such plans with an "Estimates of Expenditure on Development Account," a document the Malawi Parliament approved every year as a component of the national budget. It supplemented this with a "three-year rolling program," which itemized public sector development projects whose sources of funding the government had already identified.[4]

The exchange introduced here is relevant because it helps us understand not only the economic trajectory of postcolonial Malawi, particularly as it evolved between the 1960s and the 1970s, but also how the state responded to the demands of the many Western state and non-state institutions, and the development ideas they projected to the LDCs. It also provides a window from which to make sense of the plight of the poor in the 1970s, which is the focus of this chapter. As noted earlier, scholars emphasize how the postcolonial state in Malawi perfected colonial tactics of exploitation and domination.[5] The literature depicts the state as having deliberately pursued policies whose aim was to extract economic surplus from the peasantry, a rent-seeking behavior that was ruinous to the rural farming communities but enriching for the largescale estate farmers. The chapter argues that although state policy in the 1970s was increasingly predatory for many ordinary farmers, to a considerable extent, that behavior was less an adoption of colonial economies of exploitation than a response to the immediate postcolonial developments, which included the conflictual interaction taking place between Malawi, the WB, and the ODM.

Throughout the 1960s, the state in Malawi planned its development activities in ways that would break with the colonial tradition. To a considerable extent, colonial economies rendered the interests of ordinary farmers subservient to those of the settler community. After independence, the Malawian state emphasized the significant role smallholder agriculture would play in growing the country's economy and raising the living standards of the poor communities. Such planning, as noted in chapter one, was in line with the ideas that circulated within the WB and the ODM circles, the two institutions interacting with Malawi in matters of development. But Malawi was equally interested in financing infrastructural "development" projects, which, unfortunately, did not win the confidence of its Western partners. As noted,

Britain's ODM committed to assisting former colonies to grow their economies. Coming back to power (in 1964) after the highly criticized projects of the 1947–1951 period—which sacrificed the goals of colonial development and welfare—the last thing the Labour Government needed was to have British aid diverted to projects whose benefits for the poor or the economy generally remained questionable. Again, the WB was already transitioning towards projects that had direct effects on the poor. To ensure that foreign aid, whether in the form of grants or loans, yielded the best effects, the two institutions increasingly policed its use in Malawi, a decision that brought them in constant confrontation with both Banda and the team of expatriate staff he had retained in the civil service after independence.[6] Following the early 1970s global oil crisis, the declining budgetary support from Britain, the mounting pressure from both the ODM and the WB, and concerns over achieving political and economic autonomy, Malawi increasingly focused on intensifying cash crop production (particularly tobacco) by supporting large-scale capitalist farmers. The latter often enjoyed state subsidies whose resources, as some scholars have noted, were drawn from smallholder sector. Unlike smallholder agriculture, large-scale capitalist estates held the potential to instantly generate foreign exchange with which to balance its fiscal budget and direct the surplus towards other pressing needs of the economy Western aid agencies did not support. It was the same estate agriculture that inadvertently condemned ordinary Malawians to an exploitative visiting tenancy system and wage labor. The WB, the ODM, and the state in Malawi, least expected such an outcome.

The analysis in this chapter is intellectually rewarding. It challenges the existing scholarship for reading historical events based on the late 1970s outcomes as opposed to state intentions, and how such intentions played out in practice. It affords us a break from predictable analyses that link the colonial past with the postcolonial present while ignoring the daily routines of the historical processes that defined the state's behavior in the 1960s and 1970s. A careful search of the records at the World Bank Group Archive, the Malawi and the British National Archives as well as sources at the Bodleian Library of Commonwealth and African Studies, allows me to reflect more deeply on the intervening developments, particularly as they relate to how the state in the country interacted with its Western aid partners and the results of that encounter.

Two themes clarify the argument in question. The first reflects on the privileged position ascribed to Malawi's rural communities in the incipient development plans. Even though large-scale commercial farming was part of the plan to create wealth for the nation right from the 1960s, it was emphasized as one among several priority areas and not as an overarching policy direction in agriculture. The state planned its agriculture-based economy in ways that accommodated smallholder farmers as significant economic players. From the mid to the late-1960s, moreover, state bureaucrats jealously guarded the interests of the rural farmers by ensuring that such interests were not rendered incidental to those of the estate sector or urban communities. This position changed from the early 1970s, precisely for reasons introduced above.

The second theme relates to two significant aspects. The first examines how policy differences pitted Britain's ODM, the WB, and, to a lesser extent, UNDP development experts, against the local political leaders and their technical advisors in Malawi. It highlights how experts from these institutions (ODM, WB, UNDP) criticized Malawi's bureaucracy on various policy decisions (including the rejection of formal development planning in 1967) and the response the latter presented. In general, the predominantly white expatriate staff in Malawi displayed an ambivalent attitude towards their colleagues, often challenging them for intruding into affairs of a sovereign country. Intradepartmental correspondence suggests that this group saw foreign experts as a threat to their privileged position as advisors to the Malawi leader and stewards of the country's economy. This experience resembles that which the staff under the Department of Agriculture displayed in the colonial past.

The other aspect of the second theme highlights the opposition Western experts launched against Dr. Banda's infrastructural development projects which he packaged through the *Gwelo* plan.[7] Among others, the plan included shifting the capital from Zomba to Lilongwe, constructing the new campus of the University of Malawi in Zomba, and linking Malawi and the Indian Ocean by rail through the Mozambican railway line. The chapter reflects on how the Western financiers rejected some of these projects, the mounting pressure they exerted on the country's fiscal management, and the response of the Malawian state, which, inadvertently, negated rural agriculture. It is by understanding the dynamics in question that a better appreciation of how the war on poverty failed in postcolonial Malawi could be achieved.

DEVELOPMENT PLANNING IN MALAWI AND ITS SKIRMISHES, 1960S–1970S

The state in Malawi adopted two strategies for development after independence in 1964. The first targeted agriculture through the agency of rural agricultural projects and large-scale estate farming. With over 90% of her four million population living in the rural areas by 1964, such interventions, particularly the rural agricultural projects, would potentially uplift the living standards of the rural poor, while contributing to the country's economic growth. Already, this population was growing, and the need to keep pace with it was urgent.[8] The second strategy encouraged secondary industry, both publicly and privately financed. The success of both agriculture and secondary industry was contingent on developing basic infrastructure such as a well-developed road and railway network, plants for electricity supply, office blocks, and education facilities. Given that Malawi lacked the most basic infrastructure at independence, the state sought simultaneously to confront multiple goals of development, often relying on external financing.

Although independence came in 1964, agricultural planning for the postcolonial state should be traced to 1962 when Africans became part of the transitional government, with Dr. Banda appointed the Prime Minister.[9] The 1961 Malawi Congress Party (MCP) Manifesto, the 1962–1965 and 1965–1969 Development Plans, and the 1971 Statement of Development Policies, present us with some clues on what the state planned to achieve through agriculture. In all these documents agricultural planning emphasized two aims. The first sought to improve the people's living standards and welfare and the second, generating funds with which to facilitate the overall economic development of the country.[10] What requires clarifying is whether agricultural development would proceed along the colonial lines in which a few capitalist elites dominated the agricultural economy or through the agency of smallholder farmers, or both. The three options had both merits and demerits. Because of the high capital involved and other advantages such as the use of advanced technology, the large-scale estate sector held much promise as a strategy of generating resources for the country. Nevertheless, it would disadvantage the rural farming communities by condemning them to the role of wage laborers on agricultural estates. Again, estate agriculture required vast tracks of land. That path entailed converting customary to leasehold land, in the process shrinking the amount of cultivable land available for ordinary farmers. Given the immediate historical past, this direction was politically sensitive. The second option would avoid the political challenges associated with the first. Given the limitations of peasant-based agricultural systems, such as overdependence on family labor and a lack of appropriate farm technology, it did not have the immediate potential to generate enough income that could be plowed back to the other areas of the economy. A combination of the two strategies would mitigate weaknesses associated with them.

In general, the development plans and other instruments emphasized a combination of the two options. The framers of the plans were careful to ensure that both the estate and smallholder agriculture sectors would thrive without prejudicing one over the other. Such an approach would avoid replicating the colonial tradition of exploitation. The 1961 MCP manifesto, for instance, did not propose a dual economy in which smallholder or rural agriculture was rendered subservient to the estate sector.[11] Rather, it sought to stamp out what its framers saw as economic inequalities that had characterized the colonial period. One of its main objectives was to "reduce inequalities in the distribution of wealth and economic power" either between the rich and poor Malawians, the rural and urban communities, or the estate and the peasant sectors.[12] The 1962–1965 development plan highlighted the problem of inequalities in question and sought to "commercialize farming and make it a source of income for the masses."[13] These early documents do not point to a state eager to perpetuate the colonial economic tradition.

Both the 1961 MCP Manifesto and the 1962–1965 Development Plan benefited from the input of Dunduzu Chisiza, whose ideas these documents cited at length. Chisiza distinguished himself as one among the critical intellectuals of the MCP and helped to conceptualize much of what the MCP-run government planned to achieve before his death in a car accident of September 1962.[14] Chisiza shopped for development ideas from the US and other Western countries. Serving as the Parliamentary Secretary to the Ministry of Finance in Nyasaland's transitional government, he went to the US in late 1961 where he visited Walt Whitman Rostow, who was then serving at the White House before he moved to the State Department. Rostow was an American Economist and intellectually famous for his five stages of economic growth thesis. Chisiza accessed a draft copy of Rostow's *The Stages of Development: A Non-Communist Manifesto* before Cambridge University Press published it in 1963. During this visit, Chisiza also discussed with Rostow the possibility of organizing an economic development conference in Nyasaland.[15] While in the US, Chisiza flew to Kingston, Jamaica, to visit Arthur Lewis, a West Indies-born British Economist trained in the field of Development Economics. At the time, Lewis was serving as the Vice Chancellor of the University of the West Indies.[16] Among others, Lewis' studies focused on the problem of poverty in developing countries and how to achieve a market-oriented agricultural sector to sustain industrial growth. Chisiza had wanted to have a personal discussion with Lewis for a possible application of his ideas to Malawi. That visit proved fruitless as, unbeknown to Chisiza's US companions, perhaps, Lewis was out on holiday. Chisiza also forged contacts with Peter Thomas Bauer (later Lord Bauer), a Hungarian-born British Development Economist. Bauer distinguished himself as a leading critique of the state-led development. He disliked protectionism and foreign aid, regarding them as perpetuating rather than alleviating poverty in the LDCs. As such, he helped to lay down the foundation to the Neo-liberal tradition way before the World Bank and the IMF advocated it in the 1980s.[17] In July 1961, Chisiza organized the Nyasaland economic symposium to which, upon his request, the Ford Foundation contributed US$45,000.[18] In his 1962 work, Chisiza projected what he called a "pragmatic pattern of development" whose basic objectives included raising the living standards of the people; widening economic opportunities to arrest unemployment; and promoting "entrepreneurial activities among the less privileged sections of the community."[19]

Chisiza believed that for agrarian societies such as Malawi, industrial development needed to benefit from modernized agriculture in which the masses participated mostly through wage employment. Commercialization of agriculture on a massive scale would widen economic opportunities for many people by reducing unemployment.[20] Chisiza was aware that some segments of the society were less likely to benefit from this type of agriculture. Therefore, he also advocated for local participation in agricultural activities that were less capital-intensive as an avenue to reducing "inequalities in incomes, wealth, and income power."[21] Anticipating the position the ODM adopted a few years later, he advised African governments (Nyasaland included), "to allocate development resources not only to those enterprises which are likely to yield monetary profit, but also to those . . . which are essential to the welfare of the people even if they are not likely to yield monetary gains."[22] Chisiza's ideas, particularly those on safeguarding the interests of the rural or urban communities while not ignoring agricultural commercialization, found a place in the development instruments introduced above and others that emerged later.

Between 1965 and 1967, the government, still pondering on the two options, did not seriously intrude into the farming communities and barely assisted them through the provision of extension services, markets, and related interventions. This "non-interventionist" approach, Chipande postulates, came in the wake of the unpopular colonial soil conservation and settlement schemes which attracted opposition from Africans such that the best the state could do was to avoid the previous mistakes.[23] The absence of meaningful state intervention in rural agriculture during the early years of independence should not symbolize a rejection of an agricultural strategy based on peasant agency, nor should we mistake it with the state's propensity towards supporting estate agriculture. Such political fears notwithstanding, bureaucrats, especially Dr. Banda's expatriate staff, were already proposing certain rural agricultural schemes, having convinced Britain in 1965 to finance a small rural development project aimed at intensifying agriculture among rural farmers in southern Lilongwe. Besides, it was around the same period that proposals towards the 1967 land legislation, which was introduced in chapter two and is discussed at length in chapter five, were raised.[24]

The early years of independence, therefore, were marked less by a well-formulated agricultural policy than the debate on the right approach to follow in agricultural intensification. This debate was not only manifest in the incipient planning documents discussed earlier, but also the subsequent plans. Between 1967 and the early 1970s the country did not have any formal development plan, having relied on a "three year-rolling program," which was revised annually depending on the availability of development resources. But the initial drafts of the Statement of Development Policies, preparations for which began in 1970, present us with a comprehensive discussion of the country's plans for development, and the bureaucrat's faith in local participation.[25] The introductory chapter of the Statement of Development Policies drafted by D.S. Pearson (the Chief Economist), resonates well with what the previous frameworks spelled out. "Malawi's basic development strategy" reads the draft, "may be summed up in the phrase 'grass-roots development,'" further arguing that even though the country did not rule out implementing large-scale projects, it would only do so hoping they would raise "material welfare [of] the population at large."[26]

This approach deemphasized the privileged role accorded to what Pearson called the "Big Push" development program, according to which planners concentrated resources in a few capital-intensive projects, often through high-tech industry such as mechanized agricultural estates. For Pearson, although estate agriculture was rewarding regarding the capacity to raise a country's Gross Domestic Product (GDP), such projects left out much of the population and would therefore not arrest poverty.[27] It is, therefore, not surprising that although the state promoted some selected state-run and privately-owned large-scale farms, the state planned and implemented several agricultural projects that specifically targeted rural farmers. These projects fell into three categories. The first comprised four "large-scale" integrated programs with the highest level of funding, much of it from external sources. They included, as detailed in Map 4.1, the Lilongwe Land Development Project (LLDP); the Shire Valley Agricultural Development Project (SVADP); The Central Region lake-shore Development Project (CRLDP); and the Karonga-Chitipa Rural Development Project (K-CRDP). They were called integrated projects because they aimed at addressing several challenges confronting rural agriculture often through a concerted effort from multiple government departments. A complete package had to do with the provision of a credit facility, agricultural inputs, market outlets, health facilities, water supply, and better rural roads, among others. Land consolidation was also a significant component in some. Estimates indicate that the four projects were planned to raise a consolidated net family income by US$125 million while providing the country with an exportable surplus of US$11 million every year.[28]

All these projects evolved as state-led programs, where experts guided Africans with modern ways of farming. While encouraging farmers' participation in the agricultural process, the approach adopted was predominantly top-down and represented the dominant ideas of the time—of seeking to achieve development through external tutelage as opposed to faith in community development which became dominant in the late-1980s. The WB-financed LLDP, discussed in the next chapter, was a 500,000-acre project targeting over 60,000 families in central Malawi. It aimed at increasing

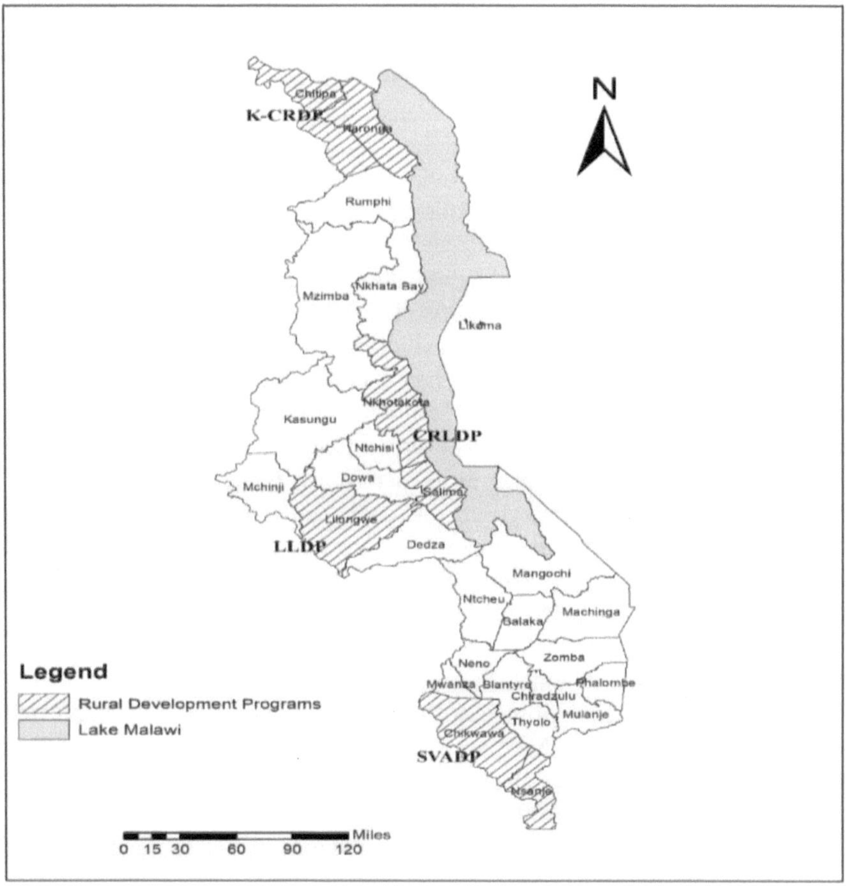

Map 4.1. Integrated rural development projects in Malawi, 1960s–1970s
Source: Drawn by Dr. Park Muhonda, Oregon State University.

per capita production of maize and groundnuts both as food and cash crops. The SVADP had similar objectives but targeted cotton and cocoa production. The latter was not attempted. The CRDP, which the former Federal Republic of Germany financed, focused on tobacco, cotton, groundnuts, maize, and rice production. It sought to experiment with new varieties of these crops. In the Northern Region, the K-CRDP, like the CRDP, focused on the production of all the other crops except for tobacco.

Under the second category were 16 irrigation and settlement schemes which the state planned and developed as integrated rural development projects between 1966 and 1979. Most of the projects targeted rice production as both a food and cash crop. Besides, the Malawian state envisaged that the project areas would become nuclei of rural towns, thereby arresting rural-urban migration. As settlement schemes, they also served political objectives. By bringing together settlers from diverse ethnic backgrounds, they would help to build a national identity at the local stage.[29] The state established these schemes across selected districts of the country. One of them was the Limphasa rice scheme introduced in chapter three. It was the Republic of China (Taiwan) that provided technical and financial support to selected irrigation schemes. This followed Dr. Banda's visit to that country in August 1967.

Following that visit, the Republic of China's (ROC) deployed an Economic Mission to Malawi in November 1967. The Mission proposed a "model villages" approach as best suited to intensify rice crop production in the country. According to that approach, which had a more comprehensive application across the country, the Taiwanese Technical Mission deployed about 6–10 experts in some selected irrigation schemes. One group, comprising agronomists, irrigation engineers, and farm mechanics, remained in Zomba, the Mission's headquarters. This group was deployed to the schemes from time to time to provide technical support. The personnel in the field cultivated designated model rice plots while providing agronomic lessons to the local communities and some selected groups such as the members of the Malawi Young Pioneers.[30] The latter would help to teach local farmers once the mission had checked out. In general, the team presented an opportunity for rural farmers to learn by emulation from these more experienced Taiwanese rice growers.[31] The Taiwanese Mission envisaged that through double cropping (production in both rainy and dry seasons), the demonstration plots would produce a total of 5000–8000 metric tons of rice per annum for export. This tonnage was higher than the 4,500 metric tons of rice Malawi exported through the existing schemes.[32]

Added to these two categories were a set of three Smallholder Authorities designed to intensify cash crop production through the agency of rural farmers. Established between 1967 and early 1970s, they included the Smallholder Tea Authority (STA), Smallholder Coffee Authority (SCA), and the Kasungu Flue-cured Tobacco Authority (KFCTA).[33] Smallholder Authorities were quasi-commercial state-owned enterprises, operating with a special board and their own staff. The state established the Authorities in areas whose climate favored the production of specific crops such that the KFCTA operated in Kasungu District of central Malawi, which is conducive to tobacco production. The STA catered for the tea-growing districts of Thyolo, Mulanje, and Nkhata-Bay.[34] Almost all these Authorities benefited from the Commonwealth Development Corporation's funding and management skills. In 1963 the Colonial Development Corporation (CDC) changed into the Commonwealth Development Corporation, conveniently acronymed here as CmDC to distinguish it from the previous corporation. The CmDC provided both technical support and loans towards government-supported development projects in former British colonies and others. The concept of the smallholder authorities was CmDC's brainchild, first implemented in Kenya's tea growing districts and other countries, including Malawi and Zambia.[35]

The STA provides a glimpse of how the smallholder authorities operated, especially with input from the CmDC. Although it was established in 1967, it had a long history going back to 1963 when the colonial state (under the transitional government) requested the CmDC to help design the Authority for the tea-growing districts of Thyolo and Mulanje. The idea at the time was to include local Africans in the tea industry, where large-scale cultivators, most of whom were British nationals, had hitherto dominated. A working party appointed by both the CmDC and the colonial state recommended that a smallholder authority be established to facilitate both the production and marketing of tea, primarily grown on customary land.[36] After independence, the government did not abandon these plans. It resolved to expand production along the lines of this model to the Northern Region district of Nkhata-Bay, targeting 300 acres with a projected expenditure of £35,000.

By 1976, the CmDC and the Malawi government jointly managed the Authority. While the government provided technical services to farmers, the CmDC financed the planting component.[37] In the words of Chirwa and Kydd, "the main business model under the STA involved provision of inputs and technical services to smallholder farmers (in which seedlings were provided free under the planting program) [sic] and the STA in turn provided transport for collection of green leaf from the smallholder farms to factories in estates."[38] The state envisaged that with time, the STA would become independent of the estate sector. That dream was realized in 1975 when the Authority teamed up with the state marketing board (the Agricultural Development and Marketing Corporation, ADMARC) to establish a tea processing factory, the Malawi Tea Company (MATECO), to which farmers, through the STA, sold their tea.[39] This model was replicated, with some variations, in all the Smallholder Authorities.

The KFCTA also emerged out of the CDC's Kasungu flue cured tobacco estate of central Malawi, itself a component of Britain's post-war economic offensive aimed at stabilizing the British economy. Established in the 1950s, the estate met a similar fate several of the CDC-run projects faced in British Africa. In 1962, the estate was written-off and transferred to the post-colonial state. It was initially a training ground for local farmers seeking to grow flue-cured tobacco before the CmDC provided a loan that helped to establish the KFCTA in 1968. Like the STA, it operated as a quasi-commercial state-owned enterprise, providing training to local farmers and facilitating tobacco marketing at the auction floors.[40] Other than the three categories in which the government took an active role to promote rural farmers as agents of agricultural intensification, the state supported the rest of the farmers in the country by providing them with extension services, markets, and credit facilities, among other services. This also included the *Achikumbe* Farmer Program, which was less of a program than a system of incentivizing farmers, and one that was similar to the colonial Master Farmers Scheme.[41] Hard-working farmers were awarded certificates of achievements irrespective of whatever means they used to produce positive results. Achikumbe farmers could be identified across the country.

Having had an application beyond the irrigation schemes, the Taiwanese village model became handy in providing shape to agricultural interventions directed at uplifting farmers untouched by the three programs discussed above. The government established model villages in all the districts of the country, targeting villages as opposed to individuals, as was previously the case with the colonial Master Farmers' Scheme. The Taiwanese model would ultimately create progressive farmers. But these were supposed to emerge from village communities. The model was not novel, however. "From the agricultural viewpoint," remarked one government official, "the Chinese Mission's conception of the model village is sensible and realistic" because it resembled "an existing extension approach" already underway in the Central Region.[42] The central component of the approach the government officer referenced was the idea of farm clubs first developed in the early 1960s in Lilongwe, Dowa, Kasungu, and Mchinji Districts.[43] Farm clubs had a committee, clubhouse, and demonstration plots which agricultural extension officers supervised. The clubs obtained credit from existing credit facilities to purchase agricultural inputs such as fertilizer and seed, and agricultural technology, mostly in the form of work oxen. These clubs later evolved into Village Planning Committees, which supervised one to three villages. The planning committees had the mandate to consolidate plots to "allow for better use of ox-drawn implements."[44] Such an approach fundamentally differed from the colonial land consolidation projects in which experts took the leading role in land reorganization. The approach, moreover, was in line with state plans to enhance local participation in the development process, which it hatched as early as 1965.

In that year, the government introduced the District Development Committees, followed by the Area and Village Action Groups (AVAGs) in 1966.[45] The District Development Committees constituted the following members: The District Commissioner, District's Members of Parliament, District Chairperson of the Malawi Congress Party, a member of the League of Malawi Youth and League of Malawi Women. The latter two were organs established under the Malawi Congress Party. Other members included the chairperson and clerk of the District Councils, supervisor of the Farmers Marketing Board, an Agricultural Officer, the District Education Officer, and

Community Development Worker. The AVAGs comprised local members of the communities with chiefs as chairpersons. These committees represented government's attempts to decentralize development activities in the country. In theory, the committees were expected to operate under the Ministry of Development and Planning, whose functions were taken over in 1967 by the Ministry of Economic Affairs. Critics have condemned this decentralized structure as representing a mere smokescreen and less inclined to any serious form of "decentralized development strategy."[46] Instead of responding to the District Development Committees, the central government, through the Office of the President and Cabinet (OPC) assumed control over the AVAGs. This reading, however, should not cloud our judgment about what the state sought to achieve and how, in the early years of independence. This level of centralization, where the AVAGs fell under the OPC, represented the government's attempt to project its authority in the countryside by directly engaging with chiefs in the work of political challenges of the time. A notable event is the failed 1967 Yatuta Chisiza's insurrection against the Banda regime, which compelled the government to project its authority in the countryside. And a retreat from a functional decentralized structure was a much later development and corresponded with the overall neglect of the peasantry from the mid-1970s onwards. A decentralized development strategy can serve as a double-edged sword. While decentralizing the state, it can also consolidate state power in rural areas, which is exactly what happened in the case of Malawi.[47]

At independence, therefore, the state committed itself to ending poverty among rural farmers and growing the economy through deliberate agricultural planning, all the while encouraging local participation in the development process. Within the framework of rural agriculture, the approach adopted was a patchwork of multiple ideas—from the CmDC, as in the conception of Smallholder Authorities; the WB and Malawi's expatriate staff, most of whom had sound colonial experience; and the Taiwanese, particularly the concept of model villages.

At the level of large-scale commercial agriculture, the state took deliberate steps to promote the existing estate sector while opening other farms without necessarily sacrificing the interests of small-scale farmers. Besides tea and tobacco production, which was predominantly under the European and Asian estates, the government opened two estates in the 1960s, the General Farming and Press Farming Ltd. The two companies mostly specialized in tobacco production in the central and northern regions, where climatic conditions favored the crop. In the 1960s, the government welcomed the Lonrho International Corporation, which invested in sugar production at Nchalo in the Lower Shire Valley. In 1968, the government partnered with the CmDC to establish the

Sugar Company of Malawi (SUCOMA) at Nchalo.[48] Thus, by the close of the 1970s, the country was dotted with specific agricultural projects.

Even though the approach adopted, particularly at the rural development level, was based on ideas shopped from different directions, it did not lack a well-articulated shape.[49] It was one that reflected faith in stimulating development through specific growth points, an idea that displayed South African influence. Having rejected the Hill report cited in the introduction to this chapter, Dr. Banda welcomed a South African Economic and Physical Planning Mission in 1967 whose report he consistently praised in his speeches.[50] One section from it resonates well with the overall agricultural outlook described here:

> In a young developing country such as Malawi, with a marked shortage of skilled labor and capital, the only practical procedure lies in co-ordinated development around focal points or growth points. All projects and studies should be geared towards the sound socio-economic advancement of the selected points. This approach must percolate through to all departments, thinking and activities. In this manner, scarce capital and man-power can be best utilized. Priorities in the sectoral investments and activities will then be directed towards these focal points."[51]

Agricultural planning in Malawi seems to have taken this shape, targeting, as it did, specific localities. As the following table illustrates, investment in smallholder agriculture and the estate sector remained significant components in the economic growth of the country.

These projections illustrate the high importance the government attached to the smallholder sector which it saw as meaningfully contributing to the country's economic growth.[52]

Nowhere was the policy of encouraging smallholder agriculture more clearly articulated than the country's "Statement of Development Policies (DevPol)"

Table 4.1. Projections in monetary GDP by selected industrial origin (MK million)

	Actual	*Projected*		*Average Growth Rate/ Annum (%)*
	1970	*1975*	*1980*	*1970–1980*
Smallholder Agriculture	26.6	46	78	11.4
Estates (including Government-led estates)	14.5	22	28	6.8

Source: World Bank, *Recent Economic Developments and Prospects of Malawi*, Report No. 67a-MAI. March 30, 1973, 14, http://documents.worldbank.org/curated/en/858961468054566315/pdf/multi0page.pdf.

covering the years from 1971 to 1980. The early draft of the DevPol shows that in promoting smallholder agriculture, the state aimed at reducing the gap between the urban and rural dwellers. Pearson's views on rural-urban disparities deserve citing at length especially because he was a key figure in the production of the document:

> The distribution of income between urban and rural areas is an important factor in Malawi's income and prices policy. It would be contrary to this broad policy to create a privileged position for urban wage earners by artificially inflating their incomes since this would be reflected in increased prices of manufactured goods and cause a reduction in the real price of farmers. Not only would this be contrary to the objectives of raising the living standards of the mass of the population but would also act as a disincentive to increase effort in the agricultural sector and hence undermine the basic development strategy. . . . These policies have been followed since independence.[53]

Earlier in 1968, Pearson struggled to defend what he saw as a development policy that all government officials shared. He was critical of the Farmers Marketing Board's (FMB) decision to reduce the producer price for rural farmers' crops, through more stringent grading procedures. In his opinion, such a deflationary policy was unnecessary as it affected the agricultural sector upon which most of the population relied.[54] FMB did not share that view, with one of its officials describing Pearson's memo as "scandalous, dangerous, critical, malicious, and contemptuous piece of work . . . with a bad motive."[55] More revealing in Pearson's memo is a reference to the "political projects"—preliminary work on the development of a new capital in Lilongwe, the Nacala Rail link, and the presidential place (Sanjika) in Blantyre. For Pearson, these projects strained the otherwise weak economy, an observation that was true for both the ODM and the WB.

The development planning documents discussed so far reveal the mind of the Malawian state. The 1971 Statement of Development Policies, however, was also the outcome of the pressure that the Western aid actors exerted on local experts and politicians in Malawi.[56] As early as 1968, various aid agencies faulted the country for abandoning formal development plans in 1967. In 1969, for example, the WB Mission to Malawi questioned President Banda on the country's rejection of formal development planning. Instead, Banda argued against that kind of planning. "I realize that at some stage there was a widespread belief that comprehensive development plans prepared in detail for a fixed term of years were a form of panacea . . . to development," Banda wrote the president of the WB, Robert McNamara, further referencing the idea as outmoded.[57] For Banda, the country did not have enough resources of its own for any possible projection of development projects. Instead, he referenced the country's preference for the rolling development program described above.

Banda's statements reflected the general tenor in the Malawian state bureaucracy even though it is far from clear who might have influenced the other. Although Banda is portrayed as the main architect of the country's development policy at the time, many of his white expatriate staff shared these ideas, and it is difficult to ignore the influence this group had over the overall direction of the country's economic landscape in the early years of independence. One passage from the Chief Secretary's memos is illustrative:

> It has been suggested from [several] sources that the Malawi Government should prepare some formal document, setting out its long-term development plan. Most of the views to this effect have been expressed by government and international agencies. . . . It would appear desirable for Malawi Government to state categorically that it does not accept the validity of the argument that national prosperity and rapid economic growth depend upon detailed prints of long-term economic planning, tailored to fit into academic theories.[58]

Earlier on April 4, 1970, the IMF Consultative Mission to Malawi challenged the expatriate staff to reconsider its position. The Mission argued that a development plan would strengthen Malawi's ability to negotiate foreign financing for her projects. In March 1970, the WB advisor on planning organization (Development Service Department) requested the Malawi Government to submit its development plan. It warned that Malawi was the only country out of a list of 70 without one. During the 1970 Malawi-London financial discussions, the ODM expressed a similar opinion. It noted that Malawi would have been most successful in attracting aid had it possessed clear plans of what it sought to achieve.[59] The ODM was, in fact, reiterating its well-established principles on aid. The 1965 aid prospectus (the White Paper) clearly stated that "British and any other aid will be most effective where it forms an integral part of a coherent and cooperative effort to implement a well-prepared development plan."[60] As early as 1952, a report by a Harold Wilson-chaired committee under the Association for World Peace had already emphasized to the British audience how well-articulated development plans would contribute towards arresting poverty in British dependencies and others. Since the mid-1940s, moreover, development plans had become a well-established tradition, with Britain insisting that colonies receive funding only upon submission of long-term development plans.[61] With time, the Secretary to the Treasury, K.J. Barnes, listened to the voice of reason and encouraged his expatriate colleagues to move towards formal planning. Even with that, he did not believe a formal development plan of the type produced by other countries would be in any way useful. He saw it as more necessary for soliciting aid than anything else.[62]

By September 1970, the drafting of the Statement of Development Policies covering the years 1971–1980 had commenced. Statement of Development Objectives, Manufacturing, Export Projections, Agricultural Policy, Human Resources and Social Services, Distribution of Transport, and finally, Progress to Date were the significant areas it targeted. This work notwithstanding, pressure from outside never ceased. The UNDP did not consider the proposed document a plan worth the name. It expressed that opinion through its 1971 Background Paper on Malawi which the UNDP Resident Representative had raised.[63] The paper criticized the country's casual approach to development and condemned it for abolishing, in 1967, the Ministry of Development and Planning. Set up in 1965, the ministry aimed at coordinating development effort in the country. When the state dropped formal development plans, the ministry was rendered less useful. State bureaucrats challenged the UNDP's argument, however. In commenting on the paper, the Development Division of the Office of the President and Cabinet trashed it for its "inaccuracies and misconceptions." It further emphasized that "any suggestion of resuscitating the old Ministry of Development and Planning should be shot down at once: it was an unmitigated failure [sic]." The comment on raising a formal development plan other than the one already attempted is illustrative: "Such a plan would not make the slightest difference to 'determine and maintaining priorities' [sic]," noted the Secretary to the OPC who viewed the plan as creating "inflexibility in the planning process."[64]

For the UNDP Resident Representative, failure to plan was indicative of a state whose bureaucrats lacked the capacity to channel the country towards real planned development. The OPC captured that mood better: "[This Background Paper] does give the impression that we are a pretty lame duck, that there isn't much hope for us, but probably, we will be able to jog along at a fairly impoverished level and not to be a bother to anyone else. [We must resist these assumptions]."[65] Mostly, the UNDP saw such failures not only crippling the government's activities but also stalling its development effort in Malawi. Such sentiments often attracted responses that implicitly reminded the UNDP about the country's sovereignty. As the Secretary to the Treasury complained, "one agency [the UNDP] is sufficiently honest to acknowledge that a formal development plan would facilitate its own work (as though the governments of developing countries were for the convenience of the UN agencies) [sic]. Others feel that they have the jurisdiction and competence to dictate policy to a member government."[66] Bureaucrats in Malawi, it appears, were reluctant to accept the patronizing tendencies of their colleagues in Western aid institutions. Most of them had acquired practical experience through colonial service and considered themselves competent enough to provide direction to the country's progress. One would postulate that since most of these expatriates had short-term contracts in Malawi, they were mindful of generating some quick results to their credit other than relying on rigid long-term plans. In any case, this kind of antagonism, as described here, characterized the developmental state throughout the early period of independence. But the major confrontation manifested through capital intensive infrastructural projects, part of the Gwelo dream Dr. Banda so tirelessly defended.

THE CONTESTED GWELO PLAN[67]

Without trivializing the agency of the white expatriate staff the country retained following independence from the British in July 1964, Dr. Banda took the overall leadership for the development direction of the country after the 1964 Cabinet Crisis.[68] Taking advantage of the parliamentary vote of confidence in him after the crisis, Banda sought to push through the developmental aspect of the dream he had envisioned while in Gwelo Prison in Southern Rhodesia where he was incarcerated between March 1959 and April 1960. The political component of his dream, which bordered on dissolving the Central African Federation, had been accomplished by 1963. As noted earlier, construction of the lake-shore road and the Nacala railway link connecting landlocked Malawi to the Indian Ocean through Mozambique, and moving the capital from Zomba to Lilongwe, ranked among the significant aspects of his development dream. The other aspect had to do with constructing a new campus of the University of Malawi in Zomba. Banda saw all these projects related to his overall vision of holistically "developing" the country.

At independence, however, Malawi did not have resources with which to embark on these large-scale projects. The task fell on Banda who looked to outside financiers, most of whom did not share his development vision. Both the ODM and the WB were critical of Banda's ambitions on the new capital and Nacala projects. As noted above, absorbing most of the functions previously managed by the CO, the ODM became a significant organ through which Britain channeled much of her aid to former colonies or protectorates and other parts of the world. Between 1964 and 1977, HMG was the largest financier for Malawi, with the WB taking the second place.[69] Before the Conservative Government established the Overseas Development Administration in 1971, it was the ODM that engaged Malawi in financial negotiations. In 1965, the ODM deployed an Economic Mission to the country to investigate its economic status with the view of determining areas that required British financial support. The ODM also tasked the Mission to comment on the feasibility of moving the capital following the £11million application Malawi had raised soliciting support from HMG.[70]

Led by C. de N. Hill, formerly the Permanent Secretary of the Ministry of Finance in Tanzania, and at the time, the Deputy Bursar of Sussex University, the mission produced a report critical of the country's large-scale infrastructural projects. As expected, the ODM respected the report which triggered Banda's response cited in the introductory section of this chapter. It argued that "it would be economically and administratively absurd to build a new capital from the scratch on a barren site eight miles outside the existing township of Lilongwe."[71] Moreover, the project, including the Nacala one, would not yield immediate benefits for the economy. On the contrary, they would divert resources away from other productive areas, particularly the agricultural sector. But Banda argued for the economic benefits of the projects and emphasized how the transfer of the capital to a central point would contribute to the fair distribution of development projects across the country.

What Banda should also have highlighted is that the decision to shift the capital did not lack historical antecedents. Earlier, the colonial state had planned to move the capital to a better place, citing the problem of floods and water-borne diseases that made Zomba unsuitable as a colonial headquarters. At several points, notably in 1922, 1924, 1925, 1934, and 1947, the state suggested moving it either to Lilongwe in the center or Limbe and Blantyre in the far South (See Map 4.2 below). The colonial project failed because of lack of adequate resources at the time.[72] Banda, it appears, was preoccupied with reasons that appealed most to the would-be financiers—the economic justification of the projects. He argued that moving the capital to Lilongwe would spread and accelerate development in the country because Lilongwe was centrally located. Again, Lilongwe was in the Central Region, which he considered the chief agricultural area of the country. On a lighter note, he saw Lilongwe as located in the main traffic line between Nairobi and Johannesburg and, therefore, more suitable for building an international airport than Zomba or Blantyre. In his 1965 speech in Parliament, he impressed upon the parliamentarians to support the project by appealing to the language of development: "This scheme of moving the capital is worth carrying out even if we haven't got £20 million," further noting that it would facilitate development of common farmers and not "theoretical development of people sitting in the universities."[73] A similar language of development was not lacking in other proposed projects. Banda argued that other than providing jobs to Malawians, the Nacala rail link (see Map 4.2 below) would service the yet to be established Viphya Pulp Mill, which will be discussed in the sixth chapter of the book.[74] Such justifications did not persuade either the ODM or the WB to alter their position. As a result, Banda contemplated turning to the

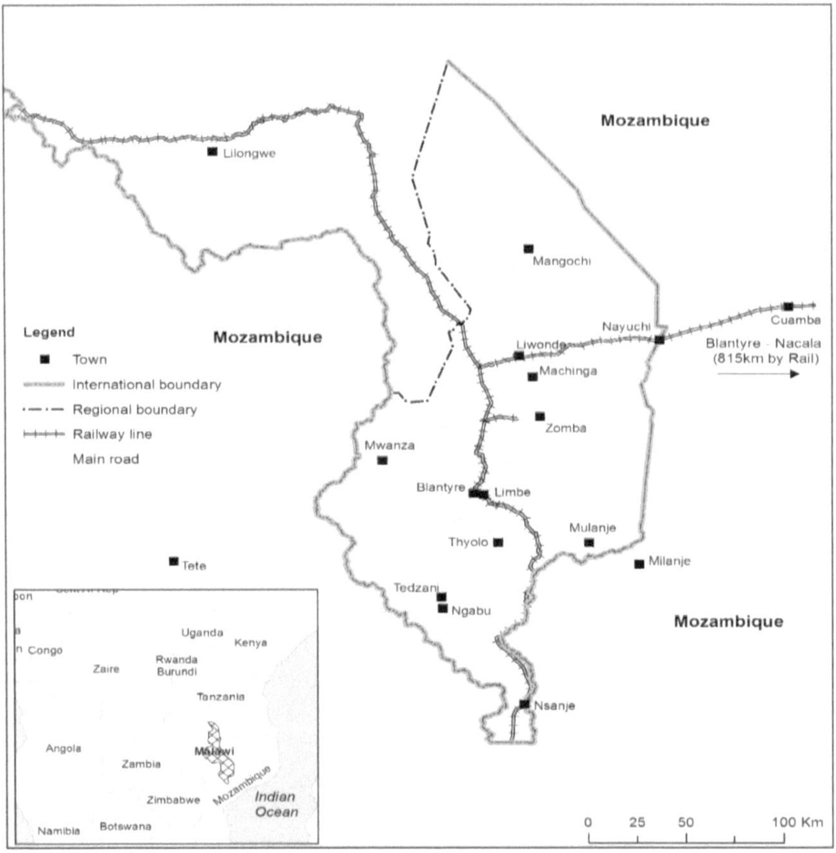

Map 4.2. Central and Southern Malawi towns and Nacala Rail Link
Source: Drawn by Mr. Jonathan Gwaligwali, University of Malawi.

apartheid government in South Africa, a politically sensitive decision, at least as the British and other players saw it.

Sensing Banda's intentions to source funding from South Africa, which he eventually did, the ODM became anxious about the possible implications Banda's actions would have on British aid to Malawi. British policy on aid did not dictate to sovereign countries the potential sources of loans and grants. But the ODM held the view that Banda should be prevented from obtaining funding from South Africa even if it meant using aid as a political lever.[75] During the 1966 Malawi-ODM financial talks in London, ODM officials tabled the objection the Minister of Overseas Development, Barbara Castle, had raised for Dr. Banda the previous year:

> I feel I must point out to you quite frankly that if financial and other resources are to be devoted during this period to the move of the capital, which can only be done at the expense of more immediately productive investment which would more quickly reduce the need for external budgetary aid, this would make it increasingly difficult for the British Government to justify to the public opinion in this country continuing aid to Malawi on the scale we have now proposed.[76]

A year later, that position had not changed. "While these decisions [about the move of the capital] are for Malawi Government to decide," stated the chair of Malawi-ODM negotiations meeting in London, "they might lead us into a situation in which we should reluctantly have to reconsider justification for devoting so much aid to Malawi."[77]

Banda questioned the ODM's intention to use the capital project to dictate the outcome of the discussions. "I am shocked," he wrote the Minister of Overseas Development, "to hear that you or your officials are raising [the] question of our decision to move [the] capital in present financial talks."[78] Similar levels of criticisms from other quarters might have contributed to the harsh tone in Banda's pronouncements. In 1966, the United States warned Banda's ambassador in New York against receiving aid from apartheid South Africa for the move of the capital. Among others, the US State Department saw such a decision as unpopular and one that would not command the support of both the Organisation of African Unity (OAU) member states and liberal opinion in the US and Britain.[79]

Banda did not hide his frustration, noting that "this hypocrisy [was] unnecessary" because the US and Britain had significant relations with South Africa and yet they prevented the small states from doing the same.[80] While keeping the South African card a top secret in the hopes of influencing Britain, such pressure was further pushing Banda towards the white-dominated South Africa as an exit option.

It was evident among some quarters in London that the ODM could not stop Banda's ambitions to move the capital because, in the wake of the 1964 Cabinet Crisis, political factors were as much important as economic motives. Three months after independence in July 1964, Banda fired three of his cabinet ministers, forcing the other three to resign. The ministers, who later fled to neighboring countries of Tanzania and Zambia where they organized anti-Banda campaigns, accused Banda of dictatorial tendencies. They also faulted his slow Africanization policy of the civil service and the proposal to introduce user fees in the country's public hospitals.[81] On his part, Banda accused his colleagues of wanting to infiltrate the country with communist ideologies, further blaming the People's Republic of China (PRC) for sponsoring the dissidents. Henry Masauko Chipembere, who was of Yao ethnicity from Mangochi, Southern Region (See Map 4.2 above), resigned in protest of Banda's decision against colleagues, and subsequently organized an unsuccessful insurrection in 1964. He was spared of execution when, wanting to pacify Malawi, both Britain and the US arranged for his asylum in California where he died in 1975. His Moto Village in Mangochi (South), however, was not spared of Banda's onslaught. In 1965, Banda ordered the arrest of all the members of the village who had joined Chipembere in his attempted coup against his government and set on fire the entire village. As noted, Yatuta Chisiza, Banda's former Minister of Home Affairs, and a brother to Dunduzu Chisiza (both of the Tumbuka ethnic group from the Northern Region) had organized another revolt against Banda's regime in 1967. He was executed just like many of Chipembere's followers who were captured earlier, including the popular Madison Silombera, whose body was displayed for public viewing at Zomba prison.

M.M.M. McMullen, a member of the United Kingdom's Commonwealth Relations Office, questioned ODM's insensitivity to these political dynamics in its opposition to transferring the capital. It was necessary, he suggested, to move the capital to Lilongwe in the Central Region, far from the Southern Region, the political bedrock of Chipembere and where Banda enjoyed little political support. For him, the shock administered to Banda by the revolt of the ministers triggered the urgent transfer of the capital to a safe base among his Chewa people in the Center. Efforts aimed at preventing Banda from implementing such a critical project would only meet with intense opposition and reduce Britain into a neocolonial power bent at dictating the domestic affairs of her former colonies. He was, therefore, of the view that the Hill report should have omitted this contentious issue.[82] McMullen was joined by many of Banda's sympathizers in London who supported the latter's ambitions. Notable among these were Duncan Sandys, a former Colonial and Commonwealth Secretary, and Nigel Fisher, a former Under Secretary for Colonies, both serving, at the time, as Conservative Members of Parliament in the House of Commons. These individuals questioned ODM's position as unfortunate given that Banda was friends with "capitalist" Britain.[83]

It is not clear whether political motives were a significant factor in Banda's decision. There is evidence to that thesis, however. In his interview with Richard Kettlewell later in the mid-1980s, Peter Youens, the former Secretary to the Prime Minister and Cabinet in Malawi from 1964 to 1966, narrated the disturbances that locked Zomba down for ten days during the cabinet crisis. In a show of solidarity with Chipembere, the civil servants and the crowd at the market threatened to burn down Banda's house. It took Secretary Youens' intervention to contain the group, almost risking his own life in the process.[84] Elsewhere, Debora Kaspin has hinted on how the transfer of the capital was a gift to the Chewa ethnic group (Banda's co-ethnics) in the Central Region of the country. Again, Deborah Potts has suggested how Banda appealed to the language of development to move the capital that would serve certain personal interests.[85]

Whatever the motive, external opposition to Banda's policies never stopped. Throughout the 1960s, the WB raised similar concerns. During the 1968 financial discussion with the Minister of Finance, Mr. John Tembo, the African Department of the WB blamed the country's weak public sector financial position on wasteful projects such as that on the capital and railway line. Since plans on these projects had already advanced, the officials noted that there was little gain in criticizing the government. "But the fact remains that as a result of government policies," one Bank official emphasized, "Malawi's financial prospects are so bad [as to not warrant further provisions of bank loans]. When the situation improves, the Bank will consider further operations."[86]

The WB was right. With the declining British direct financial support towards the recurrent budget, the country was already experiencing budgetary deficits. Dr. Banda acknowledged this in his 1968 speech in Parliament, where he advised the people to "to work hard in the fields in order to free ourselves from dependence on others outside our country. For balancing both our recurrent and development budgets," he emphasized,

> we depend on friends and well-wishers. This year, those friends on whom we greatly depend for our recurrent budget, for circumstances beyond their control, are themselves, in or under great financial difficulties. Therefore, they have not been able to and are not in a position to help us on our recurrent budget as they have been able and were in a position to help us in the past. The deficit on our recurrent account, which the Minister of Finance told the House on Friday is, in fact, a measure of the extent to which our friends have not been able to help us this year.[87]

This excerpt from Banda's speech sounds apologetic in the way it rules out "behind the curtain" politics as a contributing factor to the 1968 economic position. Banda knew that his policies on infrastructural projects were closing off some economic opportunities but stuck to them, often countering the ODM and WB criticism through expert advice from elsewhere.

In the same address, for instance, Banda praised the 1967 South African Economic and Physical Planning Mission to Malawi for presenting a report that contradicted the ODM's Hill report.[88] Banda invited the Mission to assess the country's developmental potential following South Africa's pledge to finance the capital project. "In my experience since I entered government in 1961," he stated, "of all the experts we have had in this country, the ones we had last year [from South Africa and the Republic of China] are the best . . . because all of them have written reports which are realistic, practical, and far-sighted."[89] For Banda, experts from Britain and the UN agencies were unnecessarily academic and less practical, "men living in the air" whose expertize was limited to "lecture rooms, in a college or university or to the administrative desk in the office of one or other former colonial territories. . . . This is the problem we have had—some people claiming expertize simply because they came from the United Nations."[90]

Unlike the WB and the ODM, the Rautenbach-led South African Mission maintained the position noted earlier, of achieving development in the country by targeting specific focal points.[91] It saw Banda's move to shift the capital to the Central Region as a necessary step for that purpose. The Mission argued that earlier criticisms against the decision on the capital were based on "short-term reasoning and monetary criteria," with little regard to how the project fit into the overall schema of the country's development. The project presented opportunities to "generate optimism and development in an otherwise predominantly rural region." Besides, the Mission praised the decision to erect a pulp mill in the Viphya Plateau because it held the potential to stimulate development in the north just like the Blantyre-Limbe complex (colonial commercial centers) did for the Southern Region.[92] In other words, by appealing to South Africa's expertise, Banda hit back at his Western financiers with little regard to the financial consequences of his decisions.

Moreover, South Africa's commitment was mostly towards the capital project and, later, Banda's Sanjika palace in Blantyre. Banda's 1968 speech is particularly revealing about the next steps he took to contain the growing external pressure. Noteworthy is how this pressure was impacting Banda's attitude towards European- and Asian-owned businesses in the country. The Asians, particularly Indians, like white settlers from Britain, had plied their trade in the country since the colonial times. After independence, some of these groups remained in the country and engaged in both retail and wholesale trade. By 1968, these groups controlled over 90% of consumer and capital goods businesses in the country, sometimes plying their trade in rural areas. Banda tolerated this state of affairs in the past. The 1968 deficit, however, forced him to rethink that position:

> The vast majority of businessmen in the country dealing in either consumer or capital goods [are] not Africans. It is either Europeans or Asians. As a result, all money that is made in trade and commerce in this country goes to the pockets of other people than Africans [and] goes outside the country. . . . It is very difficult for an African to enter business and succeed [because, among other reasons], the country is flooded by traders of other races [who] have built shops even in villages where Africans should start trading among their own people. . . . I am determined to see to it that [this trend] is reversed.[93]

In consequence, the government restricted European or Asian businesses to urban areas, mostly in Blantyre, Zomba, Limbe, and Lilongwe. The policy, as will become clear, also extended to the commercial agricultural sector, where it targeted both European and Asian estates, predominantly in the central and southern regions.[94]

The 1968 recurrent account deficit exerted pressure on Banda, and perhaps this explains FMB's behavior that Pearson condemned. However, that was a secondary layer of pressure, the primary one being external opposition to his infrastructural projects, which never ceased. The WB/IDA, for one, did not relent in its criticism of the country's development policy. Its position was clear in a leaked memo the Malawi UN Embassy accessed in 1969. In their discussions, the WB officials criticized Malawi's traditional projects cited above—Nacala, the new capital, and others. They added to that list the country's quest to construct yet another hydroelectric power plant at Tedzani when it already had one at Nkula, both along the Shire River in the South (see Map 4.2 above). They also questioned the Farmers Marketing Board for drawing bank overdrafts to finance its activities. Reiterating their earlier position on Nacala, the WB officials doubted the capacity of the Nacala line to generate enough revenue to pay back the South African loan. "If the railway cannot pay," read the leaked minute, "then the Government will be responsible for the debt [thereby denying resources to other essential areas of the economy]."[95] In his covering letter, the Malawi Ambassador to the UN captured better the feeling at the Bank:

> I am also informed that the officials of the Bank/IDA are generally very concerned with the amount of loans Malawi has received and those that are still in the pipe-line. They say that they may have no say in the procurement of those loans that Malawi is getting from other sources, but the feeling in the Bank/IDA circles is that in the end Malawi may find that she is biting more than she can chew.[96]

He was right. Earlier in 1968, financial discussions taking place in Washington between the Minister of Finance and the Director of the Africa Department of the WB stalled. The former was seeking a loan to finance the Tedzani project. The WB questioned the legitimacy of the request, further emphasizing its dissatisfaction with Malawi's "economic and financial policies." When asked to elaborate on that phrase, it cited Malawi's careless borrowing towards projects which, in the WB's view, would not provide immediate economic benefits to the country.[97]

When the leaked memo reached Dr. Banda's desk, it was returned with a minute equally revealing about Malawi's attitude towards the IDA. In paraphrasing it, the Acting Secretary for Foreign Affairs advised his colleague in

New York: "H.E.'s [His Excellency's] comment was that I should inform you [Mbekeani] to ignore what IDA tells you. The truth, as is known to Malawi, is that the African section of the Bank is under the charge of an Arab who, for obvious reasons, is not in our favour."[98] In essence, Banda questioned the very image of a Bank that boasted of being apolitical, thereby reducing it to a neocolonial body as many leaders in the LDCs did. What Banda's minute ignored, however, is that with McNamara at the helm of the Bank, the institution was transitioning away from financing projects that had only indirect benefits to the poor, towards those that directly addressed the plight of the poor. In undertaking such an assignment, the Bank's legitimate expectation was that Malawi would reciprocate with a similar concern. Though interested in the welfare of the poor, Malawi leadership considered the Bank's approach paternalistic and resented it every time an opportunity presented itself.

One opportunity came earlier in 1967. The World Bank Mission to Malawi questioned the country's overall failure to maintain appropriate foreign exchange reserves and borrow in local currency from commercial banks. In his letter to Banda, the WB's Vice-president warned Malawi against the tendency to draw on foreign currency deposits for purchases abroad following the non-availability of outside finance.[99] Banda couched his response in the language of political sovereignty and it deserves a lengthy citation. "The whole business," he argued,

> is, in fact, a vicious circle. As you know, we were a colony for seventy years [yet] with no economic or industrial development to [show for it]. As a country, we feel we are the best judges of what to be done [sic], what projects are to be or should be undertaken to accelerate economic and industrial development. . . . We reserve the right to reject any suggestion or any proposal with which we do not agree. . . . We are not prepared to accept any loan from anyone if that loan is tied to unfair and humiliating conditions.[100]

When Knapp briefed the President of the WB on Banda's concerns, George Woods suggested that the World Bank slow down its operations in the country, a piece of advice which, as noted above, had undoubtedly influenced the Bank's position on Malawi.[101]

In 1975, Kathryn Morton argued that British aid to Malawi had produced positive results, noting how it sustained the country's economic growth in the 1970s. Morton pitched her argument against the well-established doctrine which Professor Peter Bauer inaugurated, and one that blamed Western aid for the failure of development in Africa.[102] This literature argued that aid substituted the framing of well-articulated development plans for African countries and often failed to develop local institutions that would have supported continued economic growth. In contrast, Morton argued that the British aid to

Malawi did not substitute the country's development strategy. Britain, however, provided checks and balances which helped in the successful utilization of development aid.

A year later, Leon Gordenker presented an opposite view. He argued that the international aid organizations had a limited effect on Malawi, Zambia, and Tanzania in the sense that the national governments always prevailed each time officials from these organizations challenged domestic decisions.[103] This study is concerned with Morton's argument, especially the view that aid in Malawi did not provide an alternative development framework. What Morton overlooked, however, is that the same checks and balances, including the selective manner in which aid was presented, threatened Malawi's autonomy and forced its leadership to adopt development policies that resisted outside interference. Banda, it appears, chose greater political autonomy at the expense of economic priorities. Although Banda was generally an authoritarian leader, pressure from outside and the economic hardship the government had to endure were pushing his regime towards a greater level of authoritarianism. Similarly, Gordenker was right in associating the state in Malawi with non-compliant behavior. Even though such behavior was a necessary corrective to outside interference, much more significant were the practical steps Malawi took to contain that pressure.

For a state under constant pressure to achieve economic sovereignty, a shift to predatory economic policies discussed in the literature becomes less surprising. As noted earlier, by 1969, British direct budgetary support to Malawi had declined tremendously, from £6 million in 1965 to £2.8 million in 1969.[104] The post-1973 global oil crisis era added another layer of pressure on Malawi. Under such circumstances, the country had to choose either to rely on both the smallholder and existing estate agriculture at the pre-1968 rate or emphasize one over the other. The choice between the two options depended on which sector promised the best results in the short-term. As noted, the smallholder sector, especially the manner in which it was reorganized, held a lot of economic promise. However, it would take time to train local farmers to participate in production activities that would potentially help to raise the country's GDP. Besides, lack of appropriate farm technology meant that agricultural intensification relied mostly on the use of family labor. In view of this, estate agriculture held a lot of promise. Deliberate support to such a sector became necessary because of the potential it held to quickly generate the sought-after foreign exchange with which to resolve the problem of balance of payment deficits and redirect the surplus towards the projects external institutions refused to fund. The policy shift began in 1968 amidst intense pressure from both the WB and the ODM.

In general, when Banda advised Parliament in 1968 to indigenize the economy by placing it under the control of Africans, he was also determined to expand estate agriculture which, at the time, did not command strong African presence save for the Press Farming/General Farming Limited and other selected estates. Not surprisingly, from 1969, Banda launched a campaign to purchase European-owned estates and land, often under compulsion, for distribution to his ministers, politicians, and other elites, while expanding the General Farming and Press Farming Companies' landholdings. It is also on record that between 1970 and 1974, Central Region European and Asian estate holders had their tobacco licenses revoked to pave way for African commercial farmers.[105] Banda emphasized that land acquired by the government would only be granted to "those people or those companies that can raise money to run them properly, can employ managers to supervise the estates," which effectively restricted the land in question to large-scale farmers. In fact, several of his politicians were "allocated plots in smallholder tea and rice schemes, where they used African labour to work them," in the process defeating the whole idea of using these schemes to empower local farmers.[106] From 1973, when the oil shock had created another layer of pressure, leasehold estates for the willing large-scale Africans were created out of customary land, often supported under loans from commercial banks, the Reserve Bank of Malawi, and the State Marketing Board, ADMARC. The latter, as others have noted, benefited from the surplus it extracted from smallholder and rural development projects because of the monopoly it enjoyed over the marketing of agricultural produce. It is this kind of rent-seeking behavior that has led scholars to reduce the postcolonial state into a leviathan or predatory one.[107]

As Kydd observes, it was the years 1973–1978/9 that witnessed the golden age of estate agriculture and corresponded with the decline of the smallholder sector.[108] Mkandawire and colleagues estimate that the number of leasehold estates grew from 229 in 1970 to 876 in 1979.[109] What equally grew was the acreage under estate cultivation as Figure 4.1 illustrates. The decline in estate agriculture corresponds with the economic crisis of the early 1980s.

As the estate sector expanded, the previous projections relative to the leading economic role the state attached to the smallholder sector (see Table 4.1 above) was reversed. If the estate sector registered growth in the 1970s, that was not true with the smallholder sector whose negative growth is remarkably clear under Table 4.2.

The trend demonstrates that even beyond the time frame of this study, the postcolonial state became increasingly reliant on estate agriculture as opposed to the smallholder sector, a departure from previous intentions. The rise of agricultural estates in the early 1970s which scholars have discussed elsewhere did not represent a premeditated state plan aimed at perpetuating the colonial tradition. Nor should they represent, as Ayres has passingly noted elsewhere, the political elites' lack of concern for the majority poor.[110] Adopting such an argument reduces all that the state tried to achieve for rural

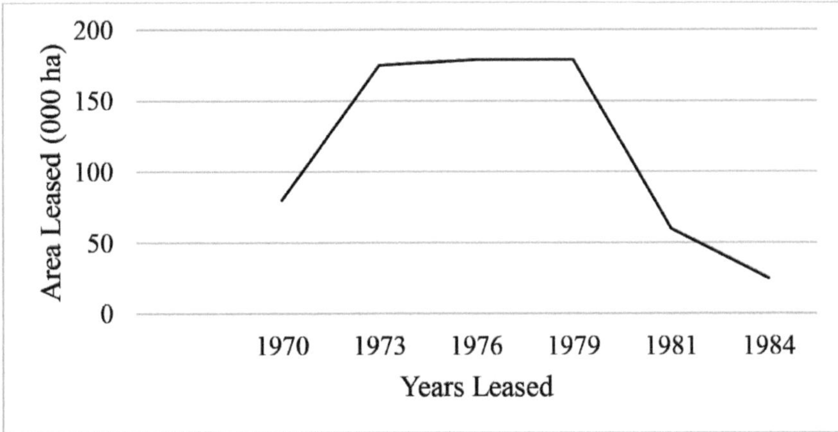

Fig. 4.1. Expansion of leasehold estates in Malawi, 1970–1984

Source: Adapted from Mkandawire et al., "Beyond 'Dualism': The Changing Face of Leasehold Estate Subsector of Malawi: A Report for the Institute for Development Anthropology," Binghamton University, 1990, 16.

Table 4.2. Annual agricultural GDP growth rates (%), 1973–1994.

Sector	*1973–1980*	*1980–87*	*1987–94*	*1973–1994*
Estate	8.6	4.1	5.3	5.6
Smallholder	4.0	1.8	1.0	0.7

Source: Adapted from World Bank, Malawi Agricultural Sector Memorandum: Strategy Options in the 1990s (Vol. 2), Report No. 12805-MAI, March 8, 1995, 26, http://documents.worldbank.org/curated/en/251811468774612825/Main-report.

farmers in the early years of independence and after into development with a conspiratorial touch—the whole idea that the state conspired to support the rural farmers for some ulterior reason. It also reads these events in hindsight based on outcomes rather than state intentions. This kind of predictable analysis, moreover, ignores the daily routines of the historical processes that defined the state's behavior in the 1960s, the result of which was mostly felt in the 1970s.

The tobacco estates seem to have paid some economic dividends, with Banda reporting to parliament in 1975 that "we have balanced our recurrent budget this year . . . because of, among other things, the tobacco estates."[111] But these estates had their own dark side in that they subjected rural Malawians to the tenancy system and wage labor, the very outcome that both the ODM and the WB least expected to see under the new poverty-oriented approach. "In many countries," warned McNamara in his 1973 speech, "tenants have to hand over to the landlord 50–60% of their crop as rent, and yet in spite of this are faced with the constant threat of eviction. The result is that their incentive to become more productive is severely eroded. [We must reverse this trend]."[112]

By the close of the 1970s, that was the exact position for Malawi, where many of the tobacco estates (as Kydd has illustrated statistically) were bankrolled through the surplus extracted from the peasant sector.[113] The overall picture of exploitation was not that different from what the Fabian Society sought to address in the colonial past. The factors leading to such state behavior in the immediate postcolonial present, however, were different. They were a product, among others, of postcolonial interactions between development actors and politicians, each making claims on knowledge about the country's development direction. The power imbalance produced by that interaction made the state in Malawi switch to policies that seemingly contradicted the previous goals of mitigating poverty and economic disparities. Such a conclusion should question analyses that draw a simple continuity in colonial and postcolonial state behavior without due consideration to the historical forces that gave rise to the later developments.

It is worth emphasizing that in the late 1970s, faith in raising the economy through large-scale capitalist farms had collapsed. The once praised Malawian economy of the 1970s was registering negative growth.[114] As a consequence, between 1981 and 1983, the IMF disbursed two Structural Adjustment Loans to Malawi to reverse what had by then become apparent as an economic crisis. It is perhaps not an exaggeration to affirm that the reforms these loans brought about as a condition for receiving them made a mockery of the objectives of arresting poverty that the ODM, the World Bank, and the state in Malawi tirelessly defended. These reforms, to use the language of Ayres, "involve[d] a contraction of public credit as well as other measures, [including] holding the line on wage increases, reducing food and other subsidies and *in the process worsening the plight of the very poor placed under the care of the ODM, WB, and the state in the country* [italics added]."[115]

CONCLUSION

From the 1960s, different societies of the world and institutions believed in the discourse of the war on poverty. The World Bank, Britain's Ministry of Overseas Development, and the state in Malawi were no exception to this trend. For the WB, the war on poverty represented, among others, a retreat away from the late 1940s and 1950s faith in development practices that did not have direct impact on the poor. The ODM had relatively similar interests. The Labour Government, which established the ODM, was yet to recover from the criticisms many of its post-war development projects attracted. This was true especially in how the postwar development projects supported under the Overseas Resources Development Act of 1948 sacrificed the objectives of ending poverty in the colonies to meet metropolitan economic concerns. Coming back to power in 1964, the ex-colonies became a space through which to mend the previous image by safeguarding the interests of the poor through aid. The state in Malawi had similar intentions and planned its activities in ways that would address poverty of its predominantly rural population. However, it also registered faith in large-scale infrastructural development projects which it saw as necessary for the long-term development of the country.

Without doubt, some of these projects, including presidential palaces, were wasteful, at least in the eyes of the British and the World Bank financiers. Such projects contradicted the goal of ending rural and urban poverty in the country. As a result, a conflictual relationship between the Malawian government and external aid agencies defined the first two decades of independence as planners, state bureaucrats, and politicians tried to reconcile somewhat contradictory development aims. The intentions of the ODM and the WB were legitimate—the need to end poverty in the country. Moreover, the state in Malawi shared that development discourse. The strategy for achieving this goal, however, involved age-old notions of British trusteeship and paternalism or, newer ones, such as the American modernization drive, which emphasized external tutelage as a necessary step towards alleviating global poverty. Hidden in this kind of trusteeship was what Duffield and Hewitt call a "paternalistic and educative design of power."[116] It is to this kind of power that the state in Malawi objected, either at the highest level of governance or at the technocratic decision-making level because it prevented a positive interaction among seemingly equal actors. The strategy they adopted, however, had negative consequences for the poor such that the outcomes point to the very ambiguity of development practice.

As noted in chapter one, as a deliberate intervention to guide progress and create wealth, development can create progress or unleash disorder. With Malawi, it created both in the 1970s. The expansion of estate agriculture contributed to economic stabilization while empowering the estate owners. This economic stabilization, however, also helped to disempower smallholder farmers, exactly what the state least envisaged. As noted, throughout the 1960s, the Malawian state consciously planned its agricultural economy in ways that would safeguard the interests of the poor while growing the economy. Developments of the late 1960s and early 1970s forced the state to turn to estate agriculture and further to draw, albeit indirectly, surplus from the smallholder sector in the process reneging from the previous effort to protect poor farmers. It is this failure to reconcile the objectives of protecting the poor while growing the economy that has been at the center of the development discourse from the distant colonial past to the immediate postcolonial present. Forces leading to that failure have changed over time, but the dilemma has remained intact. Such a conclusion does not suggest that the poor have suffered in silence or have been inactive players of the development process. As the subsequent chapter illustrates, the beneficiaries of rural development programs often participated in the projects, but mostly on their own terms as opposed to those envisioned by the planners. Such divergent interests created yet another force complicating the war on poverty.

NOTES

1. H. K. Banda speech, *National Assembly Parliamentary Debates,* January 18, 1966, 411.
2. From 1971, it was Britain's Overseas Development Administration (ODA), under the Conservative Government that constantly interacted with Malawi on matters of aid. Most of the cases I discuss, however, fell under the ODM.
3. R. B. S. Purdy (for Secretary to the President and Cabinet) to Secretary to the Treasury, October 23, 1971, MNA 4-14-1F/33764.
4. See D. S. Pearson (Chief Economist), The Development Plan, 25, 1973, H. K. Banda Archive, Indiana University Library, Box 2, Folder 9.
5. See Mhone, "The Political Economy of Malawi," 1–33; Jonathan Kaunda, "Malawi: The Post-Colonial State, Development, and Democracy," *Africa: Rivista trimestrale di studi e documentazione dell'Istituto italiano per l'Africae l'Oriente, Anno* 50, no. 3 (1995): 316.
6. After independence in 1964, Malawi pursued a slow Africanization policy of the civil service. It retained former white staff while recruiting additional foreign staff, mostly from Britain. These occupied top-government positions until later in the mid-1970s when Africans were entrusted with similar positions. Estimates indicate that by 1972, the country had over 900 expatriate civil servants under short-term contracts. See Africa Publications Trust, *Malawi: Dialogue and Development* (London: Africa Publications Trust, 1973), 21.
7. This related to the loose ideas about what Dr. Banda wanted to achieve for Malawi upon his release from Gwelo prison in Southern Rhodesia, where he was incarcerated following his arrest during the 1959 Nyasaland State of Emergency. He was released in April 1960.
8. Malawi had 2.9, 4, and 4.7 million people in 1950, 1964, and 1969, respectively. 2019 Population and Housing Census put her population at 18.6 million people. See live data of the Population pyramids of the world, 1950–2100, https://www.populationpyramid.net/malawi/1964/, Accessed on January 4, 2020.
9. As noted in the introduction, the transitional government came after the 1961 General Elections where the MCP scooped all the 20 seats of the Lower Roll of the Legislative Council and went on to dominate the Executive Council, with Dr. Banda serving as the Prime Minister. The position of the governor remained intact until 1964 when Malawi fully gained her independence from the British.

10. G. H. R Chipande, "Smallholder Agriculture as Rural Development Strategy: The Case of Malawi," Ph.D. Dissertation, University of Glasgow, United Kingdom, 1983, 44.

11. "Dual economy" as used here connotes the idea of pursuing two development policies, one supporting the estate sector, the other exploiting the peasantry. Literature discussing this trend usually carries the term "dualism" as in the following examples: Richard Mkandawire, Steven Jaffee, and Sandra Bertoli, *Beyond "Dualism": The Changing Face of Leasehold Estate Subsector of Malawi*: A report for the Institute for Development Anthropology, Binghamton University, 1990; David E. Sahn and Jehan Arulpragasam, "Development through Dualism? Land Tenure, Policy, and Poverty in Malawi," Working Paper 9, Cornell Food and Nutrition Policy Program, March 1991.

12. Malawi Congress Party, *Malawi Congress Party Manifesto for the General Elections* (Limbe: MCP Publication, 1961), 15.

13. Nyasaland Protectorate, *Nyasaland Development Plan*, 1962–1965 (Zomba: Government Printer, 1961), 53.

14. Although now disapproved by some scholars such as Joey Power, rumor held it that Chisiza's death was a staged one to contain his growing popularity. See Joey Power, "Remembering Du: An Episode in the Development of Malawian Political Culture," *African Affairs* 97, no. 388 (1998): 369–96; Joey Power, *Political Culture and Nationalism in Malawi: Building Kwacha* (Rochester: University of Rochester Press, 2010), 162–69.

15. See J. D. Hennings, British Embassy, Washington DC to J. K. Neale, Nyasaland, January 15, 1962, TNA CO 1015/2498.

16. While serving Britain as the secretary of the Colonial Economic Advisory Committee in the 1940s, Lewis suggested a deliberate policy of industrializing the West Indies, one that would help to address the problem of unemployment in the region. His ideas were not accepted, and, in protest, he resigned from that committee. See Arthur Lewis, *Theory of Economic Growth* (London: Allen and Unwin, 1955); Hodge, *Triumph of the Expert*, 266.

17. Little surprising that Margaret Thatcher, the Prime Minister of Britain from 1979 to 1990, and a supporter of neoliberalism, made Bauer a Lord. See Peter T. Bauer, *Dissent on Development* (Cambridge, MA: Harvard University Press, 1972); See also his *Development Aid: End it or Mend It* (San Francisco: ICS, 1993).

18. Conference on Economic Development in Blantyre, Nyasaland, 1960–1962, TNA CO 1015/2498.

19. Dunduzu K. Chisiza, *Africa: What Lies Ahead* (New York: The African-American Institute, 1962), 28.

20. Ibid., 28.

21. Ibid. Chisiza's ideas tilted towards Arthur Lewis' concept of the "Dual Economy" model according to which economic growth in developing societies resulted from promoting capital-intensive and profit-oriented agriculture on the one hand, without ignoring traditional agriculture (less-capital intensive) on the other. The latter, however, was regarded as a transitional phase.

22. Ibid., 29–30.

23. Chipande, "Smallholder Agriculture as Rural Development Strategy: The Case of Malawi," 46.

24. Thomas A. Blinkhorn, "Lilongwe: A Quiet Revolution," *Finance and Development* VIII, no.2 (1971): 28.

25. Memo by R. B. S. Burdy (for Secretary of the President and Cabinet), June 2, 1970, MNA 1-8-9R/17839.

26. Draft Statement of Development Objectives, Circulated October 7, 1970, MNA 1-8-9R/17839. The final copy left out several of the initial ideas that circulated among the bureaucrats. See Malawi Government, *Statement of Development Policies, 1971–1980* (Zomba: Government Printer, 1971).

27. Draft Statement of Development Objectives.

28. See Hodge, "British Colonial Expertise," 40; Sinoya J. Nankhumba, "Evolution of Agricultural Policy in Malawi and the National Rural Development Program: A Historical Overview, 1891–1980," Department of Agricultural Economics, University College of Wales, Aberystwyth, May, 1981, 31–37.

29. See Gift Wasambo Kayira, "The Plight of Small-scale Irrigation Farming in Malawi: Lessons from Wovwe Rice Scheme, 1964–2007," MA Thesis, University of Malawi, Zomba, 2010, 158.

30. Development Plan and Projects (Malawi), 1965–1969, MNA 15-12-6R/15077. The Malawi Young Pioneers was formed in 1965 through the Young Pioneers Act. As a state organization, it aimed at training the youth in basic discipline, civics, agriculture, and community development. About 2000 MYP trainees went through training in these subjects every year and 700 graduates were deployed to the settlement/irrigation schemes.

31. See Development Plan and Projects (Malawi), 1965–1969, MNA 15-12-6R/15077. On ROC's aid objectives in the late 1960s and early 1970s see Gerald Chan, "Taiwan as an Emerging Aid Donor: Developments, Problems, and Prospects," *Pacific Affairs* 70, no. 1 (1977): 37–56.

32. Development Plan and Projects (Malawi), 1965–1969, MNA 15-12-6R/15077.

33. In 1978, the Government established the Smallholder Sugar Authority (SSA) in Dwangwa (Nkhota-Kota District), the same year it established the Dwangwa Sugar Company (DWASCO).

34. See Chipande, "Smallholder Agriculture as Rural Development Strategy," 48.

35. See Michael McWilliam, *The Development Business: A History of the Commonwealth Development Corporation* (London: Palgrave, 2001).

36. Report of Government/CDC Working Party, "African Tea Development Projects," April 1963, MNA 15-12-6R/15077.

37. Ephraim W. Chirwa and Jonathan Kydd, "Farmer Organization for Market Access: Study on Farmer Organization in Smallholder Tea in Malawi," April 2005, 1, Accessed on December 28, 2019, https://pdfs.semanticscholar.org/0709/13593a59a7bfd43074de85d59e512f2b1466.pdf.

38. Ibid., 2.

39. Ibid., 2.

40. McWilliam, *The Development Business,* 102, notes that successes under the KFTA influenced the CmDC to support a similar Smallholder Authority in Zambia.

For a brief history of the KFTA see H. K. Banda speech delivered during the opening of Nairobi Agricultural Show, September 27, 1967, H. K. Banda Archive, Indian University Library, Box 2, Folder 2.

41. For details See Lemson S. Chitsamba, "Malawi and the Politics of Foreign Aid," Ph.D. Thesis, The London School of Economics and Political Science, University of London, 1990, 185–86.

42. Model Villages in Malawi, Circular No. 3/68, Department of Agriculture, Ministry of Economic Planning, Zomba, 1968, MNA 15-12-6R/15077.

43. Such an observation checks Kishindo's work which traced the history of Farmer Clubs in Malawi to 1978 when the government rolled them out across the country. The idea of farmer clubs should be traced to the early 1960s and was reinforced after the 1967 Taiwanese Economic Mission to Malawi. See Paul Kishindo, "Farmer Clubs and Smallholder Agricultural Development in Malawi," *Development Southern Africa* 5, no. 2 (2008): 491–507.

44. Model Villages in Malawi, Circular No. 3/68, Department of Agriculture, Ministry of Economic Planning, Zomba, 1968, MNA 15-12-6R/15077.

45. See R.A. Miller, "District Development Committees in Malawi: A Case Study in Rural Development," *Journal of Overseas Administration* 9, 2 (1970): 131; Gift Wasambo Kayira and Paul Chiudza Banda, "Chiefs and the Politics of Local Government in Malawi: A Historical Perspective," *Journal of Public Administration and Development Alternatives 3*, no. 1–1 (2018): 92.

46. Asiyati L. Chiweza, "The Ambivalent Role of Chiefs: Rural Decentralization Initiative in Malawi," in L. Buur, and H. M. Kyed, eds. *State Recognition and Democratization in Sub-Saharan Africa* (New York: Palgrave Macmillan, 2007), 53–78; Diana Cammack, Edge Kanyongolo, and Tam O'Neil, "'Town Chiefs' in Malawi," Working Paper No. 3. United Kingdom: Overseas Development Institute, 2009.

47. Kayira and Chiudza Banda, "Chiefs and the Politics of Local Government in Malawi," 92; Immerwahr, *Thinking Small*, 98–99.

48. Blessings Chinsinga, "The Green Belt Initiative, Politics and Sugar Production in Malawi," *Journal of Southern African Studies* 43, no. 3 (2017): 504.

49. This tendency of shopping development ideas from multiple directions after independence was not unique to Malawi. Abou B. Bamba has described how Ivory Coast borrowed industrial development ideas from France and the US all the while combining or, as he puts it, triangulating them with their own. See Abou B. Bamba, *African Miracle, African Mirage: Transnational Politics and the Paradox of Modernization in Ivory Coast* (Athens: Ohio University Press, 2016), 44–66.

50. The 1967 South African Mission was led by Dr. P. S. Rautenbach who served as an Economic Advisor to the South African Prime Minister. See *Johannesburg Post in English*, December 2, 1977, 19. Cited in United States Foreign Broadcast Information and Service, *Sub-Saharan Africa Report, 2743–2816*, June 21, 1986, 30. https://books.google.com/books?id=T2AEAQAAIAAJ&printsec=frontcover&source=gbs_ViewAPI#v=onepage&q&f=false, accessed Jan 2, 2020. I have been unable to access the Mission's report but have had to rely on Banda's speech where it is cited at length.

51. Cited in H. K. Banda address to the Malawi Parliament, January 29, 1968, H. K. Banda Archive, Indian University Library, Box 2, Folder 2.

52. Coming in 1969 or 1970, these projections illustrate the confidence state bureaucrats registered in the smallholder agricultural sector.

53. Draft Statement of Development Objectives. The statement challenges the assertion that there was an "urban bias" in development strategies prior to the 1970s. See Lipton, *Why Poor People Stay Poor*, 66–70.

54. Pearson to Robert J. Dewar (Secretary of Economic Affairs), June 27, 1968, MNA 15-12-6R/15077.

55. FMB to Dewar, July 2, 1968, MNA 15-12-6R/15077. As discussed below, Pearson had a point. 1968 was a bad year for Malawi because of the huge deficit the country suffered when external budgetary support was not forthcoming. FMB's actions aimed at compensating for such shortfalls.

56. Such an observation departs from that which Frederic Pryor projected. He argued that the *Statement of the Development Policies: 1971–1980* was a brainchild of President Banda. As this section shows, such an assertion, if not insensitive to the contribution of the white expatriate staff to the country's economic planning, ignores the political context that gave rise to the document. See Frederic L. Pryor, *The Political Economy of Poverty, Equity and Growth: Malawi and Madagascar* (Oxford: Oxford University Press, 1990), 63. It was the World Bank that commissioned Pryor's study.

57. Banda to R. McNamara, June 28, 1969, WBGA, File No. 1860299, Box 107-03/158-2-6.

58. Memo by B. C. Roberts, April 17, 1970, MNA 1-8-9R/1783.

59. See IMF Report on Malawi, 1970, MNA 1-8-9R/17839; Memo by K. J. Barnes (Secretary to the Treasury), April 8, 1970, MNA 1-8-9R/17839.

60. Great Britain, *Overseas Development*, Cmnd. 2736, 7.

61. See *War on Want*, 68–69; Morgan, *The Official History of Colonial Development*, Vol. III (London: Macmillan, 1980), 26.

62. Memo by K. J. Barnes (Secretary to the Treasury), April 8, 1970, MNA 1-8-9R/17839.

63. See UNDP Background Paper on Malawi, March 1971, MNA 4-14-1F/33764.

64. R. B. S. Purdy (for Secretary to the President and Cabinet) to Secretary to the Treasury, October 23, 1971, MNA 4-14-1F/33764.

65. Ibid.

66. Memo by S. W. Foot, April 26, 1972, MNA 4-14-1F/33764.

67. This section and some parts of the introduction benefitted from the following prior publication: Gift Wasambo Kayira, "Limits to State Power in the Post-independence Development in Malawi, 1964–1983," in Kenneth Ross, Wapulumuka Mulwafu, Kings M. Phiri, and Klaus Fiedler (eds.), *Politics, Christianity, and Society in Malawi* (Mzuzu, Malawi: MZUNI Press, 2020), 266–92.

68. The "Cabinet Crisis" took place in September 1964 following disagreements between Dr. Hastings Banda, the then Prime Minister and some of his ministers. These differed mostly on domestic and foreign policies. Consequently, Dr. Banda fired his three Cabinet Ministers forcing three others, including Henry Masauko Chipembere, to resign in solidarity with their colleagues. See Colin Baker, *Revolt of the Ministers: The Malawi Cabinet Crisis, 1964–1965* (London: I. B. Tauris Publishers, 2001).

69. Kathryn Morton, *Aid and Dependence: British Aid to Malawi* (London: Croom Helm, 1975), 1–10. Between 1958 and 1965 Malawi was only second to Kenya among the major recipients of British direct loans and grants to Africa. See statistical figures in Great Britain, *Overseas Development,* 58–59.

70. *The Observer*, October 16, 1966, Newspaper Cutting, TNA/DO 208/3.

71. Extract from C de N. Hill, Economic Mission to Malawi Report, 1965, TNA DO 183/839.

72. Removal of Zomba, 1947, MNA FS/2/19/1; Mulwafu, *Conservation Song*, 189–91. The cost of shifting the capital in 1947 was estimated at £500,000.

73. Excerpt of H. K. Banda speech, July 1965. H. K. Banda Archive, Indiana University Library, Box 6, folder 14. Also reprinted in *Malawi at War against Poverty, Disease and Ignorance* (Same file); See also H.K. Banda Address in Parliament, September 27, 1968, H. K. Banda Archive, Indiana University Library, Box 2, Folder 2.

74. H. K. Banda speech, February 1, 1966, TNA. DO 208/1. See also Banda's speech during the opening of Nacala Rail Link, July 4, 1970, H. K. Banda Archive, Box 2, folder 3.

75. Memo by Anthony Greenwood (Minister of Overseas Development), July 26,1966, TNA DO 208/3.

76. Castle to Banda, December 17, 1965, TNA DO 208/3.

77. Record of the financial meeting, November 8, 1966, TNA DO/208/10.

78. Banda to Arthur Bottomley (Minister of Overseas Development), 1966, TNA DO 208/10.

79. Dispatch by British High Commissioner (Zomba) to Commonwealth Office (London), August 29, 1966, TNA DO 208/3.

80. Record of Banda's personal communication with the American Ambassador to Malawi, August 29, 1966, TNA DO 208/3.

81. See Baker, *Revolt of the Ministers*, 91–93. The ministers were right on Banda's recruitment policy. McMaster notes that of the 2,357 senior positions in the 1970s, the expatriate staff occupied 915 of these in 1970. And, out of the 158 senior posts Malawi had in 1972, 25 were occupied by the expatriate staff. This also included 4 Permanent Secretaries. See McMaster, *Malawi*, 87.

82. Memo by M. M. M. McMullen, February 4, 1965, TNA DO 183/839.

83. *The Observer*, October 16, 1966, Newspaper Cutting, TNA DO 208/3.

84. Peter Youens' interview with Kettlewell, Feb 9, 1985, BLCAS, MSS.Afr.s. 1742 (38).

85. Debora Kaspin, "The Politics of Ethnicity in Malawi's Democratic Transition," *The Journal of Modern African Studies* 33, no. 4 (1995): 605; Deborah Potts, "Capital Relocation in Africa: The Case of Lilongwe in Malawi," *The Geographical Journal*, 51, no. 2 (1985): 188.

86. Record of the meeting, October 5, 1968, WBGA, File No. 1860298.

87. H. K. Banda address to the Malawi Parliament, January 29, 1968, H. K. Banda Archive, Indiana University Library, Box 2, Folder 2.

88. He also praised the 1967 Taiwanese Economic Mission for providing guidance on how to intensify agricultural production among rural farmers through the model village approach.

89. H. K. Banda address to the Malawi Parliament, January 29, 1968, H. K. Banda Archive, Indian University Library, Box 2, Folder 2.

90. Ibid.

91. Dr. P. S. Rautenbach, a Town Planner and at the time serving as Economic Advisor to the South African Prime Minister, and Chairperson of the Resources and Planning Advisory Council of the Republic of South Africa, led negotiations between Malawi and South Africa which resulted into the latter providing a loan of R8 million in 1968. The loan was used to kickstart construction work for the new capital in Lilongwe. See *Johannesburg Post in English*, December 2, 1977, 19. Cited in United States Foreign Broadcast Information and Service, *Sub-Saharan Africa Report, 2743–2816*, June 21, 1986, 30.

92. Cited verbatim in H. K. Banda address to the Malawi Parliament, January 29, 1968, H. K. Banda Archive, Indiana University Library, Box 2, Folder 2. See also Malawi, *National Assembly Parliamentary Debates*, January 29, 1968, 229.

93. H. K. Banda address to the Malawi Parliament, January 29, 1968, H. K. Banda Archive, Indiana University Library, Box 2, Folder 2.

94. At the time Malawi had about 10,000 Indians, some of which were also part of the 7,000 British citizens, including those that served in the government service. See Paul Chiudza Banda, "The Indian Community in Malawi: Historical Contributions in the Country's Political and Socio-economic Development," *Diplomatist Magazine, Special Report on Malawi*, 2019, 22–24. In 1971, Banda's government revised the 1965 [Property] Forfeiture Act and used it to impound property of foreign nationals at any slightest excuse. For a discussion of how British citizens suffered under that Act see cases in Forfeiture Act of Government of Malawi, 1971, TNA/FCO 45/1047; 1048. Chapter six reflects on how this political behavior influenced British decisions on aid towards Malawi. In general, Britain provided aid towards certain development projects as one way of protecting its citizens subjected to Banda's cruelty.

95. The leaked document is cited verbatim in a memo from N. W. Mbekeani (Malawi's UN Ambassador, New York) to J. Kachingwe (Acting Secretary for External Affairs, Lilongwe), February 7, 1969, MNA 11-11-5F/39566.

96. Ibid.

97. Reported in memo from K. J. Barnes (Secretary to the Treasury) to Kachingwe, May 26, 1969, MNA 11-11-5F/39566.

98. Kachingwe to Mbekeani, February 18, 1969, MNA 11-11-5F/39566. Because of the racial sensitivity of Banda's remark, the name of the Arab figure in question has been concealed.

99. John Burke Knapp to H. K. Banda, August 23, 1967, WBGA, File No. 1860298.

100. Banda to Knapp, September 27, 1967, WBGA, File No. 1860298.

101. Nevertheless, there were some exceptions. For example, at the insistence of McNamara who, unlike George Woods, enjoyed a relatively better relationship with Banda, the Bank provided US$5,250,000 in 1970 towards the Tedzani project. See MNA/1-8-9R/1784.

102. Morton, *Aid and Dependence,* 164–74; Peter T. Bauer, *Dissent on Development*; Bauer, *Development Aid.*

103. See his *International Aid and National Decisions: Development Programs in Malawi, Tanzania, and Zambia* (Princeton: Princeton University Press, 1976).

104. This reduction was part of an agreed schedule. Nevertheless, government officials often cited it as contributing to economic stress with 1968 registering the major deficit in the country's recurrent budget. See MNA 11-11-5F/39566.

105. See Simon Thomas, "Economic Developments in Malawi since Independence," *Journal of Southern African Studies* 2, no. 1 (1975): 41–42; Pryor, *The Political Economy of Poverty, Equity and Growth,* 81.

106. H. K. Banda speech, March 16, 1971, cited in Africa Publications Trust, *Malawi: Dialogue and Development*, 20.

107. Thomas, "Economic Developments in Malawi since Independence," 41–42; Martin Prowse, "A History of Tobacco Production and Marketing in Malawi, 1890–2010," *Journal of East African Studies* 7, no. 4 (2013), 10; Jonathan Kydd, "Malawi in the 1970s: Development Policies and Economic Change" in *Malawi: An Alternative Pattern of Development*, 295–380. ADMARC succeeded the FMB in 1971. On the specific figures regarding the exorbitant net profit the State Marketing Board (FMB, later ADMARC) earned by virtue of monopolizing the marketing of smallholder produce, see Thomas, "Economic Developments in Malawi since Independence," 41

108. Kydd, "Malawi in the 1970s," 295–380. In contrast to the projections under Table 4.1, Kydd argues that the smallholder sector headed towards real crisis in the 1980s. Having constrained the many ordinary farmers in favor of a the few state-sponsored elites, the country would not achieve economies of scale which often result from widening the production base.

109. See Mkandawire, et al., *Beyond "Dualism,"* 13.

110. Ayres, *Banking on the Poor,* 57.

111. H. K. Banda Address to the Malawi Parliament, March 11, 1975, H.K. Banda Archive, Indiana University Library, Box 2, Folder 4.

112. McNamara's address to the World Bank Board of Governors, Nairobi, Kenya, September 24, 1973.

113. See Kydd, "Malawi in the 1970s," 357–69.

114. Ibid.

115. Ayres, *Banking on the Poor*, 53.

116. Mark Duffield and Vernon Hewitt, "Introduction," in *Empire, Development and Colonialism: The Past in the Present*, eds. Mark Duffield and Vernon Hewitt (London: James Currey, 2013):12.

Chapter Five

Experts, Planners, and the Tampered Rural Development, 1960s–1981

Chapter Four introduced several integrated rural agricultural programs through which the Malawian state attempted to raise the living standards of the poor communities after independence in 1964. One of them was the Lilongwe Land Development Project (LLDP), which the World Bank funded and helped to manage between 1967 and 1981 through staff that was attached to the Agricultural Development Service (ADS) in Kenya. The ADS was formed in 1965 as a World Bank affiliate headquartered in Nairobi, Kenya. Specifically targeting the agricultural sector, it brought together experts that were qualified enough to provide technical and managerial assistance to most of the WB-funded projects in East and Southern Africa. Typically, the ADS-deployed technical staff, most of whom had gained experience through colonial service, were seconded to African governments while maintaining ties with ADS headquarters in Kenya. The staff in question interacted with other WB experts such as those from the Bank's Permanent Mission in Kenya and the Washington, DC, head office, all of which periodically reviewed rural development projects.[1]

In the case of Malawi, the top leadership of the LLDP was under the staff associated with the ADS. Its first manager, Peter Nottidge, was an ADS employee seconded to the Malawi government. The LLDP, which takes center-stage in this chapter, was an integrated project that evolved at the height of global concern for the poor noted in the first chapter. Its integrated nature was not in question. Though primarily targeting increased production of maize and groundnuts by providing credit and agricultural extension services, it also sought to provide clean water through boreholes; good health through rural health centers; and market and better feeder roads to facilitate produce marketing. Moreover, the state marketing board, ADMARC, constructed several market depots within the project area. Later, the project aimed at building institutional capacity by integrating local personnel in its WB-dominated management team. This rural intervention, therefore, presents an opportunity to understand how the discourse of poverty played out at a local setting from the 1960s onwards. Because of its integrated nature, the LLDP attracted special attention from the WB experts, who looked to it and others for lessons worth applying elsewhere. Having evolved between 1967 and 1981, the project's lifespan corresponded with McNamara's years at the WB. The ideas behind it, however, had a long history. Among others, both the WB and the state in Malawi earmarked it for purposes of piloting the 1967 land legislation which provided for private rights in land as a gateway to spurring agricultural productivity. These ideas, as noted in Chapter Two, were debated at length throughout the colonial period. When proposals towards land registration were made in the 1950s, they did not win the confidence of some segments of the African society. To what extent the new players realized the dream of their colonial predecessors is another aspect this chapter explores.

In general, by the time the scheme was wound up in 1981, it had failed to address poverty. Moreover, around the same time, there was a shift in development discourse; one that moved away from state-driven development towards faith in the power of unregulated markets and community-driven development projects.[2] Within this context, the LLDP presented readily available data for those scholars trained in neo-classical economics with their insatiable desire for unregulated markets. The WB consultants and economists such as B.H. Kinsey (Consultant), and Uma Lele (Chief Economist of Eastern and Southern African Division of the WB), benefitted from the evaluation data the project generated. Considering the LLDP as a knowledge laboratory, these economists were interested in understanding the relationship between commodity prices and the declining trends in the yields of groundnuts and maize in the project.[3] Concerned with matching objectives with outcomes, they argued that poor macro-economic policies such as low producer prices militated against the success of the project.[4] They criticized state marketing boards as a big part of the problem, functioning effectively as a tax on farmers, by keeping prices artificially low. In the 1980s, scholars in Malawi projected this thesis across the country, discussing it as part of the exploitation school focusing mainly on the market component.

In significant ways, this literature helps us to understand how poor market policies hamstrung rural agriculture and, with it, state efforts to alleviate poverty. This generalized rendering, however, closes opportunities for alternative explanations lying beyond state policies and market failures. Again, drawing mostly on the exploitation narrative, it shares similar weaknesses of reducing the state to a leviathan entity with little concern for the welfare of the people placed under its care. It also draws a sharp binary between the state and society, and forces one to analyze rural development through the eyes of the elites, the masters of the academic language of markets, or through the eyes of the "subaltern," who are depicted as autonomous and adversarial to the state. Though market policies matter, they rarely evolve outside the complexities of both the local and international context. As Hodge has observed elsewhere, "state projects are themselves responses to social, economic, and political crises" such that analyses that ignore the historical contexts in which such seemingly self-referential economic policies and their corresponding projects unfold are less helpful as a lens with which to dissect the histories of rural development.[5] In other words, it is difficult to present matters of economy as though they were a separate enclave set apart from matters political as economists such as Arthur Lewis at one point believed. While serving as an advisor to Kwame Nkrumah in Ghana, Lewis criticized his boss for using development projects to further some political ambitions.[6] This chapter uses the LLDP to shed light on these queries. The chapter historicizes the LLDP, fleshing out individual and group agency while emphasizing the wider social-political environment in which the project evolved. What emerges, therefore, is a history of development that emphasizes what Cullather describes as the "politics of memory" which helps us to retrospectively give meaning to development projects.[7] It is in telling the intricate history of the Lilongwe project that a fuller picture of the discourse on rural development in Malawi becomes clear. The analysis is framed around three thematic areas.[8]

The first theme reflects on how the WB experts interpreted the outcome of the LLDP. Although the market story was the most dominant one, other factors were also important, chief among them being the political nature of the project. For a state that boasted well-qualified and experienced staff, the dominance of the WB staff in the project's top management team contradicted the quest for national sovereignty. The LLDP, therefore, provided yet another space for the conflictual interactions between the state in Malawi and WB experts, results of which were discussed in the fourth chapter. The second theme analyzes the voices of the project's recipients and argues that experts were not the only ones that dictated the course of the LLDP, nor did they dominate the interpretation of its outcomes. Participating farmers helped to reshape project blueprints, forcing excerpts to respect local people's cultural interests in implementing it. Thus, interpreting LLDP's outcomes based solely on its original aims is an incomplete exercise. Again, contemporary memories of farmers who participated in the scheme contradict the story of failure prevalent in the official reports on the LLDP. Theirs is an alternative explanation that considers the scheme as having produced successful results in several areas. Such stories illustrate the capacity of local farmers to project certain claims to knowledge about the social engineering projects of the postcolonial period.[9] The final theme points towards rethinking the success story discussed under the second theme. Selected groups, notably women, remember the scheme for the negative cultural and social consequences it produced in the microcosm society under study. The chapter discusses these themes in this order, beginning with a brief history of the LLDP.

PLANNING THE LLDP, 1964–1969

The Lilongwe Land Development Project (LLDP) evolved in Central Malawi starting from 1967 and ran until 1981.[10] During its conception, the project fell within the "property rights discourse" and extended the debate on land that started during the late colonial period. As described in the second chapter, preparatory work for the project started as early as 1965 when the ODM proposed land titling reforms through the Hill report. At the time, Dr. Banda resisted such reforms. One reason for that resistance centered on the way proposals towards customary land registration were presented to Banda. They were a component of the Hill report which, as noted in Chapter Four, Banda rejected. Meanwhile, the British financed a small rural development project whose aim was to intensify agriculture among rural farmers in Southern Lilongwe.[11] Motivated by its successes, the government raised a proposal to extend the project to over 60,000 farmers cultivating 500,000 acres (202,300 hectares) in Lilongwe. The British white expatriate staff Banda had retained in his government after independence seized on this opportunity and convinced Banda of the need for land titling reforms then buried under the Hill report. Both the British and the WB were reluctant to support such a colossal project without appropriate structural changes in land ownership. The WB, for one, considered private property in land as a first step to improving agricultural productivity. Land certification would provide tenure security to farmers and hence motivate them to invest more in its productivity than was otherwise the case with communal land tenure system. It is within this context that Banda accepted the idea to have Simpson—previously a Land Advisor at the Colonial Office and then serving the ODM under the same post—work out a land legislation proposal. The choice of Simpson was deliberate. He had constantly advised the colonial state in its aborted land reform plans of the 1950s. Serving at the CO, he was also kept abreast with similar land titling reforms proposed and implemented in Kenya in the 1950s.

Both the Malawian government officials (including Banda) and the WB experts who insisted on land consolidation, were unaware of the exact work Simpson would undertake. In fact, when in 1966 Simpson presented what became the three sets of bills Banda would propose to the Parliament the following year, Robert J. Dewar (a senior member in the Ministry of Natural

Resources and another white expatriate staff) thanked him accordingly: "when you [Simpson] arrived, we had only vague ideas of what we wanted and yet by the time you left we had volumes of legislation."[12] Simpson should not have accepted such praise because, as outlined earlier in Chapter Two, his exceptional but attractive proposed land legislation was an outcome of a long history of colonial debates on land. Simpson learned the lessons from previous experience and with much ease produced the three sets of legislation that was passed in the Malawi Parliament in 1967. With the 1967 Customary Land Legislation in place, the state in Malawi aligned itself with Western strategies of development and attracted the praise of the WB and other donor agencies that financed the LLDP.[13]

Once this legal framework was set out, the government, through technical support from the WB's ADS and FAO experts, reworked the proposal on a thirteen-year agricultural scheme. Divided in four phases, it was designed to intensify maize and groundnuts production in the same land unit of 500,000 acres in the Lilongwe District of the Central region of Malawi (See Map 5.1). The new proposal targeted a similar number of farming families—60,000. The plan also included consolidating land and granting individual or family land titles to farmers.[14] The phased nature of the project reflected the degree to which external experts influenced its conceptualization. As Kinsey has observed elsewhere, it represented modernization thinking with W.W. Rostow's "take-off" stage playing out at the local level.[15] The initial years would concentrate inputs and technical support crucial to sustaining a "take-off into sustained growth."[16] While providing the country with an exportable annual surplus of £2.3 million, so experts envisaged, the project would raise net family income by 60 percent. The overall net annual income the project would contribute to the nation was pegged at £1.3 million.[17]

In 1967, the government submitted the proposal to IDA for funding, with an estimated budget of US$21.2 million, which constituted 37 percent of the US$58 million budget the WB committed towards Integrated Rural Development projects in the country.[18] Subsequent negotiations on credit took place the same year. The Minister of Finance, John Tembo, led the Malawi negotiation team which included Messrs. J. K. Barnes (Secretary to the Treasury), R. J. Dewar (Secretary of the newly created Ministry of Economic Affairs), R. Katengeza (General Manager of the Farmers Marketing Board, which changed to ADMARC after negotiations), and Peter C. R. Nottidge (Chief Agricultural Development Officer).[19] Other than Messrs. Tembo, Katengeza, and Nottidge, the rest were British white expatriates Dr. Banda retained in his government in keeping with his policy on slow Africanization of the civil service. As noted, Nottidge was an ADS employee who had previously worked for the colonial state in Kenya but seconded to the Malawi government to manage the LLDP.[20]

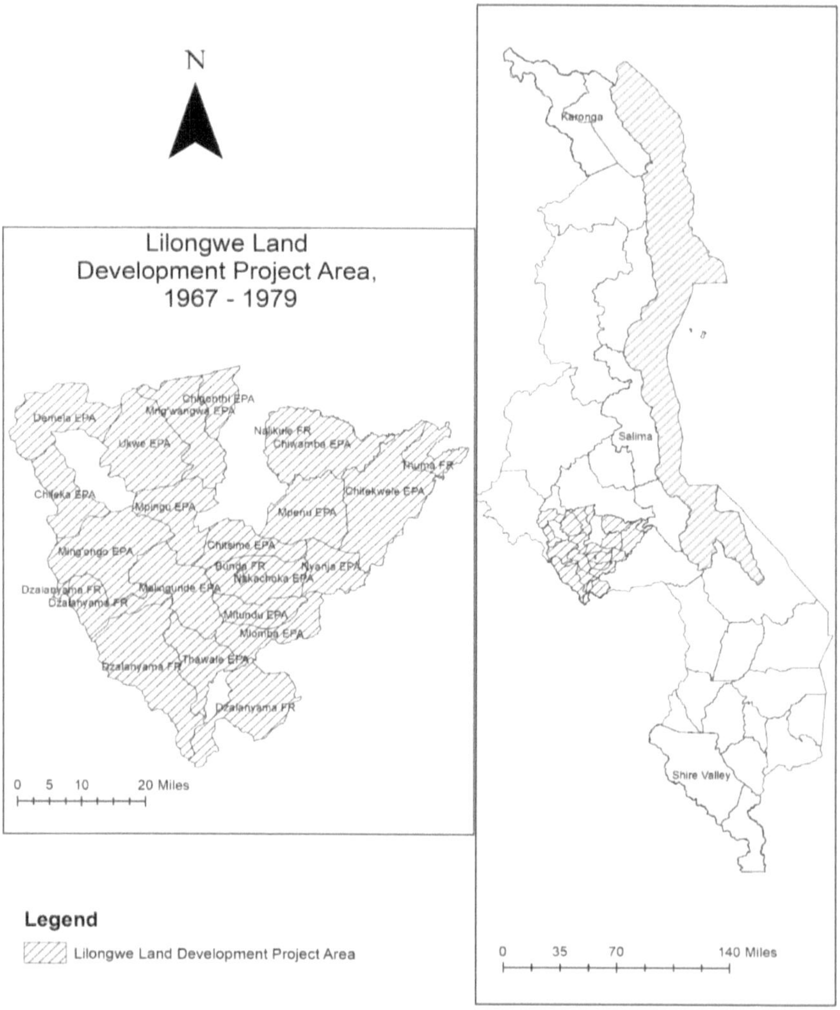

Map. 5.1. Rural development projects in Malawi, 1967–1979
Source: Drawn by Dr. Park Muhonda, Oregon State University.

The IDA approved the project in January 1968 and committed to providing US$6 million for the first four-year phase (1968/–1971/72). Subsequent funding would be released upon satisfactory performance of the preceding phases, in which case, Malawi would raise fresh proposals. Under the second and third phases (1972–1974/5 and 1975–1978/79), IDA provided, respectively, US$7.25 and US$8.5 million. The last phase (1979/1980–1985) aimed at consolidating the gains of the project.[21] In keeping with the loan agreement, the government would repay the borrowed funds in semi-annual installments (with ten years of grace) beginning on April 1, 1978, to October 1, 2017.

Apart from IDA, the United Nations Capital Development Fund (UNCDF) also provided a grant of US$1.6 million to support the health component of the third phase. With time, what started as a small project expanded greatly, with 103,600 farm families under its support cultivating about 1,200,000 acres (485,623 hectares) of land.[22] Although holding much promise, it became clear with time that the project would do little to transform the living standards of the rural communities as earlier envisaged. Instead, evaluation reports on its outcomes created anxiety among WB experts.

THE CONTESTED OUTCOMES OF THE LLDP, 1970S–1981

Between 1973 and 1975, the WB undertook two independent evaluation studies on the LLDP. The first was the routine Project Performance and Audit Study (PPAS) whose aim was to evaluate the successes, challenges, and other related aspects of a particular phase of the Lilongwe project. In this case, this study aimed at determining the extent to which the second phase of the LLDP had performed. It was the Bank's staff particularly those attached to the Bank's regional development service, the ADS, and the Bank's Permanent Mission in Nairobi, who periodically carried out these studies. The second study is simply referenced in the Bank documents as the "rural development research project" of the ADS or simply the "research project." For convenience purposes, I will reference it as the "ADS research study." The ADS research study, which was carried out by B.H. Kinsey, the consultant, was part of the WB's ongoing research on rural development projects that directly targeted the local people. It aimed at soliciting data from the LLDP whose status as an integrated project had gone well ahead of the WB's new direction in rural development. In 1975, for example, the WB's "Rural Development Policy Paper" popularized the LLDP as an early prototype, describing it as falling under "comprehensive crop and integrated farming systems together with Comilla in Bangladesh and Caqueta in Colombia."[23] The LLDP, therefore, presented the WB with an opportunity to draw some lessons worth applying elsewhere. Kinsey relied on the data which the local evaluation unit of the LLDP had compiled over time. Reports from both studies were submitted by 1975 and, disappointingly, projected a bleak future for the LLDP. Yields for both maize and groundnuts, as figure 5.1 shows, were far below the projected outputs despite periodic oscillations with each successive growing season.

Although the data in figure 5.1 only includes the produce channeled through official ADMARC markets, there was a considerable discrepancy between projected and actual figures for both maize and groundnuts. The 1972/73 figures could be outliers because of erratic rains in those years.

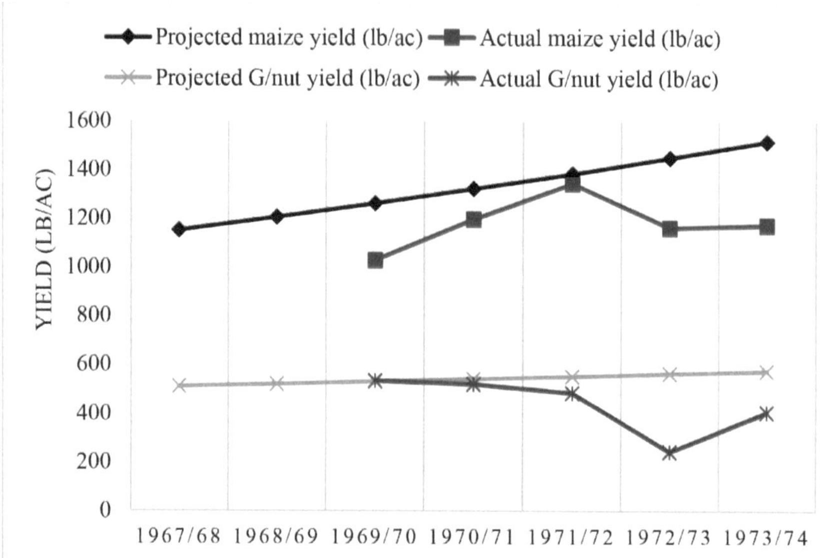

Fig. 5.1. Projected and actual yields for maize and groundnuts, 1967–1974
Source: World Bank, Project Performance Audit Report on the Lilongwe Land Development Program 1975, WBA, Credit 113-MIA.

However, much clearer are the low production figures even in the normal years. Elsewhere, scholars have discussed at length the probable causes of such an outcome.[24] The most popular explanation borrows from Robert Bates' rational choice thesis. It cites "bad" state pricing policies and poor leadership of the country as the major causes of the project's failure. With Erik Green's work being the only exception for attributing poor yields to the problem of labor, scholars typically argue that the state deliberately kept the price of maize and groundnuts low, thereby inadvertently forcing farmers to concentrate on tobacco production where prices were better.[25] The argument is similar to that of "urban-bias" which Michael Lipton has popularized—the whole idea that African states have used marketing boards to siphon off resources from the rural sector to be used in secondary industries and to keep prices of food low for urban consumers.[26] Statistics on the price ADMARC set for tobacco grown by African farmers in the 1970s, just like that of groundnuts, have been hard to find. Available figures are those compiled in the 1980s such that we can only use them with caution. Nevertheless, save for annual increases, it is doubtful that the 1980s price deviation displayed below under Table 5.1 represented any real break from the 1970s trend.

Because the price of maize and groundnuts compared unfavorably to that of tobacco at ADMARC markets, this kind of pricing policy received condemnation from the WB officials and consultants, who saw it as forcing farmers within

Table 5.1: Real ADMARC Producer Prices in the 1980s (tambala/kg)

Year	*Maize*	*Groundnuts*	*Tobacco*	*Beans*
1980/1	5.98	29.92	41.70	12.69
1984/5	7.02	40.27	58.70	23.01
1987/8	4.82	29.66	41.80	17.40

Source: Adapted from World Bank, Malawi Agricultural Sector Memorandum: Strategy Options in the 1990s, Report No. 12805-MAI, March 8, 1995, 35.

the LLDP to shift their attention towards Burley tobacco production, the crop which farmers were forbidden to grow under the terms of the Lilongwe project.[27] In keeping with the policy of encouraging production of food crops both for consumption and sale, planners, both the WB experts and those employed by the Malawian state, designed the project to discourage tobacco production. The idea was to protect farmers from overdependence on tobacco and hence reduce the risk of famine. Contrary to planners' expectations, farmers appear to have depended more on tobacco than maize because the former enjoyed better prices on the market. The price distortion thesis, as detailed above, dictated much of the debate at the WB as experts sought to make sense of the results. It should not have been the only one, however. Inappropriate technology copied from Kenya was also a big part of the problem for it caused harm to the otherwise delicate soils of the area. To contain soil erosion, experts recommended using bulldozers. But the strategy also helped to wash away the fertile soils in the consolidated plots. Again, a futile land consolidation and registration exercise did little to serve the otherwise precious resources.[28] As will become clear later in this discussion, out of the 500,000 acres initially earmarked for registration, only 13,000 acres were registered.

The story of markets, therefore, should be considered as an incomplete explanation that represented the experts' failure to provide a comprehensive analysis of the project's outcomes. The project evaluation reports generated a heated debate among WB bureaucrats and consultants as they sought to make sense of the declining production trends. Of significance here is how the debate reveals anxieties among people who had confidence in McNamara's pro-poor integrated rural development approach. If the Bank was searching for success stories to further consolidate the turn to integrated rural development, the reports on Malawi discredited the LLDP. As the reports revealed the disappointing results of the project, hopes of using Lilongwe as a reference point collapsed. Not willing to accept such negative outcomes, officials at the Bank contested the reports, and often blamed consultants and local players for the setbacks.

In June 1975, for example, the Bank's Regional Office for East Africa deployed Dennis Anderson (a member of the Development Economics Department) on a technical assistance mission to Lilongwe. Anderson, a

British national who joined the Bank in 1969 as a Senior Economist, was tasked to discuss with LLDP management the problem of monitoring and evaluation of the program, focusing primarily on providing further clarification on the declining maize and groundnuts yields.[29] Upon receipt of Anderson's report, Leif E. Christofferson (Assistant Director of Agriculture and Rural Development) wrote Montague Yudelman, his senior, stating that:

> It can now be seen where previous reports went wrong was that (a) they did not examine the yield data closely enough to allow for disease, rats, [and] prices; (b) most of the sampling information came from outside the development areas of the program; (c) they ignored the evidence on the very substantial response of the farmers to the program as reflected in greatly improved husbandry.[30]

His concluding remarks should have been comforting to Yudelman: "For these reasons, previous studies have presented an incomplete and rather biased picture; the program's impact has been much better than they have reported. I suggest that we recommend this paper [Anderson's report] for distribution to the Executive Directors [of the WB]."[31]

There is little evidence to suggest that the new findings shifted the WB's thinking over the outcomes of the project. When Anderson's report reached Benjamin King, who was then the Director of the Development Economics Department (East Africa Division), the latter was less than convinced and was frustrated by the entire exchange. He was equally worried about the disagreements and controversies the project reports generated. King suggested a fresh, substantive inquiry on the LLDP.[32] That inquiry never materialized. Instead, B.H. Kinsey, the consultant behind the "ADS research study" introduced earlier, was tasked later in 1980 to revise his work. He would be supported by R.A. Read, who had once headed the local evaluation unit of the LLDP in Malawi before his resignation from the WB in 1974.

Meanwhile, seeking to use the existing data for his publications, Kinsey was eager to see the 1975 report approved and questioned the idea of revising the report. Affirming confidence in it, he did not hide his anxiety from J. Uma Lele, who had previously supervised the ADS research study before becoming the Bank's Deputy Chief of the Agriculture Projects Division in East Africa. Kinsey wrote:

> I understand that the [ADS Research Study] report is still considered controversial and that this is probably the reason for its limited circulation. . . . I do feel that there are considerable issues of wider interest in the report and that these should not be suppressed because certain individuals may feel protective towards LLDP. [Moreover, a] full account was taken of all comments received before the report was revised.[33]

Despite Kinsey's insistence to have his report released, the WB never published it, obviously because it discredited the LLDP.

When Kinsey submitted a fresh report on January 30, 1981, a committee the WB set up to evaluate the work trashed it and argued that "the dissemination of this report leaves much to be desired."[34] If some members doubted the competencies of Kinsey, an argument difficult to sustain given his sound academic record and experiences, others questioned its conclusions.[35] The latter blamed LLDP Evaluation Unit in Lilongwe for poorly collecting data on the project. The impasse was resolved, but in ways that shifted the blame towards the WB officials seconded to Malawi and who were managing the LLDP. Anticipating such a resolution, both Andrew Mercer, a staff member of the Bank's ADS but seconded to Malawi to manage the LLDP, and Read, who resigned later, challenged the WB experts' insistence that Lilongwe data was disorganized. When the Bank experts raised the issue during the proposal development stage, they responded that the Lilongwe data was specific to the LLDP and could, therefore, not be used in meeting the broader WB objectives. They argued that such criticisms were insensitive to the best effort the local team made to collect that data amidst intense challenges. Mercer and his colleague cited inadequate funding, local political pressure, and the attitude of individual evaluators and others, as ranking among such problems.

Relating to the latter points, Mercer quizzed his colleagues: "Whose position becomes most relevant or valid [in evaluation]? That of implementing field officers, the project management, the national government, the donor agency or the academics?"[36] Even though the management of the LLDP, the WB and academics considered anthropological and sociological data important, he argued, it was "hardly relevant [to] field officers and regional interests, and study of them was strictly forbidden by presidential edict." For Mercer, a straight-jacket implementation and/or evaluation strategy was irrelevant. Instead, he preferred a more flexible approach. "It might even be necessary," he concluded, "to introduce new short-term objectives and drop others."[37] Such an exchange speaks to the very debate about expertise, what Donna Mehos and Suzanne Moon have described as claims to expertise based on place-based knowledge and experience on the one hand, and claims to expertise based on training and theory, leading to the acquisition of technical knowledge that is supposedly universal and portable, on the other.[38]

By virtue of their previous experience, many British ex-colonial officials who later served the WB in different positions possessed place-based knowledge. The WB staff seconded to the Malawi government to manage the LLDP were no exception. This staff, however, constantly liaised with colleagues either in East Africa or Washington, DC, offices of the Bank, many of whom acquired their expertise through university training. In general, experts with portable knowledge looked down upon their colleagues as possessing little training to do the right job, the case in point being that of disorganized data of the LLDP. On their part, officers working on the ground often ridiculed their colleagues in the research department, describing them as "misplaced academics who never built a dam or laid a road," with much of their work appealing more to the academy than the local players.[39] WB experts were not a monolithic group nor were their interests and ambitions always the same. But Mercer's complaint also speaks to the multiple pressures the WB staff had to face on the ground. Operating separately from the WB bureaucracy yet maintaining ties with it presented its own challenges.

The 1975 reports were not the only ones generating divergences among different interest groups. Equally contentious was the phase III Project Performance and Audit Report (PPAR) which came out in 1981. Unlike the previous reports, David Brown, a member of the World Bank's Economic Development Institute (EDI) who carried out the study, presented the physical project as "unquestionably a success and worth replicating elsewhere."[40] Among others, the "physical project" of the LLDP constituted aspects such as the construction of agricultural infrastructure (storage facilities, office space, and staff houses), land reorganization, provision of extension services, credit, and health facilities in project areas. Brown's report argued that the LLDP had succeeded in providing services in a number of these items. Nevertheless, he pointed out some glaring issues to the "development project" which, for most WB officials, contradicted the success story.[41] Among others, this project of the LLDP had to do with building local institutional capacity for future conception and implementation of similar projects.

Brown argued that the project had failed to build institutional capacity in the country, a significant addendum to the program's objectives under phase III. His report showed that the LLDP was not fully integrated within the country's Ministry of Agriculture and Natural Resources. Again, Brown criticized the WB for running a semi-autonomous administrative structure in the country, a scenario that helped to perpetuate the country's dependence on foreign experts. The program had, therefore, failed to create an internally generated, self-sustained development process.[42] Similarly problematic, the report pointed out, were the ADS-supervision missions the WB deployed from time to time. It regarded single-man missions to Lilongwe as inappropriate. Other than the short time provided to examine the projects, the report argued that such missions lacked adequate skills to supervise the multidisciplinary LLDP.[43] Confirming the earlier reports, however, Brown acknowledged a declining trend in maize and groundnuts production but attributed this to poor producer prices that ADMARC fixed on farmers' crops.

Such criticisms did not escape the attention of Malawi government officials in Lilongwe and the WB headquarters, with each taking turns to condemn the report. Malawi took issue with Brown's insistence that the country lacked qualified personnel to plan and supervise similar development projects. R.S.A. Moyo's memorandum is illustrative: "We do not agree with the view that Malawi is still dependent on outside technical assistance for conceptual work."[44] Moyo's concerns came after Brown's report had already circulated among the Executive Directors of the WB. However, he insisted that authorities present Malawi's response as an addendum while withdrawing erroneous statements. The final report reflects such amendments.

Officials at the WB wondered why Brown described the project as successful considering the many shortfalls he had highlighted. In his cable to Robert J. Dewar (then Chief of Agriculture Division, Eastern Africa office of the World Bank), Jan Wijnand, his deputy, questioned the report's claims about the success of the LLDP.[45] In fact, Wijnand noted, "the reader is left with the impression that this success is marred by very serious shortcomings and failures which reduce its significance."[46] He further noted that the report's tone was surprising given the overwhelming evidence in circulation that the WB had underestimated the implementation difficulties of such projects. Wijnand downplayed the potential of a four-year project to eliminate the country's institutional weaknesses. Moreover, the problem was not just unique to Malawi and, together with poor pricing policies, "was the root of underdevelopment in Africa." Wijnand's conclusion contrasted sharply with Mercer's concerns over the rigidity of evaluation teams:

> We do not see how supervision mission can be blamed for putting excessive emphasis on quantitative targets in the appraisal report since it is one of their duties to review progress by comparison with such targets. . . . Moreover, LLDP was under attack in headquarters throughout most of this period precisely for the poor quality of its technical monitoring data.[47]

In this way, Wijnand shifted the blame away from the top WB officials to the local players in Malawi, including its overall economic policy environment. If the regional office remained defensive in its tone, the top leadership of the WB was not. It welcomed the report, arguing that it raised design and policy issues that the WB and the country needed to address through a more detailed analysis.[48]

Other than its incriminating nature, Brown's report, unlike the previous two reports, had room for "successes" which officials at the WB should have celebrated.[49] It is not clear why officials emphasized the negative side of Brown's report more than the positive side. Perhaps answers could be located in the changes taking place at the Bank in the 1980s, which might have forced WB experts to read the report selectively. In other words, we cannot appreciate official reaction to Brown's report through events on the ground (the periphery) alone. The wider changes taking place at the Bank (the center) and beyond must be considered as well.[50] With the departure of McNamara in June 1981 and the subsequent appointment of A.W. Clausen as the WB president, there was a shift in the strategies of development at the Bank. Unlike McNamara whose pro-poor development strategy minimally departed from Britain's colonial welfare development, Clausen struggled to balance the two roles of the Bank. On the one hand was the WB's role as a commercial entity concerned with investments that generated a 10 percent minimum rate of return and, on the other, a Bank concerned with McNamara's rural development drive whose activities—mostly targeting social goals of income distribution, provision of basic needs and social services—could hardly be said to have been economically rewarding to economists at the Bank who were trained to interpret projects in terms a positive rate of economic return.[51]

Such a dilemma coincided with the overall shift in the international discourse of development, itself precipitated by the 1973 Oil Shock and the rising debt that LDCs accumulated thereafter. With the worsening economic situation of the late 1970s, African finance ministers requested the WB to investigate the bottlenecks to development in Sub-Saharan Africa. In response, Ernest Stern, the WB's Vice President of operations, commissioned Elliot Berg to undertake the investigation. The Michigan economics professor produced a report in 1981, titled *Accelerated Development in Sub-Saharan Africa*, which criticized state-led development.[52] Influenced by neo-classical economic theories, Berg questioned such things as state control over commodity prices and wasteful statutory corporations. State Marketing Boards such as ADMARC received stern condemnation from Berg's report for their monopoly over the marketing of peasant products. The antidote to these changes, the neoliberal policy reforms which brought with them Structural Adjustment Programs, were an antithesis to McNamara's pro-poor development approach which had confidence in state institutions and personnel as development actors.[53] Within this changing economic climate, officials at the WB were free to criticize rural development projects in ways not possible during McNamara's era. It is, therefore, less surprising that the LLDP "success story" presented under Brown's report never won the support of some Bank officials. Instead, experts celebrated failures in ways that reified market liberalism which the report emphasized. It is tempting to argue that it is this selective reading of the LLDP that helped to magnify its shortcomings while downplaying its successes. In this way, the Lilongwe data directly fed into the broader concerns cited above and provided experts with readily available evidence to support neoliberal policies.

Undoubtedly, the government's pricing policy influenced the project outcomes. However, such policies had a political context worth acknowledging. The previous chapter showed how the Malawian state's bias towards the estate sector in the 1970s was an outcome of certain historical forces, at the center of which was the state's quest to balance the objectives of political and economic sovereignty. Placed within this framework, it becomes less surprising that the state pursued policies that contradicted goals of rural development despite expressing faith in it. The LLDP became a mechanism by which the WB undermined the country's political autonomy. As highlighted, the project had a long history that predated the WB's intervention. In its original conceptualization, the state designed the project to operate under the Agricultural Development Branch within the Department of Agriculture, with the Program Manager responsible to the former. Over time, however, and as Brown's report rightly highlighted, the project operated semi-autonomously with the ADS appointing the Program Manager and other officials. As noted earlier, its first manager, Peter Nottidge, was a WB employee under the ADS but seconded to the Malawi government to manage the LLDP. Even though it was the Malawi government that paid salaries for such staff as Nottidge, these officials reported to both the ADS and the Malawi government. Through this arrangement of lending out its personnel, the Bank was able to track the project's progress. But it also ensured that Malawi benefited from the best expertise from the Bank. For Malawi, however, the arrangement represented a compromise and one that came after protracted negotiations.

As early as 1964, Malawi claimed it had its own well-qualified experts to run rural development projects. Most of these, whose role was discussed in the previous chapter, had previously worked for the colonial government and had been retained after independence under Dr. Banda's policy of gradual Africanization of the civil service. Save for Nottidge (Chief Agricultural Development Officer at the time, and first manager of the LLDP), the loan negotiation team that accompanied Tembo to Washington was a clear show of that expertise. Proud of this team, Dr. Banda resisted WB attempts to impose its personnel on his government and selectively accepted only those who had sound colonial experience in the region.[54]

After independence in July 1964, the WB had, through its country missions to Malawi, periodically sought to impress on Dr. Banda the need to rely on technical experts from the WB, a suggestion that never won his attention. In December 1964, Pierre L. Moussa, the Director of the WB's Department of Operations in Africa, sought to use Dr. Banda's December 10 visit to Washington as a forum to raise such matters. In his note to Burke J. Knapp, the Vice President of IBDR/IDA, Moussa anticipated Banda's silence on such an emotive issue. "If Dr. Banda does not raise the option of technical assistance, I suggest that we might be guided by the general tenor of the discussions for raising this question ourselves," he advised.[55] Moussa was right. It was Knapp who raised it only to get a disappointing response. Banda argued he was not against the WB sending him experts. However, he wanted experts who would approach development issues from a practical angle, arguing that his (Banda's) experience with theoretical economists had been unsatisfactory. "An experience, say, in Latin America or India," Banda argued, "might not necessarily qualify an economist for good service in Malawi where conditions and economic problems are different. If the WB has a practical economist, I would not object to his assignment to Malawi."[56] In essence, Banda took a side in the debate about the two models of expertise, shunning university-trained experts with portable knowledge in favor of those with place-based expertise. For Banda, Malawi needed the latter and not the former. Even with that, those who had previously served in British Africa were desirable.

When Knapp briefed Moussa about Banda's response, the latter suggested closing the chapter until a time when Malawi would make a special request on the same. That moment came when no proposal on rural development would win the confidence of the technical departments of the ODM, WB, FAO, and the UNDP without the input of Western experts. With the LLDP, technical experts helped not only to fine-tune the proposal but also run the project, with most of its top managerial positions held by ADS deployed staff. If considered within the context of the politics of the 1960s and 1970s, as detailed in the previous chapter, it becomes necessary to move beyond the "story of prices" in analyzing the outcomes of the LLDP. Political considerations are as significant as economic matters in guiding our understanding of the project's outcomes.

On several occasions, for instance, the WB tried to convince the Malawi government to raise the price of maize, groundnuts, and other peasant commodities. Such calls proved unsuccessful.[57] The demands were not necessarily in the best interest of the country, which sought to wean itself from the paternalism of Western financiers, despite some selected government officials subscribing to the WB's concerns.[58] If understood within the politics of the 1970s, raising the price of subsistence crops in the country would have without doubt reduced the outflow of local labor towards estate agriculture where better tobacco leaf was produced. More significantly, it was important that many peasants grow food crops as the estate sector was redirected towards tobacco production necessary to generate foreign exchange with which to address problems of balance of payment deficits in the country and achieve real economic sovereignty. It is within this context that Jonathan Kydd's observation on Banda's position holds true—"you [Western aid agencies] pursue your objectives and we'll pursue ours."[59]

The interaction between pricing stories and politics helps one to understand the project outcomes. An exclusive focus on these two aspects, however, might mislead us into viewing the LLDP only through the eyes of the elites, hence silencing the voice of the project's beneficiaries. I argue that to the extent that diverse interpretations exist on the LLDP's outcomes and failures, it is equally significant to analyze the "view from below," the very voice of the project participants, and the role they played in the evolution of the Scheme. Theirs is a story that does not lend itself to the above description. On the contrary, it presents an alternative interpretation of the project's outcomes.

LOCAL VOICES AND THE TAMPERED LLDP

Like experts, local farmers actively participated in the conceptualization, implementation, and evaluation of the LLDP such that a focus on their voices provides a vantage point from which to understand the project through the eyes of its beneficiaries. Three explanations clarify their participation in the project. The first centers on how the local participants altered experts' master plans, effectively making the project conform to their traditions. The second reflects on how the project beneficiaries remember the LLDP. Theirs is a story of success that contradicts a rather gloomy picture noted in the project evaluation reports. Finally, the section pays attention to women, whose reminiscence of the project displays its adverse cultural and social effects, the success story notwithstanding. By focusing on these three aspects, this section puts on display how Africans, often considered as marginal and powerless recipients in stories of rural development, projected their voice, and made certain claims to knowledge in ways that contradict Scott's concept of "State High Modernism" introduced in the introductory chapter of the book. Scott's notion reduces rural development projects' beneficiaries into helpless victims of the modernizers' machinations.[60]

Three sets of land legislation that were passed in Malawi Parliament in 1967 provide context to the first point. As noted earlier, the Customary Land Act sought to provide for individual land ownership in the project in line with the interests of WB and British experts. When in 1967 the Malawi government submitted a proposal to IDA for funding, it emphasized the land consolidation and registration aspects of the project. It also impressed upon the would-be financiers the need to provide funding for land registration and certification, an aspect which the 1967 Registered Land Act emphasized. Successful implementation of these reforms in Lilongwe would provide data on how to roll out land registration across the country.[61] Also provided in the law was registration of family land under family heads or representatives, particularly for land that could not be easily sub-divided. The interpretation of family units remained ambiguous, and officials struggled to understand how such leases could facilitate land markets.[62]

If the land legislation aimed at creating individual or family titles, evidence does not point to this direction. Instead, it was the male lineage heads (*Mwini Mbumba*) that were title holders in a few areas where land certification took place. In the Chewa custom of Central Malawi, these were the heads of the entire matrilineage of multiple households and not a single family as understood in the land legislation.[63] Andrew Mercer, the Program Manager, admitted this anomaly and isolated village land committees as having persuaded management to reconsider plans on individual land registration because they "would not fit at this stage [and conflict] with the people's cultural structure." The land committees, which Mercer saw as constituting a "good sounding board in formulating policy," proposed registering land under *Mwini Mbumba* and helped to stave off "what could have been a serious mistake."[64] A careful analysis of oral sources, however, shows that land registration was made under *Mwini Mudzi* (a traditional leader or chief) and not Mwini Mbumba as Mercer held it. One reason for this confusion relates to the fact that many of the Mwini Mbumbas were also chiefs.[65]

Just like Sara Berry has described at length elsewhere, the proposed changes in land brought about competing claims to chieftainship. Evidence suggests that Lilongwe District administrators periodically resolved boundary disputes among chiefs who considered a title deed a necessary document with which to secure their rights over village land.[66] Interestingly, villagers considered a chiefly title as *Ndunda*, which in Chewa lexicon, simply means village land under chiefly custodianship with several households cultivating it. Within the context of the LLDP, local memories of Ndunda resonate with chiefly titles which the project brought about. Ndunda, which should be appropriately defined as customary estate, was further sub-divided into smaller units placed under lineage heads.[67] Farmers respected these chiefly titles because, in their opinion, they insured villagers against landlessness coming in the wake of population pressure. For the project beneficiaries, besides asserting the authority of their chiefs, such titles were flexible and land under it could easily be sub-divided to accommodate all members of the village than otherwise would be the case under individual titles.[68]

If advocates of property rights saw economic advantages in individual land titles, villagers considered them a threat to their economic and cultural life. Like chiefs who served in the local land committees, they too defended the status quo, a scenario similar to what Derek Peterson has described as "ethnic patriotism" among the Luo peoples of Kenya.[69] There, the Luo rejected the excesses of Christian revivalists whose condemnation of African customs threatened the very survival of the Luo tradition. What emerged, instead, was a sense of ethnic patriotism in which the Luo revived their old customs and practices, further projecting themselves as a distinct interest group in Kenyan politics. Such patriotism helped them to object to the attempts the state made to consolidate Luo land in Nyanza in the 1950s. The Luo, including those who lived in urban areas, argued that such an exercise did not conform to their historical traditions of land ownership.

Given that chiefly titles are synonymous to communal or corporate titles, the Lilongwe intervention did not mark a significant break with the past. Corporate titles have more recently attracted the interest of the donor community, for their capacity to caution the landless. At that time, however, the idea represented a departure from official thinking regarding how land registration would proceed in the area. Moreover, because land was not registered under individuals or families, *Mkamwini* (husbands who married into the project area) lost their land upon the death of their wives. As one member of the community acknowledged: "It was not traditionally possible for Mkamwini to be given [sub-] Ndunda. Under this program [LLDP], Ndunda was given through his wife. Mkamwini has no rights to land here. The program respected that."[70] It was this bias against such men that the 1967 legislation sought to check as the tradition stood counter to the principles of security of land. Husbands, for example, would not adequately invest in land productivity without the assurance of tenure security. These shortfalls notwithstanding, for WB officials such as Andrew Mercer, the arrangement represented a necessary compromise. Winning the confidence of the people who were not interested in individual land registration was crucial to the success of the project.[71]

Mercer had a point. In fact, the decision to register land in the manner they did was made much earlier when Nottidge managed the scheme before he left for Kenya late in 1969 to replace Alexander Storrar as head of the ADS. No account captures Nottidge's frustration with the LLDP better than the one D. E. Warren of the Directorate of Overseas Surveys in Britain presented when he toured Lilongwe on an ODM's technical assistance mission in 1968:

> Nottidge says they all have a completely open mind on the way [land registration] will be tackled. I think this is a euphemism for saying they don't really know. At present they say they intend to register in family units. Four or five family units to a village and ten or so villages to a chief. The villages which are the responsibility of the chiefs will be a registration unit. Each village will be about 300 acres.[72]

A 1969 ODM confidential report which Messrs. I. E., Morgan (a British land expert) and J. T. Fleming (a British land tenure specialist seconded to the Kenyan government) prepared clarifies this dilemma. It also explains Nottidge's anxiety about how land registration would proceed despite having a clearly laid out procedure under the 1967 Customary Land Act.[73] "Public demand for individual tenure," the report argued,

> arises from several factors among which are extreme pressure on land, the inadequacy of existing forms of tenure, expensive land litigation and the breakdown of traditional forms of tenure brought about by these circumstances. At

the moment, there is little evidence of these factors in Malawi. . . . We were unable to find any evidence of public demand for individual tenure such as existed in Kenya. . . . Another indication that customary forms of tenure are still adequate for the immediate needs of the rural population is that although there are frequent land suits principally over the boundaries of family units, these disputes are settled by *Amweni Dziko* [*Eni Dziko,* chiefs]. . . . Furthermore, because the normal factors which give rise to a demand for individual tenure are absent, there is, understandably, a marked degree of ignorance as to its purpose and effect.[74]

The Morgan and Fleming report, moreover, predicted frustration among traditional leaders if the project disregarded their concerns. In essence, the report suggested a scenario synonymous to the colonial Indirect Rule. Seeking not to antagonize the traditional leaders, whose support was needed for a successful land reform program, the experts tolerated the interests of chiefs as they did in the colonial past.

On their part, chiefs took advantage of the lack of demand for land titling reforms among the populace to tamper with project blueprints. Together with the other members of the land allocation committees, they projected a narrative that depicted land individualization as a practice that conflicted with their traditions. In this way, they joined educated Africans of the late colonial period to immobilize custom, all the while essentializing it to defend their unique interests. In keeping with what others have argued elsewhere, chiefs harvested custom as a precious resource, and threw it back on the experts to preserve their authority.[75] What this discussion also illustrates is that communities attach diverse meanings to land beyond what advocates of the property rights school advocate. Land is a site for power, belonging, and identity such that acknowledging these diverse interests is a first step towards achieving a workable reform strategy.

The case of the LLDP, therefore, speaks to the very dichotomy of preservative and transformative trusteeship and the difficulties of breaking it. During the colonial era, members of the Fabian Society at the metropole believed in the former, with support from the colonial administrators in Nyasaland who saw preservative colonialism serving their political interests better. Seeking to protect Africans from capitalist exploitation, they found answers in preserving what they saw as African custom. To obstruct the land reform proposals of late colonialism, African elites challenged that argument using a similar language of a preservative trusteeship. Freed from the political excesses of the colonial era, both the WB and the ODM pursued transformative trusteeship. While defending the interests of ordinary Africans, they also believed in transforming "traditional societies," reforming them in ways that would make them receptive to institutions which they believed promoted economic progress. Following resistance from the local people, the new trustees, like their colonial predecessors, inadvertently preserved "custom."

Although it became clear that the modernization drive had taken a different course from what was previously planned, experts retained their confidence and were convinced that with time, "family units in the present schemes will break up into individual holdings much sooner than is anticipated."[76] Whether by design or default, the LLDP represented a classic case of a watered-down vision of modernization which emphasized integrating local communities as active actors in development projects.[77] By 1981, the country had abandoned the reforms, effectively shuttering plans to create registered titles in Malawi's customary land.

WB officials on the ground were not the only ones to align project goals with local interests, however. A move away from individual or family tenure also fit well with aspirations of the country's political leadership. Banda's 1967 parliamentary speech on the land legislation was unequivocal about the challenges African tenure system presented. But it was also ambiguous. "Even though [the] government has decided to permit individual land ownership in the country," he stated, "[the] government will not impose ownership of land on everyone all over the country. No! But [it] will have the power to create opportunities for those who want to own land, either as an individual or as head of the family."[78] It is easy to explain why Banda took a less radical position on matters of land. Like the WB officials on the ground, he too believed in a gradual process of change and one that would not drastically upset the country's traditions. Unlike the WB officials who concerned themselves with winning local support towards the project, Banda's self-acclaimed title of "guardian of Malawian tradition"—*Nkhoswe* Number One (defender and protector of Malawian women and culture)—militated against a land program that should have otherwise been radical.[79] In fact, in his *Our African Way of Life*, the book he co-authored with Thomas Cullen Young while still in London, Banda affirmed his respect for African traditions showing how Malawian social organizations such as the system of guardianship in marriage contracts, uxorilocal family practices, and family labor had worked to the good of society.[80] Such ideas could also explain the Customary Land (Development) Act's provision on family land. Given that the land reform program also threatened some of these aspects—such as uxorilocal land arrangements[81]—any radical change would not have won Banda's interest.

Political considerations might also have helped to compromise the robust implementation of the land reforms. Following the Cabinet Crisis in 1964, many of Banda's former ministers (now dissidents) were scattered in the neighboring countries of Zambia, Tanzania, and others. Any drastic changes to African tradition would have given his enemies leverage over the rural society. Moreover, Yatuta Chisiza's 1967 insurrection discussed in the previous chapter coincided with the Customary Land Legislation. Hatched when Banda was consolidating his power, the land reform program had to be tactfully handled in ways that did not alienate the masses against him, least of all, his own Chewa people in the central region of the country.

It appears, therefore, that both the WB officials on the ground and post-colonial leaders (represented in the figure of Banda) had succumbed to local pressure, albeit for different reasons. Unlike the WB, the local leadership anticipated some of these challenges. For example, the Local Lands Board Act, which would have replaced the traditional land allocation roles of chiefs, legally recognized the position of traditional leaders in land allocation committees. Even with that, little progress was registered. It would be much later in 1998 when similar plans would be revived, again under the influence of the World Bank, albeit with little success. Similarly, the 2016 Customary Land Reform Act, which achieved exactly what was envisaged under the 1967 Act, was caught up in a witches' brew of contestations, effectively crippling its implementation until it was amended in 2022. It is difficult to predict whether it will achieve any better results than those of the distant colonial past, or immediate post-colonial present. What is clear, however, is that failure to reconcile diverse interests has played a crucial role to suffocate the effective implementation of such plans. In any case, if rural development projects represent "state high modernism" as Scott once contended, the LLDP experience illustrates the very limits of state paternalism.[82] Instead, it points to the ways in which the local people negotiated the project without necessarily opposing it as scholars of colonial development projects often contend.[83] In the case of the LLDP, project beneficiaries sought to derive some benefits from the project, although not in ways experts envisaged. This latter point deserves some emphasis in the next section.

MEMORIALIZING THE LLDP

As noted earlier, WB reports on the LLDP were overly negative and highlighted how the project had failed to achieve its intended aims. In contrast to this failure story, project beneficiaries remembered the project in positive terms, citing how it brought about agricultural inputs, markets, a road network, and income. Most significant is how villagers related the project to the contemporary agricultural input subsidy program. Introduced in the mid-1990s and revised several times over the years, the program aims at assisting rural farmers across the country to access agricultural inputs, whose market price is significantly higher than the average income of most farmers.[84] Under the program, farmers receive coupons with which they purchase fertilizer and seeds at less than half the cost price.

The program generated much optimism in the early years. A member of the household would purchase two 50kgs-bag (110.23lb) of maize fertilizer, one for basal and the other top dressing. With time, two farmers have had to share a bag of fertilizer with others hardly accessing inputs despite receiving coupons. The program has generated anger in the villages. For Lilongwe farmers, flashbacks of the LLDP contrast sharply with the contemporary intervention. "We fail to understand why the government abolished the Ndunda [LLDP] program," complained one participant of the Lilongwe project, further stating that "we had money in our pockets in those days. How we wish the government resumed that project."[85] For some farmers, the previous project brought in readily available extension workers who could advise them on best farming practices and worried that such personnel is hard to find these days. One village headman outrightly dismissed the contemporary input subsidy program, challenging state officials to abolish and "replace it with Ndunda [LLDP] because it only targets some selected people."[86] Two women corroborated such sentiments and wondered why the government entertained a program that does not provide adequate fertilizer and seeds. In reminiscing about the benefits of the previous credit facility, they challenged the government to simply provide them with input credit and allow them fetch inputs on the market.[87]

It appears, therefore, that farmers remembered the past in the shadow of the present interventions, which have done little to better their lives. Many of them wished the LLDP was revived and praised Dr. Banda for what they termed as his sound agricultural policies. These sentiments are similar to how the local communities remember the Cahora Bassa Dam in Mozambique. Despite promising a lot for the local communities, such expectations were never fulfilled, forcing Barbara and Allen Isaacmam to describe the project as representing the delusion or lie of development. The experience resonates with the Copperbelt experience in Zambia, which Ferguson describes at length. There, many of the people who flocked to the copper mines ended up returning to their home villages when urban life could not provide the expected modernity.[88] With Malawi, however, the illusion has less to do with exclusion from the perceived fruits of development than cries over an economically viable promising project that was short-lived.

The perceived benefits of the LLDP become apparent when measured against tobacco production. One aspect that frustrated experts was the continued production of the crop against policy prescription. When asked why the authorities proscribed barley tobacco production, none of the farmers remembered that policy. In fact, they wondered why the authorities would have taken that position on a crop they had produced since the colonial times and which other farmers produced elsewhere.[89] Instead, they argued that the project supplied input credit for all the crops, a claim which official documents do not corroborate.

The fact that none of the people interviewed remembered that policy (on tobacco production) shows how elusive it was. It tangentially affected the seasonal farming behavior of farmers, hence allowing them to switch labor and resources towards crops of their choice, depending on their rational calculations.[90] It is within this context that we can place the role of prices. Similarly to what Robert Maxon has illustrated among the Gusii wattle bark growers of colonial Kenya who held the last word for the success of wattle production there, tobacco production in central Malawi presented a natural exit option for farmers.[91] As international business experts and politicians debated the prospects for a wattle bark industry in western Kenya, farmers resorted to cutting down the trees for charcoal production and building poles rather than banking on a rather uncertain future of the industry.[92] In the case of Malawi, a sound rural development strategy should have acknowledged the historical role of the tobacco crop among the "peasant" communities, and the threat of suppressing it would have presented to the new project.

It is worth emphasizing that farmers appear to have participated in the project on their terms rather than those of planners and experts. Not surprisingly, their interpretation of the project outcomes deviates from that of the planners. One other reason for such divergences borders on officials' obsession with matching objectives with outcomes. The WB's causal model of project assessment assumed that agricultural inputs and other support mechanisms would give rise to increased production (output) and income (for farmers).[93] In fact, data in Figure 5.1 capture the outputs very well—which registered a disappointing trend. But it is silent on the income side. Experts often assumed that decreasing output was equivalent to the low income that farmers obtained. However, the success story that farmers told does not readily fit that framework. One reason for the discrepancy has to do with the way officials told the failure story. Theirs, as noted, was an explanation that mostly confined farmers to the two project crops without due consideration to the overall economic environment of the area. Farmers measured success in several ways, emphasizing, as they did, the agricultural extension services, an efficient marketing system, and better roads. Such an extension of nodal points from which to view the project—a holistic farmer-centered perspective—affords us a break from the "price stories" and accommodates other significant elements described above.

Notwithstanding the extent that farmers regarded the project as a success, it was not all positive. Women in particular lost the privileges they previously enjoyed over land allocation. Traditionally, the Chewa society is matrilineal (uxorilocal) and land passes through the female line from one generation to the next. According to custom, married women have rights over the land which they cultivate with their husbands (married uxorilocally). It is this aspect that, among others, justified the 1967 land legislation. It had the potential to grant such husbands security of tenure. But land registration did not achieve this objective. However, while traditional interests mediated the official plans, custom itself was not left intact.

The legitimate expectation of the people where land registration took place was that chiefs and lineage heads (under whose names Ndunda was registered) would own land on trust without destabilizing the existing tradition of land ownership. However, many of these chiefs and headmen were men and not women. Besides, they were able to allocate land (sub-ndundas) to their male children with little regard to women's interest over land or land custom generally.[94] This practice was traditionally wrong because male children did not have permanent rights to land in their father's villages. Though not owning it, male children had guaranteed access to land (usufruct rights) until such a time when they moved to a different village after marriage. By letting fathers transfer Ndunda to sons, the LLDP made a mockery of the matrilineal tradition.[95] Land registration potentially robbed women the traditional rights they exercised over land and its allocation.

CONCLUSION

When the LLDP was wound up in 1981, the World Bank argued that the project would have succeeded had there been a proper reconciliation between the macro- and micro-economic policies of the country. According to the Bank, the project failed because state policy was less oriented towards the welfare of peasants in the country. The state in Malawi, in the eyes of the WB, did not adjust to McNamara's concerns for the poor. This chapter does not challenge the exploitation school directly, particularly as it relates to the market component, nor does it attempt to achieve this. What it does show, however, are the inadequacies of such a framework as a lens with which to analyze the 1960s and 1970s rural development practice. By interpreting these projects within the confines of the market tradition, we gloss over the complex ways in which multiple forces combined to frustrate the best efforts of the WB, the ODM, and the state in Malawi into confronting poverty. Much less clear is how the beneficiaries of rural development projects interpreted their participation in them.

The LLDP was a space that brought together diverse interest groups and, therefore, presents us with an opportunity to analyze the failures of the war on poverty by casting the net beyond rational choice theories and the exploitation narrative. Deserving emphasis here is how the multiple interests involved reconciled and with what results. In doing so, there is a need to pay attention to the overall political environment of the country without ignoring the world in which the farmers lived. Literature has thus far restricted the agency of the latter group to the colonial period, mostly reducing them, if not to victims of development projects, then as obedient servants of the postcolonial state. As a result, we tend to understand postcolonial histories of development through the "high" modernizer's view, with much emphasis placed on the writings of experts, civil servants, and top politicians. Even though this chapter has articulated the latter's view, it has also emphasized the agency of the local people, many of whom worked side-by-side with planners before and during the project's implementation. Like the experts, they too held certain ideas about development practice which commanded the planners' attention. By deciphering their voices, the chapter presents a more nuanced understanding of the nature of the postcolonial developmental state and its limitations. The developmental state in Malawi was not an undifferentiated entity but one in which different groups, including ordinary farmers, pulled in opposite directions, depending on their best interests. Analyzing how such contending interests were reconciled or failed to reconcile is the first step towards understanding the failure of the Integrated Rural Development programs of the 1960s and 1970s. The challenges went beyond technical and market inadequacies, the two themes most prevalent in the rural development and political economy literature. The difficulties also center on the problematic ways in which experts, planners, politicians, and development project recipients interacted as each sought to achieve certain interests. Similar contending interests foiled an otherwise promising pulp and paper producing industry.

NOTES

1. See Charles Ziegler interview with Alexander Storrar (Head of WB's ADS, Kenya, 1965–1969), August 19, 1986, Oral History Program Interview Transcript 79135, WBGA, https://oralhistory.worldbank.org/transcripts/transcript-oral-history-interview-alexander-storrar-held-august-19-1986. Accessed on December 2, 2019.

2. Robert Bates is one scholar who popularized the doctrine of the market in the early 1980s. His work coincided with the World Bank report by Elliot Berg. See Robert H. Bates, *Markets and States in Tropical Africa: The Political Basis of Agricultural Policies* (Berkeley: University of California Press, 1981); Elliot Berg, *Accelerated Development in Sub-Saharan Africa: An Agenda for Action* (Washington, DC: World Bank, 1981).

3. The notion of Africa and its projects, landscape, or people as a laboratory has received immense scholarly attention with the most recent work being that of Tilley, *Africa as a Living Laboratory.* Other works include: Christophe Bonneuil, "Development as Experiment: Science and State Building in Late Colonial and Postcolonial Africa, 1930–1970," *Osiris* 15 (2000): 258–81; Maurits W. Ertsen, "Controlling the

Farmer: Colonial and Post-Colonial Irrigation Interventions in Africa," *Journal for Transdisciplinary Research in Southern Africa* 4, no. 1, (2008): 209–36.

4. Neo-classical economic theorists considered peasants as having a potential to favorably respond to markets depending on their intelligent calculations. Bad markets would potentially produce a poor peasant response. Such a theoretical tradition did not escape Kinsey's World Bank report on the LLDP. See B.H. Kinsey, *Rural Development in Malawi: A Review of the Lilongwe Land Development Program* (Washington, DC: World Bank, 1975); Uma J. Lele's work was equally influential in shaping the World Bank's direction in rural development. See preface to her book. The preface was written by the World Bank President, Robert McNamara. Uma J. Lele, *Designing Rural Development Programs: Lessons from Past Experience in Africa* (Ithaca, NY: Center for International Studies, 1975); See also Uma J. Lele, *The Design of Rural Development: Lessons from Africa* (Baltimore: Published for the World Bank by Johns Hopkins University Press, 1984).

5. Hodge, "Writing the History of Development," 449; See also Corinna Unger, "Histories of Development and Modernization," 20.

6. Corinna Unger, "Histories of Development and Modernization," 20.

7. Cullather, *The Hungry World*, 9.

8. The analysis here employs a historicist/historical approach to studying histories of development—one that historicizes individual agency as well as development discourses and practices rather than using economic or development models to inform development history. See Hodge, "British Colonial Expertise," 24–46; Cullather, "Development? It's History," 641–653.

9. On the agency of project recipients along the lines described here see also Cooper, "Writing the History of Development," 6–23; Stacey Leigh Pigg, "'Found in Most Traditional Societies': Traditional Medical Practitioners Between Culture and Development." In *International Development and the Social Sciences,* 259–90; Cullather, "Development? It's History," 650.

10. A good description of the project is presented by Chipande, "Smallholder Agriculture as Rural Development Strategy."

11. Blinkhorn, "Lilongwe: A Quiet Revolution," 28.

12. Robert J. Dewar to S.R. Simpson (Land Tenure Advisor to the ODM), December 6, 1966, TNA DO/31/039. The legislations that were passed into law included the Customary Land (Development) Act—No. 5. 1967; Registered Land Act—No. 6, 1967; and Local Boards Land Act—No. 7, 1967.

13. The FAO was the first organization to be involved in this project. Having been motivated by a land intensification project it financed in Lilongwe in the early 1960s, FAO later helped to produce a survey for the LLDP before the WB financed its major components. It was FAO that also financed the health components of the LLDP, including the drilling of boreholes and construction of some facilities. There is evidence, also, suggesting that the WB had very high praise for Malawi's credit worthiness in the early years of independence. The land legislation is cited as an example. See BLCAS MSS Afr.s. 1742/38, 1985. Specific contents of this file cannot be cited without copyright permission.

14. World Bank Report No. P-582, Recommendations of the President to the Executive Directors on a Proposed Development Credit to the Republic of Malawi for LLDP, January 22, 1968, 2, http://documents.worldbank.org/curated/pt/873781468046744947/text/multi0page.txt; World Bank Report No. TO-610a, Lilongwe Development Project in Malawi, January 3, 1968, http://documents.worldbank.org/curated/en/998211468300594184/text/multi-page.txt.

15. I introduced Rostow's ideas in chapter four when discussing how Dunduzu Chisiza admired them. Suffice it to state that Kinsey is highlighting Rostow's "take-off" stage for illustration purposes only relative to this localized project because in Rostow's conceptualization, take-off denoted a period in which a given country (not just a region within it) enters into a stage of self-sustaining growth of 5 percent or more annually. In highlighting Rostow's ideas, Kinsey was also emphasizing that the LLDP properly fit the modernization drive of the 1950s to 1970s.

16. B. H. Kinsey, "Integrated Rural Development, Agricultural Growth and Equity in Malawi: Redefining Development Strategies and Tactics for the 1980s," *Agricultural Administration* 15, no. 1 (1984): 48.

17. Interview with Andrew Mercer (LLDP Manager), cited in Magazine Cutting: *Backgrounder*, December 12, 1969, 4, MNA 3-11-99/18949.

18. Much of this amount was directed to such areas as rural infrastructure investment, credit provision, land surveying, land conservation, and others. See Hodge, "British Colonial Expertise," 40.

19. World Bank, Report and Recommendations of the President to the Executive Directors on a proposed Credit to the Republic of Malawi for the Lilongwe Agricultural Project, Report No. P-582, January 22, 1968:2.

20. Charles Ziegler interview with Alexander Storrar (Head of WB's ADS, Kenya, 1965–1969), August 19, 1986, Oral History Program Interview Transcript 79135, WBGA.

21. World Bank, Report and Recommendations of the President to the Executive Directors on a Proposed Credit to the Republic of Malawi for the Lilongwe Agricultural Project, 2.

22. Nankhumba, "Evolution of Agricultural Policy in Malawi and the National Rural Development Program," 32. See also Hodge, "British Colonial Expertise," 40.

23. World Bank, Rural Development Sector Policy Paper, PUB-588, 1975: 8, http://documents.worldbank.org/curated/en/688121468168853933/pdf/PUB5880PUB0Box0er0Rural0Development.pdf; See also Ayres, *Banking on the Poor*, 28.

24. See for example, Kinsey, "Integrated Rural Development, Agricultural Growth and Equity in Malawi"; Lele and Meyers, *Growth and Structural Change in East Africa*; Erik Green, "State-led Agricultural Intensification and Rural Labour Relations: The Case of the Lilongwe Land Development Programme in Malawi, 1968–1981," *International Instituut voor Sociale Geschiednis* 55, no. 3 (2010): 413–46.

25. Bates, *Markets and States in Tropical Africa.* The contribution from the following studies seem to confirm Bates' concerns in the case of Malawi: Kinsey, "Integrated Rural Development"; Lele, *Designing Rural Development Programs.*

26. Lipton, *Why Poor People Stay Poor*, 66–68.

27. B. H. Kinsey has illustrated through statistical data how despite government's policy to wean farmers away from tobacco production, its sales at ADMARC remained higher than those of maize and tobacco throughout the 1970s. See his "Integrated Rural Development, Agricultural Growth and Equity in Malawi," 51.

28. Hodge, "British Colonial Expertise," 40.

29. Memo by Leif E. Christofferson, October 22, 1975, WBGA, File No. 30136805.

30. Leif Christofferson to Montague Yudelman, October 22, 1975, WBGA, File No. 30136805.

31. Ibid.

32. Benjamin D. King to M. Weiner, (Date illegible. Possibly October 1975), WBGA, File No. 30136805.

33. B. H. Kinsey to Uma Lele, June 1, 1979, WBGA, File No. 30136805.

34. Minutes of the Committee set up to evaluate the ADS Research Study Report, July 15, 1982, WBGA, File No. 30136805.

35. At the time, Kinsey was a Professor at the School of Development Studies, University of East Anglia.

36. Andrew Mercer to Uma J. Lele, October 17, 1975, WBGA, File No. 30136805.

37. Ibid.

38. Mehos and Moon, "The Use of Portability: Circulating Experts in the Technopolitics of Cold War and Decolonization," 44. Mehos and Moon present the example of the UN's Expanded Program of Technical Assistance (EPTA) which was formed in the 1950s and drew experts from several UN agencies. Its *modus operandi* emphasized "portable experts with portable knowledge" who, having been employed from different parts of the world, could be deployed in any country to provide technical skills, regardless of the experience they had. Established at the height of the Cold War, this approach was preferred to using place-based experts who, by virtue of their experience in a particular area, were prone to ideological biases that could negatively affect their work. To avoid this problem, the EPTA sent its experts on short-term missions to the countries requesting its services.

39. Ayres, *Banking On the Poor*, 29, 30.

40. Malawi LLDP Project Performance Audit Report, Phase III, World Bank Restricted Report No. 3414, April 1981, 24, http://documents.worldbank.org/curated/en/998211468300594184/text/multi-page.txt. Although plans to create it were mooted in 1951, the Word Bank's Economic Development Institute was established in 1955. It aimed at training government officials from LDCs, especially those responsible for formulation and administration of policies, equipping them with knowledge and skills that would help them do their work better. The Institute's training center was opened in Washington, DC. David Brown taught at the Institute. For details see A Brief History of the World Bank Institute (WBI/Economic Development Institute (EDI), not dated, http://documents.worldbank.org/curated/en/372291468129005130/pdf/936580WP0EDI0h0Box385399B00PUBLIC00.pdf. Accessed on January 14, 2019.

41. See LLDP Project Performance Audit Report, No. 3414, April 1981, iv.

42. LLDP Project Performance Audit Report, No. 3414, April 1981, 4.

43. Ibid., 10

44. R. S. A. Moyo (for Secretary of Treasury, Malawi) to the Director, Operations Evaluation Department (Washington, DC), March 24, 1981, WBGA, File No. 30178835.

45. In the 1960s, Robert J. Dewar served as the Secretary of Economic Affairs in the Malawi Government. He was an ex-colonial expert in British Africa.

46. Jan Wijnand to Robert Dawar, February 10, 1981, WBGA, File No. 30178835.

47. Ibid.

48. Donald C. Pickering, Asst. Director of Agriculture to S. Kapur, Director, Operations Evaluation Department (OED), March 25, 1981. WBGA. File No. 30178835.

49. Successes in the "physical aspects" of the LLDP described above.

50. I am using the terms "center" and "periphery" in very loose terms and for illustration purposes only and not to point readers to the dependency school or world systems theory.

51. For a contrast between McNamara and Clausen era, see Ayres, *Banking on the Poor*, 252–54.

52. Howard Stein, Bretton Woods Project, September 29, 2008, https://www.brettonwoodsproject.org/2008/09/art-562552/. Accessed on January 17, 2019; Elliot Berg, *Accelerated Development in Sub-Saharan Africa*.

53. In the case of the LLDP, the credit facility extended to farmers was channeled through the state marketing board, ADMARC. In fact, even though the IDA credit was signed between two parties, the World Bank and the Malawi government, the FMB (later ADMARC) was always represented as a separate entity with several clauses in the agreement document relating to it. Moreover, it was the IDA that facilitated a change from the Farmers Marketing Board to ADMARC and helped to reorganize the latter in ways that would facilitate efficiency in the Bank's activities in Malawi. See The Development Credit Agreement between the Republic of Malawi and the International Development Association, February 5, 1968, WBGA, Lilongwe Agricultural Project, Credit No. 113 MAI.

54. Nottidge was an exception. Born and raised in Kenya, he had sound experience in agriculture acquired through service in that British colony. See Hodge, "British Colonial Expertise," 35, 37. Besides, as a Chief Agricultural Development Officer, he integrated well into Banda's expatriate-staff dominated civil service. Not surprisingly, when the Bank transferred him out of Malawi to head the ADS (After Alexander Storrar—the previous head—had been moved elsewhere), Banda wrote McNamara complaining about such an arrangement. In essence, Banda saw such transfers as unnecessary especially for experienced officials like Nottidge who had once constituted part of his bureaucracy. On Banda's complaint see Charles Ziegler interview with Alexander Storrar (Head of WB's ADS, Kenya, 1965–1969), August 19, 1986, Oral History Program Interview Transcript 79135, WBGA.

55. Pierre L. Moussa to Burke J. Knapp, November 20, 1964, WBGA File No. 1830078.

56. Office Memorandum by C.H. Calika, December 10, 1964, WBGA, File No. 1830078.

57. See Nankhumba, "Evolution of Agricultural Policy in Malawi and the National Rural Development Program."

58. D. S. Pearson ranked among local bureaucrats that criticized low producer prices for peasant commodities. See my discussion in the fourth chapter.

59. Kydd, "Malawi in the 1970s: Development Policies and Economic Change," 306.

60. Scott, *Seeing Like a State*, 88–89.

61. The Original proposal was highlighted in World Bank Report No. TO-610a, Lilongwe Development Project in Malawi, January 3, 1968, 10, http://documents.worldbank.org/curated/en/927741468282249880/pdf/multi0page.pdf, December 10, 2018.

62. L. G. Sewell, Some Notes on the Customary Land (Development) Act, CAP. 59 of 9/5/67, WBGA, File No. 302991. Doc No. 102003; See also the Customary Land (Development) Act, Chap. 19 (1, c), 1967.

63. Interview with a Group Village Headman, July 13, 2016. All author interviews are anonymous to protect the individuals' identities.

64. See Andrew M. Mercer, *The Lilongwe Land Development Programme: A Precis of Activities with Some Comments on Populace Participation* 1972, 14. The Village Committees under reference here comprised the Traditional Village Headman, local political party representative; the Technical Assistant of the area, three prominent women, six prominent men, and one invited "specialist" living in the vicinity and not necessarily in the village.

65. The 1998 Customary Land Utilisation Study (CLUS) corroborated the idea of chiefly titles. See Bureau pour le Developpement de la Production Agricole (BDPA)/AHT International, "Report of the Customary Land Utilisation Study: The 'Ndunda' Land Registration Component of the Lilongwe Land Development Programme." Malawi, Lilongwe, 1998, 11. The Customary Land Utilization Study is a collection of oral testimonies compiled through interviews with former project beneficiaries. The report is housed at Malawiana Section of the University of Malawi Library, Zomba, Malawi.

66. See Berry, *Chiefs Know their Boundary,* 15, 20, 36; Land Reorganization, Central Region, 1969–1970, MNA 3-11-99/18949.

67. Interview with official at the Department of Geological Survey, Lilongwe, July 14, 2016.

68. These located sentiments are cited in BDPA/AHT International, "Report of the Customary Land Utilization Study," 11. The LLDP Quarterly report, September 30, 1969, MNA 3-11-99/18949 also depicts this opposition.

69. See Derek R. Peterson, *Ethnic Patriotism and the East African Revival: A History of Dissent, c. 1935–1972* (Cambridge: Cambridge University Press, 2012), 127–51. On resistance to the 1950s land consolidation program and its relationship to Luo ethnic revival see pages 136–40, 147–49.

70. Member of the Focus Group Discussion with selected participants, July 12, 2016. Both male and female participants corroborated this view.

71. Mercer, *The Lilongwe Land Development Programme,* 14.

72. D.E. Warren to Terence D. Wright, South Africa and Malawi Department of the ODM, April 5, 1968, TNA OD 31/108. The ODM was involved in the LLDP because it was requested to advise on the setting up of a Land Registry Office in Lilongwe. Funding for establishing the Land Registry Office and staff training was

already provided for under the IDA loan. The ODM, however, would provide funding towards technical assistantship missions, covering travel expenses, surveys, and other related aspects. A Land Registry was necessary to facilitate land registration in the LLDP. Britain took a particular interest in the Land Registry Office because, once established, it would also provide security to disputed freehold land British citizens owned in Malawi.

73. The ODM deployed Morgan to advise on how to set up a new Land Registry Office in Lilongwe. It also assigned J. T. Fleming from Kenya to assist Morgan in this exercise.

74. See Appendix A of Morgan and Fleming 1969 report reprinted in TNA OD 31/108. See also Ministry of Overseas Development, *Lilongwe Land Development Project, Annex 21*, (Confidential Report), WBGA, File No. 302031, 1969.

75. Recent work include John and Jean Comaroff, "Chiefs, Capital and the State in Contemporary Africa" in John and Jean Comaroff, eds. *The Politics of Custom: Chiefs, Capital, and the State in Contemporary Africa* (Chicago: The University of Chicago, 2018), 1–48, particularly 19, 22. See also in the same volume Sara Berry, "Chieftaincy, Land, and the State in Ghana and South Africa," 79–209.

76. Appendix A of Morgan and Fleming 1969 report, TNA OD 31/108. See also *Lilongwe Land Development Project, Annex 21*, WBGA, File No. 302031, 1969.

77. See for example Immerwahr, *Thinking Small,* 4.

78. Banda's Speech, April 4, 1967. Cited in I. E. Morgan and E. J. Fleming report for the Ministry of Overseas Development, Appendix A, 1969: 9.

79. In many of his political rallies, Banda claimed that he was the defender of Malawian traditions which also became the corner-stone of his nation-building policies.

80. Thomas Cullen Young and H. Kamuzu Banda, *Our African Way of Life: Three Essays* (London: Lutterworth Press, 1946). Banda's ideas on Malawian culture are further presented by Kings M. Phiri, "Dr. Banda's Cultural Legacy and Its Implications for a Democratic Malawi" in Kings Phiri and Andrew Ross, eds. *Democratisation in Malawi: A Stocktaking* (Blantyre: CLAIM, 1998), 149–67.

81. Under Uxorilocal land arrangements in Central Malawi, husbands primarily own land through their wives and subsequently lose it upon the death of their wives. The Land reforms were aimed at providing tenure security to such individuals by having land registered in their names, an exercise that proved futile.

82. Scott, *Seeing Like a State*, 88–89.

83. The following works demonstrated how recipients of colonial development projects negotiated them during as opposed to before project implementation: van Beusekom, *Negotiating Development*; Schuknecht, *British Colonial Development Policy after the Second World War;* Li, *The Will to Improve.* The following works present relatively similar findings in the case of colonial Malawi: Beinart, "Agricultural Planning and the Late Colonial Technical Imagination"; McLoughlin, "Land Re-organization in Malawi, 1950s–1960," 128–39. For a recent discussion contrasting this position see Gift W. Kayira, "Wealth Creation, Poverty and Social Welfare in Malawi, 1940s–1980," Mariama Khan and Grasian Mkodzongi (eds.), *Africa, History and Culture* (Dubuque, IA, Kendall Hunt, 2020), 11–28.

84. See Blessings Chinsinga and Aoiffe O'Brien, *Planting Ideas: How Agricultural Subsidies are Working in Malawi* (London: African Research Institute, 2008); Ephraim Chirwa and Andrew Doward, *Agricultural Input Subsidies: The Recent Malawi Experience* (Oxford: Oxford University Press, 2013).

85. Interview: a member of Mitundu Focus Group Discussion, July 12, 2016.

86. Interview with a Group Village Headman, July 13, 2017.

87. Interview: a member of Nambuma Focus Group Discussion, July 18, 2016.

88. Allen F. Isaacman and Barbara S. Isaacman, *Dams, Displacement, and the Delusion of Development: Cahora Bassa and Its Legacies in Mozambique, 1965–2007* (Athens, OH: Ohio University Press, 2013); James Ferguson, *Expectations of Modernity: Myths and Meanings of Urban Life on the Zambian Copperbelt* (Berkeley and Los Angeles: University of California Press, 1999).

89. Interview: a member of Mitundu Focus Group Discussion, July 12, 2016.

90. See Green, "State-led Agricultural Intensification and Rural Labour Relations," 413–46.

91. Robert M. Maxon, "Where did the Trees Go? The Wattle Bark Industry in Western Kenya, 1932–1950," *International Journal of African Historical Studies* 34, no. 3 (2001): 565–84.

92. Ibid., 579.

93. Ayres, *Banking On the Poor,* 100–101.

94. "Report of the Customary Land Utilisation Study," 11–12

95. In their discussion of the effects of the 2002 Land Policy in Southern Malawi, Peters and Kambewa have arrived at a similar conclusion. See their "Whose Security?" 454. Such stories point to the need for students of development histories to pay attention to the gendered nature of development projects, an area this book has not explored.

Chapter Six

Malawi's Foreign Policy and the Fruitless Search for Investment Capital, 1960s–1980

Soon after independence in 1964, the Malawi government cleared off part of the Viphya Plateau and planted pine trees to support a Kraft Pulp Mill scheduled to produce over 180,000 metric tons of pulp per year.[1] The project presented opportunities for job creation and investment in other supporting services in the areas of health and transport infrastructure. Politically, it aimed at spreading development to the "Dead North," so named after its lack of meaningful economic activities. When in the late-1970s a syndicate of investors from Britain, Finland, Sweden, and the Federal Republic of Germany expressed interest in the project, the WB vetoed it. The WB, which had financed some feasibility studies and had promised to provide a loan to support selected components of it, argued that Malawi was yet to prove the economic returns of the mill. That decision coincided with the fall of pulp prices on the world market. Even though Malawi tried to revise upwards the economic benefits of the Viphya, the Bank was less persuaded. Instead, the Bank proposed in 1980 to support a scaled-down sawn timber project, much smaller than the original idea but which has stood to the present day. After so much money spent on feasibility studies, what appeared to have been a promising industry ended as a mirage. Beyond the WB's veto, how else should we explain the failure of the project? Why, for example, did Malawi not disagree with the Bank's position, as was the case with other decisions discussed earlier in this study, for a project whose political and economic value was immense?

This chapter addresses these questions. It seeks answers first, in the changing development climate of the 1970s in which the Bank was increasingly disinterested in industrial projects that minimally addressed the plight of the poor, and second, in the intersection between the discourses of development and the Cold War and how Dr. Banda's foreign policy mediated that intersection. The chapter argues that the WB vetoed the project because although it would potentially raise the industrial status of the country, it would only help to fulfill the interests of foreign investors rather than meeting the basic economic needs of the country. Moreover, the WB, and a network of international donor agencies it influenced, including West Germany's *Kreditanstalt für Wiederaufbau* (KfW), doubted the mill's economic returns and its capacity to address rural and urban poverty in the country. For these agencies, the Viphya was a perfect example of those showcase projects that would end up sacrificing the country's commitment to addressing poverty while enriching multinational companies. The Bank tolerated the project only in the hope that it would, with time, safeguard the country's interests. Malawi was aware of the Bank's fears and carefully aligned the economic goals of the project with the country's aspirations through backward and forward linkages.

Backward linkages included the construction of roads and a harbor at Chintheche along Lake Malawi, the aim of which was to facilitate the shipping of pulp to the Southern Region where the consignment would be forwarded by rail to the Indian Ocean through Mozambique. They also included creation of jobs for Malawians working in the Viphya plantations. Forward linkages were the potential indirect benefits the project had for Malawi. These included transforming the pulp processing area into an industrial site, thereby creating more skilled and non-skilled jobs for the local population and others, while spurring socio-economic developments; construction of health and education facilities for the workers; and facilitating the rail and shipping industry in the country. When it became clear that Malawi would not safeguard these interests through the mill, the Bank flexed its muscles as an "international economic watchdog" and blocked the project.[2] It argued that the project had a poor rate of return of less than 10 percent and would, therefore, hardly pay back for the investment made under backward linkages.

Lacking another "South Africa" to provide funding, Banda's government bowed down and accepted the Bank's proposition for a timber-selling project. Banda's decision, however, was less a result of a lack of potential funders than his rigid foreign policy which closed rather than opened investment opportunities. Throughout the search for industrial aid, Banda never consulted the Soviet Union or countries in the Eastern bloc, a deliberate decision taken not to ruin relations with the West. Although far from certainty, failure to contact the Soviet Union in the 1970s and throughout Banda's 30-year rule represented a lost opportunity, especially because increased trade exchange between the West and the East marked the economic underpinnings of the 1970s Détente.[3] Banda's decision further questions the scholarly tendency to exaggerate "political pragmatism" as dictating his decision-making behavior which is said to have brought economic dividends to the country.[4] Instead, it shows how the state in Malawi was caught up in a particular capitalist ideology which, while opening some economic opportunities, also closed others. In examining this ideology, the chapter speaks to broader debates on development and the Cold War. Rather than seeing the Cold War as an ideological confrontation, the chapter highlights, as Odd Arne Westad and Guy Laron do in their separate works, the opportunities for trade and development it created and forestalled in the Global South.[5]

The chapter analyzes these aspects around two themes. The first discusses the Viphya Pulp Mill scheme as a site for international networking, emphasizing its political dynamics and how the WB blocked it. The analysis here is woven through a transnational framework that brings into postcolonial Malawi multiple international state and non-state actors who sought to support the country's quest for industrial development. The analysis is based on recently declassified Malawi National Archives files on the project. Despite its significance in the country's history of industrial development, the Viphya Pulp Mill scheme has not attracted scholarly attention.[6] To reconstruct its history, I have relied on the Viphya files deposited at the Southern Region Records Center of the Malawi National Archives in Zomba. The files contain minutes, reports, and correspondence occurring among different government departments, foreign missions and embassies, the Viphya Pulp and Paper Corporation (VIPCOR), the ODM/ODA, KfW, and the UN development agencies such as the UNDP, FAO, and the WB. These files remain loose, unprocessed, and stacked in boxes marked either for destruction in the future or safe keeping for effective retrieval until an archivist catalogs them into archival documents, for ease of access to the public. So far, the latter is yet to materialize. Beyond its historiographical contribution, the chapter points students of Malawi's development history to the existence of these significant documents.

By emphasizing how the Viphya Pulp Mill Scheme was aborted, moreover, these sources help us to connect the project with the colonial Tung Scheme, which faced a similar fate, thereby shedding light on the cyclical nature of development discourse and practice. For some authorities, especially the staff that served under the colonial Department of Agriculture, the failure of the CDC-run Tung Scheme was a blessing in disguise because the project, and the Limphasa Scheme attached to it, did not safeguard the economic interests of Africans. Had the project succeeded, it would have benefitted the metropole more than Africans in the protectorate. These same concerns were echoed by the WB in the immediate postcolonial present, even though the methods of achieving development differed.[7] What did not change over time were the concerns experts held over creating a secondary industry that barely addressed the interests of the poor societies.

The second theme engages other primary sources, notably Dr. Banda's speeches, to discuss the country's pragmatic foreign policy in the context of continental and global politics. It broadens the existing literature on Malawi's foreign policy and development by demonstrating how that policy played out in broader international decisions beyond the African region, and the opportunities it opened or closed during the 1970s Cold War Détente; an era of increased exchange in areas of trade, industry, and development. Of emphasis here is how the country's Western ideological leanings prevented the country from seeking alternative sources of funding for its industrial project, and what the politics surrounding the Viphya teach us about the Malawian state. Given the limits of the sources under consideration, these conclusions should be understood only within the context of how some leaders in the Global South took advantage of global politics to achieve certain aims in ways that the Malawian leader did not.

THE VIPHYA PULP MILL PROJECT: A MIRACLE TURNED INTO A MIRAGE

Plans to set up a pulp and paper mill in the country date back to the early 1950s when Britain, through the CDC, sought, without success, to establish one such mill in the Nyika Plateau of the Northern Province.[8] Around the same time, the colonial government set aside about 4,250 acres of land for afforestation in the Viphya/Chikangawa plateau (Northern Province), the aim of which was to produce sawn timber for both domestic use and export.[9] It was in the early 1960s, however, that the Viphya Plateau came into the spotlight as a possible site for the paper-making industry in the country. In 1963, the colonial government deployed consultant R.G. Green to study the area under the general theme of "Utilization of Exotic Plantations." Green's report, which the FAO had commissioned, suggested further investigation into the possibility of establishing a pulp industry in the country "based upon conifers [pine trees] to be grown on the Viphya Plateau."[10] Between 1963 and early 1964, FAO deployed another expert, K.H. Kursten, to study the technical and economic feasibility of establishing a bleached long fiber sulphate kraft pulp mill producing 300 tons of pulp per day. Like Green's report, Kursten's study brought about positive results, and further identified Western Europe as the possible market for the country's pulp.[11] Following independence in 1964, the country did not abandon the proposal. With financial and technical support from Britain, Malawi stepped up the planting program at the Viphya from less than 1000 acres in 1963 to over 12,000 acres in 1967.[12]

Meanwhile, Banda launched a fierce campaign to solicit financial support for more studies on the Viphya and investment in the mill. Banda looked to his traditional funders as the British High Commissioner reported in 1966:

> Mr. Jones, the American Ambassador [to Malawi], told me yesterday that he has been under heavy pressure from Dr. Banda about the Viphya Pulpwood project. Dr. Banda had told him that he was sending a Mission to Canada at the end of May. . . . If the Canadians refused to commit themselves to any helpful forward move on Viphya, the Mission would go to the United States to seek American help.[13]

Later in 1967 Banda visited President Lyndon Johnson and impressed upon him to support the project. Banda positioned the project as an arena for international cooperation and one that would contribute to his country's industrial and socio-economic development. Convinced about its aims, Johnson promised to lobby investors towards the project. He further suggested providing funding for more detailed studies through the USA's Agency for International Development (AID) program.[14] Banda's campaign paid off. Between 1965 and 1968, five more studies were undertaken on the preliminary technical and economic evaluation of the project, mostly financed through the US and Canadian aid.[15]

The Brown & Root Inc. study came explicitly in the wake of talks Banda held with President Johnson. "I recall with very great pleasure the most useful and constructive discussion we were able to have in Washington in June of this year [1967]," Banda wrote Johnson: "One result of our discussion was that the Brown and Root team visited Malawi in August in order to investigate our Pulp/Paper project."[16] Because the report recommended a detailed technical and economic evaluation of the project, Banda advised Johnson to the effect that Malawi had since "requested the United States AID organization . . . for the [financial] assistance in undertaking this full study."[17] While these preliminary negotiations were positive, it became clear to Malawi officials that the Viphya project was far more complex than initially imagined. Already, by January 1968, Malawi had not received response on the financial request Banda highlighted in his letter to Johnson. Again, a follow-up letter which the Ministry of Economic Affairs in Malawi raised through the US Embassy in the country did not bring any immediate response.[18] Instead, some officials within the US State Department suggested that Malawi seek financial support from Israel, not least because of that country's interest in the pulp industry.[19]

Because of what Malawi saw as unnecessary delays from the US, it raised another application for funding to the UNDP while also seeking South African support towards the project. The latter sent its experts to Malawi in

1968. Other than encouraging Malawi about the "prospects for setting up a paper-making industry in [the Viphya]," there is no evidence suggesting that South Africa committed to supporting the project financially.[20] Following protracted negotiations, however, the UNDP deployed Arne Sundelin, a Swedish Forest Industries Consultant, to undertake a detailed technical and economic survey of the project. Unlike the previous studies, Sundelin's report was mostly negative on certain key aspects: "A Kraft Pulp Mill in Malawi, exporting to Western Europe, would not yield an acceptable gross return on the investments, even if the capacity is increased to 600 tons per day—i.e. [sic] about twice the size of the mill which [the existing plantation can support]," read his report. Sundelin further ruled out the Viphya's capacity to capture markets in "the countries bordering the Indian and Pacific Oceans."[21] Instead, he suggested that Malawi should focus on the regional markets within Africa, a tenuous suggestion given that Tanzania, Kenya, and Zambia were planning similar projects. Even with that, he proposed a scaled-down project producing 200–300 tons of pulp per day and set 1980 as the commencement date for the mill. Alternatively, he recommended producing sawn timber for export but as an integrated operation combined with the pulp mill. Sandelin's report further suggested a pre-investment study of the Viphya. The study would concentrate on the potential for markets the African region offered.

When officials in London received Sundelin's report, they suggested that Britain scale-down funding towards the tree planting program. They argued that there was "as yet, insufficient evidence to show that Vipya Pulp/Paper [sic] will, in fact, be viable and become a reality."[22] Because of this, the British officials feared the Viphya plantations would be used for timber as opposed to pulp-making purposes. In that regard, the existing forest was far beyond Malawi's domestic timber needs. Malawi officials, however, accepted the report and challenged both the British and UNDP to consider it favorably. For them, the Viphya mill would soon materialize "and the question [was] one of timing within the period 1975/80."[23] Malawi further cited FAO's press release of May 14, 1969, which had predicted an increase in global demand for pulp by 1975.[24]

By this time, interest in the Viphya within the UNDP was waning, and this was clear among Malawi Government officials already disappointed by the US's silence on the previous application. The UNDP never responded in time. In his discussion with some members of the UNDP in New York, the Malawi Ambassador to the UNO (Mbekeani) concluded that the UNDP was unwilling to support Malawi's second application. "Since the UNDP provided money for the consultant [Sundelin]," Mbekeani briefed his colleague, "they now feel that they have done their part on the scheme." Instead, the UNDP approached, on behalf of Malawi, the IBRD, FAO, and the United Nations Industrial Organization to fund the pre-investment study.[25] Mbekeani wondered why the UNDP contacted these organizations on Malawi's behalf when the country was a member to each one of them. Skeptical of this international networking, Mbekeani warned his colleague: "It would appear that we are now going in circles on this scheme. . . . It appears . . . there is a deal somewhere whereby Kenya and Zambia are being earmarked for assistance in this field. If we are not careful, we may be overtaken and our scheme, as I hear, will turn into an ordinary softwood plantation for building purposes."[26] Though the UNDP finally financed the pre-investment study with the IBRD as an executing agency, Mbekeani had a point.

In 1971, for example, Lennart Markila, the Chief of the FAO's Pulp and Paper Branch and a member of the FAO Forest Industries and Paper Division, visited Malawi to investigate the Viphya project even before Sundelin's second report was out. It was J. Wyatt-Smith, the Forest Advisor to the United Kingdom Overseas Development Administration (ODA) who, unsuspectingly, perhaps, suggested that Markila study the Viphya following the latter's planned visit to East Africa.[27] Markila produced a report that further damaged the Viphya's reputation. It advised Malawi to abandon the paper and pulp project since Zambia, a new entry into the field, was planning a similar scheme. Instead, Markila proposed "a study of the use of sawn timber, including export to markets in Central Africa and the Middle East."[28] By suggesting another study when Sundelin's findings were not yet out, officials in Malawi saw Markila as "deliberately spinning all these stages out . . . to give time for the Zambian project to overtake Malawi."[29] When Markila's proposal reached Dr. Banda's desk, he trashed it. Instead, he advised his officials to ignore any proposals that Zambia's Pulp and Wood Scheme would interfere with the Malawi one: "We must push as hard as possible to get a pulp mill at the Viphya."[30]

Although Markila's position would have influenced decisions within FAO and other international organizations, Sundelin's second report on the pre-investment survey somewhat ameliorated that damage. It considered a pulp mill project targeting regional markets to be feasible. Moreover, a May 25, 1971, FAO press release showed that the world paper demand would rise from 123 to 285 million tons between 1969 and 1985. The rising demand for paper, it argued, presented opportunities to developing countries interested in the pulp and paper industry.[31] Again, the report by a team of experts the UNDP deployed to Malawi following Sundelin's favorable results did not deviate from the existing findings. Moreover, a follow-up study (Pre-investment study II) which the Finland-based consultancy firm (the Jaakko Poyry and Co.) carried out in 1973 through UNDP financial support confirmed the positive results.[32]

By mid-1973, plans to establish a mill at Chintheche (along the lake shore) had become clear.[33] The mill, whose commencement date officials pushed to 1979, would produce 180,000 metric tons of bleached kraft pulp per year. They pegged the total capital required at US$117 million, with US$91 million for setting up the mill and the difference covering infrastructural components such as road and harbor construction. Convinced that the project would have direct effects on the Malawi economy, the WB agreed to support the last aspect (in the form of a loan) on condition that Malawi secured private investors. Estimates showed the project would have a gross economic return of US$17 million per year, employing over 7,000 workers in both skilled and non-skilled jobs.[34] It also held the potential to transform Chintheche and the Viphya/Chikangawa areas socio-economically. By 1973, the country boasted a pine [*Pinus Patula*) tree plantation of 24,000 hectares out of the 54,000 (134,675 acres) required to supply a mill operating at that rate. Meanwhile, Britain agreed to continue supporting the tree planting program, which registered 54,501 hectares (134,000 acres) by 1980. It was envisaged, however, that the existing plantation was enough to kick-start the project.[35]

To systematically lobby private investors towards the project, the government established the Viphya Pulp and Paper Corporation (VIPCOR) on December 1, 1973, which, equipped with a business prospectus, went in search of Western European countries and others as potential business partners. Between 1973 and 1975, Malawi visited different Western countries and financial institutions, including the Federal Republic of Germany, Sweden, and the European Investment Bank. None of these potential donors offered any meaningful prospects for funding other than to promise to liaise with prospective investors. Frustrated, Malawi turned to Iran for support, urging Tehran to participate in the project either through the Iranian Industrial and Mining Development Bank (IIMDB) or the country's private firms. "I have taken the initiative of addressing this letter in the hope that Your Majesty might consider this as an ideal opportunity to promote the interests of both our countries, by having substantive discussions between an appropriate Iranian organisation and the official representatives of the Viphya project," Banda wrote in a letter to Shahanshar Reza Pahlavi in 1974.[36] Banda hoped that the Minister of Finance, Dick Matenje, would deliver the letter to Tehran while leading a four-member delegation for discussions there, notably with officials from the Iranian bank.

For Banda, the project also presented an opportunity for cooperation between the two countries following his previous attacks on the "Arab world." In the 1960s, Banda took issue with the "Arab Casablanca group of states" which, in his view, was negatively influencing the Organization of African Unity (OAU) through its "impulsive, impatient, revolutionary [and] aggressive" behavior.[37] He was also critical of the United Arab Republic (UAR), blaming it for having helped his rebel ministers (of the 1964 cabinet crisis) to train in Algeria using UAR air services.[38] During the 1967

Arab-Israeli war, Banda condemned the Arab world as an aggressor while praising Israel, a country with which Malawi had diplomatic ties.[39] Again, later in 1969, he condemned the Arab countries for supporting a military solution to the white minority governments in Southern Africa (to force them out of power), further stating that "those people who start accusing the whites of Southern Africa ought to have the courage to take a look at the North where the Arabs practice the worst form of imperialism."[40] Even though Iran was not a member of the Arab Casablanca group, Banda's attacks were generic and targeted north Africa and the Middle East generally. Moreover, although Iran's population was predominantly Persian, the country had a sizable population of Arabs. Similarly, both Iran and Iraq, the latter with a predominantly Arab population, were once members of the Baghdad Pact, a pro-Western defensive organization that was formed in 1955 to contain the Soviet influence in the Middle East. Until the Iraq-Iranian War of 1980–1988, the relationship between Iran and the mainstream Arab world was stable such that Banda's accusations against the Arabs might have affected Iranian perception of Malawi as a trusted business ally. The turn to Iran, therefore, showed how far Banda was willing to compromise his earlier position to achieve his economic interests.

Before finalizing travel arrangements, however, Iran cabled advising Malawi about the tight schedule his Imperial Majesty had and suggested, instead, that the officials deliver the letter to the Minister of Imperial Court.[41] Banda did not have problems with that arrangement. But he was no doubt disappointed a year later when Tehran rejected the request to hold financial talks, again citing the tight schedule government officials had.[42] There is no evidence suggesting that Iran received Banda's letter and whether the delegation went to Iran at some other moment. Banda's earlier attack on the Arab World perhaps explains the failed meeting. Nevertheless, the aborted meeting meant that Malawi continued with a search for investors elsewhere.

In 1977, another opportunity presented itself when a consortium of Western investors expressed interest in the project. Led by the Jaako Poyry Engineering OY of Finland, whose sister company carried out the UNDP study on Viphya in 1973, it assembled five more private firms in the names of AEG-Telefunken AG (FRG), Costain International Limited (Britain), Deutsche Babcock AG (FRG), Ekman International (Sweden), and Sunds International (Sweden). Jaako Poyry deployed its consultancy branch to Malawi to revise its previous study. Meanwhile, the Bank expressed reservations about making decisions based on some "old economic reports" and implicitly called for a fresh study on the project's economic benefits to the country. In 1977, therefore, three new studies were undertaken. In addition to the one carried out by the consortium in question, both Malawi and the Bank commissioned separate studies. The Bank engaged the Canadian firm,

SCN-Rust, to undertake a fresh review of the project's economic benefits. Malawi solicited the services of A. Jennings, an economist attached to the University of Leicester who had previously been seconded to the country's Economic Planning Division, to revise the previous economic benefits report. Through his support, Malawi produced a report that favorably considered the Viphya. "The Viphya [project]," read the report,

> will result in the erection of 8,200 extra jobs directly. Faute de mieux, assuming the employment multiplier to be the same as the income multiplier, the total employment opportunities created by the project is estimated to be 21,000. With 4 percent of the population below the age of 15 years, and moving into the working age group, the project will make a major contribution to the possible problems of employment of new entrants to the labour force.[43]

Overall, the project's economic return by 1988 was projected to be 16 percent of the country's total GNP.

The Jaako Poyry report was equally promising to the consortium. Convinced that the two reports would appeal to the WB, the VIPCOR signed the contract with the consortium on February 23, 1978. The two parties agreed that Malawi would finance the last pre-engineering study before the consortium could move in to set up the mill. Unaware of the Bank's position, the VIPCOR launched yet another campaign in search of resources between March 6 and 22, 1978, holding discussions in West Germany with officials from the Ministry for Economic Co-operation, Economics Ministry, and the KfW—FRG's official development bank. The same team held similar discussions with officers under the European Investment Bank in Luxembourg before proceeding to Washington for talks at the WB. As a result of these talks, the FRG promised to release a grant of DM850,000 and an additional sum of MD1,150,000 to cover comprehensive engineering studies.[44]

These reports (by Malawi and Jaako Poyry) never won the confidence of the Bank officials who assessed them against the results of the SCN-Rust study. First, the WB argued against the sophisticated chemical technology of processing the pulp, which the consortium proposed. The Bank viewed such technology as inappropriate to a Less Developed Country such as Malawi. Instead, it suggested a simple, labor-intensive, and water-based pulp processing strategy. It also encouraged the use of ox-drawn carts, instead of trucks, to haul tree logs to the Chintheche plant.[45] Second, and perhaps more damaging to the Viphya Scheme, the WB argued that Jaakko Poyry had undervalued the project's investment costs (now valued at US$250 million) to display a positive picture of the economic benefits it presented to Malawi. For the WB, such a deal could help the consortium benefit from the capital Malawi would raise through international public financial institutions, hence subsidizing a private entity.[46] Moreover, the WB did not have confidence in a report whose study was undertaken by an interested party, the Jaako Poyry. Instead, the Bank valued the project at US$500 million in line with the figures in the SCN-Rust report.[47]

Third and related to the second, unlike the Malawi report which valued the economic benefits of the project at 16 percent of the country's GNP by 1988, the SCN-Rust report put it at 7 percent. The minimum economic benefit value the Bank required to support the project was a 10 percent rate of return.[48] The Bank took issue with Malawi's revised report for including infrastructural costs (such as road and harbor construction costs) as part of its contribution to the total investment package. The Bank had pledged to finance these aspects in the form of a loan. Because Malawi was to pay back the loan with interest, moreover, it was wrong to include it in calculating the project's net worth. Without the Bank's support, the project costs would be much higher than displayed.

But Malawi feared that excluding infrastructural costs would inflate the total investment package and scare off prospective investors. The standoff was not resolved. "There appears to be nothing we should be doing with respect to this project," noted an official at the WB in 1978.[49] "Should the Malawi Government be successful in securing a technical partner of any substance, and in putting together any kind of financial package," the official further briefed his colleagues at the Bank, "we will have to consider reactivating our timetable for the project."[50] Noting that the KfW was about to finance the engineering study, the last survey before setting up the plant, the WB cabled KfW advising it against releasing funds before the Malawi Government demonstrated a positive economic return of the project.[51] In response, the KfW withdrew its offer. Malawi tried to win the confidence of the WB by requesting Jennings to reconcile "his" report and that by the SCN-Rust. The WB was less persuaded but later in 1980, it proposed to support a sawn timber project which has since stood to the present day.[52] That decision also coincided with the fall of pulp prices on the world market. After so much money spent on feasibility studies, and 120,000 acres of pine trees planted, what appeared to have been a promising industry ended up being a mirage. To what extent does the WB's veto explain the failure of the project?

It is argued here that the technical challenges notwithstanding, the project evolved during an unfavorable economic period—one in which the international development community was generally averse to large-scale development projects with less direct effects on the poor. As noted in chapter one, the period after 1968 witnessed a remarkable shift in the global strategies of confronting poverty in the LDCs. The Viphya Scheme was a throwback to an earlier period when theorists believed that large-scale, capital-intensive projects would help to raise a country's GDP with the society benefiting through trickle-down economic effects. As early as 1969, the WB, as a component of a network of other UN agencies, had already doubted the economic potential of the Viphya, forcing Mbekeani to conclude in 1973 that the Viphya was tolerated because it was a "milking cow for consultants."[53] The suggestion to finance a sawn timber project, moreover, did not depart from what Sundelin's report had proposed in 1968. The WB accommodated the project because Malawi framed its other objectives in ways that addressed the concerns of the poor. It projected that the scheme was likely to create over 8,000 skilled and non-skilled jobs. Several other supportive projects such as dispensaries and schools undoubtedly captured the WB's interests as well. This explains the inflated job projection figures in Jennings' report cited above—which was meant to convince the WB because the latter jealously guarded these objectives. This also explains why the Bank was against sophisticated pulp-processing technology, which potentially replaced some of the jobs. It also explains the WB's particular focus on the SCN-Rust report, which noted the project would bring a rather insignificant economic return to the country. If understood in this context, the project's failure becomes less surprising. We could summarize it with what Ravi Gulhati has elsewhere described as "promising reforms, bad luck."[54]

Equally significant to note, however, is how the Bank was careful not to support a project that would end up enriching foreign companies. The Bank had two significant goals for the project. The first was to safeguard the fundamental economic interests of the country, which, unfortunately, were made incidental to those of multinational investors. The second centered on guaranteeing that the population derived benefits from the project, whether through direct participation or its related social services. For the Bank, the proposal on the sawn-timber project would well have provided citizens with jobs and other social services, albeit on a small scale. It was a better alternative than exposing the country to the ravages of multinational capitalism.

But why did Dr. Banda accept the WB's position when in the immediate past he had insisted on his autonomy from external influence? This question is important to note because the Viphya Scheme was very significant to Banda and his bureaucrats. As noted, the project would not only serve socio-economic purposes but also the political objectives of appeasing the people from the Northern Region, where there was minimal economic progress since the colonial times. Like the transfer of the national capital to Lilongwe, Banda viewed the Viphya Scheme as helping to spread development to the "Dead North." Already, some bureaucrats celebrated the project for its socio-economic value to the people of the Northern Region such that it was "politically embarrassing to abandon it" at that critical stage. Again, there had been rumors to the effect that people from the north were targeted for retrenchment at the Viphya plantations following the collapse of the Viphya Scheme.[55]

The following section seeks to provide answers to the questions raised here by locating Malawi within the wider global political dynamics of the 1960s and 1970s. It discusses Banda's 1970s foreign policy and how he attempted to mediate the two dominant discourses of the time—that of the Cold War and development. Rather than emphasizing how the Cold War served the objectives of counterinsurgency—which assumes an unlimited flow of resources and support from friendly governments—the discussion highlights how alignment in Cold War politics closed opportunities for searching alternative sources of funding to finance the Viphya Scheme. Although Banda claimed openness to both the West and the East, thereby potentially cultivating friendships with either side, in reality he pursued a pro-Western foreign policy that eliminated the Soviet Union and her allies. As a result, he did not seek industrial aid from the East to finance the Viphya Scheme. Because his foreign policy closed off other alternative sources of funding, objecting to the WB's decision was not a workable alternative, as was the case before when South Africa promised to fund the capital and Nacala projects. By locating Malawi within the broader global political and economic dynamics of the time, the discussion emphasizes the limits of state power in the age of post-independence development.

LIMITS TO DR. BANDA'S FOREIGN POLICY, 1964–1970S

In describing Malawi's foreign policy of the 1960s and 1970s, Bryan Roberts noted that Banda's "basic principle had been readiness to do business and to have good relations with any country with which grounds for common advantage could be found."[56] Like Roberts, both McMaster and Williams described Malawi's foreign policy as realistic and typical of a maverick state whose leadership made choices based on an intelligent search of the best economic outcomes.[57] More recently, Chiudza Banda placed Banda's foreign policy under the rational actor model, according to which, political leaders make decisions depending on the practical problems confronting them.[58] These arguments dovetail well with similar actors elsewhere. Literature on the Global South has emphasized how the Cold War era provided opportunities to some leaders to act autonomously, often switching sides between the East and West depending on their intelligent calculations. For example, when the US President, Dwight Eisenhower, rejected Sukarno's application for aid in 1956, the Indonesian leader turned to the Soviet Union, in the process securing a US$350 million loan for his country between 1959 and 1965.[59] Ragna Boden notes that although Sukarno's Indonesia profited from Moscow, it neither rewarded its patron with a political voice nor strategic gains.[60] Similarly in Egypt, Laron shows how this behavior defined Gamal Abdel Nasser's simultaneous interaction with the West and the East in the 1950s. When the US withdrew their pledge to finance the Aswan High Dam following Nasser's military pact with the Soviets, the Egyptian leader responded by nationalizing the Suez Canal to the utter shock of France, Britain, and the US.[61] Such a pragmatic foreign policy held true for Jawaharlal Nehru of India, who historian Westad describes as "a state-oriented pragmatist" who believed in a planned economy in which both the state and the private sector played a role. Nehru remained open to both the West and the Soviets, allowing India to use 94 percent of the Soviet's aid for economic development projects while maintaining ties with capitalist Britain and America.[62]

Whether explicitly or not, literature on Malawi puts Banda in the ranks of such figures as discussed above. Unlike these leaders, however, Banda reigned during the Cold War Détente of the 1960s and 1970s which, arguably, created more opportunities for trade and investment. As Robert McMahon and Werner Lippert have highlighted in their separate studies, the era saw expanding trade links and technological transfers between Western and Eastern Blocs.[63] As early as 1963, the US was already trading with the East, the case in point being that of President Kennedy's wheat exports. That wheat deal, as Lippert observes, helped to create competition for Eastern markets among the Western European countries throughout the 1970s Détente. Western Europe maintained trade ties with the Soviet Union even in the face of the weakening trade relations between the US and the Soviets. West Germany, for one, ranked among Moscow's major trading partners in the 1970s, with the former granting US$1.6 billion in credits to the Soviets for investment in the 3,500-mile Yamal-pipeline.[64] To what extent, then, did Malawi tap into this economic climate in support of her industrial interests? An Answer to this question requires tracing how Malawi's foreign policy mediated her interaction with other countries and actors at both the African regional and more global levels.

At the African regional level, Banda's "realistic" policies worked out well. On several occasions, he disagreed with other African leaders on decisions he considered not in the best interest of the country. For example, he objected to the mid-1960s OAU resolution to shun the white minority governments in Africa: South Africa, Southern Rhodesia, Mozambique, and Angola. He argued that such a decision did not conform to the country's policy of "contact, dialogue, and good neighborliness." Banda warned that shunning the white Southern African states would only help to ruin Malawi's precarious economy. Because Malawi is landlocked, Banda argued, it was impossible for it to boycott the neighboring countries with access to the sea.[65] As observed in chapter four of the book, in wanting to create a shorter communication route to the Indian Ocean, Banda relied on the goodwill of the white government in Mozambique to construct a rail link connecting Malawi to the port of Nacala. Similarly, Banda solicited loans and grants from South Africa to move the capital from Zomba in the far south to Lilongwe in the Central Region. While requesting parliamentary approval to send a mission to South Africa in March 1967, Banda emphasized that he did not believe in boycotts and that such a decision was not in the best interest of Malawi. Banda believed that he had the responsibility to stabilize the country economically and South Africa was crucial to achieving this object.[66]

Unsurprisingly, Banda challenged the OAU's proposal to wage war against Ian Smith's government in Southern Rhodesia, further doubting the organization's military capacity. Smith had unilaterally declared Southern Rhodesia (now Zimbabwe) as a self-governing territory, a decision that did not please Britain and Africans. The latter saw it as obstructing independence at a time when many African countries had achieved it already. At the time, other African countries proposed using military force to liberate the territory from white rule and their voice found a place in the OAU. For Banda, the "Rhodesian Air Force could reduce to ashes within 24 hours all the capitals of Central and East Africa."[67] Moreover, Banda saw an aggressive approach potentially uniting the white governments in Southern Africa against blacks, thereby complicating the struggle for independence in Southern Rhodesia, South Africa, Angola, Mozambique, and other areas. Earlier in 1966, he impressed upon his colleagues attending a Commonwealth Prime Ministers' Conference to allow Britain to address the Southern Rhodesian problem because it was "Britain's affair . . . I, for one, trust Britain to handle the problem the best way she sees fit."[68]

Banda became the first black president to visit apartheid South Africa between August 16 and 20, 1971; a visit that earned him condemnation from the OAU member states save for Malagasy (Republic of Madagascar), Ivory Coast, Gabon, Lesotho, and Mauritius, whose leaders, like Banda, advocated for contact and dialogue in resolving the South African problem. These countries rejected the OAU's resolution to suspend talks with South Africa.[69] Such a position often won the praise of the West, with President Richard Nixon affirming that "although we strongly oppose racial discrimination, we recognize the complexity of the problem South Africa faces. We fully agree that the present situation must change, but we cannot subscribe to oversimplified solutions to complicated and intense human problems."[70] Despite South Africa's record of racial discrimination, the US considered it a strong ally in Southern Africa which, for the most part of the 1960s and 1970s, was imbricated in Cold War politics. Western and Eastern powers and their allies fought for the control of Southern Africa, which was already caught up in wars of liberation, particularly in Angola, Mozambique, and Southern Rhodesia.

While most African countries gained independence in the 1960s, the Portuguese did not grant independence to their colonies in Angola, Mozambican, Guinea Bissau, and others. The same applied to Southern Rhodesia, where the white rule was consolidated through the 1965 Unilateral Declaration of Independence from the British. Although nominally a self-governing territory, Southern Rhodesia, like South Africa, did not share power with blacks. Realizing that the white rulers were nowhere close to handing over power to blacks, Africans in these countries resorted to wars of liberation, often securing military hardware, political training, and financial support from the Soviet Union, the US, Cuba, and the People's Republic of China. The armed liberation groups rarely fought as a united front, however. Angola presents a good example. Three groups emerged, each headed by leaders who either pursued a more nativist non-aligned policy or mostly aligned with the Eastern or Western blocs. The People's Movement for the Liberation of Angola (MPLA), The National Liberation Front of Angola (FNLA), and The National Union for the Total Independence of Angola (UNITA) were the most popular groups. Many of their leaders had long espoused socialist ideas and became good allies with the Soviet Union.

In seeking to contain the Soviet Union from influencing the decolonization process in Southern Africa, the US got involved in the regional politics and was further caught up in the civil war that broke out between these groups before and after independence in November 1975. Despite periodic oscillations, the US and China (which wanted to contain the growing influence of the Soviets) supported FNLA and UNITA while the MPLA received support from the Soviet Union and Cuba. South Africa was an important ally of the US, the latter touting itself as a policeman in the Southern African region.[71] Because of this, African governments' attempts to destabilize South Africa did not command US support. Although African states sought the support of the United Nations Organization towards "isolation of the offenders, economic measures against them, and the use of military force," as one US State Department Official put it, the US had "problems with [such an] approach."[72] In Malawi, the use of force or any other destabilizing approach on South Africa did not win the support of Banda, who located his pragmatism within the broader concerns of the West, with an eye on the economic advantages it might give to Malawi's economy. The economic growth the country registered between 1964 and 1979 has been attributed, in part, to Banda's pragmatic policies and his willingness to befriend those governments the OAU sought to isolate, and which were strategically significant to the West.[73]

Kayuni has argued that unlike Zambia and Tanzania whose leaders stuck to certain ideological leanings—Humanism for Zambia's Kenneth Kaunda and *Ujamma* for Tanzania's Julius Nyerere—Banda pursued an open-door policy of "pragmatic unilateral capitalism."[74] Banda's statements attest to this.

Addressing members of the Debating Club in the southern town of Zomba in 1964, he emphasized this openness, noting:

> Yes, I will be friendly to everyone—East or West. But so far as I am concerned, the policy of independent Malawi will be discretional alignment and non-alignment. Yes, discretional alignment and neutralism. When the West is doing what I think is the right thing—what is good for Malawi—I will align with the West. When the East is doing the right thing—what I think is good for Malawi—I will align with the East. But when either one or the other does something wrong, which is only in their own interest, and not in the interest of Malawi, then we part company.[75]

Banda emphasized such a position in international fora, stating at the UN General Assembly in December 1964, that Malawi would treat "each international situation, each internal problem or question that arises between the West and the East . . . strictly on its merit and not on the basis of previous commitments or rigid negative neutralism or subservient or cringing alignment."[76]

It is such pronouncements, in addition to Banda's regional behavior, that has prompted scholars such as McMaster to identify him with maverick behavior and Kayuni to describe his approach as "pragmatic unilateral capitalism." What needs emphasizing, however, is that Banda's realistic or practical foreign policy mostly played out at the African regional level. As someone with a Western orientation—having lived in the US and Britain for over thirty years—Banda retained faith in the role of the private sector in growing the economy, albeit assisted by a capitalist state.[77] He rejected popular policies on nationalization which the neighboring countries pursued, further questioning the notion of African Socialism which guided policy in Zambia and Tanzania. "What is African Socialism?" Banda queried: "It makes me sick. [Leaders in Zambia and Tanzania] do not know what they are talking about."[78] Instead, he acknowledged the role of the private sector in the country's economic growth. In consequence, Banda committed the country to a capitalist ideological leaning in its interactions with other international actors within the broader global village.

Banda's disposition towards the communist East, moreover, was excessively negative and contradicted claims to pragmatism and the open-door policy. Though admiring the Soviet Union's industrialization, he associated it with a communist or socialist system surviving on oppressive policies. In his 1967 speech to members of the Debating Club in Zomba, Banda admitted that "the development of Russia since 1917 [had] been phenomenal. It was a backward country with very few industries. There were no men of science to speak of, but today she runs with America. In a short space of about forty-five years, she has done it. . . . " But Banda linked this success to violence, coming "at the expense of human suffering, misery, and death." He wondered whether Malawian citizens were "prepared . . . to be conscripted by the state and have the state tell [the citizenry] how many bags of maize . . . to grow."[79]

Because of this, Banda selectively forged diplomatic ties with Western/capitalist countries, including the Republic of China (Taiwan) which he recognized as a separate country and visited between August 4 and 10, 1967. He persistently condemned the Soviet Union, the German Democratic Republic (Eastern Germany) and the People's Republic of China (PRC), reducing them to violent countries that did not believe in peace.[80] Banda mainly took issue with the PRC, especially because of what he described as Chinese imperialism. He advised African leaders to guard against "the overpopulated nation that looked to the great empty continent of Africa [to secure a space for her population]." Banda further questioned PRC's claims to Afro-Asian solidarity, arguing that the PRC should first have liberated territories under colonial rule within her backyard before reaching out to Africa.[81] These territories included Hong Kong and Macao, which remained under the British and Portuguese colonialism respectively. Like the Soviet Union, Banda saw Chinese imperialism bringing oppressive polices and subjecting Africa to a new wave of imperialism. He, therefore, resisted it whenever an opportunity presented itself. One came in 1965 when the question of admitting PRC into the UNO was raised. Banda rejected PRC's application, further emphasizing that the record of the PRC, relative to "the attitude towards armed combat, her open interference in the affairs of other nations, and her outspoken antipathy to the United Nations Organization," did not lend itself to admission into the peace-loving UNO.[82]

Political developments in the country might have helped to cement Banda's pro-Western stand and his distrust for the communist East. Dr. Banda accused the PRC for the 1964 cabinet crisis discussed in chapter four. "So, that country," he stated referencing the PRC:

> while its population is starving finds money, millions enough to corrupt African politicians. How do I know this? Ambassador of that particular country came to Malawi on two successive occasions. He told me [that] if you recognize us, we will give you six million [US dollars] now. . . . I refused. Later that very power corrupted six of my ministers—three first and then another three, and all for 18 million [US dollars].[83]

Whether PRC supported Banda's ex-ministers is not clear. However, as noted in chapter four, it was the US and not any of the countries in the East that gave asylum to Chipembere. Believing that communist propaganda was behind the 1964 chaos, Banda banned Marxist literature in the country, including Kwame Nkrumah's *Class Struggle in Africa*. He also proscribed those trade unions affiliated to the All African Trade Union Federation which had links with related unions in Eastern Europe.[84] Banda's political speeches had finally coalesced into a pro-Western foreign policy. Thus, unlike Nasser, Sukarno, and Nehru who mostly maintained an open-door policy towards both the West and the East, Banda did not. Such a disposition allowed the country to enjoy support from Western countries, ranging from the US, Britain, the Federal Republic of Germany, Canada, to the ROC. But it is this same disposition that helps us understand why Banda never consulted the East for potential funding towards the Viphya project. Simply put, Banda's "discretional alignment" with the West denied the country an opportunity to interact with other international actors on a more realist plane, particularly during the Détente era of the 1970s.

The Viphya Scheme collapsed because the WB blocked the funding for it at the most crucial stage. Deserving an explanation, however, is the question of why a pragmatic and maverick Banda simply agreed with the WB's decision, which was in complete contrast to his previous behavior. Banda's behavior in the late 1970s contrasts sharply with that of the 1960s when the Malawian leader made certain decisions based on practical problems affecting the country. For example, addressing the National Assembly on the possibility of seeking funding from apartheid South Africa against opposition from the US, Britain, and the WB, Banda impressed upon the parliamentarians that "in matters of this kind, we must not allow political or ideological considerations to cloud our judgment."[85] Earlier in January 1966, he had suggested to the house the possibility of securing South African loans, further stating that "I don't mind alliances with the devil."[86] In his 1967 address at the Nairobi agricultural show in Kenya, Banda had this to say when he responded to critics who condemned him for his diplomatic relations with apartheid South Africa:

> The United States of America, Britain, France [West] Germany are capitalist countries. They do not believe in communism. The Soviet Union, Czechoslovakia, Yugoslavia and Poland are communist countries, or more respectably, socialist countries. They do not believe in capitalism. Yet, the United States, Britain, France and Germany trade with the Soviet Union, Czechoslovakia, Yugoslavia and Poland. The United States, Britain, and France at least, have established diplomatic relationships with the Soviet Union, Czechoslovakia . . . Poland [and also] with Malawi. The fact that Malawi trades with South Africa, Rhodesia and Mozambique does not mean that she approves the political views of the Governments of South Africa, Rhodesia and Mozambique.[87]

When the WB used its influence to quash the Viphya Scheme in 1978, one would have expected Banda to widen his search for industrial aid for such a significant project by possibly seeking the assistance of the East, particularly the industrial Soviet Union which was already hungry for allies. This would have been consistent with Banda's maverick character. Yet, he did not.

I argue that though the Cold War provided opportunities for aid and investment capital for countries in the Global South, it closed other available alternative options, especially for those countries whose leaders, like Banda, allowed the Cold War politics to dictate their foreign policy objectives. It is in this context that Westad's observation holds, that "in many cases, the Third World leaders' choices of ideological allegiance brought them into collaboration with one or the other of the superpower, [decisions that] proved disastrous for their own people."[88] Given the economic benefits that came with Western aid in the 1960s and 1970s, "disaster" is perhaps too strong a word to align with Malawi.[89] Perhaps Banda made an intelligent opportunity cost analysis which eliminated the East in favor of the West and its related economic institutions, which at times limited the development and opportunities for his country.

It is difficult to appreciate the relevance of such an argument, however, because most of the aid and loans Malawi received in the 1960s and 1970s came from its traditional partners, with Britain and the WB/IDA taking the lead. Both Britain and the Bank could not be said to have been primarily motivated by Cold War considerations. It was colonial ties that primarily connected Britain to Malawi just as the economic mandate dictated WB's aid to the country.[90] This chapter does not suggest that the Soviets would have, with certainty, provided Malawi with investment resources to finance the Viphya Scheme. Instead, it points to how Banda's proclivity towards the West foreclosed alternative options for setting up such a costly project. In this way, the discussion dissents from Chiudza Banda's recent conclusions on the effects of the Cold War on Banda's regime and his ambitions.[91] Rather than seeing Dr. Banda as benefiting from the politics of the Cold War with the Western politicians and development experts supporting his ambitions until the end of the Cold War era in the late 1980s, the chapter argues that in more subtle ways, Cold War politics limited opportunities for investment aid that ran counter to Western interests, particularly for an industrial project that Banda so highly valued. Moreover, as detailed, much of the investment loans and aid that Malawi received in the 1960s and 1970s were not so much influenced by Cold War considerations than by the country's traditional ties with Western countries and institutions. Even if we accept that Britain and America gave aid to Malawi in exchange for Banda's pro-Western stand, as Chiudza Banda maintains, such a thesis would mostly apply to the 1960s. By the 1970s, it appears, Banda's foreign policy had fully tilted towards the West such that it did not require sustenance through "Western Cold War aid."

CONCLUSION

This chapter has examined the struggles that the post-independence state in Malawi endured in its quest to set up a pulp-producing industry in the country. The idea behind the Viphya Scheme first evolved during the last decade of British colonial rule, around the 1960s. The Viphya Plateau, which had once accommodated the failed attempt at Tung production initiated by the colonial state, became an automatic site for the pulp industry. By the late 1970s, however, it was clear to state officials and politicians in Malawi that the Viphya dream would not materialize. The chapter has argued that the WB veto frustrated the project at the most crucial stage. That veto came because Malawi did not convince the WB about the economic returns the Viphya presented to the country. In clarifying the WB's resolution, the chapter has located the Viphya within the 1970s economic and development policy environment. Persuaded that development should help address the interests of the poor, the WB was loath to support an industrial project whose economic return would primarily privilege the interests of foreign investors. Three factors influenced this decision: a shift on what constituted as significant development projects; insignificant economic benefits of the Viphya to Malawi; and the falling pulp prices on the world market.

The Viphya case helps to clarify important aspects of the early postcolonial state in Malawi. First, the state in Malawi was not as autonomous as scholars often emphasize. It was amorphous and subject to multiple pressures which limited its power. In making sense of what it achieved or failed to accomplish, one should take into consideration the multiple players with which it interacted, both state and non-state actors. It is in that interaction that answers to the failure of the war on poverty in the country could be found. Second, the Viphya illustrates how the discourses of development and the Cold War intersected. Undoubtedly, Cold War politics facilitated the transfer of capital and aid to certain countries. Even with that, the scholarly tendency to emphasize its positive economic aspects should not be exaggerated. Countries that "benefitted" from the Cold War politics were mostly those whose geopolitical position fed into the interests of the superpowers involved. Malawi did not pose any threat of flipping to the Eastern side as was the case with India, Indonesia, Egypt, and the former Portuguese colonies in Southern Africa. Even though Banda's prominent political position in global politics gave him political capital with which to drum up the support of either Western or Eastern powers, his rigid and overly pro-West foreign policy sentenced the country to working with its traditional donors only. As Westad has observed, the Cold War was a double-edged sword—it could either open or close economic opportunities. It did the latter for Malawi in the 1970s.

Finally, we should not use the Viphya case to justify well-trodden notions of neocolonialism in the form of multinational companies taking over the economic control of former colonies after independence. In fact, in this case, the state tried, without success, to attract foreign companies to the country. By vetoing the Viphya, however, the WB played the role we associate with the Fabian Society in the colonial past. While they failed to block similar undertakings in the distant past, the Fabians condemned the Chamberlainites for their obsession with projects that treated colonial interests incidental to those of the metropole. In undertaking that duty, they were joined, in the 1940s and 1950s, by the staff serving under the Department of Agriculture in colonial Malawi, who criticized the CDC-run Viphya Tung Scheme for its failure to accommodate African interests. These parallels should remind us about the cyclical nature of the development discourse and practice. Methods of achieving development have varied over time. Its aims and the concerns of development experts, however, have remained relatively the same.

NOTES

1. UNDP Report, Viphya Pulp Mill Project, May 7, 1973, MNA 11-11-3F/39560B.

2. In the WB's assessment, because the project had a poor rate of return (less than 10 percent), it would hardly pay back for the investment made under backward linkages.

3. Werner D. Lippert, "European Long-Term Investments in Détente: The Implications of East-West Cooperation," Oliver Bange and Poul Vilaume, eds. *The Long Détente: Changing Concepts of Security and Cooperation in Europe, 1950s–1980s* (Budapest, Hungary: Central European University Press, 2017), 77–93; Robert J. McMahon, *The Cold War: A Very Short Introduction* (Oxford: Oxford University Press, 2003), 122,131.

4. McMaster, *Malawi*, 93–94, 162; Happy M. Kayuni, "Malawi's Economic and Development Policy Choices from 1964 to 1980: An Epitome of 'Pragmatic Unilateral Capitalism,'" *Nordic Journal of African Studies* 20, no. 2 (2011): 112–13; Williams, *Malawi*, 261–300. See pages 266–67 for the statistical figures on the country's economic growth between 1964 and 1972. The projected growth should not negate the balance of payment problems of 1968–1973 discussed in chapter five.

5. Guy Laron, *Origins of the Suez Crisis: Postwar Development Diplomacy and the Struggle over Third World Industrialization, 1945–1956* (Washington, DC: The John Hopkins University Press, 2013); Odd Arne Westad, *The Global Cold War: Third World Interventions and the Making of Our Times* (Cambridge: C.U.P., 2009).

6. The only secondary source available, at least to the author's knowledge, is D. Giles and A. Jennings, "Project Appraisal and the Multiplier: The Case of the Pulp Mill Project in Malawi," *Oxford Economic Papers* 34, no. 2 (1982): 390–402. The two once worked for the Malawi Government.

7. It was a public corporation, the CDC, that managed the Viphya Tung Scheme while the Pulp Mill Scheme would have operated as a private entity, with the government, through the VIPCOR, as one among the shareholders.

8. McCracken, *History of Malawi,* 242.

9. Precis for the Executive Council, Chikangawa/Viphya Forest Reserve, June 4, 1951, MNA FS 2/9/1/3.

10. R. G. Green, FAO EPTA Report No. 1739, "Utilization of Exotic Plantations," 1963, MNA 11-11-3F/39560.

11. K. H. Kursten, FAO Report No. 1851, "The Feasibility of an Export Pulp Industry," 1964, MNA 2-19-6F/17842.

12. The Viphya Project, MNA 2-19-6F/17842. See also Giles and Jennings, "Project Appraisal and the Multiplier," 390–402.

13. The British High Commissioner, Malawi, to Russell, Deputy High Commissioner, Malawi, May 13, 1966, TNA DO 208/6.

14. Record of discussion, President Lyndon Johnson and N. W. Mbekeani (Malawi's Ambassador to UNO), September 25, 1967, MNA 11-11-3F/39560.

15. The Viphya Project, MNA 2-19-6F/17842. These included "The Preliminary Study of Proposed Pulp and/or Paper Industry in Malawi," by Stadler Hurter International Ltd., Montreal, Canada, 1964; "Malawi Forest Industry: Report to Canada External Aid Office," by Spartan Air Services Ltd., Canada, 1966; "A Preliminary Study for a Pulp Mill in the Republic of Malawi," by Brown & Root Inc., Houston, Texas, 1967; Two private studies included one by St. Regis Pulp and Paper Co., New York City, and Owens of Illinois and Toledo of Ohio. The last three had an explicit object of exploring possible investment in a pulp mill.

16. Banda to President Johnson, November 13, 1967, MNA 11-11-3F/39560.

17. Ibid.

18. Permanent Secretary, Ministry of Economic Affairs, Malawi, to Marshall P. Jones, US Ambassador, Malawi, January 4, 1968, MNA 11-11-3F/39560.

19. Memo by Mbekeani (Malawi Ambassador, UNO) to J. R. Ngwiri (Permanent Secretary, Ministry of External Affairs, Malawi), February 19, 1968, MNA 11-11-3F/39560.

20. South African Pulp and Paper Industry visitors, February 6, 1968, MNA 11-11-3F/39560.

21. Arne Sundelin, Report to the Administrator of UNDP (Special Fund) on the Viphya Pulp/Paper Project in the Republic of Malawi, November 1968, 7–1, MNA 2-19-6F/17842.

22. R. G. Cormack, London, to R. C. Kite, British High Commissioner, Malawi, January 16, 1969, MNA 2-19-6F/17842.

23. Ibid. Cormack's letter details Malawi's position.

24. FAO Press Release (Note to Correspondents) on Pulp and Paper, May 14, 1969, MNA 2-19-6F/17842.

25. Mbekeani, New York, to John Ngwiri (Secretary for the Treasury), Malawi, January 3, 1969, MNA 11-11-3F/39560.

26. Ibid.

27. Lennart Markila to B. R. Fuller (Director of Forestry and Game, Malawi), February 12, 1971, MNA 2-19-6F/17842.

28. Record of the meeting to discuss the Viphya project, Blantyre, Malawi, April 29, 1971, MNA 2-19-6F/17842. In attendance at the meeting were the ODA Forestry Adviser (Mr. Wyatt-Smith), Mr. Windsor, British High Commissioner; Mr. Bannister, Secretary for Agriculture and Natural Resources, among others.

29. Ibid.

30. Minute by Dr. Banda, May 3, 1971, MNA 2-19-6F/17842.

31. FAO Press Release, "Rising Demand for Paper Could Help Developing Countries' Economies," May 25, 1971, MNA 2-19-6F/17842.

32. See the Jaakko Poyry main report, "Prefeasibility Study for Industrial Utilization of the Viphya Forest Resources in Malawi," June 1973, MNA 10-10-10F/32582.

33. Located along Lake Malawi, Chintheche's position would allow for easy transportation of the pulp via the lake before connecting to the Nacala rail link to Mozambican port on the Indian Ocean coast.

34. See A Confidential report by the UNDP experts, May 7, 1973, MNA 11-11-3F/39560.

35. Ibid.

36. Banda to Shahanshar Reza Pahlavi, January 6, 1974, MNA 2-19-6F/17842.

37. McMaster, *Malawi*, 157. The Arab Casablanca group of states was an active bloc in the 1960s operating as an informal association and advocating for Pan-Africanism and the total liberation of Africa. It comprised Egypt, Algeria, Ghana, Guinea, Libya, Mali, and Morocco.

38. Ibid.

39. Ibid.

40. Extract from *Noticia da Beira*, July 9, 1969, Newspaper Cutting, H.K. Banda Archive, Indiana University Library, Box 4, Folder 6. More details in the subsequent section.

41. Iranian Ambassador (K. Niamir) to Ethiopia and Malawi, Addis Ababa, to John Ngwiri, Secretary for External Affairs, Malawi, January 16, 1974, MNA 11-11-3F/39560.

42. Record of discussion between Malawian Ambassador (Ethiopia) and Iranian Ambassador (Ethiopia/Malawi), January 20, 1975, MNA 11-11-3F/39560.

43. Economic Planning Division, "The Viphya Pulp Mill Project in Malawi: Economic Appraisal," July 1977, MNA 9-13-95/52288.

44. Record of discussion on the visit of Treasury and Viphya Corporation officials to Germany, Washington, and Luxembourg, March 6–22, 1978, MNA 30-10-10F/34582.

45. The local communities would obviously be the likely candidates to man the oxcarts.

46. Confidential memo by Austin H. Madinga (Alternate Executive Director, WB) to D. T. Matenje (Minister of Finance, Malawi), March 22, 1978. Economic Planning Division, "The Viphya Pulp Mill Project in Malawi: Economic Appraisal," July 1977, MNA 9-13-95/52288. Madinga attended the WB meeting on Viphya. Also, in attendance at the meeting were two officials from Malawi, Messrs. Lihowa and Kalinga.

47. The figure was reported in a memo from J.Z.U. Tembo, Chairman, VIPCOR to Dr. Banda, February 18, 1980, MNA 9-13-9F/52288.

48. Memo by P. M. O. Mbisa (Chief Economist), February 21, 1978, MNA 30-10-10F/34582.

49. Memo by Sivaram P. Nayar to Andrew J. Ewing, World Bank, Washington, DC, February 16, 1978, MNA 30-10-10F/34582.

50. Ibid.

51. WB to KfW, originating department and personnel illegible, telex number 74021, March 17, 1978, MNA 30-10-10F/34582.

52. Later, Jennings published an article justifying the Viphya to an academic audience. See Giles and Jennings, "Project Appraisal and the Multiplier," 390–402.

53. Mbekeani (Malawi Ambassador, Ethiopia) to Secretary of External Affairs, Blantyre, July 31, 1971, MNA 111-11-3F/39560. By that time, more than ten studies had been undertaken on the Viphya with little to show for it. These included: 1963: FAO/EPTA/R. G. Green, "Utilization of Exotic Plantations"; 1964: FAO/K. H. Kurten, "Report to the Government of Nyasaland on the Feasibility of an Export Pulp Industry"; 1965: Stadler Hurter International Limited, "Preliminary Study of Proposed Pulp and/or Paper Industry in Malawi"; 1966: Spartan Air Services Ltd., "Malawi Forestry Industry: Report to Canada External Aid Office"; 1967: FAO/UNDP, "Timber Marketing: Report to the Government of Malawi"; 1967: FAO/UNDP, "Investigating Wood Requirements: Report to the Government of Malawi"; 1967: Brown and Root Inc., "A Preliminary Study for a Pulp and Paper Mill in the Republic of Malawi"; 1971: Department of Forestry and Game (Malawi), "Viphya Pulpwood Plantations: Project Summary and Progress to Date"; 1968: A. Sundelin, "Report to the Administration of UNDP Special Fund on the Viphya Pulp/Paper Project in Malawi"; 1970/71: A. Sundelin, "Paper and Pulp Marketing Survey for IBRD."

54. Ravi Gulhati, *Malawi: Promising Reforms, Bad Luck* (World Bank: Washington, DC, 1989).

55. T. N. Msusa (Commissioner for Town and Country Planning) to Co-ordinating Officer, VIPCOR, December 4, 1980, MNA 9-3-95/52288. Msusa's letter clearly articulates the political objectives of evenly spreading development across the country. Also, an investigation on the rumor in question revealed that there was no targeted retrenchment based on one's region or ethnic group. Because many of the people involved in the plantation scheme were from the north, they were also retrenched in large numbers. See the District Commissioner's (North) report, "Potential Political Issues on the Viphya Labor Force," submitted to the Secretary of the President and Cabinet, Lilongwe, April 17, 1980, MNA 9-13-9R/52288;

56. Bryan Roberts, "Malawi Progress and Problems Since Independence," *African Affairs* 69, no. 274 (1970): 62.

57. McMaster, *Malawi,* 93–95; Williams, *Malawi,* 5.

58. Paul Chiudza Banda, "Hastings Kamuzu Banda: How the Cold War Sustained Bad Governance in Malawi," in Baba G. Jallow, ed. *Leadership in Postcolonial Malawi: Trends Transformed by Independence* (New York: Palgrave Macmillan, 2014), 28; See also Stephen Chan, *Kaunda and Southern Africa: Image and Reality in*

Foreign Policy (London: British Academic Press, 1992), 3–4. Chan's work discusses at length the rational actor model.

59. Ragna Boden, "Cold War Economics: Soviet Aid to Indonesia," *Journal of Cold War Studies* 10, no. 3 (2008): 115–16; Cullather, *The Hungry World,* 136.

60. Ibid., 127–28.

61. Laron, *Origins of the Suez Crisis,* 152.

62. Westad, *The Global Cold War*, 81; Boden, "Cold War Economics," 121. India also secured the Soviet military aid towards the Sino-Indian war of 1962 and the Kashmir crisis of that decade.

63. McMahon, *The Cold War*, 122, 131; Lippert, "European Long-term Investments in Détente," 77–93.

64. Lippert, "European Long-term Investments in Détente," 80, 83, 88, 92.

65. Malawi: A Brief Statement of Domestic and Foreign Policies, July 24, 1968, MNA 12-10-7R/28381; H. K. Banda address, UNO General Assembly, December 2, 1964, MNA 12-10-3F/28408.

66. *Rhodesian Herald*, March 24, 1967, Newspaper Cutting, MNA 12-10-3F/28408; See also McMaster, *Malawi*, 94.

67. Banda's address to the Malawi Parliament, November 11, 1967. Cited in *Ethiopian Herald*, Newspaper Cutting, MNA 12-10-3F/28408.

68. H. K. Banda speech, Lagos, Nigeria, cited in Press Release no 22/66, Malawi, January 13, 1966, MNA/ 12-10-3F/28408.

69. See "The Unholy Alliance," *The Nationalist* (Tanzania), August 7, 1971, Newspaper Cutting, MNA 12-10-5R /28394.

70. Cited verbatim in speech by David D. Newsom (Assistant Secretary of State for African Affairs, USA), Atlanta Press Club, September 21, 1971, MNA 12-10-7R/28381.

71. Westad, *Global Cold War*, 207–49.

72. Newsom speech, Atlanta Press Club, September 21, 1971, MNA 12-10-7R/28381.

73. Kayuni, "Malawi's Economic and Development Policy Choices from 1964 to 1980," 112–31. Many of the projects of that era—M1 Road, Nacala Rail Link, the new capital, Hydro Electric Power station, Agricultural schemes, and so forth—were bankrolled through loans from Western countries and South Africa.

74. Ibid., 122.

75. H. K. Banda speech, "A Threat to World Peace," April 29, 1964, H. K. Banda Archive, Indiana University Library, Box 2, Folder 4.

76. See H. K. Banda address, UNO General Assembly, December 2, 1964, MNA 12-10-3F/28408.

77. See H. K. Banda speech, H. K. Banda Archive, April 29, 1964, Indiana University Library, Box 2, Folder 4.

78. Cited in *East Africa and Rhodesia*, "Dr. Banda's Criticisms of other African Leaders," July 6, 1966, Newspaper Cutting, TNA, DO 208/1.

79. See H. K. Banda speech, "A Threat to World Peace," April 29, 1964.

80. See H. K. Banda address, UNO General Assembly, September 27, 1965, MNA 12-10-3F/28408.

81. "Prime Minister Warns against China's Advances," *Malawi Times*, September 17, 1965; On Afro-Asian solidarity see H. K. Banda speech during his visit to the Republic of Malagasy, September 16, 1965, MNA/12-10-3F/28408.

82. H. K. Banda address, UNO General Assembly, September 27, 1965, MNA 12-10-3F/28408.

83. H. K. Banda speech during his visit to Malagasy, September 16, 1965, MNA/12-10-3F/28408.

84. See Paul Chiudza Banda and Gift Wasambo Kayira, "The Contested Legacies of Malawi's Decolonization Process, 1944–1994," in Kenneth R. Ross and Wapulumuka O. Mulwafu, eds. *Politics, Christianity and Society in Malawi: Essays in Honour of John McCracken* (Mzuzu, Malawi: MZUNI Press, 2020), 215–42.

85. *National Assembly Parliamentary Debates*, August 23, 1966, 30.

86. *National Assembly Parliamentary Debates,* January 18, 1966, 411.

87. H. K. Banda Speech delivered during the opening of Nairobi Agricultural Show, September 27, 1967, H. K. Banda Archive, Indiana University Library, Box 2, Folder 2.

88. Westad, *The Global Cold War*, 3.

89. For statistical figures on Malawi's economic growth between 1964 and 1972 (despite the balance of payment challenges of 1968–1973 see Williams, *Malawi*, 266–67; Kayuni, "Malawi's Economic and Development Policy Choices from 1964 to 1980," 112–13. Kayuni relies on William's data.

90. After independence, for example, Britain had some of its citizens (particularly, British Indians), plying their businesses in Malawi. Britain's presence in the country was also necessary to protect this group which was a constant target of Dr. Banda's 1965/1971 The [Property] Forfeiture Act. British officials often used aid to bargain for compensation of those whose property was confiscated. These relations, whatever the nature they took, had little to do with Cold War politics. See cases in Forfeiture Act of Government of Malawi, 1971, TNA/FCO 45/1047; 1048.

91. Chiudza Banda, *The State, Counter-insurgency and Political Policing in Colonial and Post-colonial Malawi.*

Conclusion

Some Reflections on the State and the War on Poverty

In more recent years, scholars have emphasized the need for writing development histories that are more imperial, global, and transnational in approach.[1] This book has responded to this call by documenting the struggles, dilemmas, and anxieties that the state in Malawi endured in fulfilling the task of arresting rural poverty. The result is an imperial and transnational study that speaks to broader debates about British colonial development and welfare, how they played out in colonial Malawi and their legacies for the postcolonial society. A significant argument pursued in this book is that political independence in Malawi did not mark a complete break with the past, at least at the level of economy. Instead of looking at colonial legacy in overly negative terms, the book has zeroed in on many of the seemingly positive ideas and practices of development the British pursued which continued to influence the postcolonial state, albeit without much success. In adopting this argument, the book does not seek to rehabilitate colonialism but rather to show how overemphasis on negative colonial legacy robs society an opportunity to improve on current interventions on development by retracing their historical roots to the original ideas that birthed them and the unique historical context that gave to their rise or frustrated their implementation. I have demonstrated that postcolonial attempts to reform customary land use practices for the benefit of the rural poor, or to create inclusive secondary agricultural industries that did not disadvantage the poorer segments of the society, or greater still, promote rural development interventions to address rural poverty, were first tried and failed under British colonialism. In emphasizing these commonalities, the book tells a story that displays first, the cyclical nature of development histories and second, how state power was contested in ways that frustrated the aims of arresting poverty in the country. These cycles and contestations, and the changes they display over time, become remarkable through an analysis that taps on the fruitful dialogue between a prospective and retrospective examination of the state and what it sought to achieve for the poor. More significantly, the changes were brought about by national, imperial, and transnational players and, therefore, deserve a comment as I conclude this study.

When the CO proposed land titling reforms in 1939 and later 1947, it was aware that the reforms were politically sensitive, having created chaos in other parts of the British Empire in the past. The rejection of these proposals by colonial authorities in Nyasaland did not come as a surprise to the CO. What the CO least anticipated was that following the political uncertainties of the 1950s, local bureaucrats would appropriate the idea, repackage it, and use it for purposes of securing settlers' interests in land. Aware of such motives, Africans, particularly those serving in the Legislative Council, blocked the land reform proposals, only to support them later in 1967 after calls for political independence became a reality. By this time, they had the support of the World Bank, which advocated private rights to land. Freed from the political debates of the colonial era, the new players supported the Lilongwe project within the overall framework of the 1960s war on poverty. The confidence experts espoused soon waned when chiefs rejected land individualization. In consequence, development experts were forced to compromise and accept corporate or village titles, which only helped to reinforce the very customs they sought to break. The fact that Dr. Hastings Banda never helped to roll out the 1967 customary land legislation across the country shows that the dilemmas colonial bureaucrats faced in the 1930s and 1940s were as real for the postcolonial present as they had been for the colonial past.

These connections in the development process and the political dynamics involved were not unique to land reform proposals. This book has emphasized how attempts by the postcolonial state to support the pulp mill industry were predicated on deeper historical interests to turn the Viphya Plateau into an economic hub for northern Malawi, which was dubbed the "Dead North." The Viphya became a space where various industrial ideas were tested and failed. Of significance is how both the pulp mill and the tung oil schemes reveal the way power was contested and why. During the colonial period, the DOA was careful not to support a tung oil industry that excluded Africans. Real colonial trusteeship involved protecting Africans from the ravages of markets while granting them economic opportunities necessary to raise their living standards. Participation in tung tree production and later, the production of rice in the Limphasa Scheme of the CDC, was a necessary step towards that direction. I have argued, however, that such claims to defend the interests of Africans should not be exaggerated. Bureaucrats within the DOA also used the "African card" to contain the growing influence of planters who were slowly usurping the Department's power to set the economic agenda of the colonial state. This resistance was also apparent in the way authorities debated the CDC-run Viphya Tung Scheme, often accusing its personnel of promoting unrealistic economic ventures.

The pulp mill project was no exception to these dynamics. The WB supported the project in the hope that it would safeguard the country's economic interests and secure jobs for Malawians. It became clear, however, that the mill as designed would benefit foreign investors far more than ordinary Malawians. As a result, the Bank frustrated the project. But the policing role the Bank played was not unprecedented. Many of the members of the Fabian Society in the colonial past also accused Joseph Chamberlain of promoting metropolitan economic interests over the welfare of the colonial people. Between 1947 and 1951, moreover, the Labour Government too received intense criticisms for promoting similar projects in the colonies, which it supported through the ORDA. Furthermore, in the immediate postcolonial present, both the WB and Britain's ODM condemned Dr. Banda for promoting capital intensive development projects, which they regarded as straining the economy. Also, scholars in Malawi have taken over the role the Fabians played in the past and criticized the state for supporting large-scale commercial private estates at the expense of promoting the welfare of peasants.

These debates, however, should not reify the popular arguments that assume a simple continuity from the colonial past to the postcolonial present, nor reduce the state to one that was necessarily leviathan. Malawi's development history should not be read backward based on outcomes, as is the trend with the existing literature. Instead, it needs to be interpreted based on intentions and attempt to trace how such intentions played out. Such an approach helps us read this history beyond the exploitation narrative, all the while escaping the fallacy of leapfrogging legacies. It also helps us pay attention to the contours of development history and avoid presenting it deterministically.

The connections in development history, as articulated in this study, remind us about the contradictions of the development process itself. Development can create both progress and crisis. The fear of creating the latter dictated debates on colonial and, later, postcolonial development and welfare—from the Liverpool School to the Fabians, to the World Bank, Britain's Ministry of Overseas Development, and the Malawian state. Development actors, politicians, and state bureaucrats shared a belief in the principle of trusteeship and worked to ensure that development did not condemn ordinary Africans to the exploitation of other classes. The real dilemma, however, centered on how to reconcile the goals of achieving high production on the one hand and ameliorating poverty of the poor on the other. Strategies employed varied over time and oscillated between the two goals. Specific forces acting on the state, however, determined which direction the pendulum of state policy would swing. If the 1930s and 1940s represented an era of colonial development and welfare within the British Empire, the economic pressures arising from the Second World War created countervailing forces that forced a reversal of that policy. Similarly, at independence, the Malawian state planned to support both small-scale and large-scale farmers. However, concerns over its economic sovereignty coming in the wake of intense pressure asserted by the ODM and the WB, not to mention the oil shock of the early 1970s, forced the state to reorient its agricultural policy towards the more economically promising estate sector.

It is this story of how Malawi's development history unfolded over time that this study has sought to tell. In doing so, the book affords scholars and others a better understanding of the behavior of the state that helped to shape this history. Although the state in Malawi was becoming increasingly authoritarian and leviathan, it was also weak, fluid, and malleable. The state was certainly weak because it failed to measure up to well-decentralized and better democratized states that fit in neo-Weberian model of the state. But the state was also weak because of the several contending development actors that undermined its autonomy, in the process pushing it towards more authoritarianism. I have argued that none of the developmental actors discussed—whether state bureaucrats, local politicians, or international actors from aid institutions—had complete control over the country's development process. Even Dr. Banda, whom scholars praise as having controlled the development process of the country, did not enjoy unlimited power. While chapter four shows that Banda triumphed over the WB and the ODM in his decisions on the capital and railway projects, his failure to challenge the WB over the Viphya Pulp Mill project shows the limits to his power. In the colonial past, although the Department of Agriculture officials helped to obstruct the Nyasaland Tea Growers' Association from accessing government funds for a corporate tung oil extraction mill, their attempts to block planters' interests in the Viphya Tung Scheme failed. It was planters such as Barrow and Tait-Bowie, who guided the experimental Viphya Scheme. Both these groups finally lost out when the CDC personnel took over the management of the Viphya Scheme.

The land debate displays similar dynamics. As noted, neither the CO nor the local administrators had complete control over this debate and its associated practices. Attempts to promote land improvement schemes as an alternative to land tenure reforms failed as ordinary Africans rejected the schemes. What is more, while colonial administrators appear to have triumphed over the colonial office's policy recommendations on land in the 1940s, African elites blocked proposals on land reforms the government proposed later in the 1950s. Similarly, plans by the postcolonial state and the WB to introduce titling reforms after independence foundered when local Africans rejected such proposals even as they accepted the Lilongwe land project for the benefits it presented in other areas of their economic life. In recognizing the kaleidoscopic ways in which power relations played out in Malawi, the study questions the "vertical power relations" at the center of the "politics of domination" which poststructuralist development scholars often associate with the development project.

It appears, therefore, that there are significant similarities in the way both the colonial and postcolonial states sought to achieve autonomy from outside players and how local forces challenged state power. Undoubtedly, the colonial state was an extension of the British imperial state, with the CO exercising enormous control over its decisions. The debates on the 1950s land tenure reforms and the Viphya tung oil industry show how the governor in Nyasaland periodically liaised with the CO on matters relating to these areas. The rejection of the S/S/C's policy recommendations of 1939 and 1947, however, illustrates how the colonial state defended its autonomy in some decisions. After independence, the postcolonial state was an autonomous entity. But its weak economic position forced it to continue engaging with Britain on various aspects of its economy. Similar considerations connected it to the various UN agencies, including the World Bank. These ties limited the power the state exercised over the development process. Both Britain's Ministry of Overseas Development and the World Bank significantly constrained state actions. Other than these broader power dynamics, both the colonial and postcolonial states faced internal pressures that further limited state autonomy.

By displaying how various players contested state plans, therefore, this book presents a better understanding of how the war on poverty failed in Malawi. For a country already exposed to multiple impediments to development, including a lack of mineral resources with which to generate revenue, its landlocked status which naturally increased the cost of transportation, and the oil shock of the 1970s, it is tempting to suggest that the war on poverty probably failed even before it started. Government bureaucrats always worried about how to address the general economic weaknesses of colonial and later postcolonial Malawi, before paying attention to the specific problems of the poor. Besides, for most of the colonial period, the country did not have a research station worth the name such that officials' knowledge of such aspects as the general climatic conditions and soil status remained shallow. These problems combined with limited or lack of farm technology to frustrate the zeal planners had. Such challenges notwithstanding, the state remained optimistic and constantly theorized or raised specific development interventions directed at mitigating poverty among the poor communities. The contending but irreconcilable intensions of the many groups involved in this war, however, further weakened the state's capacity to address the problem of rural poverty. It is impossible to frame development plans that will command the support of all the segments of society. Recognizing the roles various groups played to frustrate or strengthen state projects in the past is a necessary step to smoothen the development process in contemporary and future interventions.

This book opened with the contrasting stories of coffee and tobacco farmers, whose experiences partly influenced research towards it. As I wind it off, it is worth emphasizing that tobacco production was liberalized in the mid-1990s, allowing both large- and small-scale farmers to produce the crop and sell it directly at the auction floors. Over time, tobacco has consistently fetched bargain-basement prices on the market, forcing rural farmers to pull out of its production. In contrast, coffee production in the north has remained promising and given rise to one of the country's most forward-looking farmers' unions, the Mzuzu Coffee Planters Cooperative Union Limited. Constituting six coffee cooperatives with more than 3000 farming families from the country's northern region, it aims to assist farmers afford decent accommodation, achieve food security, and attain better education by promoting sustainable coffee production, processing, and marketing.[2] The union boasts the Mzuzu Coffee brand, which has attracted international recognition for its quality. In 2019, Malawi lost its fairtrade certification.[3] A fairtrade label on a product symbolizes, among others, that the product is produced under fair practices which provide better returns to farmers while promoting climate-friendly production strategies. Non-reinstatement of this certification to the country spells disaster for coffee farmers. It will close off international markets for the brand and reverse the gains coffee farmers have achieved over time. The Malawian state requires some level of dynamism to mediate such contemporary forces that threaten the livelihood of local coffee and related farmers, fully recognizing the diverse interests at stake and how to accommodate them.

NOTES

1. Engerman and Unger, "Introduction: Towards a Global History of Modernization," 2009, 375–85; Hodge, "Writing the History of Development," 127–74.
2. Mzuzu Coffee Planters Cooperative Union Limited, https://www.mzuzucoffee.org/, Accessed on July 27, 2022.
3. "Malawi Coffee Industry Embroiled in Unfair Trade Practices," May 27, 2022, *The Independent*, https://independentmw.com/malawi-coffee-industry-embroiled-in-unfair-trade-practices/, Accessed on July 27, 2022.

Bibliography

PRIMARY SOURCES

From the Malawi National Archives (MNA)

1-8-9R/17841, World Bank IDA Aid to Malawi, 1971.

1-8-9R/17841, UK Financial Talks, 1971.

2-19-6F/17842, Kursten, K. H. FAO Report No. 1851, "The Feasibility of an Export Pulp Industry," 1964.

2-19-6F/17842, Sundelin, Arne, Report to the Administrator of UNDP (Special Fund) on the Viphya Pulp/Paper Project in the Republic of Malawi, November 1968.

2-19-6F/17842, The Viphya Pulp Project, 1968–1971.

1-8-9R/17839, Draft Statement of Development Policy, 1970.

1-8-9R/17839, IMF Report on Malawi, 1970.

1-8-9R/17839, National Development Plan, Malawi, 1970–1971.

3-11-99/18949, Interview with Andrew Mercer (LLDP Manager), *Backgrounder*, December 12, 1969, Magazine Cutting.

3-11-99/18949, Land Reorganization, Central Region, 1969–1970.

3-11-99/18949, The LLDP Quarterly Report, September 30, 1969.

4-14-1F/33764, Memoranda by R. B. S. Purdy (for Secretary to the President and Cabinet), October 23, 1971.

4-14-1F/33764, UNDP Background Paper on Malawi, March 1971.

6-6-4F/17864, Papers for London Talks, 1968.

9-13-95/52288, Economic Planning Division, "The Viphya Pulp Mill Project in Malawi: Economic Appraisal," July 1977.

9-13-95/52288, Economic Planning Division, "The Viphya Pulp Mill Project in Malawi: Economic Appraisal," July 1977.

10-10-10F/34582, Viphya Project Papers, dating from 1978.

11-11-3F/39560, Green, R. G. FAO EPTA Report No. 1739, "Utilization of Exotic Plantations," 1963.

11-11-3F/39560, Viphya Pulpwood Project, Minutes, Reports and Correspondence, 1967–1975.
11-11-3F/39560B, Viphya Pulp Mill Project, 1973.
11-11-5F/39566, World Bank Schemes in Malawi, 1971.
12-10-3F/28408, *Ethiopian Herald*, November 11, 1967, Newspaper Cutting.
12-10-3F/28408, H. K. Banda address, UNO General Assembly, December 2, 1964.
12-10-3F/28408, H. K. Banda address, UNO General Assembly, September 27, 1965.
12-10-3F/28408, *Rhodesian Herald*, March 24, 1967, Newspaper Cutting.
12-10-3F/28408, H. K. Banda speech during his visit to Malagasy, September 16, 1965.
12-10-3F/28408, H. K. Banda speech, Lagos, Nigeria, cited in Press Release no. 22/66, Malawi, January 13, 1966.
12-10-3F/28408, H. K. Banda address, UNO General Assembly, December 2, 1964.
12-10-5R/28394, *The Nationalist* (Tanzania), August 7, 1971, Newspaper Cutting.
12-10-7R/28381, Address by David D. Newsom (Assistant Secretary of State for African Affairs, USA) at the Atlanta Press Club, September 21, 1971.
12-10-7R/28381, Malawi: A Brief Statement of Domestic and Foreign Policies, July 24, 1968.
15-12-6R/15077, Development Plan and Projects (Malawi), 1965–1969.
15-12-6R/15077, Model Villages in Malawi, Circular No. 3/68, Department of Agriculture, Ministry of Economic Planning, Zomba, 1968.
15-12-6R/15077, Report of Government/CDC [CmDC] Working Party, “African Tea Development Projects,” April 1963.
FS 1/6/1, Post-War Development, Agenda and Minutes, 1945.
FS 2/9/1/3, Precis for the Executive Council, Chikangawa/Viphya Forest Reserve, June 4, 1951.
FS 2/19/1, Removal of Zomba Capital, Nyasaland, 1947.
PCS 1/16/1, Land Resettlement, Nchacha, Chikwawa, 1956–1958.
PCS 1/16/8, Land Usage Schemes—Namphota, 1956.
PCS 1/16/9, Memorandum, Provincial Commissioner (South) to District Commissioners (South), specific date not legible, 1954.
S12/1/2/2, Native Land Tenure Conferences, Nyasaland Protectorate, 1947–1949.
S12/1/12/2, Rice Production in the Limphasa Valley, Nyasaland, 1942.
S12/1/18/1, Tung Production, Nyasaland, 1929–1949.
S12/1/18/3, Minutes, Correspondence in Tung Development, Nyasaland, 1944–1946.
S12/1/18/4, Tung Production, Nyasaland, 1939–1941.
S19/1/1/1, Projects, Colonial Development, Nyasaland Viphya, 1947–1948.
S43/1/11/1, Native Land Tenure, Nyasaland Protectorate, 1939–1940.

From the British National Archives (TNA)

CO 525/178/10, Land Bank, Nyasaland, 1939.
CO 525/208/4, Nyasaland Post-war Development Plan, 1945–1955 (Revised 1947).
CO 1015/622, Progress Reports by the Colonial Development Corporation on the Limphasa Dambo Farm of Nyasaland, 1951–1953.
CO 1015/674, Quarterly report of the Limphasa Scheme, June 1952.
CO 1015/901, Land Tenure, Nyasaland, 1954–1956.
CO 1015/850, *East Africa and Rhodesia*, Magazine cutting, May 27, 1954.
CO 1015/1407, African Land Tenure, Nyasaland, 1957–1959.
CO 1015/1742, The Nyasaland African Congress, 1957–1959.
CO 1015/2188, Titles to Land, Nyasaland, 1960–1962.
CO 1015/2498, Conference on Economic Development in Blantyre, Nyasaland, 1960–1962.
DO 183/110, African Land Tenure and Land Policy in Nyasaland, 1960–1965.
DO 183/839, United Kingdom Economic Mission, Malawi 1965.
DO 208/1, H. K. Banda speech, February 1, 1966.
DO 208/3, Financial Decisions, 1966, Malawi.
DO 208/6, Political Relations between Malawi and the United States of America, 1966.
FCO 45/1047; 1048, Forfeiture Act of Government of Malawi, 1971.
OD 31/108, Request for Advice in the Establishment of a Lilongwe Land Registry, 1967–1969.
OD 31/039, Visit and Report of Mr. S. R. Simpson (Land Tenure Advisor, ODM) to Malawi, 1966.

From the World Bank Group Archive (WBGA) in Washington, DC, and its online database documents

Lilongwe Land Development Project (03), Malawi-Credit P001598/550 MAI, Correspondence, Vol. 5, 1977–1981, Box 1-4-16, File No. 30178835.
Malawi LLDP Project Performance Audit Report, Phase III. World Bank Restricted Report No. 3414. April 1981, http://documents.worldbank.org/curated/en/998211468300594184/text/multi-page.txt.
Malawi: General Negotiation—Correspondence. Vol. 1, 1964, File No. 1830078.
Malawi: General Negotiation, Volume 1, 1968–1971, Box 107-03/158-2-6, File No. 1880299.
Malawi: General Negotiation—Correspondence, Vol. 2, 1967, File No. 1860298.
Malawi: General Negotiations, Vol. 1. 1969–1971, File No. 1860299, Box 107-03/158-2-6.
McNamara's address to the World Bank Board of Governors, Nairobi, Kenya, September 24, 1973, http://documents.worldbank.org/curated/en/930801468315304694/pdf/Address-to-the-Board-of-Governors-by-Robert-S-McNamara.pdf.

Ministry of Overseas Development, *Lilongwe Land Development Project, Annex 21*, 1969, File No. 302031.

Research Product Output (RPO) 670–93, Evaluation, LLDP, 1975–1982, File No. 30136805.

Sewell, L. G. Some Notes on the Customary Land (Development) Act, CAP. 59 of 9/5/67. No., File No. 302991 (102003).

The Development Credit Agreement Between the Republic of Malawi and the International Development Association, February 5, 1968, World Bank Lilongwe Agricultural Project, Credit No. 113 MAI, http://documents.worldbank.org/curated/en/376411468277503973/pdf/Credit-0113-Malawi-Lilongne-Agricultural-Development-Project-Credit-Agreement.pdf.

World Bank Research Program Completion Reports and Evaluation, Lilongwe Land Development Project, 1975–1982, File No. 30136805.

World Bank Institute (WBI/Economic Development Institute) (EDI), not dated, http://documents.worldbank.org/curated/en/372291468129005130/pdf/936580WP0ED I0h0Box385399B00PUBLIC00.pdf.

World Bank, Lilongwe Development Project in Malawi. Report No. TO-610a, January 3, 1968, http://documents.worldbank.org/curated/en/998211468300594184/text/multi-page.txt.

World Bank, Rural Development Sector Policy Paper, PUB-588, 1975: 8, http://documents.worldbank.org/curated/en/688121468168853933/pdf/PUB5880PUB0B ox0er0Rural0Development.pdf.

World Bank, Republic of Malawi Poverty Assessment. Washington, DC, World Bank Group, 2016, https://openknowledge.worldbank.org/bitstream/handle/10986/26488/MalawiPovAssess.pdf?sequence=1&isAllowed=y. Accessed on July 26, 2022.

World Bank, Report and Recommendations of the President to the Executive Directors on a proposed Credit to the Republic of Malawi for the Lilongwe Agricultural Project, Report No. P 582, January 22, 1968, http://documents.worldbank.org/curated/pt/873781468046744947/text/multi0page.txt.

Ziegler, Charles interview with Alexander Storrar (Head of WB's ADS, Kenya, 1965–1969), August 19, 1986, Oral History Program Interview Transcript 79135, WBGA, https://oralhistory.worldbank.org/transcripts/transcript-oral-history-interview-alexander-storrar-held-august-19-1986. Accessed on December 2, 2019.

From the Bodleian Library of Commonwealth and African Studies (BLCAS), Oxford.

Beaver, William interview with Richard Kettlewell, October 11, 1979, William Beaver papers, MSS.Afr.s.22.28.

MSS Afr.s. 1742/38, 1985. Specific contents of these papers cannot be disclosed without copyright permission.

Transcript of Land Colloquium on Malawi, November 22, 1980, MSS.Afr .s.1742.22.28.
Transcript of the Nyasaland Colloquium on Finance, 1982, MSS.Afri.s.1742 m-40.
Youens, Peter interview with Richard Kettlewell, Feb 9, 1985, Peter Youens papers, MSS.Afr.s.1742 (38).

From Dr. H. K. Banda Archive, Indiana University Library

Extract from *Noticia da Beira*, July 9, 1969, Newspaper Cutting, Box 4, Folder 6.
H. K. Banda address to the Malawi Parliament, January 29, 1968, Box 2, Folder 2.
H. K. Banda speech, Nairobi Agricultural Show, September 27, 1967, Box 2, Folder 2.
H. K. Banda address to the Malawi Parliament, September 27, 1968, Box 2, Folder 2.
H. K. Banda speech during the opening of Nacala Rail Link, July 4, 1970, Box 2, folder 3.
H. K. Banda address to the Malawi Parliament, March 11, 1975, Box 2, Folder 4.
H. K. Banda speech, "A Threat to World Peace," April 29, 1964, Box 2, Folder 4.
H. K. Banda speech, July 1965, Box 6, folder 14.
Malawi at War against Poverty, Disease and Ignorance, Box 6, folder 14.
The Development Plan (Malawi), 1973, Box 2, Folder 9.

Government Publications and Others

Abrahams, Sidney. *Nyasaland Land Commission*, Vol. 1. Zomba: Government Printer, 1946.
Africa Bureau. *Reflections on the Report of the Royal Commission on East Africa.* London: Africa Bureau, 1956.
Africa Publications Trust. *Malawi: Dialogue and Development*. London: Africa Publications Trust, 1973.
Appalachian Regional Commission. *Moving Appalachia Forward: Appalachian Regional Strategic Plan, 2005–2010*. Washington, DC: The Appalachian Regional Commission, 2004.
Association for World Peace. *War on Want: A Plan for World Development*. London: Association for World Peace, 1952.
Berg, Elliot. *Accelerated Development in Sub-Saharan Africa: An Agenda for Action.* Washington, DC: World Bank, 1981.
Brain, Christopher and Michael Cable. *Pioneering Development: CDC Diamond Jubilee, 1948–2008*. London: CDC Group plc, 2008.
Bureau pour le Developpement de la Production Agricole (BDPA)/AHT International, "Report of the Customary Land Utilisation Study: The 'Ndunda' Land Registration

Component of the Lilongwe Land Development Programme." Malawi, Lilongwe, 1998.
Colony and Protectorate of Kenya, *A Plan to Intensify the Development of African Agriculture in Kenya.* Nairobi: Government Printer, 1954.
Great Britain. Colonial Development Act, 1929. London: HMGSO, 1929.
Great Britain, *Overseas Resources Development Act, 1948*. London: HMSO, 1948.
Great Britain. *Overseas Development: The Work of the New Ministry*, Cmnd. 2736. London: HMSO, 1965.
Great Britain, *Parliamentary Debates* (Commons), 5th Series 482 (December 13, 1951), https://www.theyworkforyou.com/debates/?id=1951-03-13a.1317.7, Accessed January 18, 2020.
Great Britain. *Report of the Conference on African Land Tenure in East Africa and Central Africa, February 1956.* London: HMSO, 1956.
Great Britain. *Role of United Kingdom in Commonwealth Development*, Cmnd. 237. London: HMG, 1957.
Great Britain. *The East Africa Royal Commission Report*, 1953–1955, Cmd. 9475. London: HMSO, 1956.
Hailey, Lord. *An African Survey: A Study of Problems Arising in Africa South of the Sahara*. London: Oxford University Press, 1938.
Hinden, Rita. *Plan for Africa: A Report Prepared for the Colonial Bureau of the Fabian Society*. London: George Allen and Unwin, 1941.
Kettlewell, Richard W. *An Outline of Agrarian Problems and Policy in Nyasaland.* Zomba: Government Printer, 1955.
Labour Party. *The Empire in Africa: Labour's Policy.* London: The Labour Party, 1926.
League of Nations. *Covenant of the League of Nations*, April 28, 1919. Amended in December 1924.
Malawi Congress Party. *Malawi Congress Party Manifesto for the General Elections*. Limbe: MCP Publication, 1961.
Malawi Government. Customary Land (Development) Act—No. 5; Registered Land Act—No. 6; and Local Boards Land Act—No. 7, 1967. Zomba: Government Printer, 1967.
Malawi Government. *1977 Statistical Survey*. Zomba: National Statistical Office, 1977.
Malawi Government. *Malawi in Figures.* Zomba: National Statistical Office, 2019. http://www.nsomalawi.mw/images/stories/data_on_line/general/malawi_in_figures/2019%20Malawi%20in%20Figures.pdf, Accessed on January 28, 2019.
Malawi Government. *Malawi in Figures*. Zomba: National Statistical Office, 2019.
Malawi Government. *Statement of Development Policies, 1971–1980*. Zomba: Government Printer, 1971.
Malawi Government. *National Assembly Parliamentary Debates*, January 18, 1966.
Malawi Government. *National Assembly Parliamentary Debates*, August 23, 1966.
Malawi Government. *National Assembly Parliamentary Debates,* January 18, 1966.
Malawi Government. *National Assembly Parliamentary Debates*, January 29, 1968.
Mercer, Andrew, M. *The Lilongwe Land Development Programme: A Precis of Activities with Some Comments on Populace Participation.* Lilongwe,1972.
Mitchel, Philip. *The Agrarian Problem in Kenya*. Nairobi: Government Printer, 1948.

National Statistical Office. *Integrated Household Panel Survey, 2010–2013: Household Socioeconomic Characteristics Report*. Zomba, Malawi: National Statistical Office, 2014.

Nyasaland Government. *Annual Report of the Secretary for African Affairs*: *1958*. Zomba: Government Printer, 1958.

Nyasaland Protectorate. *Nyasaland Annual Report, 1946*. Zomba: Government Printer, 1948.

Nyasaland Protectorate. *Nyasaland Development Plan, 1962–1965*. Zomba: Government Printer, 1961.

Nyasaland Protectorate. *Nyasaland Native Trust Land Order-in-Council, 1936*. Zomba: Government Printer, 1936.

Nyasaland Protectorate. *The Tung Ordinance no. 11 of 1946*. Zomba: Government Printer, 1946.

Nyasaland Protectorate. *Proceedings of the Legislative Council*, 71st Session, February 7, 1957.

Nyasaland Protectorate. *Proceedings of the Legislative Council*, 69th Session, May 3, 1955.

Ormsby-Gore, William, Church, A.G. and Linfield, F.C. *Report of the East Africa Commission*, Cmd. 2387. London: HMSO, 1925.

"Science and Administration in East Africa," *Nature* 115 (January 10, 1925): 37–38, https://doi.org/10.1038/115037a0, Accessed January 19, 2020.

United Nation Economic Commission for Africa. *The Cooperative Movement in Africa*. Addis Ababa: UNECA, 1962.

United States Foreign Broadcast Information and Service, *Sub-Saharan Africa Report, 2743–2816*, June 21, 1986, 30. https://books.google.com/books?id=T2AEAQAAIAAJ&printsec=frontcover&source=gbs_ViewAPI#v=onepage&q&f=false, Accessed Jan 2, 2020.

Unpublished Dissertations, Theses, Seminar, and Working Papers

Cammack, Diana, Edge Kanyongolo and Tam O'Neil. "'Town Chiefs' in Malawi." Working paper no. 3. United Kingdom, Overseas Development Institute, 2009.

Chipande, G. H. R. "Smallholder Agriculture as Rural Development Strategy: The Case of Malawi." PhD Dissertation, University of Glasgow, United Kingdom, 1983.

Chirwa, Ephraim W. and Jonathan Kydd. "Farmer Organization for Market Access: Study on Farmer Organization in Smallholder tea in Malawi." April 2005, 1, Accessed on December 28, 2019, https://pdfs.semanticscholar.org/0709/13593a59a7bfd43074de85d59e512f2b1466.pdf.

Green, Erik. "Peasant Production and Limits to Labour." PhD Dissertation, University of Lund, Sweden, 2005.

Griffiths, Christopher A. "Land Tenure in Malawi and the 1967 Reforms." MA thesis, Department of Law, University of Malawi, 1981.
Kayira, Gift Wasambo, "The Plight of Small-scale Irrigation Farming in Malawi: Lessons from Wovwe Rice Scheme, 1964–2007." MA Thesis, University of Malawi, Zomba, 2010.
Mandala, Elias C. "The Kololo Interlude in Southern Malawi, 1861–1895." MA thesis, University of Malawi, 1977.
Nankhumba, Sinoya J. "Evolution of Agricultural Policy in Malawi and the National Rural Development Program: A Historical Overview, 1891–1980." Department of Agricultural Economics, University College of Wales, Aberystwyth, May, 1981.
Nthenda, Louis-James. "H. M. Treasury and the Problems of Nyasaland Public Finance, 1919–1940." PhD Dissertation, Oxford University, United Kingdom, 1972.
Phiri, Canaan, R. K. "The Viphya Tung Scheme, 1945–1968: A Futile Strategy to 'Awaken the Dead North." History Seminar Paper, no. 6. Chancellor College, University of Malawi, 1987/88.
Sahn, David E. and Jehan Arulpragasam. "Development through Dualism? Land Tenure, Policy, and Poverty in Malawi." Working Paper no. 9, Cornell Food and Nutrition Policy Program, March 1991.
Snyder, Joseph M. "The Fabianization of the British Empire: Postwar Colonial Summer Conferences and Community Development in Kenya and Uganda, 1948–1956." PhD Dissertation, West Virginia University, USA, 2017.

Oral Testimonies

Focus Group Discussions with former LLDP beneficiaries in the following areas:

Chitsime (Unit 1 of LLDP), July 12, 2016.
Mitundu (Unit 24), July 12, 2016.
Mpingu (Extension Planning Area Center), July 18, 2016.
Nambuma (Unit 21), July 18, 2016.

Key Informant Interviews with the following:

Group Village Headmen, Lilongwe, July 13, 2017.
Key Informant Interview with an official at the Department of Geological Survey, Lilongwe, July 14, 2016.

SECONDARY SOURCES

Abbott, George C. "Re-examination of the 1929 Colonial Development Act." *The Economic History Review* 24, no. 1 (1971): 68–81.

Acharya S. N. "Development Perspectives and Priorities in Sub-Saharan Africa." *Finance and Development* 18, no. 1, (1981b): 16–24.

Agrawal, Arun. "Poststructuralist Approaches to Development: Some Critical Reflections." *Peace and Change* 21, no. 4 (1996): 464–47.

Ake, Claude. *Democracy and Development in Africa*. Washington, DC: Brookings Institution, 1996.

Almond, Gabriel A. "The Return to the State." *American Political Science Review* 82, no. 2 (1988): 853–74.

Amin, Samir. "Underdevelopment and Dependence in Black Africa: Historical Origin." *Journal of Peace and Research* 9, no. 2 (1972): 105–119.

Ayres, Robert, L. *Banking on the Poor: The World Bank and World Poverty.* Cambridge: The MIT Press, 1984.

Baker, Colin. *Development Governor: A Biography of Sir Geoffrey Colby*. London: I. B. Tauris, 1994.

Baker, Colin. *Revolt of the Ministers: The Malawi Cabinet Crisis, 1964–1965*. London: I. B. Tauris Publishers, 2001.

Baker, Colin. *Seeds of Trouble: Government Policy and Land Rights to Nyasaland, 1946–1964*. London: British Academic Press, 1993.

Baker, Colin. "The development of Agricultural Administration in Malawi." *The Quarterly Journal of Administration 8*, no. 3 (1973/4): 261–86.

Bamba, Abou B. *African Miracle, African Mirage: Transnational Politics and the Paradox of Modernization in Ivory Coast*. Athens, OH: Ohio University Press, 2016.

Banda, Paul Chiudza and Gift Wasambo Kayira. "The Contested Legacies of Malawi's Decolonization Process, 1944–1994." In Kenneth R. Ross and Wapulumuka O. Mulwafu, eds. *Politics, Christianity and Society in Malawi: Essays in Honour of John McCracken.* Mzuzu, Malawi: MZUNI Press, 2020, 215–42.

Banda, Paul Chiudza. "Hastings Kamuzu Banda: How the Cold War Sustained Bad Governance in Malawi." In Baba G. Jallow, ed. *Leadership in Postcolonial Malawi: Trends Transformed by Independence.* New York: Palgrave Macmillan, 2014, 27–44.

Banda, Chiudza, Paul. *The State, Counterinsurgency and Political Policing in Colonial and Post-colonial Malawi, 1891–1994*. Lanham, MD: Lexington Books, 2020.

Banik, Dan and Blessings Chinsinga. *Political Transition and Inclusive Development in Malawi*. London: Routledge, 2016.

Bates, Robert H. *Markets and States in Tropical Africa: The Political Basis of Agricultural Policies*. Berkeley: University of California Press, 1981.

Bauer, Peter T. *Development Aid: End it or Mend It*. San Francisco: ICS, 1993.

Bauer, Peter T. *Dissent on Development*. Cambridge, MA: Harvard University Press, 1972.

Bayart, Jean-François. *The State in Africa: The Politics of the Belly*. Cambridge: Polity Press, 1993.

Beinart, William. "Agricultural Planning and the Late Colonial Technical Imagination: The Lower Shire Valley, 1940–1960." In *Malawi: An Alternative Pattern of Development: Proceedings of a Seminar Held in the Centre of African Studies,* University of Edinburgh, 24 and 25 May, 1984, 93–148.

Berman, Bruce, J. *Control and Crisis in Colonial Kenya: The Dialectic of Domination*. London: James Currey, 1990.

Berry, Sara. "Chieftaincy, Land, and the State in Ghana and South Africa." In John and Jean Comaroff, eds. *The Politics of Custom: Chiefs, Capital, and the State in Contemporary Africa*. Chicago: The University of Chicago, 2018, 79–209.

Berry, Sara S. "Debating the Land Question in Africa." *Comparative Studies in Society and History* 44, no. 4 (2002): 638–68.

Berry, Sara. *No Condition Is Permanent: The Social Dynamics of Agrarian Change in Sub-Saharan Africa*. Madison, WI: University of Wisconsin Press, 1993.

Berry, Sara. *Chiefs Know Their Boundaries: Essays on Property, Power, and the Past in Asante, 1896–1996*. Portsmouth, NH, Oxford, 2001.

Blinkhorn, Thomas A. "Lilongwe: A Quiet Revolution." *Finance and Development VIII*, no. 2 (1971): 26–31.

Boden, Ragna. "Cold War Economics: Soviet Aid to Indonesia." *Journal of Cold War Studies* 10, no. 3 (2008): 110–128.

Bonneuil, Christophe. "Development as Experiment: Science and State Building in late Colonial and Postcolonial Africa, 1930–1970." *Osiris* 15 (2000): 258–81.

Chabal, Patrick and Jean-Pascal Daloz. *Africa Works: Disorder as Political Instrument*. Oxford: James Currey, 1993.

Chambers, Robert. *Rural Development: Putting the Last First*. London: Routledge, 2014.

Chan, Gerald. "Taiwan as an Emerging Aid Donor: Developments, Problems, and Prospects." *Pacific Affairs* 70, no. 1 (1977): 37–56.

Chan, Stephen. *Kaunda and Southern Africa: Image and Reality in Foreign Policy*. London: British Academic Press, 1992.

Chanock, Martin. *Law, Custom and Social Order: The Colonial Experience in Malawi and Zambia*. Cambridge, C.U.P, 1985.

Chanock, Martin. "A Peculiar Sharpness: An Essay on Property in the History of Customary Law in Colonial Africa." *Journal of African History* 32, 1 (1991): 65–88.

Chanock, Martin. "Paradigms, Policies, and Property: A Review of the Customary Law of Land Tenure." In Kristin Mann and Richard Roberts, eds. *Law in Colonial Africa.* London: James Currey, 1991, 61–84.

Chazan, Naomi. "Patterns of State Society Incorporation and Disengagement in Africa." In Donald Rothchild and Naomi Chazan, eds. *The Precarious Balance: State and Society in Africa*. Boulder: Westview Press, 1988, 121–48.

Chinsinga, Blessings and Aoiffe O'Brien. *Planting Ideas: How Agricultural Subsidies are Working in Malawi*. London: African Research Institute, 2008.

Chinsinga, Blessings. "The Green Belt Initiative, Politics and Sugar Production in Malawi." *Journal of Southern African Studies* 43, no. 3 (2017): 501–515.

Chirwa, Wiseman. "'The Garden of Eden': Sharecropping on the Shire Highlands Estates, 1920–1945." In Alan H. Jeeves and Jonathan Crush, eds. *White Farmers Black Labour: The State and Agrarian Change in Southern Africa, 1910–1950*. Portsmouth, NH: Heinemann, 1997, 265–80.

Chirwa, Ephraim and Andrew Doward. *Agricultural Input Subsidies: The Recent Malawi Experience*. Oxford: Oxford University Press, 2013.

Chisiza, Dunduzu K. *Africa: What Lies Ahead*. New York: The African-American Institute, 1962.

Chiweza, Asiyati L. "The Ambivalent Role of Chiefs: Rural Decentralization Initiative in Malawi." In L. Buur and H. M. Kyed, eds. *State Recognition and Democratization in Sub-Saharan Africa*. New York: Palgrave Macmillan, 2007, 53–78.

Christiansen, Robert. "Financing Malawi's Development Strategy." In *Malawi: An Alternative Pattern of Development: Proceedings of a Seminar Held in the Centre of African Studies*, University of Edinburgh, 24 and 25 May, 1984, 407–71.

Comaroffs, John and Jean. "Chiefs, Capital and the State in Contemporary Africa." In John and Jean Comaroff, eds. *The Politics of Custom: Chiefs, Capital, and the State in Contemporary Africa*. Chicago: The University of Chicago, 2018, 1–48.

Constantine, Stephen. *The Making of British Colonial Development Policy, 1914–1940*. London: Frank Cass, 1984.

Cooper, Frederick. *Africa since 1940: The Past of the Present*. Cambridge: Cambridge University Press, 2019.

Cooper, Frederick. "Writing the History of Development." *Journal of Modern European History* 8, no. 1 (2010): 5–23.

Cooper, Frederick. *Decolonization and African Society: The Labor Question in French and British Africa*. Cambridge: Cambridge University Press, 1996.

Cooper, Frederick. *Colonialism in Question: Theory, Knowledge and History*. Berkeley, CA: University of California Press, 2005.

Cooper, Frederick. "Development, Modernization, and the Social Sciences in the Era of Decolonization: The Examples of British and French Africa." In Jerónimo Miguel Bandeira and Pinto António Costa, eds. *The Ends of European Colonial Empires: Cases and Comparisons*. New York: Palgrave Macmillan, 2015, 15–50.

Cowen, Michael and Robert W. Shenton. *Doctrines of Development*. London: Routledge, 1996.

Cowen, Michael and Robert Shenton. "The Origin and Course of Fabian Colonialism in Africa." *Journal of Historical Sociology* 4, no. 2 (1991): 143–74.

Cowen, Michael. "Early Years of the Colonial Development Corporation: British State Enterprise Overseas During Late Colonialism." *African Affairs* 83, no. 330 (1984): 63–75.

Cullather, Nick. *The Hungry World: America's Cold War Battle Against Poverty in Asia*. Cambridge: Cambridge University Press, 2013.

Cullather, Nick. "Development? It's History." *Diplomatic History* 24, no. 4, (2000): 641–53.

Duffield, Mark and Vernon Hewitt. "Introduction." In Mark Duffield and Vernon Hewitt, eds. *Empire, Development and Colonialism: The Past in the Present*. London: James Currey, 2013, 1–15.

Ekbladh, David. *The Great American Mission: Modernization and the Construction of American World Order*. Princeton, NJ: Princeton University Press, 2011.

Engerman, David C. et al., (eds.). *Staging Growth: Modernization, Development, and the Global Cold War*. Amherst, MA: Amherst College Press, 2003.

Engerman, David C. and Corinna R. Unger. "Introduction: Towards a Global History of Modernization." *Diplomatic History* 33, no. 3 (2009): 375–85.

Ertsen, Maurits W. "Controlling the Farmer: Colonial and Postcolonial Irrigation Interventions in Africa." *Journal for Transdisciplinary Research in Southern Africa* 4, no. 1, (2008): 209–36.

Escobar, Arturo. *Encountering Development: The Making and Unmaking of the Third World*. Princeton, NJ: Princeton University Press, 1995.

Ferguson, James. *Expectations of Modernity: Myths and Meanings of Urban Life on the Zambian Copperbelt*. Berkeley and Los Angeles: University of California Press, 1999.

Ferguson, James. *The Anti-Politics Machine: "Development," Depoliticization, and Bureaucratic Power in Lesotho*. Minneapolis: University of Minnesota Press, 1994.

Finnermore, Martha. "Redefining Development at the World Bank." In Frederick Cooper and Randall Packard, eds. *International Development and the Social Sciences: Essays on the History and Politics of Knowledge*. Los Angeles: University of California Press, 1997, 203–227.

Flint, John. "Planned Decolonization and its Failure in British Africa." *African Affairs* 82, no. 328 (1983): 389–411.

Gilbert, Rist. *The History of Development: From Western Origins to Global Faith*. London: Zed Books, 1997.

Giles, B. D. "Economists in Government: The Case of Malawi." *Journal of Development Studies*, 15, no. 2 (1979): 216–32.

Giles, B. D. and A. Jennings. "Project Appraisal and the Multiplier: The Case of the Pulp Mill Project in Malawi." *Oxford Economic Papers* 34, no. 2 (1982): 390–402.

Gilman, Nils. *Mandarins of the Future*. London: John Hopkins, 2007.

Gordenker, Leon. *International Aid and National Decisions: Development Programs in Malawi, Tanzania, and Zambia*. Princeton: Princeton University Press, 1976.

Green, Erik. "Modern Agricultural History in Malawi: Perspectives on Policy-choice Explanations." *African Studies Review* 50, no. 3 (2007): 115–33.

Green, Erik. "State-led Agricultural Intensification and Rural Labour Relations: The Case of the Lilongwe Land Development Programme in Malawi, 1968–1981." *International Instituut voor Sociale Geschiednis* 55, no. 3 (2010): 413–46.

Green, Erik. "A Lasting Story: Conservation and Agricultural Extension Services in Colonial Malawi." *Journal of African History* 50, no. 2 (2009): 247–68.

Green, Erik. "Indirect Rule and Colonial Intervention: Chiefs and Agrarian Change in Nyasaland, ca. 1933 to the Early 1950s." *International Journal of African Historical Studies* 44, no. 2 (2011): 249–74.

Gulhati, Ravi. *Malawi: Promising Reforms, Bad Luck*. World Bank: Washington, DC, 1989.

Gupta, Partha Sarathi. *Imperialism and the British Labour Movement, 1914–1964*. London: MacMillan, 1975.

Hadfield, L. A. and John Aerni-Flessner. "Introduction: Localizing the History of Development in Africa." *International Journal of African Historical Studies* 50, no. 1 (2017): 1–9.

Hall, Catherine. *Civilizing Subjects: Metropole and the Colony in the English Imagination, 1830–1867*. Chicago: University of Chicago Press, 2002.

Havinden, Michael and David Meredith. *Colonialism and Development: Britain and its Tropical Colonies, 1850–1960*. London: Routledge, 1993.

Hinden, Rita. "Socialism and the Colonial World." In Arthur Creech Jones, ed. *New Fabian Colonial Essays*. New York: Praeger, 1959, 9–18.

Hoben, Alen. "The Political Economy of Land Tenure in Somalia." In R. A. Downs and S. P. Reyna *Land and Society in Contemporary Africa*. Hanover, NH: University of New Hampshire, 1988, 192–220.

Hodge, Joseph and Gerald Hödl. "Introduction," In Joseph M. Hodge, Gerald Hödl, and Martina Kopf. *Developing Africa: Concepts, Practices and Twentieth-century Colonialism*. Manchester: Manchester University Press, 2014, 1–34.

Hodge, Joseph, Morgan. "Writing the History of Development (Part 2: Longer, Deeper, Wider)." *Humanity: An International Journal of Human Rights, Humanitarianism, and Development* 7, no. 1 (2016): 125–74.

Hodge, Joseph, Morgan. "Science, Development, and Empire: The Colonial Advisory Council on Agriculture and Animal Health, 1929–43." *Journal of Imperial and Commonwealth History* 30, no. 1 (2002): 1–26.

Hodge, Joseph M. "Colonial Experts, Development and Environmental Doctrines, and the Legacies of late Colonialism." In Christina F. Ax, Niels Brimnes, Niklas T. Jensen, and Karen Oslund, eds. *Cultivating the Colonies: Colonial States and Their Environmental Legacies*. Athens, OH: Ohio University Press, 2011, 300–326.

Hodge, Joseph Morgan. *Triumph of the Expert: Agrarian Doctrines of Development and the Legacies of British Colonialism*. Athens, OH: Ohio University Press, 2007.

Humphrey, David H. "Malawi's Economic Progress and Prospects." *The Eastern Africa Economic Review* 5, no. 2, (1973): 71–104.

Hydén, Göran. *Beyond Ujamaa in Tanzania: Underdevelopment and an Uncaptured Peasantry*. Berkeley: University of California Press, 1980.

Iliffe, John. *The African Poor: History*. Cambridge: Cambridge University Press, 1987.

Immerwahr, Daniel. *Thinking Small: The United States and the Lure of Community Development*. Cambridge, MA: Harvard University Press, 2015.

Iriye, Akira and Pierre-Yves Saunier. *The Palgrave Dictionary of Transnational History*. New York: Palgrave Macmillan, 2009.

Isaacman, Allen F. and Barbara S. Isaacman. *Dams, Displacement, and the Delusion of Development: Cahora Bassa and Its Legacies in Mozambique, 1965–2007*. Athens, OH: Ohio University Press, 2013.

Kalinga, Owen J. M. "The Master Farmers' Scheme in Nyasaland, 1950–1962: A Study of a Failed Attempt to Create a 'Yeoman' Class." *African Affairs* 92, no. 368 (1993): 367–87.

Kandawire, Kamchitete J. A. *Thangata: Forced Labor or Reciprocal Assistance? A Case Study of the Conversion of a Traditional African Institution into a Colonial Institution of Production with Special Reference to Southern Malawi.* Zomba, Malawi: Research and Publication Committee of the University of Malawi, 1979.

Kaspin, Debora. "The Politics of Ethnicity in Malawi's Democratic Transition." *The Journal of Modern African Studies* 33, no. 4 (1995): 595–620.

Kaunda, Jonathan M. "Malawi: The Postcolonial State, Development, and Democracy." *Africa: Rivista trimestrale di studi e documentazione dell'Istituto italiano per l'Africae l'Oriente, Anno* 50, no. 3 (1995): 305–324.

Kayira, Gift W., "Wealth Creation, Poverty and Social Welfare in Malawi, 1940s–1980," In Mariama Khan and Grasian Mkodzongi (eds.), *Africa, History and Culture* (Dubuque, IA, Kendall Hunt, 2020), 11–28.

Kayira, Gift Wasambo. "Limits to State Power in the Post-independence Development in Malawi, 1964–1983." In Kenneth Ross, Wapulumuka Mulwafu, Kings M. Phiri and Klaus Fiedler (eds.), *Politics, Christianity, and Society in Malawi*. Mzuzu, Malawi: MZUNI Press, 2020, 266–92.

Kayira, G. W. and P. C. Banda. "Chiefs and the Politics of Local Government in Malawi: A Historical Perspective." *Journal of Public Administration and Development Alternatives* 3, no. 1–1 (2018): 84–97.

Kayuni, Happy M. "Malawi's Economic and Development Policy Choices from 1964 to 1980: An Epitome of 'Pragmatic Unilateral Capitalism.'" *Nordic Journal of African Studies* 20, no. 2 (2011): 112–13.

Kelemen, Paul. "Planning for Africa: The British Labour Party's Colonial Development Policy, 1920–1964." *Journal of Agrarian Change* 7, no. 1 (2007): 76–89.

Kelemen, Paul. "Individualism is, Indeed, Running Riot: Components of the Social Democratic Model of Development." In Mark Duffield and Vernon Hewitt, eds. *Empire, Development and Colonialism.* Woodbridge, UK: Byodell and Brown, 2009, 188–201.

Kettlewell, Richard W. *Agricultural Change in Nyasaland, 1945–1960*. Stanford, CA: Stanford University Press, 1965.

Kinsey, B. H. "Integrated Rural Development, Agricultural Growth and Equity in Malawi: Redefining Development Strategies and Tactics for the 1980s." *Agricultural Administration* 15, no. 1 (1984): 45–63.

Kinsey, B. H. *Rural Development in Malawi: A Review of the Lilongwe Land Development Program*. Washington, DC: World Bank, 1975.

Kishindo, Paul. "Farmer Turnover at Settlement Schemes: The Experience of Limphasa Irrigation Rice Scheme, Northern Malawi." *Nordic Journal of African Studies* 5, no. 1 (1996): 1–10.

Kishindo, Paul. "Farmer Clubs and Smallholder Agricultural Development in Malawi." *Development Southern Africa* 5, no. 2 (2008): 491–507.

Krasner, Stephen D. *Defending the National Interest: Raw Materials Investments and U.S. Foreign Policy*. Princeton, NJ: Princeton University Press, 1978.

Kydd, Jonathan. "Malawi in the 1970s: Development Policies and Economic Change." In *Malawi: An Alternative Pattern of Development: Proceedings of a Seminar Held in the Centre of African Studies,* University of Edinburgh, 24 and 25 May, 1984, 295–380.

Kydd, Jonathan and Robert E. Christiansen. "Structural Change in Malawi Since Independence: Consequences of a Development Strategy Based on Large-scale Agriculture." *World Development* 10, no. 5 (1982): 355–75.

Lamport-Stokes, H. J. "Land Tenure in Malawi." *The Society of Malawi Journal* 23, no. 2 (1970): 59–88.

Laron, Guy. *Origins of the Suez Crisis: Postwar Development Diplomacy and the Struggle over Third World Industrialization, 1945–1956*. Washington, DC: The John Hopkins University Press, 2013.

Latham, Michael E. *Modernization as Ideology: American Social Science and "Nation Building" in the Kennedy Era*. Chapel Hill: The University of North Carolina Press, 2000.

Latham, Michael E. *The Right Kind of Revolution: Modernization, Development and U.S. Foreign Policy from the Cold War to the Present*. Ithaca, NY: Cornell University Press, 2011.

Lele, Uma J. *Designing Rural Development Programs: Lessons from Past Experience in Africa*. Ithaca, NY: Center for International Studies, 1975.

Lele, Uma J. *The Design of Rural Development: Lessons from Africa*. Baltimore: Published for the World Bank by Johns Hopkins University Press, 1984.

Lewis, Arthur. *Theory of Economic Growth*. London: Allen and Unwin, 1955.

Li, Tania Murry. *The Will to Improve: Governmentality, Development, and the Practice of Politics*. Durham, NC: Duke University Press, 2007.

Lipton, Michael. *Why Poor People Stay Poor: Urban Bias in World Development*. Cambridge, MA: Harvard University Press, 1977.

Lippert, Werner D. "European Long-term Investments in Détente: The Implications of East-West Cooperation." In Oliver Bange and Poul Vilaume, eds. *The Long Détente: Changing Concepts of Security and Cooperation in Europe, 1950s–1980s*. Budapest, Hungary: Central European University Press, 2017, 77–93.

Lonsdale, John and Bruce Berman. "Coping with Contradictions: The Development of the Colonial State in Kenya, 1895–1914." *Journal of African History* 20, no. 4 (1979): 487–505.

Lottholz, Philipp and Nicolas Lemay-Hébert. "Re-reading Weber, Re-conceptualizing State Building: From Neo-Weberian to Post-Weberian Approaches to State, Legitimacy and State Building." *Cambridge Review of International Affairs* 29, no. 4 (2016): 1467–1485.

Low, D. A. and J. M. Lonsdale, "Introduction: Towards the New Order 1945–1963." In D. A. Low and Alison Smith, eds. *History of East Africa*, vol. 3. Oxford: Clarendon Press, 1976, 1–63.

Lugard, Lord. *The Dual Mandate in British Tropical Africa*. London: Archon Books, 1923/1965.

Lund, Christian. *Law, Power and Politics in Niger: Land struggles and the Rural Code.* Hamburg: LIT Verlag, 1998.

Lund, Christian. "A Question of Honour: Property Disputes and Brokerage in Burkina Faso." *Africa* 69, no. 4. (1999): 575–94.

Malawi: An Alternative Pattern of Development: Proceedings of a Seminar Held in the Centre of African Studies, University of Edinburgh, 24 and 25 May, 1984.

Mamdani, Mahmood. *Citizen and Subject: Contemporary Africa and the Legacy of Late Colonialism*. London: James Currey, 1996.

Mandala, Elias. *The End of Chidyerano: A History of Food and Everyday Life in Malawi, 1860–2004.* Portsmouth, NH: Heinemann, 2005.

Mandala, Elias. *Work and Control in a Peasant Economy: A History of the Lower Tchiri Valley in Malawi, 1859–1960*. Madison: University of Wisconsin Press, 1990.

Mandala, Elias. "The Triumph of the Peasant Option and the Parasitic Cotton Sector in Malawi, 1891–1995." In Karin Hofmeester and Pim de Zwart, eds. *Colonialism, Institutional Change and Shifts in Global Labour Relations.* Amsterdam: Amsterdam University Press, 2018, 173–203.

Maxon, Robert M. "Where Did the Trees Go? The Wattle Bark Industry in Western Kenya, 1932–1950." *International Journal of African Historical Studies* 34, no. 3 (2001): 565–84.

McCracken, John. *A History of Malawi*, 1859–1966. Oxford: James Currey, 2012.

McCracken, John. "Planters, Peasants and the Colonial State: The Impact of the Native Tobacco Board in the Central Province of Malawi." *Journal of Southern African Studies*, 9 no. 2 (1983): 172–92.

McCracken, John. "Experts and Expertise in Colonial Malawi." *African Affairs* 8, no. 332 (1982): 101–116.

McLoughlin, Peter F. M. "Land Re-organization in Malawi, 1950s–1960: Its Pertinence to Current Development." In Sayre P. Schatz, ed. *South of the Sahara: Development in African Economies*. Philadelphia: Temple University Press, 1972, 128–39.

McMahon, Robert J. *The Cold War: A Very Short Introduction*. Oxford: Oxford University Press, 2003.

McMaster, Carolyn. *Malawi: Foreign Aid and Development*. London: Julian Friedman Publishers, 1974.

McWilliam, Michael. *The Development Business: A History of the Commonwealth Development Corporation*. London: Palgrave, 2001.

Meek, Charles Kingsley. *Land Law and Custom in the Colonies.* Oxford: Oxford University Press, 1946.

Mehos, Donna C. and Suzanne M. Moon. "The Use of Portability: Circulating Experts in the Technopolitics of Cold War and Decolonization." In Hecht Gabrielle, ed. *Entangled Geographies: Empire and Technopolitics in the Global Cold War.* Cambridge: MIT Press, 2011, 43–72.

Metcalf, Thomas R. *Ideologies of the Raj*. Cambridge: Cambridge University Press, 1994.

Mhone, Guy C. Z. "The Political Economy of Malawi: An Overview." In Guy Mhone, ed. *Malawi at the Crossroads: The Postcolonial Political Economy*. Harare: SAPES Books, 1993, 1–33.

Mhone, Guy (ed.). *Malawi at the Crossroads: The Postcolonial Political Economy*. Harare: SAPES Books, 1993.

Migdal, Joel S. *State in Society: Studying How States and Societies Transform and Constitute One Another*. Cambridge: Cambridge University Press, 2010.

Mitchell, Timothy. "The Limits of the State: Beyond Statist Approaches and their Critics." *The American Political Science Review* 85, no. 1 (1991): 77–96.

Mkandawire, Richard, Steven Jaffee, and Sandra Bertoli. *Beyond 'Dualism': The Changing Face of Leasehold Estate Subsector of Malawi.* Binghamton, NY: Institute for Development Anthropology, 1990.

Miller, R. A. "District Development Committees in Malawi: A Case Study in Rural Development." *Journal of Overseas Administration* 9, 2 (1970): 129–42.

Moon, Suzanne. *Technology and Ethical Idealism: A History of Development in the Netherlands East Indies*. Leiden: CNWS Publications, 2007.

Moon, Suzanne. "Imperial Knowledge, Scientific Authority, and Native Development: The Controversy over Sugar/Rice Ecology in the Netherlands East Indies, 1954–1914." *Environment and History* 10, no. 1 (2004): 59–81.

Morel, E. D. *Affairs of West Africa*. London: Frank Cass & Co., 1968.

Morgan, David John. *The Official History of Colonial Development*, Vol. III. London: Macmillan, 1980.

Morton, Kathryn. *Aid and Dependence: British Aid to Malawi.* London: Croom Helm, 1975.

Mulwafu, Wapulumuka Oliver. *Conservation Song: A History of Peasant-State Relations and the Environment in Malawi, 1860–2000*. Cambridge: White Horse Press, 2011.

Ng'ong'ola, Clement. "The Design and Implementation of Customary Land Reforms in Central Malawi." *Journal of African Law* 26, no. 2 (1982): 115–32.

Ng'ong'ola, Clement. "The State, Settlers, and Indigenes in the Evolution of Land Law and Policy in Colonial Malawi." *International Journal of African Historical Studies* 23, no. 1 (1990): 27–58.

Nordlinger, Eric A. *On the Autonomy of the Democratic State*. Milton Keynes, UK: Lightning Source, 1981.

Norris, Jacob. *Land of Progress: Palestine in the Age of Development*. Oxford: Oxford University Press, 2013.

Nworah, Kenneth Dike. "The Liverpool 'Sect' and British West African Policy, 1895–1915." *African Affairs* 7, no. 281 (1971): 349–64.

Nworah, Kenneth Dike. "The Politics of Lever's West African Concessions, 1907–1913." *International Journal of African Historical Studies*, 5 no. 2 (1972): 248–64.

Olivier, Lord. *Imperial Trusteeship*. London: The Fabian Society, 1929.

Pachai, Bridglal. *Land and Politics in Malawi, 1875–1975.* Kingston, Ontario: Limestone Press, 1978.

Pachai, Bridglal. "Land Policies in Malawi: An Examination of the Colonial Legacies." *Journal of African History* XIV, no. 3 (1973): 681–98.

Palmer, Robin. "Working Conditions and Worker Responses on Nyasaland Tea Estates, 1930–1953." *Journal of African History* 27, no. 1 (1986): 105–126.

Pearce, Robert Desmond. "The Colonial Office and Planned Decolonization in Africa." *African Affairs* 83 no. 330 (1984): 77–93.

Peters, Pauline E. and Daimon Kambewa. "Whose Security? Deepening Social Conflict Over 'Customary' Land in the Shadow of Land Tenure Reform in Malawi." *Journal of Modern African Studies* 45, no. 3 (2007): 447–72.

Peterson, Derek R. *Ethnic Patriotism, and the East African Revival: A History of Dissent, c. 1935–1972*. Cambridge: Cambridge University Press, 2012.

Phillips, Anne. *The Enigma of Colonialism: British Policy in West Africa*. London: James Currey, 1989.

Phiri, D. D. *History of Malawi,* Vol. 2. Blantyre, Malawi: College Publishing Company, 2010.

Phiri, Kings, Wapulumuka O. Mulwafu and John McCracken (eds.). *Malawi in Crisis: The 1959/60 Nyasaland State of Emergency and its Legacy*. Zomba: Kachere Series, 2012.

Phiri, Kings M. "Dr. Banda's Cultural Legacy and its Implications for a Democratic Malawi." In Kings Phiri and Andrew Ross, eds. *Democratisation in Malawi: A Stocktaking*. Blantyre, Malawi: CLAIM, 1998, 149–67.

Pierce, Steven. *Farmers and the State in Colonial Kano: Land Tenure and the Legal Imagination*. Bloomington, IN: Indiana University Press, 2005.

Pigg, Stacey Leigh. "'Found in Most Traditional Societies': Traditional Medical Practitioners Between Culture and Development." In Frederick Cooper and Randall Packard, eds. *International Development and the Social Sciences: Essays on the History and Politics of Knowledge*. Berkeley: University of California Press, 2013, 259–90.

Place, Frank and S. E. Migot-Adholla. "The Economic Effects of Land Registration on Smallholder Farms in Kenya: Evidence from Nyeri and Kakamega Districts." *Land Economics*, 74, no. 3 (1998): 360–73.

Porter, Bernard. *Critics of Empire: British Radicals and the Imperial Challenge*. London: I. B. Tauris, 2008.

Potts, Deborah. "Capital Relocation in Africa: The Case of Lilongwe in Malawi." *The Geographical Journal* 51, no. 2 (1985): 182–96.

Power, Joey. "'Individualism is the Antithesis of Indirect Rule': Cooperative Development and Indirect Rule in Colonial Malawi." *Journal of Southern African Studies* 18, no. 2 (1992): 317–47.

Power, Joey. "Remembering Du: An Episode in the Development of Malawian political Culture." *African Affairs* 97, no. 388 (1998): 369–96.

Power, Joey. *Political Culture and Nationalism in Malawi: Building Kwacha*. Rochester: University of Rochester Press, 2010.

Prowse, Martin. "A History of Tobacco Production and Marketing in Malawi, 1890–2010." *Journal of East African Studies* 7, no. 4 (2013): 691–792.

Pryor, Frederic L. *The Political Economy of Poverty, Equity and Growth: Malawi and Madagascar.* Oxford: Oxford University Press, 1990.

Pugh, Patricia. *Educate, Agitate, Organize: 100 Years of Fabian Socialism*. London: Mathuen, 1984.

Ranger, Terence. "The Invention of Tradition in Africa." In E. Hobsbawm and T. Ranger, eds. *The Invention of Tradition*. Cambridge: Cambridge University Press, 1983, 211–62.

Riley, Charlotte. "The Winds of Change are Blowing Economically: The Labour Party and British Overseas Development, 1940s–1960s." In W. M. Smith and Chris Jeppesen, eds. *Britain, France and the Decolonization of Africa.* London: UCL Press, 2017, 43–61.

Reader, Luke. "'Not Yet Able to Stand by Themselves': Leonard Woolf, Socialist Imperialism, and Discourse of Race, 1925–1941." *Trans-Script* 1 (2001): 102–130.

Roberts, Bryan. "Malawi Progress and Problems Since Independence." *African Affairs* 69, no. 274 (1970): 60–64.

Robinson, Kenneth. *The Dilemmas of Trusteeship.* London: Oxford University Press, 1965.

Rostow, Walt Whitman. *The Stages of Development: A Non-Communist Manifesto.* Cambridge: Cambridge University Press, 1963.

Sachs, Wolfgang (ed.). *The Development Dictionary: A Guide to Knowledge as Power*. London: Zed Books: 1992.

Saunier, Pierre-Yves. *Transnational History*. New York: Palgrave Macmillan, 2013.

Schmidt, Heide-Irene. "Pushed to the Front: The Foreign Assistance Policy of the Federal Republic of Germany, 1958–1971." *Contemporary European History* 12, no. 4 (2003): 473–507.

Schneider, Leander. *Government of Development: Peasants and Politicians in Postcolonial Tanzania*. Bloomington: Indiana University Press, 2014.

Schuknecht, Rohland. *British Colonial Development Policy After the Second World War: The Case of Sukumaland, Tanganyika*. London: Global Book Marketing, 2010.

Scott, James, C. *Seeing Like a State: How Certain Schemes to Improve the Human Condition Have Failed.* New Haven: Yale University Press, 2008.

Scott, David. "Colonial Governmentality," *Social Text.* 13, no. 2 (1995):191–220.

Shaw, Bernard George. *Fabian Essays in Socialism.* Gloucester, MA: Peter Smith, 1889.

Shepperson, George and Thomas Price. *Independent African: John Chilembwe and the Origins, Setting and Significance of the Nyasaland Native Rising of 1915*. Edinburgh: University of Edinburgh, 1963.

Shipton, Parker and Mitzi Goheen. "Understanding African Land-holdings: Power, Wealth and Meaning." *Journal of the International African Institute* 62, no. 3 (1992): 307–25.

Simon, Thomas. "Economic Developments in Malawi Since Independence." *Journal of Southern African Studies* 2, no. 1 (1975): 30–51.

Sindima, Harvey J. *Malawi's First Republic: Economic and Political Analysis*. Lanham: University Press of America, 2002.

Skocpol, Theda, Peter B. Evans and Dietrich Rueschemeyer (eds.). *Bringing the State Back In.* Cambridge: Cambridge University Press, 1986.

Skocpol, Theda. *States and Social Revolutions: A Comparative Analysis of France, Russia, and China*. Cambridge: Cambridge University Press, 1979.

Stanfield, Michael Edward. *Red Rubber, Bleeding Trees: Violence, Slavery and Empire in Northwestern Amazonia, 1850–1933*. Albuquerque: University of New Mexico Press, 1998.

Stephens, Michele McArdle. *In the Lands of Fire and Sun: Resistance and Accommodation in the Huichol Sierra, 1823–1930*. Nebraska: University of Nebraska Press, 2018.

Tilley, Helen. *Africa as a Living Laboratory: Empire, Development, and the Problem of Scientific Knowledge, 1870–1950*. Chicago: University of Chicago, 2011, 69–216.

Tomlinson, Jim. "The Commonwealth, the Balance of Payments and the Politics of International Poverty: British Aid Policy, 1958–1971." *Journal of Contemporary European History* 12, no. 4 (2004): 413–29.

Turchetti, Simone, Néstor Herran and Soroya Boudia. "Introduction: Have we Ever Been 'Transnational'? Towards a History of Science Across and Beyond Borders." *British Journal for the History of Science* 45, no. 3 (2012): 319–36.

Unger, Corinna R. "Modernization à la Mode: West Germany and American Development Plans for the Third World." *GHI Bulletin*, no. 40 (Spring 2007): 143–59.

Unger, Corinna R. "Histories of Development and Modernization: Findings, Reflections, Future Research." In H-Soz-Kult 09.12.2010, 1–22. https://www.hsozkult.de/literaturereview/id/forschungsberichte-1130. Accessed on March 17, 2019.

Unger, Corinna R. *International Development: A Post-war History*. Bloomsbury, PA: Bloomsbury Academic, 2018.

Vail, Leroy. "The Making of an Imperial Slum: Nyasaland and its Railways, 1895–1935." *Journal of African History* 16, no. 1 (1975): 89–112.

Vail, Leroy. "Railway Development and Colonial Underdevelopment: The Nyasaland Case." In Robin Palmer and N. Parsons, eds. *The Roots of Rural Poverty in Central and Southern Africa.* Los Angeles: University of California, 1977, 365–95.

Vail, Leroy. "The State and the Creation of Colonial Malawi's Agricultural Economy." In Robert I. Rotberg, ed. *Imperialism, Colonialism and Hunger: East and Central Africa*. Lanham, MD: Lexington Books, 1983, 39–88.

Van Beusekom, Monica M., and Dorothy L. Hodgson. "Lessons Learned? Development Experiences in the Late Colonial Period." *Journal of African History* 41, no. 1 (2000): 29–33.

Van Beusekom, Monica M. *Negotiating Development: African Farmers and Colonial Experts at the Office Du Niger, 1920–1960*. Portsmouth, NH: James Currey, 2002.

Vaughan, Megan. *The Story of an African Famine: Gender and Famine in Twentieth-Century Malawi*. Cambridge: Cambridge University Press, 1987.

Wallerstein, Immanuel. *The Modern World System*. New York: Academic Press, 1974.

Weber, Max et al. *From Max Weber: Essays in Sociology.* New York: Routledge, 1967.

Westad, Odd Arne. *The Global Cold War: Third World Interventions and the Making of Our Times.* Cambridge: Cambridge University Press, 2009.

White, Nicholas J. "Reconstructing Europe Through Rejuvenating Empire: the British, French, and Dutch Experiences Compared." *Past and Present* Supplement 6 (2011): 211–36.

Wicker, E. R. "The Colonial Development Corporation, 1949–1954" *Review of the Economic Studies* 23, no. 3 (1955–1956): 213–28.

Williams, S. G. B. "The Beginnings of Mzuzu with Some Biographical Notes on Some of the Viphya Tung Project Managers." *The Society of Malawi Journal* 22, no. 1 (1969): 46–50.

Williams, T. D. *Malawi: The Politics of Despair*. Ithaca: Cornell University Press, 1978.

Wood, Alan. *The Groundnut Affair*. London: The Bodley Head, 1960.

Woods, Tony. "The Myth of the Capitalist Class: Unofficial Sources and Political Economy in Colonial Malawi, 1895–1924." *History in Africa* 16 (1989): 363–73.

Young, Crawford. *The African Colonial State in Comparative Perspective*. New Haven: Yale University Press, 1997.

Young, Crawford. *The Postcolonial State in Africa: Fifty Years of Independence, 1960–2010*. Madison: University of Wisconsin Press, 2012.

Young, Cullen. Thomas and Banda Hastings, Kamuzu. *Our African Way of Life: Three Essays*, London: Lutterworth Press, 1946.

Zeleza, Tiyambe. "The Political Economy of British Colonial Development and Welfare in Africa." *Transafrican Journal of History* 1, no. 141 (1985): 139–61.

Zimmerman, Andrew. "Africa in Imperial and Transnational History: Multi-Sited Historiography and the Necessity of Theory." *Journal of African History*. 54, no. 3 (2013): 331–40.

Index

About the Author

Gift Wasambo Kayira is senior lecturer in history at the University of Malawi. He holds a doctorate in history from West Virginia University, US. His research interests revolve around the history of development, British imperial history, and histories of ethnicity in twentieth and twenty-first century Malawi. He has published on these themes extensively in the *Journal of Southern African Studies*, *Journal of Eastern African Studies*, *Journal of Public Administration and Development Alternatives*, *African Studies Quarterly*, *Society of Malawi Journal*, and others. Some of his contributions have also appeared in edited volumes. Kayira runs a postgraduate seminar in African Economic History at the University of Malawi. He also teaches courses in Modern African History, World History, and Evolution of Development Thinking at the undergraduate level.

www.ingramcontent.com/pod-product-compliance
Ingram Content Group UK Ltd.
Pitfield, Milton Keynes, MK11 3LW, UK
UKHW040858081026
15587UKWH00016B/757

9 781666 921656

Probability and Mathematical Statistics (Continued)

PURI and SEN • Nonparametric Methods in General Linear Models
PURI and SEN • Nonparametric Methods in Multivariate Analysis
PURI, VILAPLANA, and WERTZ • New Perspectives in Theoretical and Applied Statistics
RANDLES and WOLFE • Introduction to the Theory of Nonparametric Statistics
RAO • Asymptotic Theory of Statistical Inference
RAO • Linear Statistical Inference and Its Applications, *Second Edition*
ROBERTSON, WRIGHT, and DYKSTRA • Order Restricted Statistical Inference
ROGERS and WILLIAMS • Diffusions, Markov Processes, and Martingales, Volume II: Îto Calculus
ROHATGI • Statistical Inference
ROSS • Stochastic Processes
RUBINSTEIN • Simulation and the Monte Carlo Method
RUZSA and SZEKELY • Algebraic Probability Theory
SCHEFFE • The Analysis of Variance
SEBER • Linear Regression Analysis
SEBER • Multivariate Observations
SEBER and WILD • Nonlinear Regression
SEN • Sequential Nonparametrics: Invariance Principles and Statistical Inference
SERFLING • Approximation Theorems of Mathematical Statistics
SHORACK and WELLNER • Empirical Processes with Applications to Statistics
STOYANOV • Counterexamples in Probability
WHITTAKER • Graphical Models in Applied Multivariate Statistics

Applied Probability and Statistics

ABRAHAM and LEDOLTER • Statistical Methods for Forecasting
AGRESTI • Analysis of Ordinal Categorical Data
AGRESTI • Categorical Data Analysis
AICKIN • Linear Statistical Analysis of Discrete Data
ANDERSON and LOYNES • The Teaching of Practical Statistics
ANDERSON, AUQUIER, HAUCK, OAKES, VANDAELE, and WEISBERG • Statistical Methods for Comparative Studies
ARTHANARI and DODGE • Mathematical Programming in Statistics
ASMUSSEN • Applied Probability and Queues
*BAILEY • The Elements of Stochastic Processes with Applications to the Natural Sciences
BARNETT • Interpreting Multivariate Data
BARNETT and LEWIS • Outliers in Statistical Data, *Second Edition*
BARTHOLOMEW • Stochastic Models for Social Processes, *Third Edition*
BARTHOLOMEW and FORBES • Statistical Techniques for Manpower Planning
BATES and WATTS • Nonlinear Regression Analysis and Its Applications
BHATTACHARYA and WAYMIRE • Stochastic Processes with Applications
BECK and ARNOLD • Parameter Estimation in Engineering and Science
BELSLEY, KUH, and WELSCH • Regression Diagnostics: Identifying Influential Data and Sources of Collinearity
BHAT • Elements of Applied Stochastic Processes, *Second Edition*
BHATTACHARYA and WAYMIRE • Stochastic Processes with Applications
BLOOMFIELD • Fourier Analysis of Time Series: An Introduction
BOLLEN • Structural Equations with Latent Variables
BOX • R. A. Fisher, the Life of a Scientist
BOX and DRAPER • Empirical Model-Building and Response Surfaces
BOX and DRAPER • Evolutionary Operation: A Statistical Method for Process Improvement
BOX, HUNTER, and HUNTER • Statistics for Experimenters: An Introduction to Design, Data Analysis, and Model Building

*Now available in a lower priced paperback edition in the Wiley Classics Library.

Applied Probability and Statistics (Continued)

BROWN and HOLLANDER • Statistics: A Biomedical Introduction
BUCKLEW • Large Deviation Techniques in Decision, Simulation, and Estimation
BUNKE and BUNKE • Nonlinear Regression, Functional Relations and Robust Methods: Statistical Methods of Model Building
BUNKE and BUNKE • Statistical Inference in Linear Models, Volume I
CHAMBERS • Computational Methods for Data Analysis
CHATTERJEE and HADI • Sensitivity Analysis in Linear Regression
CHATTERJEE and PRICE • Regression Analysis by Example
CHOW • Econometric Analysis by Control Methods
CLARKE and DISNEY • Probability and Random Processes: A First Course with Applications, *Second Edition*
COCHRAN • Sampling Techniques, *Third Edition*
COCHRAN and COX • Experimental Designs, *Second Edition*
CONOVER • Practical Nonparametric Statistics, *Second Edition*
CONOVER and IMAN • Introduction to Modern Business Statistics
CORNELL • Experiments with Mixtures, Designs, Models, and the Analysis of Mixture Data, *Second Edition*
COX • A Handbook of Introductory Statistical Methods
COX • Planning of Experiments
DANIEL • Applications of Statistics to Industrial Experimentation
DANIEL • Biostatistics: A Foundation for Analysis in the Health Sciences, *Fourth Edition*
DANIEL and WOOD • Fitting Equations to Data: Computer Analysis of Multifactor Data, *Second Edition*
DAVID • Order Statistics, *Second Edition*
DAVISON • Multidimensional Scaling
DEGROOT, FIENBERG, and KADANE • Statistics and the Law
*DEMING • Sample Design in Business Research
DILLON and GOLDSTEIN • Multivariate Analysis: Methods and Applications
DODGE • Analysis of Experiments with Missing Data
DODGE and ROMIG • Sampling Inspection Tables, *Second Edition*
DOWDY and WEARDEN • Statistics for Research
DRAPER and SMITH • Applied Regression Analysis, *Second Edition*
DUNN • Basic Statistics: A Primer for the Biomedical Sciences, *Second Edition*
DUNN and CLARK • Applied Statistics: Analysis of Variance and Regression, *Second Edition*
ELANDT-JOHNSON and JOHNSON • Survival Models and Data Analysis
FLEISS • The Design and Analysis of Clinical Experiments
FLEISS • Statistical Methods for Rates and Proportions, *Second Edition*
FLURY • Common Principal Components and Related Multivariate Models
FRANKEN, KÖNIG, ARNDT, and SCHMIDT • Queues and Point Processes
GALLANT • Nonlinear Statistical Models
GIBBONS, OLKIN, and SOBEL • Selecting and Ordering Populations: A New Statistical Methodology
GNANADESIKAN • Methods for Statistical Data Analysis of Multivariate Observations
GREENBERG and WEBSTER • Advanced Econometrics: A Bridge to the Literature
GROSS and HARRIS • Fundamentals of Queueing Theory, *Second Edition*
GROVES • Survey Errors and Survey Costs
GROVES, BIEMER, LYBERG, MASSEY, NICHOLLS, and WAKSBERG • Telephone Survey Methodology
GUPTA and PANCHAPAKESAN • Multiple Decision Procedures: Theory and Methodology of Selecting and Ranking Populations

Continued on back end papers

*Now available in a lower priced paperback edition in the Wiley Classics Library.